AMERICAN
WOMEN
IN JAZZ

AMERICAN
WOMEN
IN JAZZ

1900 to the Present
Their Words, Lives, and Music

SALLY PLACKSIN

Seaview Books

NEW YORK

Seaview Books/A Division of PEI Books, Inc.

Library of Congress Cataloging in Publication Data

Placksin, Sally.
  American women in jazz.

  Bibliography: p.
  Discography: p.
  Includes index.
    1. Jazz musicians—United States. 2. Jazz music—
United States—History and criticism. 3. Women musicians
—United States. 4. Women composers—United States.
I. Title.
ML3508.P58 1982   785.42'092'2 [B]   81–50324
ISBN 0–87223–756–7   AACR2

Designed by Tere LoPrete

The author and publisher gratefully acknowledge permission to reprint excerpts from the following:

"Hustlin' Blues"
Words and music by Malissa Nix and T. Dorsey.
© Copyright 1928 by Northern Music Company, New York, N.Y. Rights administered by MCA Music, a division of MCA Inc., New York, N.Y. Copyright renewed. Used by permission. All rights reserved.

"Don't Fish in My Sea"
Words and music by Bessie Smith and Ma Rainey.
© Copyright 1928 by Northern Music Company, New York, N.Y. Rights administered by MCA Music, a division of MCA Inc., New York, N.Y. Copyright renewed. Used by permission. All rights reserved.

Satchmo and Me. Riverside RLP 12–120. Courtesy Fantasy Records.

Treat It Gentle by Sidney Bechet. Reprinted by permission of Hill and Wang, a division of Farrar, Straus & Giroux, Inc. Copyright © 1960 Twayne Publishers Inc. and Cassell & Company, Ltd. Reprinted by Da Capo Press, Inc., 1975.

"Ma Rainey" in *The Collected Poems of Sterling A. Brown,* selected by Michael S. Harper. Copyright 1932 by Harcourt, Brace, Jovanovich, Inc., renewed © 1960 by Sterling A. Brown. Reprinted by permission of Harper & Row, Publishers, Inc.

Hear Me Talkin' to Ya edited by Nat Shapiro and Nat Hentoff. Copyright © 1955 by Nat Shapiro and Nat Hentoff. Reprinted by permission of Holt, Rinehart and Winston, Publishers.

Dinosaurs in the Morning by Whitney Balliett. Lippincott, 1962. Originally in *The New Yorker;* © 1961. Reprinted by permission of *The New Yorker.*

The booklet accompanying *Mary Lou Williams: The History of Jazz,* Folkways Records, FJ 32860. © 1978 by Folkways Records & Service Corp. Used by permission.

"In Search of Our Mothers' Gardens," © 1974 by Alice Walker. Reprinted by permission.

"Jazz and the White Critic," © 1963 by Maher Publications, a division of John Maher Printing Co. First published in *down beat* magazine. Used by permission.

Cadence Jazz and Blues Magazine, © 1978 by Robert D. Rusch. Reprinted by permission.

The National Endowment for the Arts' Jazz Oral History Project at the Institute of Jazz Studies at Rutgers University.

Grateful acknowledgment is also made to the following for the loan of photographs used in the book: Jane Sager, Ruth McMurray, Audrey Hall Petroff, Flo Dreyer, Fagle Liebman, Marge Creath Singleton, Clora Bryant, George Clarke, Floyd Turnham, Jr., Andy Kirk, Dr. Albert Vollmer, Bridget O'Flynn, Corky Hale, and Evelyn McGee Stone.

And to the following for making available material from their catalogs: Biograph Records, Folkways Records, Inner City Records, Pablo Records, Spivey Records, New Music Distribution Service, and Mr. Bill Barry of VJM Records.

For my father
Samuel Zadek Placksin
(1908–1980)

Contents

FOREWORD AND ACKNOWLEDGMENTS   xiii

A NOTE ON SOURCES   xviv

PREHISTORY (1619–1900)   3

THE TWENTIES   7

    The Blues Women   7

       Gertrude "Ma" Rainey   12

       Bessie Smith   16

       Mamie Smith   21

       Ethel Waters   24

       Ida Cox   28

       Rosa Henderson   32

       Victoria Spivey   33

       Alberta Hunter   36

       Clara Smith   39

    The Instrumentalists   41

       Edythe Turnham (piano/leader)   47

       Mary Colston Kirk (piano)   49

       Marge Creath Singleton (piano)   51

       Lil Hardin Armstrong (piano/leader/composer)   58

       Dyer Jones and Dolly Jones (trumpets)   64

       Irma Young (alto sax/B-flat soprano sax/baritone
          sax/ukulele/tap dancer)   66

       Doris Peavey (piano/organ/accordion)   71

       Norma Teagarden (piano/leader)   73

Audrey Hall Petroff (reeds/violin/piano/leader)   78
Peggy Gilbert (reeds/vibes/vocals/leader)   82

THE THIRTIES   85

Ernestine "Tiny" Davis (trumpet/leader)   90
Valaida Snow (trumpet/vocals/violin/piano/leader/
    dancer)   93
Ina Ray Hutton and Her Melodears   95
Betty Sattley Leeds (tenor saxophone)   99
Estelle Slavin (trumpet/leader)   101
Jane Sager (trumpet)   103
Irene Kitchings (pianist/leader/composer)   109
Maxine Sullivan (vocalist)   116
Helen Oakley Dance (writer/producer)   122

THE FORTIES   127

The International Sweethearts of Rhythm   132
    Pauline Braddy Williams (drums/vocals)   134
    Evelyn McGee Stone (vocalist)   138
    Helen Jones Woods (trombone)   141
    Helen Saine Coston (reeds)   143
    Anna Mae Winburn (leader/vocalist/guitar)   145
Eddie Durham's All-Star Girl Orchestra   149
Clora Bryant (trumpet/composer)   152
Fagle Liebman (drums/arranger/vocals)   156
Flo Dreyer (trumpet/valve trombone/leader)   161
Norma Carson (trumpet)   164
June Rotenberg (bass)   167
Bridget O'Flynn (drums)   171
Rose Gottesman (drums)   173
Lucille Dixon (bass/leader)   175
Melba Liston (trombone/composer/arranger/
    leader/vocals)   179
Mary Osborne (guitar/vocals)   184
Carline Ray (Fender bass/guitar/piano/acoustic
    bass/vocals)   187
Dorothy Donegan (piano)   193
Sarah McLawler (piano/organ/vocals)   195
Norma Shepherd (piano/vocals)   202

Martha Young (piano)   206
Jane Jarvis (piano/organ/producer/composer)   208
Sheila Jordan (vocalist)   213

THE FIFTIES   221

Willene Barton (tenor saxophone/leader)   227
Jean Davis (trumpet)   231
Dottie Dodgion (drums)   235
Dorothy Ashby (harp/piano/composer)   239
Corky Hale (harp/piano/organ/flute/piccolo/cello)   243

THE SIXTIES   248

Carla Bley (composer/keyboards/saxophone/leader)   251
Barbara Donald (trumpet/composer/leader)   255
Vi Redd (alto sax/soprano sax/vocals/leader)   259
Patti Bown (piano/composer/leader)   260

THE SEVENTIES   266

Ann Patterson (reeds/leader)   269
JoAnne Brackeen (piano/composer)   273
Fostina Dixon (reeds/leader/composer)   276
Erica Lindsay (reeds/leader/composer)   279
Jane Ira Bloom (tenor sax/alto sax/soprano sax/
    leader/composer)   281
Janice Robinson (trombone/leader/composer)   285

EPILOGUE   293

NOTES   295

SELECTED DISCOGRAPHY   303

SELECTED BIBLIOGRAPHY   323

INDEX   325

Foreword and
Acknowledgments

Bessie and Billie were basic, always (as was Billie's primer, "Bessie for feeling, Louis for style"—and both of them for sound). As far as the singers were concerned, for every Count, King, and Duke in jazz, I knew there had been an Empress, a Queen, a Divinity. On piano, too, there were women whose names, it seemed, had alway been known to me—Mary Lou Williams, Hazel Scott, Cleo Brown, Dorothy Donegan, Barbara Carroll, to name but a few.

Then one day in 1978 I happened to hear a 1928 record by a singer I'd never heard before: It was Rosa Henderson, belting out a song called "Strut Yo' Puddy" on an anthology of rare and hot female vocals, and she was wonderful. Who was she? I wondered. Were there other records? I turned to the standard jazz encyclopedias: There was little to be found. (My discovery of Henderson predated the publication of Sheldon Harris's *Blues Who's Who*.) After a search, I was able to put together an outline of her life, and learned that during the 1920s, the heyday of the Classic Blues, Henderson had been one of the most popular entertainers and had made nearly a hundred recordings.

Shortly after discovering Henderson and some of her female peers in the early years of jazz—Ida Cox and her Raisin' Cain Company, pianist Sweet Emma Barrett, trumpet players Dyer and Dolly Jones—I heard a 1928 record of the great Ma Rainey singing "Traveling Blues":

> I went down to the deh-pot
> Looked up and down the board.
> I went down to the deh-pot
> Looked up and down the board.
> I asked the ticket agent,
> Is my town on that road?

The lyric seemed to me an ironic metaphor for all the names, lives, and music I wanted to know more about but could not readily find. Their towns were on the road, to be sure, but where, and in what context?

As one name led to another, I decided to undertake a systematic search for information on female contributors to jazz. I turned to liner notes, obituaries, clippings from the black and white press of the day, discographies, recordings (both in and out of print), periodicals, books, and—most importantly—the musicians themselves, or those who remembered them.

It soon became clear that not only did women have a rich and extensive history as vocalists and pianists, they also had a long (although thoroughly obscured) history as players of the instruments that had always been considered "unacceptable" or "inappropriate" for women: brass, reeds, drums, bass. The heritage stretched back to Congo Square in the early nineteenth century. It could be traced back to the nineteenth-century black all-woman brass bands, through the eras of ragtime, vaudeville, swing, bop, free jazz, and "new" music, a small measure of it preserved on record, some on film, but most of it simply vanished, for many of the instrumentalists I interviewed had never been recorded, and some were no longer actively playing; thus, it was impossible to hear what they had sounded like. The very fact that so many of them had never been recorded, however, represented another important aspect of their collective and individual history. As the women spoke, the very rhythms of their speech, in a sense, became their music, and in the end, the dearth of recorded history would make their stories no less valid.

While I have included singers and pianists in the book, the instrumentalists, in particular, fascinated me. Behind the myths and glamorized facades presented to the public, what had been the true texture of their lives in a largely unsupported—even unpopular and slightly disreputable—American art form considered for the most part solely the province of the men? How had they started out and survived? How had they been affected by the deeply ingrained western tradition which held that women should not even play brass or reeds, let alone become important leaders, soloists, or innovators on the instruments? How had conditions, prospects, and the attitudes of women in the field changed over the decades? As far as the singers were concerned, what were the real stories behind the commercial successes and the years of "hanging in there"?

Having interviewed nearly fifty female and twenty-five male musicians, I was struck by the great diversity of backgrounds from which the women had come into the jazz world. They represented all races and religions; some had college or conservatory degrees, while others learned their craft directly on the road; some quit young to raise their families, and others never left, taking their children on the road. Perhaps the most striking and universal characteristic I encountered was the sense of commitment and the spirit and skill for survival these women possessed. Among the hundreds of women who made up the "hidden history" of America's classical music, there were consummate musicians, show-women, entertainers, creators, educators, writers, and astute business-women who, despite a society and chosen field that discouraged their self-expression and artistic individuality, managed to survive and contribute to the greatest degree possible at the time they were "out there."

As I talked to these women about their lives and experiences, I discovered that, inevitably, they would tell me of other jazz women they knew whose stories and accomplishments deserved to be told. For reasons of time and length, however, it became necessary to limit the scope of this book. What has emerged after two and a half years of research is a combined narrative/oral-history portrait of a representative group of women who played and continue to play important roles in jazz but who have rarely, if ever, had a chance to talk openly and honestly about their lives. In addition to providing a perspective on the history of American women in jazz over seven decades, it is my hope that this book has also provided an open forum for some of these women to talk about how they do what they do; an introduction to a rich and largely unexplored facet of America's musical history; an invitation and point of departure for further exploration and documentation; and, finally, a tribute to the many women who have spent years or lifetimes working to perpetuate jazz, often without public fanfare or adequate recognition or remuneration.

During the time I worked on this project, there were many people whose generosity and assistance in a great variety of contexts were invaluable to me. I would like to thank my agent, Katinka Matson, for encouraging me to write this book; my editor, Anne Kostick, and her assistant, Cameron Barry, for their support and cooperation while I did; and my copy editor, Susan Philipson, for her careful eye and meticulous attention to detail.

Most of all, I am indebted to those women who shared their lives and recollections with me, and without whom this history would not exist. Their warmth, outspokenness, enthusiasm, and enormous generosity of time and spirit were truly without equal. I would like to extend my gratitude to: Marge Creath Singleton, Irma Young, Norma Teagarden, Audrey Hall Petroff, Peggy Gilbert, Ernestine "Tiny" Davis, Betty Sattley Leeds, Estelle Slavin, Jane Sager, Maxine Sullivan, Helen Oakley Dance, Pauline Braddy Williams, Evelyn McGee Stone, Helen Jones Woods, Helen Saine Coston, Anna Mae Winburn, Lorraine Brown, Clora Bryant, Fagle Liebman, Flo Dreyer, Norma Carson, June Rotenberg, Bridget O'Flynn, Rose Gottesman, Lucille Dixon, Melba Liston, Mary Osborne, Carline Ray, Dorothy Donegan, Sarah McLawler, Norma Shepherd, Martha Young, Jane Jarvis, Flo Jones, Hetty Smith Pasco, Sheila Jordan, Willene Barton, Jean Davis, Dottie Dodgion, Dorothy Ashby, Corky Hale, Gloria Coleman, Della Griffin, Lodi Carr, Barbara Donald, Patti Bown, Ann Patterson, JoAnne Brackeen, Fostina Dixon, Erica Lindsay, Jane Ira Bloom, and Janice Robinson.

Other musicians and people who were not the principal subjects of this book were also equally generous in sharing their recollections and insights with me, and without their contribution, the total picture would have been far less complete than it is. I wish to extend my deep appreciation to Clyde Bernhardt, Andy Kirk, Eddie Durham, Roy Eldridge, Doc Cheatham, Jonah Jones, Dick Vance, George Clarke, George James, George Kelly, Lee Young, Paul Quinichette, Eddie Barefield, the late Snub Mosley, Floyd Turnham, Jr., Tommy Benford, the late Walter "Foots" Thomas, Jimmy Rowles, Ikey Robinson, Jesse Stone, Francis Williams, Walter Bishop, Sr., Hollis M. Peavey, Arthur Herzog, Jr., Leonard Kunstadt, Callie Arter, Irv Kratka, Dianne Gregg, Elden Kitchings, and Joseph Attles.

For their enormous dedication and expertise in maintaining a unique jazz archive, and for their many kindnesses to me during the course of researching this book, I am particularly indebted to Dan Morgenstern, director of the Institute of Jazz Studies at Rutgers University, curator Ed Berger, Bob Kenselaar (who has since left), Marie Griffin, Jeanette Gayle, and Ron Welburn, coordinator of the National Endowment for the Arts' Jazz Oral History Project at the Institute. I am especially grateful to Vincent Pelote and Walter Parker of the Institute for their infinite patience and valiant assistance during last-minute fact checking. In addition, I wish to acknowledge the staffs of the Music Division and the Rodgers and Hammerstein Archives of Recorded Sound at the Lincoln Center Library for the Performing Arts; Mr. Ernest Kaiser and the staff of the Schomberg Center for Research in Black Culture; Frankie Mac-Cormick and the Songwriters Hall of Fame; Cobi Narita and the Universal Jazz Coalition; Dianne Gregg and Carol Comer of the Women's Jazz Festival, Inc.; and Deborah Morgan and the J & R Music World Jazz Outlet.

My thanks also go to others who gave generously of their time, knowledge, and support: Jeff Atterton, David Chertok, the late Jon Saunders, Pastor John Garcia Gensel and Saint Peter's Church, Stanley Dance, Kenn Freeman, Diane Reverand, Dr. Albert Vollmer, Peter Carr, Arthur Newman, Jack Bradley, Alan Sukoenig, Raymond Ross, James K. Davis, Carol Sloane, Sidney Placksin, Frances Ehrlich, Mary Lyn Maiscott, Yale Evelev, Morton Savada, Max Herman, Emil Faustin, Cynthia Kelsh, Judy Small, Charlotte Watson, and José Escalero. I am particularly indebted to Dr. Jo Grieder for her sensitive and constructive comments on the manuscript; Phil Schaap for directing me to important sources; Brooks Kerr, for his enthusiastic aid in tracking down a number of important individuals, and for making available recorded material from his private collection; Janie Rockhold and Carroll Conover for their thoughtfulness and assistance during particularly difficult times; and most especially Judy Ehrlich, for her steady support and friendship.

Finally, there are five people who deserve special gratitude: my father, Samuel Placksin, who did not live to see this book completed, but whose enthusiasm, support, and total belief in the project were unfailing from its earliest days; my mother, Edith Chochlow Placksin, for her constant support and her thoughtfulness in being ever on the alert for relevant leads and information; and Donald Bogle, Phyllis Gaudia, and Eddie Durham, whose friendship, encouragement, and great generosity in sharing with me their knowledge, insights, and wisdom are gifts which, in Duke Ellington's words, extend truly "beyond category."

A Note on Sources

Quotes from unidentified clippings at the Institute of Jazz Studies at Rutgers University will be identified in the text with the abbreviation (IJS).

Quotes from unidentified clippings at the Lincoln Center Library for the Performing Arts will be identified in the text by the collection in which the clippings were found:

Billy Rose Theatre Collection: (LCL-T)

Music Division: (LCL-M)

Quotes from transcripts in the National Endowment for the Arts' Jazz Oral History Program at the Institute of Jazz Studies at Rutgers University will be followed in the text with the abbreviation (JOHP).

All other unidentified material comes from original interviews by the author.

AMERICAN
WOMEN
IN JAZZ

PREHISTORY
(1619-1900)

... Negro music is essentially the expression of an attitude, or a collection of attitudes, about the world, and only secondarily an attitude about the way music is made.
—LeRoi Jones (Amiri Baraka)
"Jazz and the White Critic"

The main origin of American jazz was the spiritual. Because of the deeply religious background of the black American, he [she] was able to mix this strong influence with rhythms that reach deep enough into the inner self to give expression to outcries of censored joy which became known as jazz.
—Mary Lou Williams
Mary Lou Williams: The History of Jazz

Our mothers and our grandmothers, some of them: moving to music not yet written.
—Alice Walker
"In Search of Our Mothers' Gardens"

In 1619 an indentured slave named Isabelle, the first black woman to be brought to America, landed at the settlement in Jamestown, Virginia.

Since that time, North and South, sacred and secular, slave and free, black women have participated in the creation and evolution of black music in America—and out of that musical heritage and expression, jazz was born.

From Africa black men and women brought a birthright and blood rite of music—a heritage of improvisation, rhythm, call-and-response antiphony, and a musical passion that would be retained in America. (Centuries later, the two features that distinguished jazz from other dance music would be improvisation and the rhythm and phrasing that made the music "swing.") But from its earliest years in America, this African birthright of music would take on new meaning; it would take on life-and-death proportions. In the "hush harbors" where blacks would gather to pray, at secret prayer grounds—sometimes nothing more than a twisted thick-rooted muscadine bush in the woods—in factories in the cities and fields in the country, at festivals in the more lenient North, always black music held a hidden meaning, a mixture of sorrow, faith, "censored joy," spiritual and cultural affirmation far deeper than the white man could perceive. Often (as in black speech later on) there was also a practical, coded message—a slightly altered lyric or a metaphor, intended to exclude the white world from its meaning while conveying a piece of life-or-death information to blacks: the place of a voodoo or religious meeting or the time and plan of an escape route to "Canaan," which, when heard in spirituals, meant, to every slave, "the North."

In America, black women no longer improvised songs about the "poor white man . . . No mother has he to bring him milk,/No wife to grind his corn,"[1] as they had done in Africa, one leader improvising lyrics about the day's events as the group joined in. (This song was heard and written down by Scottish surgeon Mungo Park, who visited Africa in 1795.) In America, black women improvised messages along the "grapevine telegraph," the secret system of communication among the slaves. In New Orleans, where the strictly forbidden voodoo cults nevertheless flourished during the nineteenth century, "a message could be conveyed from one end of the city to another in a single day without one white person's being aware of it," wrote Lyle Saxon in *Fabulous New Orleans*. A black woman working in a kitchen, he explained, would sing a Creole song "which sounded innocuous enough to any white listener, but at the end of the verse she would sing a few words intended as a message." Another slave working nearby would listen closely and hear the message repeated at the end of the second verse. "This second servant would then go outside and attend to her duties. She would sing the same song and her voice would be heard by servants in the house next door. In this way, by means of a song, news of the meeting of a Voodoo society would be carried from one end of the city to another and upon the appointed night Negro men and women would slip from their beds before midnight and would assemble for their ceremonies."[2]

In New Orleans, not only was music important to the slaves and the women on the daily periphery of voodoo, but it also lay at the heart of the meetings and ceremonies themselves. And one group of women was central to the voodoo cults: the voodoo queens of New Orleans.

Little is known of the earliest queens—Sanité Dédé, Marie Saloppé, and the most famous and long-lived queen, Marie Laveau. Free women of color, glamorous and haughty showwomen, shrewd and clever business-women, the queens began to accrue power in the early nineteenth century, after the Louisiana Purchase (1803) eased the formerly strict rulings against voodoo in New Orleans. In Africa, "vodun" had had both a king and a queen, but in America, where it was easier for black women than for black men to attain power outside the legitimate religious hier-

archy, the cult became predominantly matriarchal. The queens functioned as important religious and spiritual leaders at a time when many
blacks were permitted no alternative religious life or emotional release.
They were also, as writer Susan Cavin has noted, influential in the
organization of the music that was part of every voodoo ceremony and
ritual and that preceded the music known as jazz. "Marie Laveau," wrote
Cavin about the woman who turned voodoo worship from the devil to
the Lord, "was not only a pivotal figure in Voodoo, but possibly in jazz
as well."[3]

After 1817, New Orleans' Place Congo (or Congo Square) was the
site where the most public voodoo ceremonies took place. On Sunday
afternoons, slaves would gather there to chant and to dance the tamer
dances that represented six African tribes. (Fearful city fathers had restricted voodoo meetings to this time and place, but the secret, more
sensual rites continued along the lakefront or at Marie Laveau's Maison
Blanche.) Creole jazzman Sidney Bechet had grown up hearing about
the music played at Congo Square. "Improvisation," he called it. "That's
what it was. It was primitive and it was crude, but down at the bottom
of it, inside it, where it starts and gets into itself—down there it had the
same thing there is at the bottom of ragtime. It was already born and
making in the music they played in Congo Square."[4]

As Susan Cavin pointed out, it has generally been "tacitly" assumed
by jazz historians and scholars that men were the only music makers in
Congo Square. But women were also there. They functioned not only as
participants but also as leaders of chants and even as drummers, playing
the instrument which, in Haitian voodoo, was the male divinity personi-
fied and which, in Africa, was reserved for tribal chiefs alone.

As early as 1819, Benjamin Latrobe attended and wrote about a dance
at Congo Square where he saw a calabash "with a round hole in it, the
hole studded with brass nails, which was beaten by a woman with two
short sticks."[5] In 1825 D. W. Buel described a lakeside ceremony run by
the first known queen, Sanité Dédé. There Buel observed "a Negress
with the leg bones of a buzzard or turkey beating an accompaniment on
the sides of a cylinder."[6]

Not only were the voodoo queens and women an important force in
the black community; at a time when black and white women in America
were ruled and manipulated by what Adrienne Rich has called a "divide
and conquer" strategy[7] devised and sustained largely by southern white
men, the secret voodoo cults also provided an early ground on which
women of both races mixed, for some of the women who attended the
secret rites were white. Newspaper accounts considered it scandalous
when white women were discovered at the ceremonies. (One man actually committed suicide the day after his wife was found at a meeting and
the news was printed in the morning paper.)

Some women argued (successfully) in court that voodoo was a "religious" practice, and the law "had no justification for its attitude towards them," while in another group, in which "several" white women were present, "the white ladies claimed that they had been unclad only because of the excessive heat, and had been present only because they had one and all collapsed simultaneously on the doorsteps of the Voodooienne."[8] (The white women, it was reported, were merely fined and then dismissed.)

"I likes 'Poor Rosy' better than all the songs," said one ex-slave woman, "but it can't be sung without a full heart and a troubled spirit."[9]

"Consider, if you can bear to imagine it," wrote Alice Walker, "what might have been the result if singing, too, had been forbidden by law. Listen to the voices of Bessie Smith, Billie Holiday . . . [or Dinah Washington, Ella Fitzgerald, Betty Carter, Sarah Vaughan] and imagine those voices [and the anonymous early voices] muzzled for life."[10]

By the turn of the century, black women had come out of a rich musical tradition to sing individually, as the group had done in Africa, about the feelings and events of daily life. By the early 1900s in America, they had begun to sing and tell the world about the blues.

THE TWENTIES

The Blues Women

You must make your whole body sing the blues from your toes
right up to the top of your head. Flat tones . . . show the freedom
in blues singing. You should never know when they come out of
you. The heart will tell the voice when.

—Victoria Regina Spivey

While the spirituals of the nineteenth-century camp meetings and the
hymns of the black churches had provided the sustenance and affirmation
that the black world needed, the people also needed something earthier,
E. Simms Campbell wrote,[1] something that touched their lives more
intimately. As freer solo expression became possible after Emancipation,
the articulation of individual isolation, hard times, abandonment, pain,
suffering, hopes, joys, humor, wisdom, mischief, and dreams was added
to the collective cry. In addition to the biblical themes, landscape, and
language of the spirituals, there was now also a smaller, human, un-
celestial setting and scale where metaphor was retained, but where the
individual and his or her feelings, everyday circumstances, and *personality* became preeminent, and he or she the hero or the victim. Black
women began to introduce and expand upon their more personal plight
and feelings, whatever they might have been, from dinner burning on the
stove to the death of a relative to the pain of loving a hard-hearted,
inaccessible man. (It was a woman singing on the road, W. C. Handy
recalls in his autobiography, *Father of the Blues,* who inspired part of his
famous composition "St. Louis Blues.")

For ten golden years of Reconstruction—the "mystic years," W. E. B.
DuBois called them—black life and culture flourished, until the concomitant rise of the Ku Klux Klan by 1877 once again subjected blacks
to new forms of violence, economic intimidation, and murder. The black
minstrel troupes, which had begun in the 1860s, continued nonetheless,

and in the late nineteenth century, as they began to open their doors to female entertainers, the stage became an important creative avenue for women. Ma Rainey's grandmother was said to have been a stage performer during Reconstruction; pianist Edythe Turnham got her start in the minstrel shows around 1900; and as early as 1902, legend has it, the great Ma Rainey herself was singing blues songs (which antedated the traditional blues form) on the stage and establishing her reputation as "the Mother of the Blues."

By the first two decades of the twentieth century, blues-singing female entertainers like Ma Rainey, Bessie Smith, Ida Cox, and others were barnstorming their way through the South, working in tents, circuses, carnivals, or in the theaters on the black TOBA (Theater Owner's Booking Association, *aka* Tough on Black Asses or "Toby time") circuit. They were singing comedy songs, novelty songs, ballads, doing comedy and dramatic routines, and also singing blues songs and the blues. Because they mixed the rural blues tradition with the more varied and sophisticated fare of the vaudeville stage, and because the blues remained their most popular drawing card and purest form of expression (particularly after 1920, when the first blues record was made), they eventually became known as "the Classic Blues Singers." The best of these artists—Rainey, Smith, Cox, Victoria Spivey, Alberta Hunter, Sippie Wallace—not only sang the songs of other composers, but also wrote their own, and their own were often their most popular and their best.

Traveling by Pullman car, bus, or automobile, the most famous of the minstrel troupes—the Rabbit Foots, Florida Cotton Blossoms, Georgia Smart Set, Silas Green of New Orleans—would hit the canebrakes and the factory towns, the theaters of the bigger cities, laying down a bedrock of blues among the people. They followed the tobacco crops in the spring, the cotton crops in the fall, hit the coal mines and the Sea Islands off Georgia, arriving in each town at the season when the people had the most money to spend and were ready to go out and party. When the troupes arrived, the tents would go up, the bands would march through town, flyers would be handed out, and soon the show would be on, the crowds so big, recalled blues singer Brother John Sellers, that "they be packed in there like rice in a bowl."[2]

While the blues and the traveling shows had been an integral part of the black world for two decades, in 1920 came a milestone event that changed both the entertainment industry and the daily texture of black life, particularly in urban areas; it also brought forth in a major way an idiomatic expression not only from the black world but also from the female world.

In 1919, when she recorded a vaudeville routine with the legendary Bert Williams, Mary Straine became the first black woman ever to make a record. But a black woman had yet to be recorded singing the blues.

In 1920, after a long and arduous struggle on the part of the black music community to persuade the white music establishment to record a black female blues vocal, entertainer Mamie Smith finally got the break: Okeh Records let her record "The Crazy Blues." With the success of the record—it sold over a hundred thousand copies in its first month of release—Okeh (which, appropriately enough, meant "so be it" or "it is so" in Chocktaw) became a serious new rival to Paramount and Columbia, and opened the door for the blues recording industry of the twenties.

The sensational reception of "The Crazy Blues" marked the official opening of the decade of the Classic Blues Singers, as white record producers discovered the new and highly lucrative "race market," as it was called—the black public eager to purchase records through mail-order catalogs, record stores in black neighborhoods, or even via Pullman porters arriving from the North with stacks of records to sell. Trombonist Clyde Bernhardt, then a young boy in Badin, South Carolina, recalls that soon after "The Crazy Blues" was released, a man came into town with 200 copies and sold them all at $1.10 apiece ($1.00 was the going price). By March 1921, Bernhardt was in Harrisburg, Pennsylvania. The song, he says, "was all you could hear on the streets, black neighborhoods, mixed neighborhoods, sometimes four and five playing the same record at different speeds in their homes. Sonoa Victrolas, wind-up."

As record companies became convinced that the vast appeal of the blues was more than just a passing phase, they started scouring city and countryside, sending out local recording units and looking for talent to build up their catalogs. Even classically trained vocalists tried their hand at the sometimes "naughty" but more lucrative blues. Some of the better known blues women took advantage of the great demand of the market by recording under four, five, or more pseudonyms for as many different labels. (There were no royalty arrangements at that time, only fees for sessions.)

Not only had Mamie Smith created a new industry and employment option for young black women all over the country; she had also paved the way for singers like Gladys Bently, blues shouter and vaudeville artist Lizzie Miles, and country blues singers like Lucille Bogan and singer/guitarist Memphis Minnie Douglas, who made over 200 recordings and created some of the most inventive sounds in blues. Smith also put the blues on a national scale and helped to bring black music and culture to people—black as well as white—who might otherwise have had little or no access to it at all. Finally, it should be noted that all the blues women, in using some of the finest jazz musicians of the day as their accompanists—Louis Armstrong, Coleman Hawkins, Sidney Bechet, Tommy Ladnier, Joe Green, Fletcher Henderson, to name but a few— made possible some of the earliest recorded jazz breaks by these great artists.

As the "royal family" of singers grew, the crowds came out to hear them all singing their hit songs: the polished and beautiful Mamie Smith; the big-voiced, petite, popular Princess White; the "Empress," Bessie Smith, personification of the blues and considered by many the first jazz singer; the dramatic Sara Martin singing "Death Sting Me Blues"; Sippie Wallace singing her own "Up the Country Blues," her high, whining "Mighty Tight Woman," and her low, solemn, gospel-inspired "Flood Blues"; Ethel Waters, with her combination of earthy blues and shakes and high-toned vaudeville fare; the more urbane Ida Cox (later called "the Sepia Mae West"); Bertha "Chippie" Hill singing "Pratt City Blues" and "Trouble in Mind," songs she had recorded with a very young Louis Armstrong; Victoria Spivey wailing her Texas moans; the magnetic Alberta Hunter; Clara Smith, whose recorded output rivaled Bessie Smith's; Trixie Smith; Laura Smith (none of the Smiths were related); Mattie Hite; Mary Stafford; Edith Wilson, Lucille Hegamin . . .

In their songs, the blues women told of a wide range of subjects and feelings, and, with their candor, broke many of the sexual and social taboos of the day. They sang of love, unrequited love, murderous revenge, anger, prostitution, jail, abandonment, loneliness, disease, alcohol, floods, travel, home, humor, trains, sex, ships, superstition, hard luck, death, dreams, voodoo, graveyards, lesbianism, male homosexuality, sadomasochism, violence, and even aching feet. They were rough, raunchy, and worldly, and their presentation and material both mirrored and dug deep into their audiences' own lives and experience.

Live, the blues queens' ritual was as mesmerizing and cathartic as the voodoo rites had been nearly a century before. (As the voodoo queens had, to some small extent, bridged a gap between black and white women, so too did the blues women, who influenced such white artists as Connee Boswell and Sophie Tucker, and also, on occasion, played to white audiences.) Each performer worked her own particular magic on the people, drawing them into the action. Women shouted recognition when the singer told about the way her man mistreated her; they shouted confirmation when Bessie Smith sang her "Young Woman's Blues" or when Ma Rainey majestically dumped her man in "Titanic Man Blues"; and they mourned with "Backwater Blues," Bessie's version of the tragic Delta flood. Men and women alike were touched and renewed by these priestesses of blues, who offered a raunchy (or elegant) release, confirming and fertilizing the spirit and core of the black world.

Some nights the shouts turned into silence as the congregations sat spellbound in the mystical presence of Ma Rainey or "Miss Bessie." Like all artists, musicians, actors, and show people in those years, the blues women were considered by many, even in the black community, the "lowest of the low"; still, they flaunted their elaborate costumes, jewels, feathers, and plumes, fulfilled fantastical images of glamour, sex, and power at a time when women approached that status in few walks of life. And the ties between performer and her congregation were electric and profound.

The blues, Albert Murray has said, are "a device for making the best of a bad situation" without compromising one's integrity, and the hero is the one who accomplishes this feat, aided by the "antagonistic co-operation" of life.[3] It was the "antagonistic cooperation" of life in America that brought out the blues queens' particular best, shaped their talents, and honed their irony (in the way they confronted and transcended racist material and stereotypes), and made these women, most of whom had run away as children to join the TOBA circuit, Olympian in any world.

Sometimes, they sang the news across the oceans, like Ida Cox in "Broadcast Blues"; sometimes, they telegraphed it, like Ma Rainey in "Rough and Tumble Blues" (this spreading of the word was a common blues device); other times, they merely sang about it "in their solitude," face turned to the wall and just the audience listening in. But whichever way they let the news be known, once they'd drawn the world in as commiserators and conspirators, they managed to conquer—or at least diminish—the very plight (or truly celebrate the joys) of which they sang. They may have been abandoned, hopeless, too passive even for suicide (or were they just sassily flaunting their temperament and basically hopeful that better days, better times, better men were just around the corner?). They may have been making a strong statement, as in Bessie Smith's "Poor Man's Blues" or Victoria Spivey's "T.B. Blues." But even if they had nothing else in the world—no other love, no other hope, no other platform—they had their song, and for the moment, they had power. With their singing of the song came the very antidote to the plague of blues.

By 1928 the nearly ten-year-long blues craze had started fading, and the market was on the way down. Many rural blacks felt divorced from their country roots, and urban audiences wanted more sophisticated fare. Recording companies terminated or failed to renew the blues queens' contracts. Adapting to the times and trends, some of the women remained active throughout the Depression, taking their own shows around the country (as did Ida Cox) or experimenting in film (as did Victoria Spivey and Bessie Smith). Others retired or survived as best they could.

By 1939 the two greatest blues women, Ma Rainey and Bessie Smith, were dead, and others—Rosa Henderson, Mamie Smith, Clara Smith—had disappeared or died. Still others—Alberta Hunter, Victoria Spivey, Sippie Wallace—would continue to contribute richly and importantly to this unique American literature, retiring for a time, but coming back to revitalize their own classic music, as well as to write, perform, and record beautiful new songs.

Gertrude "Ma" Rainey

O Ma Rainey,
Sing yo' song;
Now you's back
Whah you belong,
Git way inside us,
Keep us strong. . . . .
O Ma Rainey,
L'il an' low;
Sing us 'bout de hard luck
'Roun' our do';
Sing us 'bout de lonesome road
We mus' go. . . . .
　　　　　　—"Ma Rainey"
　　　　　　by Sterling Brown

Gertrude "Ma" Rainey is, today, the acknowledged "Mother of the Blues." Her contribution as musical innovator, poet, lyricist, composer, mentor, performer, and mystical, overwhelming presence has also been recognized. Yet, when Ma Rainey died in Rome, Georgia, in 1939, her death went practically unnoticed by the music world. Although she had been out of show business for only four years, her death certificate listed her "usual occupation" as "housekeeper."

From what is known of Rainey's life, and especially from her music—nearly one hundred songs preserved on record—we can reconstruct and appreciate the power and importance of the "Queen Mother of the Classic Blues."

The second of five children, Gertrude Pridgett was born in 1886 to Thomas and Ella Allen Pridgett, Alabamans who had relocated to Rome, Georgia. She was baptized into the First African Baptist Church, of which her brother later became a deacon. Her grandmother was supposed to have been on the stage after Emancipation and was said by trombone player Al Wynn to have been a "very stately lady,"[4] and both her parents were reported to have been minstrel-show entertainers.

Born into this environment, Pridgett was trained from childhood as a singer and dancer, and her talent was obvious early on, as was her decided flair for the flamboyance that accompanied stage acts in those days. By the time she was fourteen, she made her debut singing and dancing in *The Bunch of Blackberries,* a local talent show presented at the

Springer Opera House in Columbus, Georgia, after which, presumably, she went on to work in tent shows.

In 1902, the story goes, so stricken by the poignant song she overheard a woman singing about the man she'd lost, the young Pridgett learned the song and incorporated it into her act. She later said that she subsequently heard similar songs during her travels. Although the first official blues—W. C. Handy's "Memphis Blues"—was not published until 1914, audiences responded with special enthusiasm to the song that Pridgett called "the blues," and it was always featured as her closing number.

On April 22, 1904, Pridgett married Will "Pa" Rainey, an older vaudevillian with the famous Rabbit Foot Minstrels, and the couple toured together, the eighteen-year-old Pridgett now billed as "Madame Gertrude Rainey." Their act consisted of comedy, singing, and dancing, but Madame Rainey—affectionately known as "Ma"—was the featured player. Over the next years, the couple traveled with the Moses Stokes Show (where Bessie Smith also had her first job), the Rabbit Foot Minstrels, Tolliver's Circus (which billed them as "Rainey and Rainey, Assassinators of the Blues"), Silas Green from New Orleans, the Florida Cotton Blossoms, the Smart Set, and other minstrel troupes. By 1917 Ma Rainey was playing the South with her own group—Ma Rainey and her Georgia Smart Set—and Pa Rainey was no longer a partner in the act, or even a part of the show.

That same year, Rainey's Georgia Smart Set appeared in Badin, South Carolina, hometown of trombonist Clyde Bernhardt, who at that time was still a child. Badin was then a fast, fashionable boom town. The Alcoa plant employed nearly 6,000 people, and when the minstrel-bearing trains could not get enough track to park their cars in Badin, they would go to Albemarle, seven miles away. In one or another of the two towns, Clyde Bernhardt saw all the carnivals and circuses and heard all the blues queens. In the days before Mamie Smith's big hit, says Bernhardt, "Ma Rainey was the 'Queen of the Blues'; she's the one that had the name."

Bernhardt not only saw Ma Rainey for the first time in 1917, but also got to run errands for her, buying her Coca-Colas (several times a day) and doing whatever else she might require. "Sometimes she'd come there and play four weeks, and she'd change shows maybe two or three times a week. She had a packed tent every night, and she didn't depend on the colored people alone," he recalls, for half the tent was for blacks, the other half for whites. During the day, Rainey rehearsed the act. "She didn't read no music," says Bernhardt. "She had her own musicians that played with her. She used a piano player, a drummer, a violin player, a bass-violin player, and a cello player. She had what they called back in them days a string band. I don't know whether any of them could read music or not. I think the piano player could read music, and the rest of 'em, they had good ears and they would follow. He knew what she wanted and he would tell the other fellows in the band. . . . I saw their shows rehearsing many times. Sometimes they'd rehearse two or three hours, getting a new show to put on the next night."

Rainey also worked rehearsing the chorus girls, in this case darker than the usual "café-au-lait" line, as she did not want them to appear lighter onstage than she did. During the teens and twenties, the chorus lines provided one of the principal employment opportunities for young women in the world of entertainment, and the "café-au-lait" tradition went back as far as 1842, when British writer Charles Dickens observed mulatto women dancing at Almack's Tavern in New York City's Five Points, or tenderloin, to what was the "hot music" of the day, supplied by a trumpeter, drummer, perhaps a fiddler and a tambourine player, and performed for the exclusive carriage trade. As Clyde Bernhardt points out, women like Rainey, Cox, and Bessie Smith were of special importance because, dark-skinned themselves, they did not honor the prevailing prejudice in favor of light-skinned chorines. "They would give any kind of girl a job and a chance if she had talent and could act," Bernhardt recalls. Had it not been for them, he says, many of the women would never have gotten a break.

A typical Rainey show lasted about two hours. These were the days when flash, flamboyance, even freakishness filled the bill, and audiences were vocal and demonstrative one way or the other. One can imagine some of the elements of a Rainey performance: the audience making its pilgrimage from miles around (". . . flivverin' in,/Or ridin' mules,/Or packed in trains,/Picknickin' fools . . .");[5] the tent filling, blacks on one side, whites on the other—some demanding to be seated in the black section when the seats designated "white" were filled (most reports attest to the fact that Rainey preferred black audiences); and the great Rainey herself, making up backstage, taking over an hour to apply the greasepaint and light powder to her face—and later, says Bernhardt, taking just as long to remove it.

Out front, the audience would be waiting. The band would open with an instrumental, followed by the chorus line—in the unusual combination of light-skinned men and very dark women—dancing "Strut Miss Lizzie," "The Cutout," or maybe "Pickin' Peaches," the women dressed in just-below-the-knee-length skirts and high-heel lace-up shoes. Then came the comedians with ethnic humor and broad comedy; next, the soubrette singing a fast tune like "Ballin' the Jack," joined by the chorus. The comedians would reappear, and finally Ma Rainey herself would come on, joking about her craving for "pig meat" and for "bird liver"—young and tender men. "I'm gonna tell you about my man," she'd say, "and then probably with her jazz cats she'd start singing 'A Good Man Is Hard to Find.' "[6] (Later on, after she had started to record, she used to make her entrance from a huge Victrola, blowing kisses to the audience.) "When her last number came," recalled Artiebelle McGinty, who toured with her, "everybody would be waiting for that and it would be a blues"[7]—usually "C. C. Rider," a guaranteed showstopper.

Rainey never left her musical or spiritual roots, and although she appeared in the Midwest and the North—Chicago, New York, Philadelphia—she was primarily of and for her southern audiences. "Ma really *knew* her people," poet Sterling Brown has said. "She was a person of the folk; she was very simple and direct. She would moan and the audience would moan with her. She had them in the palm of her hand."[8]

Gertrude "Ma" Rainey's recording career came relatively late in her life as a blues queen. When the blues craze started in 1920, Rainey was already thirty-four years old, and it was not until three years later, in December 1923, that she cut her first sides for Paramount, the only label on which she ever recorded. Over the next six years she would record over a hundred songs, eighty-six of which are currently available. She wrote twenty-four of the songs herself, and over the span of her recording career, writes Rudi Blesh, it was she more than anyone else who was "responsible for the growth in variety and complexity of the accompaniments from simple guitar and piano to the full instrumental jazz accompaniments which help to give some of these records their timeless depth, breadth, and richness."[9] During her recording career, she would be paired with jazz musicians of legendary stature: Louis Armstrong, on "Countin' the Blues," "Jelly Bean Blues," and "See See Rider" (*sic*); Tampa Red, on "Daddy Goodbye Blues" and "Runaway Blues"; Tommy Ladnier and Lovie Austin, on "Boweavil Blues"; and Charlie Green, on "Chain Gang Blues."

Her subject matter ranged from Everywoman's lovesick, lonesome blues to the havoc wreaked against the men who did her wrong; from anguished desolation to murderous revenge. She counseled women to "Trust No Man"—not even their *own*—and advised men to be careful talking in their sleep; she delivered ultimatums, and she dealt frankly and boldly with homosexuality, lesbianism, sadomasochism, and sexual violence in her songs. While most of the song personas in various versions of "Hustlin' Blues" were walking the streets on "lonesome rainy nights," fearful of facing their men empty-handed, Rainey's "Hustlin' Blues" portrays a streetwalker who finally declares:

> O judge, tell him I'm through
> O judge, tell him I'm through
> I'm tired of this life,
> That's why I brought him to you.

Another Rainey song (this one written with Bessie Smith) speaks the wry, vivid poetry of the blues:

If you don't like my ocean
Don't fish in my sea,
Stay away from my valley
And let my mountain be.

And at the bottom line are the blues that are just about the blues: "Countin' the Blues" or "Blame It on the Blues."

By 1928, when Ma Rainey's contract was up, the blues had begun a slow fade, and Paramount declined to renew her contract. (One executive, questioned during the fifties, would explain, "Her down-home material had gone out of fashion."[10]) Having never stopped touring (although she had bought her family a home in Georgia and maintained a large apartment in Chicago), she continued to work on the road with her own company, the Arkansas Swift Foot Review, until it collapsed. Then she joined the Al Gaines Carnival Show, working in tents throughout the Southwest.

In 1935 both Rainey's mother and sister died, and the Mother of the Blues retired to her home in Columbus, Georgia, keeping house for her brother, Thomas Pridgett. An excellent businesswoman, she was also running the two theaters that she owned, the Lyric and the Airdrome, and had become active in church affairs. In 1939, at the age of forty-three, Rainey suffered a heart attack and died in City Hospital. She was buried in the family grave at Porterdale Cemetery in Columbus.

"Bessie (and all the others who followed in time)," wrote Dan Morgenstern, "learned their art and craft from Ma, directly or indirectly."[11] On the road, her administrative-managerial skills were first-rate (she treated her musicians well, bought them instruments, and always paid everybody off); as a "personality"—with her elaborate rhinestone gowns, twenty-dollar-gold-piece necklace, and her gold and diamond teeth—she knew what the people wanted and kept her public tantalized.

Jazz historian Charles Edward Smith once wrote of Rainey: "She was the voice of the South, singing of the South, to the South."[12] Today, Rainey has come to transcend such territorial limitations, her message resurrected fifty years after the peak of her career.

Bessie Smith

Songwriter and innovative artist, actress, comedienne, dancer, and mime, Bessie Smith was the epitome of the blues woman as mass hypnotist, as preacher, as "voodoo queen." Her voice was monumental. She could growl, barrelhouse, and embellish the blues and, at the same time, endow them with majesty and a profound simplicity and grace. She possessed a quiet, intense spirituality (and vulnerability) that merged with sure talent and a "See If I'll Care" attitude to explode onstage with the impact of some natural phenomenon—earthquake, flood, volcano.

Smith's work exerted a tremendous influence on musicians of her day and on musicians in all the decades that followed. Of the 180 songs she recorded for Columbia, 160 are currently available. Unlike any of the other blues women, Smith has had her life well documented and explored in a full-length biography, and discussions of her work and her importance have been included in jazz books from which all other women are absent. She was portrayed on Broadway by Linda Hopkins in *Me and Bessie,* and her music has been paid special tribute in recorded or live performance by such singers as Juanita Hall, Dinah Washington, and Carrie Smith.

Bessie Smith was born in Chattanooga, Tennessee, to William Smith, a part-time Baptist minister, and his wife, Laura. By the time Bessie was nine years old, her parents had died, her older sister, Viola, was raising the remaining children in what Bessie once called a "little ramshackle cabin," and Bessie herself had started singing on Chattanooga's 9th Street for nickels and dimes, with her brother Andrew accompanying her on guitar. When another brother, Clarence, joined Moses Stokes's Traveling Show, he arranged an audition for her, and in 1912 she joined the company primarily to work as a dancer. It was on the Stokes show that she first met Ma and Pa Rainey, and it is probably because of that meeting that the legends grew up about the kidnapping of the young protégée by the queen-mentor of the blues.

That same year, Bessie danced briefly in the chorus line of one of Irvin C. Miller's shows, but was dismissed because she did not fit his bill "Glorifying the Brownskin Girl." The next year, she played in Atlanta's "81" Theater, and her reputation began to grow. She trained chorus dancers by day and sang at night, dressed in street clothes, earning ten dollars a week plus tips and delivering her big number, "Weary Blues." During the late teens and early twenties she got onto the TOBA circuit, touring with such companies as the Rabbit Foot Minstrels, the Florida Cotton Blossoms, and Silas Green, and worked in various clubs, in addition to having her own revue, the Liberty Belles, in which she appeared as a singer, dancer, and male impersonator. By 1922 she had moved to Philadelphia and acquired a sizeable following throughout the South and along the Eastern Seaboard.

In 1920, when the blues craze first hit, Bessie Smith was turned down by three companies before Columbia signed her up. Emerson didn't like her; neither did Okeh, where she cut a test of "Sister Kate" with Sidney Bechet; and Black Swan (the only black-owned record company) found her "too rough" for their liking. When she did start recording, her first record was a new version of "Downhearted Blues," which Alberta Hunter had written and recorded a year before with Lovie Austin on piano. It sold extremely well, and when Smith returned to the "81" Theater shortly after the record's release, her first night was a triumph, and the second night's music went out over the air waves to a predominantly white radio audience. Over the next ten years, Smith would record a total of 180 songs.

During all the years she was recording, Smith continued to travel with her entourage in a Pullman car, appearing in tents, theaters, and revues. Frank Schiffman, owner of the Apollo Theater, once said that Bessie more than anyone knew how to control audience response. She, too, more than any other blues woman, seemed to have a religious, evangelical hold on a house. "She had a church deal mixed up in it," guitarist Danny Barker once remarked.[13] (If, in fact, the troupe got into a town in time for church on Sunday, Bessie would attend.) "She was real close to God, very religious," said drummer Zutty Singleton. "She always mentioned the Lord's name. That's why her blues seemed almost like hymns."[14] And, wrote Willie the Lion Smith, "As much as she roared, drank, and dissipated, she was always considered to be a devout religious woman— truly one of God's children. Our great gospel singer of today, Mahalia Jackson, stood outside a New Orleans theater to listen to Bessie and derived a great deal of her inspiration from what she heard."[15]

In one show, the stage set simulated a recording studio, and Bessie explained to the audience how her records were made. (Later they were on sale in the lobby.) In another act, she wore an Aunt Jemima costume (and later flew down the street in it, racing to a hotel where her husband had been reported rendezvousing with a chorine). Eventually, the costumes of beaded fringed dresses and Spanish shawls became more elaborate as she added horsehair wigs and headdresses hung with lampshade fringe. During the Depression, the helmeted gaudiness went, and a poignant simplicity took its place—plain black dresses, hair cropped short and cleanly sculpted off her face. She was ever majestic. She was what Albert Murray called "primordially regal."[16]

Onstage, Smith did not riff and jive and shoot out lines about her pig-meat men as much as women like Ma Rainey and Clara Smith did. Bessie stood "flat-footed" and sang. And whatever she sang, from fast jazz tunes like "Alexander's Ragtime Band" to the most banal Tin Pan Alley songs, to her own classic blues—"Young Woman's Blues," "Back Water Blues," "Poor Man's Blues"—the material was always defined, or redefined, by her inimitable phrasing, feeling, and style. She slid and slurred between the notes, working closely around what Richard Hadlock has called a group of "center tones" that worked best in terms of intensity and projection, as she sang without megaphone or microphone.[17] (While Hadlock is certainly correct in his evaluation of Smith's importance to the early history of blues and jazz, he is also quick to dismiss without mention any other female singers or musicians of the day with the statement that Smith "was the only woman" to contribute "significantly to the development of jazz in the twenties."[18])

The same spirit and independence reflected in her lyrics was also apparent in her life. Not only did she choose first-rate jazz players to accompany her (Coleman Hawkins, James P. Johnson, Charlie Green, Louis Armstrong) but, as Hadlock notes, it "was in her determination to do things her own way"—she rarely used a drummer, for example— that early jazz players, even in the days before Louis Armstrong hit New York, "recognized in Smith's work the sort of individuality they sought to express on their own horns and strings."[19]

As the twenties drew to a close, Bessie Smith had become a superstar— the highest-paid black artist of the decade and the first "dark diva" whose work and reputation reached and openly affected the "dominant culture."[20] Still, she never forgot where she had come from. She preferred pig-feet parties to dicty blacks or the whites who tried to court her. ("You should have seen them ofays lookin' at me like I was some kind of singin' monkey," she once commented after singing at a party at writer/photographer Carl Van Vechten's house and, after six or seven scotches, knocking his petite wife to the ground as she made her exit.[21])

As the Blues Era faded, the year of the Wall Street crash found Smith in a Broadway flop, *Pansy*, and also experimenting in the new medium, film. In the seventeen-minute short *St. Louis Blues*, Smith portrayed a woman victimized by her man and drowning her sorrows in liquor and the blues. Behind her, the Hall Johnson choir, seated at tables around the barroom, is singing, and James P. Johnson is at the piano. While at the time, the Handy family objected to the barroom setting, Smith manages to transcend the limitations of her role in what was to be the only vision of her preserved on celluloid.

During the thirties Bessie was still getting work, despite hard times for the blues queens in general. She was earning half of her former $2,000-a-week salary, rumored to be down and out, and, most painful of all, had lost her husband and adopted son. Jack Gee had left her for Broadway star Gertrude Saunders (using Bessie's money to finance Saunders's show) and had later taken Jack, Jr., away. Bessie was involved with another man, Richard Morgan, and although she still had work, the days of big money were over.

In 1933 record producer and writer John Hammond arranged an Okeh session for Smith in New York (with Bessie earning only $37.50 a side). Determined to keep up with the times and mood of a Depression audience, Bessie expressly asked for pop tunes as opposed to blues, and the session produced "Do Your Duty," "Gimme a Pigfoot and a Bottle of Beer," "Take Me for a Buggy Ride," and "Down in the Dumps."

Clearly, Smith was aware of the changing trends in music and was trying to keep in step. During 1935, '36, and '37, she appeared frequently in New York, and the *New York Age* noted in 1935 that "Bessie Smith of the old blues singing school is probably the first of her clan to modernize her type of singing."[22] In 1936 she made her only appearance on New York's "Swing Street" (52nd Street, then the home of many of the principal jazz clubs), singing at a Sunday-afternoon jam session. Smith came in, sang, and left, leaving the audience dazzled and dazed; Mildred Bailey (a good friend of Smith's) refused to sing for fear of breaking the Empress's spell.

In 1937 Bessie was touring the South in a revue called *Broadway Rastus*. On September 26, driving with Richard Morgan out of Memphis, she was killed when their car collided with a truck. The controversy surrounding her medical treatment—or lack of it because she was a black woman—mythologized her in death as she had never been in life. (It was later ascertained that she was taken "as quickly as possible" to the Afro-American Hospital, but died of internal injuries and loss of blood.)

"It was like she had that hurt inside her all the time," wrote Sidney Bechet, "and she was just bound to find it." Whether it was "her own feelings of not being wanted, or of being mad or of being happy . . . what she had was alive; she'd been through the whole book. And you can say that one way and you can say it another. If you understand it, it's there, and if you don't understand it, it's not for you. Bessie, she was great. She was the greatest."[23]

In 1970 a Philadelphia woman called to the attention of the press the fact that Bessie Smith was buried in an unmarked grave. Soon two other women had agreed to split the cost of a headstone, whatever it might be. The two were Janis Joplin and Juanita Green, who had scrubbed Bessie's kitchen floor as a child, and gone on to become a registered nurse and president of the North Philadelphia chapter of the NAACP. On August 7, 1970, the unveiling of the stone took place. Janis Joplin stayed away, not wishing to divert attention from the Empress. On the stone was carved, forty-three years after her death: "The greatest blues singer in the world will never stop singing."

"I remember at the Bijou Theater when Bessie Smith or Clara [Smith, but no relation] came in," says trumpet player Doc Cheatham, recalling the heyday of the Classic Blues, "all of the roughest type of people in Nashville would pack that theater. Once in a while I would spot a few teachers from my high school, but they would have newspapers up to their faces so nobody would recognize them. Yeah, they liked it, but they didn't want to be seen in there. . . .

"We have a lot of girl singers who are doing Bessie Smith. Here and there you run into them. There's a lot of them. But nobody can come up to Bessie Smith. I don't know why. I guess it's an individual thing, a personal thing—a personal feeling in singing the blues. She just had something that nobody could imitate, that's all."

Mamie Smith

Mamie Smith was the first black—male or female—to make a vocal recording of the blues. The wildfire success of the 1920 record "Crazy Blues" was directly responsible for the birth of the blues recording industry, and Smith, as pioneering artist, succeeded in opening an important artistic and economic avenue to black women in the early twentieth century.

Born around 1883 in Cincinnati's "Black Bottom," Mamie Smith landed her first professional job early, in 1893. Gertrude Pridgett was only seven years old when the ten-year-old Mamie began touring as a dancer with the Four Dancing Mitchells, and by the time Pridgett made her debut at the Springer Opera House in 1900, Mamie was a show-business veteran of seven years. By 1912 she was touring with the Smart Set, and in 1913 she came to Harlem with her husband, William Smith, a tenor also known as "Sweet Singing Smitty." She worked in such clubs as Barron's, Leroy's, Edmund's, and Percy Brown's, and also in a Perry Bradford revue, *Made in Harlem,* and "became one of the most popular singer-entertainers in town," recalled Willie the Lion Smith.[24]

After many efforts on the part of members of the black music world to have a black female vocalist record the blues, it was finally black songwriter and music publisher Perry Bradford who was able to arrange for Smith's 1920 record date, despite letters from northern and southern pressure groups threatening a boycott of Okeh phonographs and records if they recorded any black female vocalists. (Smith's first recording date was not to sing the blues, however, but came about when Sophie Tucker, scheduled to record, fell ill at the last minute. Bradford convinced Okeh to let Smith replace her, and the two relatively undistinguished numbers she recorded that day—with a white band accompanying her—did respectably enough that six months later she was back in the studio with a black band singing the blues.)

Pianist Willie the Lion Smith, cornetist Addington Major, trombonist Ward "Dope" Andrews, clarinetist Ernest "Sticky" Elliott, and violinist Leroy Parker were on the date, and the Lion described the session: "I taught the bandsmen their parts from the piano sheet music given to me by Miss Smith. All stood, except the Lion, in front of a large megaphone-like horn, and Mamie really let loose with her fine contralto voice."[25] Everyone was paid twenty-five dollars for the date, but, he adds, there were no royalty arrangements, and two months went by before any of the artists got their money.

The song itself, according to the Lion, was "just an ordinary old blues strain that had been used in other songs. Mamie said she had first used it in a show called *Maid of Harlem* [sic] at the Lincoln Theater under the title 'Harlem Blues.' James P. Johnson once claimed he used the same strain in his 'Mama and Papa's Blues,' which he composed back in 1916. Other pianists remembered that part of the melody came from an old bawdy song played in the sporting houses, 'Baby, Get That Towel Wet.' "[26]

Whatever the various origins of the song, "Crazy Blues" was the first version that made it onto wax, and following its success, Mamie Smith and her Jazz Hounds set out on tour. Perry Bradford replaced the Lion, who had no wish to travel through the South, and at various times Mamie's frequently shifting personnel included such legendary players as Johnny Dunn, Bubber Miley, Joe Smith, Sidney Bechet, Curtis Mosby, and even a young tenor saxophone player named Coleman Hawkins.

Pianist/arranger Jesse Stone remembers Smith's aggregation, as well as the effect her superb taste in musicians had on his own band, the Blues Serenaders, at the time: "Now, Mamie had the top black musicians in the United States at that time. Fletcher Henderson, in order to create a great, great reading band, raided her band and took these guys like Coleman Hawkins and all these great musicians from Mamie. But Mamie had these musicians first. By the way, Coleman Hawkins played with me before he worked with Mamie Smith. Tried to get me to go out as an arranger with her, but I didn't wanna go, because I wanted to have my own band. She wrecked my band, 'cause she could pay more than I could pay 'em, you know."

After the success of "Crazy Blues," Mamie Smith is reported to have been the highest-paid black artist of the day. (For a one-nighter at Billy Sunday's Tabernacle in Virginia, she received $2,000; she wore an ostrich-plume cape worth $3,000, and her New York apartment reportedly had a piano in every room.) Throughout the twenties Smith toured and recorded, and at the peak of her career, wrote Leonard Kunstadt and Bob Colton, "her name was synonymous with the word success. Her furs, jewelry, apartment buildings, lover's quarrels, gun-chasing antics were receiving much notoriety. The advent of a recording session by Mamie was nearly enough to declare a national holiday in the Negro districts of the nation."[27]

Smith remained a high-class entertainer, and her assertive, polished delivery of the blues exerted a powerful influence on audiences and singers, black and white alike. In New Orleans, a young Connee Boswell heard and was influenced by Smith in a black theater that on Friday nights was open to whites, and in Houston's City Auditorium during the early twenties, it was a Mamie Smith performance that fired young Victoria Spivey's determination to go after a career as a blues singer herself.

During the late twenties Mamie Smith married a third husband, one of the Goldberg brothers, managers and owners of the Seven Eleven troupe with whom she played (by then, using only piano, drums, and horn accompaniment). Though she continued to draw black audiences during the Depression, her fortunes started to shift. In 1931 she made her last recordings, leaving a legacy of over eighty sides, among them such titles as "You Can Have Him, I Don't Want Him, Didn't Love Him Anyhow," "Get Hot," "Don't Mess with Me," "Don't You Advertise Your Man," and "I'm Free, Single, Disengaged, and Looking for Someone to Love." Though she continued to work in New York, Florida, even Europe, she was slipping into a gradual decline.

"I think there was some sort of business conspiracy against her," Jesse Stone suggests, "because she was too intelligent in a business way for her day and time. At that particular time, women weren't supposed to know the business like she knew it. Women weren't supposed to *even* be able to go around and select all these great musicians like she did. . . . After they raided her band, she tried to be an individual singer, but she never attained the same height that she had attained when she had that band. She recorded some things after that, but it seemed to show that they were holding her down, 'cause the better recording companies wouldn't have anything to do with her after that. She was with the Okeh label at first, and she was the *only* artist with the Okeh label selling all over the United States, both white and black. I know she tried to get on with a record company called Vocalion . . . but nothing ever happened to her after that.

"The last time I saw her was on 52nd Street. I was there when they were auditioning her to go on 52nd Street with a small band, and they took another band in her place. Maxine Sullivan—they took Maxine instead of her. And Maxine and her husband [John Kirby] became very famous. That was the last I saw of her."

During the early forties, Smith made some brief appearances in films—*Mystery in Swing* (1940), *Murder on Lenox Avenue* (1941), *Sunday Sinners* (1941), and, in 1943, another soundie with Lucky Millinder, *Because I Love You*. In 1946, she died penniless in a Harlem hospital, following a long illness, and was buried in an unmarked grave in Frederick Douglass Memorial Park, Staten Island. In 1964, Gunter Boas of the Iserholm (West Germany) Hot Club, learning of the situation, collected the money for a headstone and shipped it to America. With the help of blues singer Victoria Spivey, Leonard Kunstadt, of *Record Research* magazine, veteran film actor Leigh Whipper, and such entertainers as Jimmy Rushing, Maxine Sullivan, and Lucille Hegamin, who participated in a benefit concert, the money was raised for Mamie Smith's reinterment in another cemetery. By this time, however, Kunstadt recalls, bureaucratic mishandling (and confusion in the cemetery office over *which* Mamie Smith was actually buried at the Frederick Douglass cemetery) blocked the progress of the reinterment. To this day, the situation has not been straightened out; nor has any marker been placed commemorating—as the Hot Club had reminded us—"America's First Lady of the Blues."

Ethel Waters

In *American Singers*, Whitney Balliett lists three singers who pioneered American jazz singing: Ethel Waters, Louis Armstrong, and Billie Holiday. Waters started out as a blues singer, known as "Sweet Mama Stringbean," and, never a big-voiced shouter, she brought a new style of blues singing to the twenties. The "source of her genius," one critic wrote, lay in her mixture of opposites (IJS): a combination of earthiness and deep spirituality, of rowdiness and sweetness, all of it molded and bound together by the overriding sense of drama that Waters brought to every word and every story she ever sang.

"At the time I started," Waters explained in *down beat* in the early fifties, "I was one of the first to show people that there was an individual way of doing things with lyrics and rhythms" (IJS). She didn't really sing, Waters said; she *recited* her music. "I want to tell that story. I want you to feel and live it" (IJS). With her individual approach, Waters made her songs the standard-setters for all time, and provided a jazz and popular music foundation that influenced countless other singers, from Maxine Sullivan to blues shouter Big Joe Turner, who called Waters the only singer he ever adored. Among the songs Waters introduced and virtually "owned" were "Dinah," "Am I Blue?", "Stormy Weather," and, from the vintage blues years, "Down Home Blues," "One Man Nan," "Oh Daddy," "The DaDa Strain," "You Can't Do What My Last Man Did," "The New York Glide," and "Jazzin' Babies Blues."

Ethel Waters was born in Chester, Pennsylvania, in 1896. As she wrote in her autobiography, she was always the outsider, never loved and

never really wanted.[28] Her maternal grandmother, known as "Mom,"
worked "out," desperately trying to keep her home and her three daughters and granddaughter together, and doing her best to keep Ethel away
from the vice, drinking, and lust that were rampant in the red-light district where they lived. Early on, wrote Waters, God made her "tough,
headstrong, and resilient . . . my vile tongue was my shield, my tough-
ness my armor."[29]

The one escape in Waters's early life was singing. She would listen,
she recalled, fascinated more by the stories the songs told than by anything else. Her whole family could sing, she wrote, and the families in
the alley harmonized without instrumental accompaniment. (The local
kids, she recalled, even used game-song lyrics to warn the prostitutes
of approaching cops.) Waters's first professional job came when she was
five years old and billed as "Baby Star" in a child program in a Philadelphia church. At eight she saw her first vaudeville shows and began to
imitate the songs she'd heard—"Lovey Joe" and "Barbershop Chord." By
nine she had discovered the Catholic Church, which would become her
bastion until the end of her life. At thirteen she was married and separated at fourteen, and at various times she worked as a cleaning woman,
scullion, laundress, dishwasher, and waitress. While working as a cham-
bermaid, she would spend her time in front of the mirror imagining that
she was standing before hordes of cheering people. It was about this
time, she said, that she began to adopt a theatrical manner.

In 1917 Waters made her singing debut at a local Halloween party.
Before that she had been known as Chester's champion shimmy-shaker
and could also do the split, but this Halloween was the first time she
was using her voice to win friends and admiration. Braxton and Nugent,
owners of a small vaudeville unit, were present, and they offered her a
job. Waters accepted and, wearing a dress bought at a rummage sale—
eggshell satin with buttons down the front—she became the first woman
(and the second person) ever to sing "The St. Louis Blues" in a professional setting.

From the Braxton and Nugent unit, Waters went on to work with the
Hills Sisters, singing songs like "Baby Doll" and "Come Right In and
Stay a While, There Ain't Nobody Here But Me." Yet, despite her great
success as Sweet Mama Stringbean, Waters still had one overriding
ambition: to become the personal maid of a lady who would take her
around the world. Fortunately, this dream was never realized, and
Waters continued forging the new road of blues singing, working the
southern vaudeville circuit, Chicago's old Monogram Theater, and tent
shows, often living with the other troupers in whorehouses on the road
when no one else would take them in.

In 1919 Waters went to New York to work in cabarets, as well as in
her first stage show, *Hello, 1919!* She was also heard at Edmund's Cellar
by a Cardinal Records scout, and two years later she was making her first

records, "At the New Jump Steady Ball" and "The New York Glide."
That same year, the same scout asked her to record for Black Swan, and
after the success of her first four numbers, the company sent her out on
the road with Fletcher Henderson and the Black Swan Troubadours.
Clyde Bernhardt remembers seeing her show at the Chestnut Street
Auditorium in Pennsylvania in 1921. Waters was then a lanky beauty,
and Bernhardt describes the night as he remembers it:

"Joe Smith stood up in the balcony and played the 'Bugle Call Rag'—
that was the opening number—with his beautiful, moaning tone. Then
one more instrumental. Then, 'Ladies and Gentlemen, we now going to
give you Miss Ethel Waters, the famous blues singer. Miss Ethel Waters!'
And she come walking out onstage, and she had on some tight-fitting
gown, and she opened up with 'Down Home Blues.' "

Waters sang four numbers in the show that night, her four big hits:
"Down Home Blues," "One Man Nan," "Oh Daddy," and "The DaDa
Strain." "See," Bernhardt continues, "Ethel Waters never had the strong,
shouting voice like Bessie Smith or Clara Smith or Princess White. But
she had a beautiful, *good* voice. She could do blues and fast-tempo jazz
songs, but she could also turn around and sing a sweet song, a ballad,
and sound beautiful."

Waters recorded throughout the twenties, producing hit after hit.
Whatever she sang, she sang with dignity and authority, and her voice,
her diction, her phrasing, her persona changed to suit each song. She
sang her songs, and on occasion, as she herself said, she recited them;
always, the sense of drama and intimacy was implicit in her shaping of
the material, in her colorations and the richness of her lower register.
She brought to the blues a new sophistication and class. Top white
vaudeville artists of the day came by to catch her act, and Sophie Tucker
actually paid Waters to come to her hotel room so that she could study
her style.

In 1925, when Josephine Baker left the Plantation Club to go to Paris,
it was Waters who had been asked to go abroad first and had declined.
She "preferred to see America first." As actor Joseph Attles points out,
unlike many black artists of the day who made their reputation abroad
and then came back, Waters "made it" on home turf. In 1925 she went
on the "white time" (or vaudeville circuit), first appearing in Chicago,
where the sedateness of the audience's response convinced her she had
failed—until the manager came backstage to offer her thirty-five dollars
for the following week. She eventually became the first black woman to
headline at the Palace in New York, and shared top billing with such
acts as Jack Benny, Van and Schenck, and Olson and Johnson; yet when
she was later called in to save the dying Plantation Club revue, the
white women on the show, she has said, considered her just "another
TOBA singer." The rave review of tough critic Ashton Stevens, however,

proclaimed her the Yvette Guilbert of her race, and overnight she became known as "the Ebony Nora Bayes."

During the late twenties, while she was playing the Keith and Orpheum circuits, back in New York the work she enjoyed most, she wrote, was recording for Columbia (as an exclusive artist) with such musicians as Benny Goodman, Joe Venuti, and the Dorseys, who could ad-lib the music with her and keep up with quick changes. Then in 1929, the year Bessie Smith made *St. Louis Blues,* and King Vidor made the first black musical, *Hallelujah,* Waters signed with Daryl F. Zanuck to do her first film, *On with the Show,* at a guaranteed $5,000 a month. (It was in this film that she first sang "Am I Blue?")

By 1930 Waters, age thirty-four, was tired and wanted to rest. She took her goddaughter, Algretta Holmes, to Europe and later wrote in her autobiography: "My ambition was to bring Algretta up so everyone would love her as I'd never been loved as a little girl. For once I wanted to do the little things that every other woman does each day of her life. I thought that being a wife and mother would convince me I belonged to the human race."[30]

When Ethel Waters returned to America, the Depression was in full force. But for Waters, the golden era of theater was about to begin, as her impressive list of "firsts" as well as musical and theatrical triumphs grew. First there was *Rhapsody in Black.* She became the first black woman to do serious monologs on stage, and the critics compared her to Cornelia Otis Skinner and Ruth Draper. In 1933 she introduced "Stormy Weather" in the Cotton Club revue, a song which she said mirrored her own misery at the time. "My love life, my marriage, was being stormy as hell just then. I felt I was working my heart out and getting no happiness. . . . 'Stormy Weather' was the perfect expression of my mood, and I found release in singing it each evening."[31]

In 1934 came Irving Berlin's *As Thousands Cheer,* in which Waters introduced "Supper Time," the devastating song of a black woman who has just learned that her husband has been lynched. Waters said she felt she was singing it for her people, and, stopping the show with an entirely new type of song, she became the highest-paid woman on Broadway, as well as a member of the first interracial cast to tour the South. In 1939 she played in *Mamba's Daughters,* in the first serious role for a black woman on Broadway. Waters portrayed Hagar, a woman she said "was all Negro women lost and lonely in the white man's antagonistic world."[32] Chosen for the part by director Guthrie McLintock because all she would have to do, he felt, was "give it the same understanding and timing, the same repressed emotion she puts in her songs," Waters received seventeen curtain calls on opening night.[33] "I had shown them all," she wrote years later, "what it is to be a colored woman, dumb, ignorant, all boxed up and feeling everything with such intenseness that she is half crazy." She had finally "told" the story of her mother's life "in front of the carriage trade . . ." "If I died here and now," she remarked on opening night, "it would be all right. . . . At last, I have fulfillment."³⁴

Waters's film, theater, and television credits continued to mount: *The Member of the Wedding, Cabin in the Sky, Pinky, Tales of Manhattan, At Home with Ethel Waters,* and, finally, the crusades with Billy Graham. As her art had been a projection of opposites, so her life and career had been a mixture of elation and tragedy. Debt-ridden, beset by problems with the IRS, whenever there were slumps, she resorted to her singing and appearances in clubs. Her beloved "Mom" died before seeing her granddaughter's great success, and the love of her own mother, won by Waters before she died, was the greatest gift she could imagine. Her love affairs with men were generally marked by turmoil and disappointment, and magazines like *Ebony* and *Tan* carried stories about her tragic love life.

"Into the short thirty-two-bar choruses of these brief songs, Ethel Waters could pour all her own memories of grief, sorrow, and loneliness and make them unforgettable vignettes of great dramatic intensity," wrote Langston Hughes.³⁵ The stage, says Joseph Attles, was her "throne."

Ethel Waters was part of the fountainhead of American singing. In the liner notes to *The Greatest Hits of Ethel Waters,* John S. Wilson noted that the songs, spanning the years 1925 to 1934, represented "a fascinating voyage of discovery for those who want to trace the roots of contemporary style and material." The development and progress of her career as a singer, said Whitney Balliett, mirrored the development of popular song.

Following a long illness, Waters died in California in 1977.

Ida Cox

One of the most widely admired of the blues women, Ida Cox was a trouper whose keen business sense and resilience enabled her to keep a successful career going for nearly forty years, despite the end of the Blues Era in the late twenties. Shaped more by the vaudeville and music-hall circuit than by the rural blues tradition out of which Ma Rainey and Bessie Smith emerged, Cox had an urban, sophisticated blues style, and brought a fine, wry tautness to practically everything she sang.

Some of Cox's blues were arch, worldly, and bold; others were deeply haunting and mournful. She could broadcast the ocean of her blues, so immense she needed the U.S. Navy to Mayday in and help her; then she could turn around and make the blues seem almost child's play, telling us, as though the blues didn't even have to be, "Wild Women Don't Have the Blues."

When White and Clark's Minstrels came to Cedartown, Georgia, a small town fifty miles outside Atlanta, fourteen-year-old Ida Prather packed her bags one day and ran off with the minstrel troupe, successfully hiding out in the rest room as her mother had the train searched by police. The year was 1903. One year earlier, Ma Rainey had made country blues "respectable" by bringing them onto the vaudeville stage. Though Prather had been initially lured by the dancers she saw in White and Clark's company, when she and the players arrived in Cartersville, she made her debut singing "Put Your Arms Around Me, Honey" like a pro. From that day on, her repertoire included blues, rags, and her famous "Hard, Oh Lord," a song she learned from her brother.

From White and Clark's, Prather went with Pete Werley's famous Florida Cotton Blossoms and later with the Rabbit Foot Minstrels. After her marriage to Adler Cox, the pair took over the Douglass Hotel in Macon, Georgia, next door to the famous Douglass Theater. With guests like Bessie Smith and Ma Rainey staying at the hotel whenever they played in Macon, the call of the circuit was never far away, and when Cox's mother died in 1920, she moved to Atlanta and reentered the world of entertainment. She worked at the "81" Theater on Decatur Street, accompanied by Jelly Roll Morton, and "Jelly Roll Blues" became her first big number.

In 1923 Cox became the first blues artist to record for Chicago-based Paramount Records, preceding Ma Rainey by six months (together, the two women became the biggest attraction on the label). Between 1923 and 1929 Cox cut eighty-eight sides, backed by such musicians as Lovie Austin (who headed the Paramount house band), Tommy Ladnier, and Fletcher Henderson. Her most famous numbers—"Wild Women Don't Have the Blues" and "Four Day Creep"—and a later song, "One Hour Mama," offered loud, no-nonsense proclamations of the kinds of basic survival tactics and powers celebrated and flaunted in the boldest of the female blues singer's idiom. Other numbers spoke of death, loss, superstition, and hard times.

After the Wall Street crash tolled the death knell for the blues women of the twenties, Cox was one of the few who managed to survive. She recorded her last tunes for Paramount in 1929 and went on to organize her own show, Ida Cox and her Raisin' Cain Company. Both Victoria Spivey and Lovie Austin attested to the fact that it was one of the best shows on the road: The handsome and stately Cox would have thought little of spending $1,500 on a petticoat alone; the chorus line had seventeen top chorines; Cox's husband/accompanist Jesse Crump was with her, and with the Raisin' Cain unit they toured tents and theaters throughout the country.

Doc Cheatham, who played for Cox's large show during the Depression years, recalls that the show was "terrific" and that Cox was an excellent businesswoman, who ran the whole show on her own:

"Oh, Ida was beautiful. Very, very fine woman. Ida had a responsibility with that show. You know, it was a big responsibility in those days, especially when you had to pay off your show people and had to see that they got their transportation and made the trains and got to rehearsal. Money was *tight*. These shows would scuffle; sometimes they didn't do any business in the theaters, and then they'd have to move on to the next theater and you know, the bookin' association [TOBA], they'd pay you half your money this week and promise you the other half next week . . . and after a while you'll find yourself so far behind, it's enough to make anybody evil. Very seldom you came out—you *never* came out ahead. I went out with three or four shows and I really didn't get paid, either. You just get a little money at the end of the week. You never got full salary, never. But there was nothing else for the people—show people—to do. They just took what they got, and went on and made it some kinda way."

Even the greatest of the blues queens were not immune:

"Well, you see, the stars—they were all stars—they would run into the money problems just the same. If you would draw the people, the audience, and have a full house, why, you wouldn't have to worry about your money. But some weeks you'd have a good house and some weeks you wouldn't. Well, those people just wouldn't *think* about payin' you. They'd give you something to quiet you down and send you on to the next house, and you were hoping like the devil that you could bring in the people. . . . They would rely like on the Saturdays to bail them out, because first part of the week you didn't have *anybody* in the theater. You had to be an *awful* drawing card, very big, to bring somebody in there on Monday. It was a rough life."

Rivalries among the blues women, Cheatham says, usually flared up over which one was the biggest draw:

"They were jealous in a way. I mean, if you would say Bessie [Smith] did better business, drew more people to the theater than Clara [Smith], why, then, you were in *trouble*. And it went on down the line like that. They tried to see who could bring in the largest audiences all the time."

In 1934 a show called *Fan Waves* came to the Apollo Theater, billing a mystery attraction: "the Sepia Mae West, a Chicago Sensation." ("The irony was, of course," wrote Chris Albertson, "that the white stars were actually pale versions of the black performers they imitated—Harlem had its Mae Wests and Sophie Tuckers long before those two ladies made the scene."[36]) Bessie Smith was to be in *Fan Waves*, but, at the time, even she had no idea that this "Chicago Sensation" was none other than the former blues queen Ida Cox.

Three years later, Cox was heading the *Darktown Scandals* at the Roxy Theater in Salt Lake City. The show was built around Cox, and, said *Variety* (December 1, 1937), "In Ida Cox, the unit has a star." This time she was hailed as an "ebony edition of Sophie Tucker" (who, it should be remembered, had taken her lessons from Ethel Waters). The "hefty blues warbler," the reviewer continued, gagged about her "bull hips," sang "My Handy Man," and topped it all with a shiver dance that "rocked the house."

Just two years later, Bessie Smith and Ma Rainey were both dead, and Cox was in semiretirement. At fifty, she had barnstormed all over the country and headlined in vaudeville. For nearly a decade she had been Paramount's second biggest star. She had survived the Depression, put her daughter through college, and proved herself to be one of the few performers tough, enterprising, and resourceful enough to survive the blow dealt the blues queens at the end of their golden decade. When John Hammond produced his Spirituals to Swing concert that year, dedicated to the memory of Bessie Smith, Ida Cox appeared and sang her big song, "Four Day Creep." Soon afterwards, when Barney Josephson's Café Society began to feature many of the artists who had taken part in that immensely successful concert, Cox was one of them. But when she fell ill, her replacement, the young Hazel Scott, became so popular that the club decided to keep her on. Cox continued to tour and play other dates until 1944, when she suffered a stroke while onstage in Buffalo. She retired completely, and in 1950 moved to Tennessee.

In his liner notes to the *Spirituals to Swing* album, John Hammond noted that Cox's whereabouts were unknown and that the rumors of her passing could only be hoped false. In 1961 he tracked her down; she was living with her daughter in a quiet residential section of Knoxville. Chris Albertson, then of Riverside Records, contacted her and persuaded her to come to New York for a record date. *The Afro-American* of April 15 ran an item on her comeback, and *The New York Times* carried a photo of Cox, Coleman Hawkins, and Roy Eldridge at the date—"Miss Ida's final statement," the singer called it.

The New Yorker (April 29, 1961) also covered Cox's visit: "Tallish, straight-backed, gray-haired, and handsomely proportioned, Miss Cox was wearing schoolmarm spectacles, a smart brown dress, and red bedroom slippers, and looked several decades younger than her age," the writer noted. Later, at the studio, while they waited for the rest of the musicians, he asked her how she felt about the session. She replied:

"Lord, I haven't thought about it since I finally decided to do it. At first, I felt I just couldn't. My health haven't been so good since I had a stroke in Buffalo in 1944. I walked out on a night-club floor there and it look like everything left me, everything went black. I haven't sung a note since, and I do thank God for sparing me this long. Of course, I'm here now, and I mean to do the best I can, but then I'm going back home—*whoom*, like that. I'll record some of my own blues—''Fore [*sic*] Day Creep,' 'Moanin' Groanin' Blues,' 'Cherry Pickin' Blues,' 'Graveyard Dream Blues.' I remember the words pretty well, even if most everything else—people and all what I've done in my life—it vanishes away."

Cox did remember the words, recorded the date (her voice stretched a little tauter, perhaps, to a finer bluesy whine), and then went right back home.

Ida Cox died of cancer in Knoxville on November 10, 1967.

Rosa Henderson

Like so many of the great blues singers, Rosa Henderson came out of the music-hall/traveling-show/TOBA tradition. A gifted comedienne, musical-comedy headliner, and rousing, booming-voiced singer, Henderson recorded nearly one hundred songs between 1923 and 1931 (though only a few are available on anthologies today). With the sudden death of her husband and partner in 1927, she began gradually to slip into retirement and, eventually, oblivion, but during the heyday of the Classic Blues Era, Henderson's was one of the loudest and strongest voices on record or on stage.

Born in Henderson, Kentucky, in 1896, Rosa Henderson joined her uncle's traveling show at the age of thirteen, singing a blues repertoire and playing tents and plantations throughout the South, including a five-year stretch in Texas alone. In 1918, a seasoned veteran of twenty-two, she left her uncle's show and, with her husband, comedian and showman Slim Henderson, eventually got into vaudeville in New Orleans. When Slim joined with John Mason, the new Henderson and Mason troupe played all over the country, receiving headline billing at many of the biggest theaters. Rosa Henderson also received star billing in some independent musical comedies during the twenties: *The Harlem Rounders; The Seventh Avenue Strollers;* and *Ramblin' Around,* in which she and Slim did a showstopper titled "On a South Sea Isle."

In addition to pursuing her stage career, Henderson was also busy re-

cording. Her material included everything from blues to vaudeville numbers, and she was accompanied by such top jazz musicians as James P.
Johnson, Coleman Hawkins, and Fletcher Henderson. In eight years
she recorded on nearly a dozen labels, using at least half a dozen pseudonyms, among them "Flora Dale" (on Domino), "Mamie Harris" and
"Josephine Thomas" (on Pathe and Perfect), and "Sally Ritz," her sister's
name (on Banner). Her first tune was "I Ain't No Man's Slave," and
one of her last was "I Can't Be Bothered with No Sheik," and she was
as adept handling (and triumphing over the racist implications of) a
demure number like "I'm a Good Gal but I'm a Thousand Miles from
Home" as she was singing the rousing and earthy "Strut Yo' Puddy."

In 1927, just as things were reaching their peak for Henderson as a
performer, her husband suddenly died. She did a few dates with John
Mason, and was in a Frank Montgomery production in Atlantic City,
but, essentially, her spirit and energy for the theater had begun to
dissipate. In 1932 she appeared in a New York revue called *Yeah-Man*
(Mantan Moreland was in it as well), singing a mournful ballad as a
"piece of Harlem driftwood" (LCL-T) lamenting "The Spell of Those
Harlem Nights." In 1939 she did her last recording date for Columbia,
accompanied by James P. Johnson on piano, and then settled down to
work in a New York City department store in order to provide for her
family and raise her daughter, who later became a top chorine.

In the early fifties Leonard Kunstadt, inquiring after her, was told by
Fletcher Henderson (no relation) that Rosa Henderson had died, and
nearly fifteen years went by before Kunstadt discovered that Henderson
was in fact still alive. Through her daughter, an interview was set up in
June 1963. "The comedienne is all over," Kunstadt noted in his account
of the meeting.[37] Henderson came back to sing at some charity benefits
during the sixties, and she died in May 1968 at the age of seventy-one.

Victoria Spivey

Victoria Spivey started to record in 1926. A prolific songwriter, and
consummate exponent of flat Texas tones and moans, she had one of the
longest and most varied careers of all the blues women. The people,
events, and feelings of her daily life were always her primary inspirations,
and Spivey produced nearly 1,500 songs, many of them never credited
to her. "Many of her blues were grim tales of death, despair, cruelty and
agony, underscored by her somber piano and dark Texas moans," wrote
one critic.[38] "As a performer," wrote another, "she was in turns joyous,
somber, coy, and showy."[39]

Spivey also worked in film and on stage, as a band manager, a column-ist for *Record Research* magazine, and, in 1962, became the only one of the blues queens to own her own record company. On the Spivey label, she was able to reissue some of her early classic blues, among them "The Alligator Pond Went Dry," "How Do You [They] Do It That Way?", "Telephoning the Blues," "Organ Grinder Blues," and "Murder in the First Degree"; to record such artists as Lonnie Johnson, Memphis Slim, Sonny Greer, Buddy Tate, Eddie Barefield, Danny Russo, and Brenda Bell; and to bring two of her contemporary blues sisters—Lucille Hegamin and Hannah Sylvester—back into the recording studio.

Born in Houston, Texas, in 1906, Victoria Spivey was one of eight children. Two of her sisters, Addie ("Sweet Peas") and Elton, also sang, and her father and his brothers had a string band. By the time she was eight, one of her sisters had introduced her to a small sporting house in the first ward, where she discovered her sister's boyfriend and her own earliest piano inspiration, Robert Calvin, and learned to play the blues before her feet could reach the pedals. At twelve she was playing for the silent movies at Houston's Lincoln Theater, and later worked as vocalist with the Texas jazz and blues bands of Lazy Daddy Filmore and L. C. Tolen. While most women did not go into the tough barrel-houses around Houston and Galveston, Spivey was frequently to be found in them, listening to such blues singers as Blind Lemon Jefferson, Joe Pullum, Bernice Edwards, or her cousin, Sippie Wallace.

After seeing Mamie Smith perform at the Houston City Auditorium, Spivey decided to carve out her own career singing the blues. At sixteen she traveled to St. Louis to audition for Jesse Johnson, Okeh talent scout and owner of the De Luxe Music Shop, the city's leading outlet for blues records. "I walked into that Central Station that was on Market Street," Spivey later said, "and I was frightened, but I wouldn't let anybody know it."[40]

Finding Johnson out of his shop, Spivey persisted until the woman who was there let her sit down at the piano. "I was darin', you know. So I just sit there and commence to whippin' on them ole 'Black Snake Blues.' "[41] Two days later, Johnson drove to Spivey's sister's house in Moberly, Missouri, and gave Victoria a contract, and within five days the record of "Black Snake Blues" was being pressed. It sold 150,000 copies in its first month. The song, said Spivey, had really started as a joke, its lyric inspired by her sister's disparaging nickname for her boyfriend, the pianist Robert Calvin. "I wrote the thing myself," Spivey said. "He [Calvin] had always shown me the melody, but I got the first rhythm—of blues with rhythm."[42]

With "Black Snake Blues," wrote Leonard Kunstadt, "she brought another meter to the blues, music to accompany a doubling up of lyrics, with a heretofore unknown addition of four bars to the already much-used 12-bar construction. Her off-tones and drops must have been the avant-garde of the middle 20's."[43] The song firmly established the sixteen-year-old Spivey in the blues circle, was soon being recorded by bands and vocalists, and was eventually included in the repertoires of such blues artists as Leadbelly and Josh White.

Following her "overnight" success, Spivey moved to New York and over the next three years wrote and recorded some of her most famous titles: "Hoodoo Man Blues," "Spider Web Blues," "Dope Head Blues," "Number 12 Let Me Roam," "Murder in the First Degree," and "No Papa No." The songs continued to come straight from the everyday experiences of her life: "T.B. Blues" was about the death of a childhood playmate, and a strong early protest against a society that ostracized victims of tuberculosis; and "Number 12" was about a Chicago-bound train that carried away a suitor. "When I heard that whistle blow," she recalled, "there was a sadness that came over me and I just grabbed my ukulele and started wailing a while."[44]

During the late twenties, Spivey divided her time between appearances in St. Louis, New York, and Chicago. Her name had become a weekly feature in the black press, and she recorded with some of the top jazz players of the day: Louis Armstrong, Luis Russell, Red Allen, Zutty Singleton, King Oliver, and Lonnie Johnson. She also worked as a songwriter for the St. Louis Music Company, penning at least a hundred more songs for them.

As the decade drew to a close, Spivey went to Hollywood to play the role of Miss Rose, the ingenue in King Vidor's first all-black talkie musical extravaganza *Hallelujah!* According to a review by Alain Locke and Sterling Brown, while the film offered a generally stereotypical and superficial view of black life, "most authentic of all," they concluded, "is the hypnotic effect of Victoria Spivey's wail, 'He's gone,'—a chant that recalls the weird moans that have made this young artist's name a byword among the folk."[45]

During the thirties, Spivey continued to write and record, her songs dealing with subjects that ranged from penal institutions and capital punishment to drugs and lesbianism. She managed Lloyd Hunter's Serenaders, a band out of Omaha, Nebraska, headlined in *Dallas Tan Town Topics,* worked as manager, booker, and talent scout, and later, with her husband, dancer Billy Adams, played a four-and-a-half-year run in *Hellzapoppin'.* She toured the country's clubs up until 1950, when personal obligations forced her into semiretirement for the next decade. In 1961 she came back to appear at Gerde's Folk City in New York, and in 1962 took a major step toward securing her artistic freedom by founding her own record company.

Sometimes, recalls Leonard Kunstadt, Spivey would sit in a car on the corner of 8th Street in New York City, watching the street scenes and writing the blues. Some of her early songs—the original "Black Snake Blues," or "13½ Cents a Pound"—were written in one session; in later years, says Kunstadt, she worked on some of her most powerful songs for long periods of time. "Grant Spivey," a moving blues narrative about her father, a straw boss on the Galveston wharf, took her almost a year to perfect. She wrote her lead sheets phonetically and in rhyme, and in later years began to work with a tape recorder. (Many of these tapes, Kunstadt says, will be issued at a future date.) Spivey's later compositions were, like her early ones, deeply personal and formally unconventional—"tone poems set to the blues." She recorded not only on Spivey Records but also on Folkways (*The Blues Is Life*) and Bluesville (*Woman Blues!*).

Talking about the blues, Victoria Spivey once said: "To pay too much heed to standardized blues tones and bars spoils the emotional impact inwardly for yourself. . . . You must feel in your heart most of all, not in your brains or in the interest of your pocket. Let your manager worry about your pocket. Flat tones, whether they be hard or soft, show the freedom in blues singing. You should never know when they come out of you. The heart will tell the voice when."[46]

During the last decade of her life, Spivey brought the message of her blues to Europe, to radio, to television, and to select club and college engagements. She died in 1976 at Beekman Hospital in New York, at the age of seventy.

Alberta Hunter

In 1977 Alberta Hunter made one of the most spectacular comebacks in entertainment history. At age 82 she opened at Barney Josephson's Cookery in New York after a twenty-year absence from public life, during which time she had not sung a note.

One of the first women to start recording the blues in the 1920s, Hunter was also the composer of "Downhearted Blues"—the song that was Bessie Smith's first big hit—and she came into the Cookery with a repertoire of old and new material. She sang "Downhearted Blues," and such vintage "naughty" blues as "My Particular Man" and "Handy Man" (tunes she calls "suggestive, not risqué," and which she recorded originally because they brought in the money for the recording companies). A fierce, magnetic, preaching performer, she can turn around and sing with definitive warning in her stern, lower-range vibrato, "You Reap Just What You Sow." She sings as movingly in Yiddish or French as she does in English, and the newest titles in her repertoire include a chilling, tender version of her own "Remember My Name" (composed for the Robert Altman film of the same name) and a slow, rocking "The Love I Have for You."

Since Hunter's success at the Cookery, her classic thirties recordings have been reissued (including "You Can't Tell the Difference after Dark" and her current theme song, "My Castle's Rocking"), and a new album, *Amtrak Blues,* was released in 1980. She has appeared on television and radio, has been featured in just about every major newspaper and magazine, and has received invitations to appear all over the world, including several from the White House. On one occasion, however, Hunter had to turn the White House down: The invitation, she said, was for her day off.

Born in Memphis, Tennessee, to Charles Hunter and Laura Peterson Hunter, Alberta Hunter was one of four children. As Hunter tells the story—of how she got into show business—she one day persuaded a Chicago-bound teacher to take her along, landed in the Windy City, boarded a local bus, and got off by chance in front of the very building in which the one Chicago girl she knew happened to work. It was her friend's day off, but Hunter soon located her, got herself a job peeling potatoes at six dollars a week, and then discovered she could make ten dollars a week singing in nightclubs. Having already sung some concerts in Memphis, Hunter chose the more lucrative route, and in 1912 got a job at Dago Frank's singing for the clientele of prostitutes and pimps. A piano player had taught her two songs, and she sang them in a high soprano, the contralto range still unknown to her. She didn't know one note from the other, she says, and the "sporting girls" helped her along until she eventually "made good."[47]

When Dago Frank's was closed by the police, Hunter moved on to Hugh Hoskins's, where she worked from 1914 to 1916. The clientele was slightly classier, and some of the downtown people came to hear her, for her reputation was spreading. From Hoskins's she moved on to the Panama, the De Luxe, the Pekin, and the Elite No. 2, where she worked with pianist Tony Jackson, and where stars like Al Jolson and Sophie Tucker would drop in to catch her act. By 1920 she was working in Chicago's most elaborate club, the Dreamland, where Louis Armstrong and Lil Hardin were playing in King Oliver's band. The clientele was mixed and the place was big and noisy, but, as Hunter says, the lack of microphones was never a strain on her voice; in fact, there were times when the blues singers sang so loud they had to "soften up." Hunter was earning a salary that ranged from $17.50 to $35 a week, but, after tips from the bighearted gangsters who ran the clubs, she would go home with $400 or $500 a night.

In 1921 Hunter, known as "the South Side's Sweetheart," went to New York to make her first recordings. She recorded some songs in the small Black Swan studio, and, the following year, initiated Paramount's 12000 series with her own "Downhearted Blues." "When I was a kid," Hunter explained, "I used to take one finger and just hit down on the piano to hit whatever note. If I'd hit one note and that wasn't the one I wanted, I'd hit the next one, you know, until I'd get the one I wanted. That's how I got 'Downhearted Blues.'"

Lovie Austin, pianist at the Monogram Theater and also house pianist at Paramount, heard Hunter singing the song one day and was impressed enough to encourage her to have it copyrighted. Hunter couldn't write it out, however, and because Austin set it down for her, Hunter gave her composer credit on the song. She was a "good, honest woman," Hunter says of Austin, "because somebody else might have stolen the whole thing from me."

Hunter continued to record for Paramount throughout the twenties and also toured on the Keith and Orpheum circuits. In 1923 she made her Broadway debut, replacing Bessie Smith in *How Come?* (which also featured Sidney Bechet), and from then on combined recordings, theater, and appearances at the world's most posh and cosmopolitan night spots. In 1927, after a brief marriage—the demands of her professional life and schedule, she later said, were too great for the marriage to succeed— she went to Europe on vacation. While she was there, Noble Sissle asked her to come to England to appear in concert. Oscar Hammerstein and Jerome Kern heard her there, and invited her to audition for a new production of *Showboat*. She competed against a white woman, got the part, and the show ran for eleven and a half months. By the early thirties Hunter had developed into what Chris Albertson called a "first-rate cosmopolitan chanteuse,"[48] playing such spots as Copenhagen's National Scala and replacing Josephine Baker at the Casino de Paris.

Back in the United States, Hunter did such radio shows as "The Alberta Hunter Show" (1937) and "The Chamber Music Society of Lower Basin Street," and appeared in *Mamba's Daughters* with Ethel Waters in 1939. When the United States entered the war, she took the first black USO unit to China, Burma, India, and the ETO. She toured over there, as well as at home, and also did a command performance for Eisenhower and Marshall Zhukov in Germany. "They said they didn't have no place for crybabies," Hunter recalled, "so they sent me, because they said I had a lot of nerve."

In 1954 her mother died, and Hunter decided to quit singing. "I didn't want to spoil what I had done," she told Chris Albertson. "I didn't want them to say, 'Is she still here?'" The day after her mother died, Hunter enrolled in the YWCA Nursing School on 137th Street in New York, and for the next twenty years she worked as a practical nurse in a Bronx hospital. She did do some recording during those years—with Lovie Austin in 1961, and again in 1962 with Jimmy Archey's group—but essentially, she has said, she never sang, or even hummed at home, and was keeping a low profile for fear that if her age got out, the hospital would let her go.

Still composing, Hunter says her music comes to her much the way it always did, perhaps at dawn or three or four in the morning: "I might have an idea, and lyrics will come to me," she explains. "And the tune will come right along with it. And I'll get up early and go downtown and have somebody take the music down and put the words with it."

Hunter was raised on the principle that if you respect yourself, you will command respect. As for independence, "I've always been liberated," she says, "because I've always made my own, and you know, I've always been independent and never asked anybody for anything, and never wanted anybody to give me anything."

Clara Smith

Clara Smith, "the Queen of the Moaners," was one of the most prolifically recorded women of the Blues Era. It was her material that, along with Bessie Smith's, dominated Columbia's female blues output. Today, with the exception of the two duets she recorded with Bessie Smith, and one British reissue of fourteen of her 1923 recordings, her work is unavailable in this country.

Clara Smith was born in Spartanburg, South Carolina, in 1894. Few details of her life are known. She began to work theater circuits around 1910, and by 1918 was headlining on the TOBA circuit, playing in such places as New Orlean's Lyric Theater. She began recording for Paramount in 1923, and her first song was "Every Woman's Blues." (Smith recorded 123 songs in all.) That same year, she settled in New York, working in speakeasies and cellar clubs, and also opened the Clara Smith Theatrical Club.

During the mid-twenties, Clyde Bernhardt recalls, Clara Smith was one of the "dressiest" women on stage. "And she'd keep the house laughing when she'd get out and talk about how she dressed up her man." She flirted with the men out front and told their wives, "I know I make more money than you make, and I can do more *for* him than you can."

Smith drew a tough, raucous crowd, and as Doc Cheatham says, the more "evil" her routines and singing got, the more her audiences loved it. "The worse she sang, the better she went over. Oh, she was something else. I was afraid to get near there when Clara used to come off stage."

One writer has said that by the peak of her career in the late twenties, Smith was the complete performer. She could "inject sly humor into a risqué song, generate warmth and spirit, where appropriate, and yet convey all the emotions of the blues." In this versatility, he wrote, she was unequaled "by any other contemporary artiste."[49] Carl Van Vechten, who also knew Smith's work, wrote: "Her voice is powerful or melancholy by turn. It tears the blood from one's heart."[50]

On record, Smith gives evidence of that power. The slow songs, for which she had a penchant, show her control and her instincts of phrasing and time. On songs like "I Got Everything a Woman Needs" and "Waitin' for the Evenin' Mail," her voice is rich and open, and her bent notes and colorations clearly show her slow-swinging feeling for the blues.

Despite the fact that audiences and record buyers loved her, Clara Smith seems to have shunned the publicity and attention that was attendant upon most of the other queens. It is known that in 1926 she married an ex-baseball manager named Charles Wesley, and that she, like Ma Rainey, preferred to stay close to the TOBA circuit and to the South. By the time the Depression hit, Smith was working around the East Coast in revues, clubs, and even in an all-black western, *Trouble on the Ranch,* and having a difficult time. Clyde Bernhardt recalls her wearing a plain black dress and tam, "making thirty-five dollars a week in 1932 and glad to get it." Smith would have only three more years to endure the hard life of the Depression. In 1935, she died of heart disease and was buried in Lincoln Cemetery, Macomb County, Michigan. Smith was forty-one.

The Instrumentalists

During the twenties, while star-caliber women like Bessie Smith and Ma Rainey strutted across stages shouting the blues, dancing, and playing comedy and dramatic routines, and others, like Gertrude Saunders, Florence Mills, and Adelaide Hall, were singing in Broadway hits, women who played pianos, and even horns and drums, were very much supporting players.

Western tradition regarding women and musical instruments paralleled African tradition, which held that keyboards and strings were appropriate for women whereas horns and drums were reserved for men. During the years of slavery in the South, however, no slave, male or female, had access to a piano. And while a male slave was sometimes permitted to construct such an instrument as a fiddle (or on occasion might even receive a new one from a master who found it both socially and economically profitable to own a slave with musical ability), female slaves were denied access to string—and all other—instruments. Some male slaves, it should also be noted, were eventually able to earn enough money as musicians to buy their freedom and go on to attain professional status, but for the women no such possibility existed.

Following Emancipation, black priorities were immediately apparent, and many newly freed blacks who could not yet afford furniture for their homes nevertheless managed to buy small organs or pianos, determined that their children would have access to the music and the instrument which they, as slaves, had been denied. Other women, like W. C. Handy's own mother, expressed a preference for the guitar, but were forbidden by the church from playing string instruments.

At this same time—and even earlier in an area like Philadelphia, the cultural center of free blacks in the mid-nineteenth century—keyboard and instrumental training was a part of the everyday life of young women in the black upper class, as it was for their white counterparts. As early as 1842, one observer noted, young black Philadelphia women learned to play the "pianoforte, guitar, or some other appropriate instrument."[51] This training, of course, was not intended for practical application in the professional world, but only to enhance the women's home-bound status as ladies, wives, and mothers.

Outside the upper classes, many women could not afford—or did not want—to stay at home. Employment options were limited, with nurse, teacher, factory worker, seamstress, domestic, or laundress being the most common. The world of show business, however, offered another, if less respectable, avenue, and as early as the 1860s, D. Antoinette Handy reports in *Black Women in America's Bands and Orchestras,* some black women had become pianists in minstrel bands, often working alongside husbands or other family members. Handy notes that Mrs. Henry Hart worked with her husband's Alabama Minstrels in the sixties and seventies, and Mrs. Theodore Finney worked with her husband's Quadrille Band in Detroit during the 1880s.

By the early twentieth century, many black women all over the country had studied music, either at home or in school, and had gotten experience playing in church. In addition to receiving classical and church training, some of them had also been exposed to ragtime, the syncopated music coming out of Sedalia and St. Louis, and these women were especially well prepared to fill the increasing demand for pianists in theaters and cabarets.

With the beginning of World War I, and the concomitant decrease in immigration, more women entered the labor market, working in a greater range of jobs. In some cities, black women were working not only in the usual prewar roles but also as railroad-track hands, munitions makers, inspectors, porters, ice women, and elevator operators. While a woman could earn seven dollars a week plus a two-dollar-a-month bonus working in a laundry, she could earn thirty cents an hour working with a pick and shovel on the street. Holding such jobs, as well as working in their prewar capacities, black women were on their way to becoming what W.E.B. DuBois would call in "The Damnation of Women," "a group of workers fighting for daily bread like men, independent and approaching economic freedom."[52]

Immediately following the war, there was more reason than ever to be attracted to the world of black entertainment. Many new black theaters had opened up, and the lively beat of jazz was orchestrating the postwar jubilation all over the country. By 1920 the blues queens had laid the cornerstone for the blues recording industry, and, given the limited and grueling range of other jobs available, many talented and adventurous young women were choosing the new and promising path of music. Back female pianists found their way into cabarets, tent shows, theaters, hot bands, and society bands. In cities all across the country, there were nuclei of piano-playing women who, because they had been taught to read music (while most male musicians who started out playing horns in fraternal lodges and organizations had not), were called upon to play in orchestra pits and small combos of the day. Those who had "good left hands" and could pound out a solid, steady beat, who could provide the harmonic foundation for the rest of the instruments and still be heard above the horns, were always in demand.

New Orleans could boast of Dolly Adams, Jeanette Salvant Kimball, Olivia Cook, Camilla Todd, and Billie Pierce. Edna Thomas played with Louis Armstrong at the Red Onion Café as early as 1919, and Mamie Desdoumes, who was missing two fingers on her right hand, sang and played the blues around the lavish Storyville (the red-light district) mansions and Perdido Street dance halls. Desdoumes was also the one who first sold Jelly Roll Morton on the blues, and his famous "Mamie's Blues" was based on something he'd heard her sing.

Kansas City, virtually an open city for vice and night life under the rule of political boss Tom Pendergast, was a mecca for jazz musicians in the teens and twenties. One of the most popular keyboard artists was Julia E. Lee. Lee joined her brother's band in 1920 and with him toured what was known as the "territory"—the sparsely populated areas out in the midwestern "sticks," "characterized by tiny towns [generally with very small black populations], bad roads, brutal, cold, icy and snowy winters."[53] Territory bands were the minor leagues of the big bands, the outlets where the up-and-coming youngsters could build their reputations. In 1933 Lee left the band to work as a single. She recorded extensively during the forties and fifties, scoring big hits with such *double-entendre* songs as "King Size Papa" and "You Gotta Gimme What You Got," and continued to perform her Kansas City blues-shouting style practically until her death in 1958.

Chicago was another entertainment center during the twenties. By mid-decade many of the greatest New Orleans musicians had migrated north to play at the famous Dreamland and other Chicago clubs. On 135th Street "nearly every doorway was a club," recalls saxophonist George James, and women were making important contributions to the jazz life of the city. Pianist/leader Garvinia Dickerson was working there, as was Cleo Brown, whose recording of legendary pianist Pinetop Smith's "Boogie Woogie" first popularized the eight-beat-to-the-bar style. James remembers two other female pianist/leaders of the day: Lottie Hightower, a "real ragtime, boogie-woogie, blues pianist," who led her own Eudora Nighthawks, and Ida Maples, who led the Melody Makers. "Maples," says James, "was not only a terrific pianist, but a terrific businesswoman as well."

The Windy City was also the home of much of the blues recording industry of the twenties, and one of the most highly respected musicians in this regard was Lovie Austin, house pianist at Paramount Records and the Monogram Theater. It was Austin, sitting in the pit of a TOBA theater in Pittsburgh, "conducting a group of five or six men, her legs crossed, a cigarette in her mouth, playing the show with her left hand

and writing music for the next act with her right," who inspired a young Mary Lou Williams. "She was a fabulous woman and a fabulous musician, too," Williams once said of Austin. "I don't believe there's any woman around now who could compete with her. She was greater than many men of this period."[54]

On record, Austin accompanied some of the greatest blues women of the day, using a studio band and usually doing the orchestrations herself. As leader of her own group, the Blues Serenaders (which employed some of the best contemporary jazz players and recorded many of Austin's compositions), she demonstrated her excellence as a small-band pianist.

On the East Coast, New York had the dynamic stride pianist Alberta Simmons, who reportedly taught James P. Johnson, and there was also Mazie Mullins, the famous Lincoln Theater organist who so impressed the teenaged Thomas "Fats" Waller that he hung around the theater until she taught him how to play. Washington, D.C., had Gertie Wells, remembered by Duke Ellington as a "great piano player," although she never did "anything professionally outside Washington."[55] The West Coast had Bertha Gonsoulin, who played with King Oliver's band briefly during the twenties and later went on to teach; and Texas brought forth Arizona Dranes, a blind church singer/pianist, who brought a rocking, rollicking beat to the sanctified music she recorded between 1926 and 1928. "It is easy, listening to her play," wrote Frank Driggs, "to see the relationship between gospel, blues, and boogie-woogie as practiced by roving groups of pianists in most of the larger cities in the twenties and right up to World War II."[56]

In Philadelphia around this time, another young pianist was just beginning her career, and she would develop into one of the giants of jazz. Born in Georgia, the second of twelve children, Mary Lou Williams began to learn music at the age of three from her mother, a church pianist, who would hold her daughter on her lap while she practiced. When Williams was five, the family moved to Pittsburgh, and although Williams's mother did not allow music teachers in the house (she believed formal study had ruined her ability to improvise), she did allow musicians in. One of her daughter's earliest influences was the heavy boogie-woogie piano player Jack Howard. "He taught me a lot of professional things it would have taken me years and years to learn"—for example, always to play the left hand louder than the right, "because that's where the beat and the feeling was," said Williams. "It's just like a drum keeping a steady beat."[57] By the time she was six, she was going out on professional jobs, bringing home handkerchiefs full of money, playing for society people like the Mellons, and learning the fingering off of Fats Waller's piano rolls, while her family paid her a weekly allowance for performing their favorite tunes—Irish songs, classical pieces, and boogie-woogie.

When she was in the fifth and sixth grades, she was going out on jobs with McKinney's Cotton Pickers when they came to town (tenor player Chu Berry would take her along), and at one point she ran away from home, "because I had that blood in me like a gypsy. I wanted to go out and play, be with musicians." Williams went out with the Home Talent Show and a troupe called the Hottentots, rough and raunchy vaudeville units, and described the existence as an "animal life." Before she was twenty, she married saxophonist John Williams and became a member of his Syncopators. With him she also toured with Buzz n' Harris, a vaudeville show, and later with Seymour and Jeanette on the TOBA and Keith circuits. Eventually the outfit was headquartered in Memphis, where Williams continued to work while her husband left for Texas to join the T. Holder band, which would soon be taken over by band-leader Andy Kirk. When Mary Lou went to join her husband, she quickly began to do some work with the band—sewing to earn money for band uniforms, hauling water during baseball games, giving manicures at a nickel apiece, and *also* doing some arrangements and filling in occasionally for the piano player, livening up the jobs with tunes like her own "Froggy Bottom."

In 1930 Mary Lou Williams made her historic solo piano recording of "Night Life," something she improvised on the spot, unaware that it was even being recorded. With the distinctive Williams touch and colorations, and the strong, propelling left hand, this forthright, joyful piano heralded what the thirties Kansas City "swing" style would be all about. Within a year of the recording, Williams would become a full-time member of the Kirk band and one of the music's strongest guiding forces.

While some of the piano-playing women of the twenties went on to pursue lifelong careers in jazz, others dropped out of professional life as soon as they got married and began to raise families. Often they married other musicians and retired. Many remained active musically whenever and wherever they could. Whether they stayed with jazz or turned to classics or church music later in their lives, all of them had been an integral part of the jazz network of the decade.

As keyboard was the acceptable territory of the women and girls— even Jelly Roll Morton confessed to doubts about taking up the instrument "for fear of being misunderstood"[58]—brass and other instruments that grew out of the military- and marching-band tradition were considered the province solely of the men and boys.

In New Orleans around the turn of the century, fraternal-organization brass bands appeared regularly at the city's funerals, parades, street celebrations, and lakefront picnics. Women, of course, were absent from these aggregations (so, in fact, were their "appropriate" instruments—

piano and strings). Nevertheless, enterprising black female pioneers did forge other paths on reeds, brass, and drums. As early as the 1880s, D. Antoinette Handy notes, Viola Allen was fronting the sixteen-piece Colored Female Brass Band in Michigan, and Ethel Hill was leading Hill's Astoria Ladies' Orchestra. In 1896, W. C. Handy recalled, Nettie Goff was playing trombone with the famed Mahara's Minstrels, and as time went on, women worked with vaudeville acts, like the Seven Musical Spillers, which included the gifted musician and band director Isabelle Taliaferro Spiller and drummer and reeds player Alice Calloway. Women worked with circus/carnival bands, like the Young Family Band, or got jobs on the TOBA circuit playing in pit bands or onstage.

Trombonist Clyde Bernhardt recalls seeing trombonist/violinist Della M. Sutton in a traveling show, "Roy White and his Style of Stepping." "She was the first woman I'd ever heard play a trombone," Bernhardt says. "She could sing and entertain also. They didn't give her no spot in that show. She just played down there in the pit." This was in the late teens; in the late twenties and early thirties, New York-born Sutton also led her own all-woman band.

In New Orleans, before the famous Storyville was shut down by the Navy Department in 1917, Antonia Gonzales, one of its most famous madams, billed herself as the only woman opera singer and cornet player. "Miss Antonia herself is said to have been surprisingly proficient as an instrumentalist," wrote Al Rose, "and often joined in duets with the professor" (pianist Tony Jackson);[59] but, despite offers to perform on the road, Gonzales preferred to stay in her comfortable mansion taking care of business.

Other cities offered other opportunities to black female instrumentalists. In New York, the Lafayette Ladies' Orchestra trained young women to work in orchestras playing in theaters run by the Elite Amusement Corporation. Marie Lucas, a member of the famous theatrical family (minstrel man and actor Sam Lucas was her father, and Tony Lucas, her uncle), was in charge of the program. Lucas had studied in Europe, and, back in America after World War I, became a prominent part of New York's music world. When pianist Willie the Lion Smith mentions the postwar crowd that frequented Leroy's, he includes trombonist/pianist/leader Marie Lucas among Harlem's "real talent," ranking her with such luminaries as Bill Robinson, Bert Williams, Florence Mills, and Ethel Waters.[60]

Around the same time, in Denver, Hattie McDaniel—later to play Mammy in *Gone with the Wind*—occasionally played drums with George Morrison's band; in Kansas City, Josie Williams's Union Band "could sight-read and furnish music on all occasions";[61] in Chicago, Estella Harris and Mae Brady led their own groups, and Alice Calloway played drums in a trio with saxophonist George James and trumpeter Dolly Jones.

For all these women, show business was undoubtedly an experience fraught with trials, adventure, and sometimes even danger. James recalls some of the occupational hazards of working in Chicago during Prohibition days. (On this particular job, Alice Calloway was on drums.):

"We played over in Cicero, which was the headquarters of Capone's mob. The gig was very nice. We made a lot of money. In gangster hangouts, you could make all kinds of money, especially tips and things like that. There was just the danger of something happening to you in the place, like the place bein' blown up or shot up or something on the job. If you could stomach that danger, it was all right. We stayed out there about four or five weeks, until one night somebody drove across down the highway and shot the place up. We had just gone to the back of the dining room to eat supper, and we heard all these shots and everybody was divin' for the kitchen, so we stayed there, and when we came out, all the front of the place had been shot up, because they were havin' a war as to whose beer should be used—Capone's or whoever's. So that ended the gig."

By the early twenties, the pioneer male jazz soloists had begun to emerge, starting with (on record) Louis Armstrong and Sidney Bechet. Now, ironically, women faced a new obstacle: Not only did they have to contend with the old notion of "masculine" versus "feminine" instruments; they also had to face the prevailing and deep-seated notion that women should not become important soloists. Nevertheless, at least three female instrumentalists came forth during and even before the 1920s: trumpet player Dyer Jones, her daughter Dolly Jones, and alto saxophonist Irma Young. Of the three, only Dolly Jones had the opportunity to record.

Edythe Turnham

(piano/leader)

Edythe Turnham was one of the pioneer pianist/bandleaders of the early twentieth century. Born Edythe Payne in Topeka, Kansas, around 1890, she started to play piano when she was about three years old. "She left Topeka 'round 1900," says her son, Floyd Turnham, Jr., saxophonist with Barry Martyn's Legends of Jazz, "and she come up to Spokane with her father. She went with some kind of minstrels back up in Spokane, Idaho, all up through the north there, and she played piano for them. Her sister was on the show. It was about eight or ten of them [women] on the show there, and two blackface comedians. They'd dance and sing and everything, told jokes on the corners."

Turnham married around 1907 or 1908. In 1909 her son, Floyd, was born. (Turnham also had a daughter.) "My dad was a carpenter in the section gang," Floyd recalls. "Then he started waitin' table at the Silver Girl." (He was also, eventually, drummer in the family band.) "Around 1923," Floyd says, "she started me out on saxophone. I tried to get her to learn me to play piano, but she always wanted me to play saxophone." Turnham taught her son to read music and when he forgot any of the notes, he remembers, "she got the saxophone chart book out and put how many keys to hold down to play that note on my music."

During the early twenties, Turnham was playing as a single all around Spokane; then the family migrated. "We went across the plains up from Spokane to Tacoma, and we left there and went to Seattle. Always stayed around Seattle. She worked around Seattle, played piano for a dancing school out there, my sister learned dancin' . . . Then, after that, she formed a band up there. We had five pieces working around Seattle —the Copper Kettle, the Chicken Shack, the Plantation—and finally [in 1928] we went on the Orpheum circuit to Winnipeg, Canada. Winnipeg, Calvary, Vancouver, and when we got down to Seattle, we was on the Pantages circuit, down the coast to Long Beach, Frisco, and from there to Pantages in L.A. In L.A., Pantages sent us to Salt Lake City, but we didn't have no contract, so we got stranded right here, L.A., and so we was here until she passed."

When the family first arrived in Los Angeles, a friend who was working in the studios there helped to get Turnham some jobs. "From then on," Floyd recalls, "we started hittin' around L.A., four and five pieces, then went on to ten pieces. Two trumpets, trombone, three sax, and four rhythm. [Three band members also doubled on violin.] When we first left Seattle, we called the band the Knights of Syncopation, and went [from that name] to Dixie Aces. We worked quite a few clubs, and we had the staff band at WFWB and WFOX and KGFJ. We worked at Club Alabam, Café de Paris, Oak's Tavern in downtown L.A. We used to be *loaded* with music, all the latest tunes. Every time they'd come out, they'd [the song pluggers] bring [them all] to her, and we'd play [them] right on down. Everybody could read in the band."

During the early thirties, the band was busy working around L.A. and doing pretty well, considering the effects of the Depression. "We'd make three dollars a night," Floyd says. He remembers Duke Ellington catching the band at the Jazzland Café around 1934. "Girl, you sure can play," Ellington told Turnham. "You sure are heavy."

"She was very heavy on the piano," says her son. "She would play two different styles. She liked to play with small groups, and when she got with ten pieces, she said she had to play a different style. She could read anything—'Rhapsody in Blue,' anything. Any new numbers, she could play 'em. She read music faster than I did. Like Mexican tunes, Spanish tunes for the Mexicans to dance faster—she beat me playing the lead!

"Lost my dad in '36, and she kinda give it up then, 'round '37. She worked with different groups after I left her. I worked around there myself, and I left here in the forties with Les Hite's band. She played up to about '45, and she got sugar diabetes and that's what took her away. . . . If she'd have been a man, she could have went further than bein' a woman, you know. My dad, he was on the drums and he took care of the business.

"She was really a sweetheart. . . . She always used to say that she wanted to go to Paris, to follow Josephine Baker—that was her ambition. And here I've been to Paris with the Legends of Jazz, and I thought about her many times like that."

Edythe Turnham died in 1950.

Mary Colston Kirk

(piano)

George Morrison started out organizing a boys' "string band" in Boulder, Colorado, in the early 1900s, when, he once explained, black men held a monopoly on careers in music.[62] By the 1920s he had a dance band that had become one of the top society bands in the Midwest. In a photograph of Morrison's band, taken in 1922 at the Empress Theater in Denver, there is a piano at either end of the stage and a woman seated at each keyboard. On the right is Desdemona Davis, and on the left, Mary Colston Kirk.

In Denver, Colorado, where Mary Colston grew up during the early part of the twentieth century, Wilberforce J. Whiteman, father of the twenties and thirties popular bandleader Paul Whiteman, was the music instructor in the public-school system. "In school," says bandleader Andy Kirk (who married Mary Colston during the twenties and also played in George Morrison's band), "we had music starting in the sixth grade." Students learned to read, took ear training, and studied the classics. In addition, Colston and many of the other young women she knew studied privately with a French piano teacher. But, Kirk recalls, Colston also "had a natural feeling for rhythmic things"—things like Scott Joplin's "Maple Leaf Rag." "Everybody played that, all the girls, and we had a couple of boys, too. I started on the piano, but I thought it was a girl's instrument. In the early days, it was a delicate thing. They thought that it was associated more with women than with men, because of the delicacy."

The Colstons' piano had been bought for Mary's older sister and brother, but Mary was the one with the best ear. After her sister took a lesson, Mary would sit at the keyboard and play by ear exactly what she'd heard her sister play. When her parents noticed that she was the only one paying serious attention to the instrument, "her mother decided that she'd put it all on her," Kirk says.

Colston's first professional job was with George Morrison's band. In 1920 Desdemona Davis, originally from Kansas City, joined the group. "The reason two pianos were brought together," Kirk explains, "was that he [Morrison] did a lot of society work, and sometimes there would be two or three jobs on one night, and he would spend a little time on one spot and then come over to the other one. So Desdemona would be at one spot and Mary Colston at another. At the Hotel Albany we used two pianos. That would be on weekends."

The Morrison band's repertoire included classics ("something from Wagner, and, of course, he loved Kreisler," Kirk remembers), schottishes for black dances, one-steps and two-steps and different kinds of schottishes for the wealthy white homes. After World War I, says Kirk, the music got happier and faster, and the Viennese waltz replaced the slower three-quarter-time waltz, and ragtime tunes like "The Dance of the Grizzly Bear" were popular. The band's blues and ragtime tunes were sung by Hattie McDaniel, who had moved to Denver from Wichita and gotten her start playing in family shows, minstrel shows, and for lodges and fraternal organizations. McDaniel also sat in on drums, and "broke up the house" with her recitations of the poetry of Paul Laurence Dunbar.

In 1925 Kirk and Mary Colston were married. They continued to work in Morrison's bands, each of them working at a different end of the city. When Kirk went to Oklahoma with T. Holder's band several years later, Mary followed soon after. By then she was raising a young child and no longer played professional piano. She did play in church, however, and later, when the Kirks moved to New York, she began to teach. She has continued to study over the years, and is on the staff of The Modern School, a nursery and elementary school run by Mildred L. Johnson, the daughter of composer J. Rosamond Johnson.

"She'll play something for inspiration for the kids," says Kirk of his wife. "She's a very musical woman. She always loved music. She wasn't thinking of making it a career or making money; but she loves it."

Marge Creath Singleton

(piano)

I always say, well, that's amazing. In St. Louis I was the only woman who ever played on the steamboat. The only woman who ever played!

—Marge Creath Singleton

During the 1920s Marge Creath (pronounced *Creth*) Singleton was one of the most important members of the group of women piano players who worked in and around St. Louis. (Others were Marcella Kyle, Pauline Coates, and Ruth Green, who in Marge's opinion was "better than any of us and could swing like a man on the piano.") Sister of Charlie Creath, cornet player and leader of the four major St. Louis bands of the day, Marge not only played on the riverboats and all over the city with her brother's bands, but was also indispensable in helping to run the Creath organization. Later, during her nearly fifty years of marriage to drummer Zutty Singleton, she almost single-handedly ran his business affairs. Although she had stopped performing herself, she was frequently called on to give her opinion of Zutty's various bands, and more than once saved the day when pianists failed to show up, or showed up unfamiliar with the changes (chord progression) of a tune like "Squeeze Me" or "Clarinet Marmalade."

Friends and relatives have recently begun trying to coax Singleton to retire to a quieter life in her native St. Louis. Says Singleton, "I'll come back to St. Louis when I become senile and don't give a damn about anything—but I have to be where the *action* is!"

When Marge Creath was growing up in Ironton, Missouri, it was fashionable for girls to take music lessons and learn piano, while the boys learned to play brass and reeds for the high-school bands and other outfits that entertained at the various fraternal organizations around the city.

Marge's mother had bought a piano for the two girls and horns for the three boys, but more than anything, she wanted her children to get a good education, so, she said, "they won't have to work the way I'm workin'." "She was a cook at the Aluminum Ore Company," says Marge. "Died when she was only forty-eight years old—a young woman, and so well respected and so loved. And she had worked so hard to *try* to educate us the best she could, because my father was the type who said, when he was sixteen, he was out on his own."

Marge's mother could not afford to have both her and her sister take piano lessons, so her older sister took them. But when the teacher left, Marge remembers, "I would go to the piano and play everything that she had played, because I had such an ear." Finally, her sister got so angry, she told her mother she didn't want to take the lessons anyway. Thus Marge began to study with Miss O'Leary, a black teacher who had graduated from Oberlin. At the same time, she was also going to high school and to local parties. One boy, she remembers, "had learned all this ragtime piano playing from his uncle, who was a good friend of Jelly Roll Morton's, who was in East St. Louis then. At any rate, he would teach me some of that; I would watch and play just like he played." She had absolutely no desire to play jazz professionally, however. Jazz was a "man's world," she says, and she "didn't like being around all those *men.*" Nor did she have thoughts of becoming a concert pianist. "But my mother begged me to go to Juilliard. She said, 'Even when you're old, you can teach and make a living.'"

By the time Marge had gone as far as Czerny's Book Four, Miss O'Leary told her mother that her daughter was "quite gifted" but that she couldn't do anything with her. "When O'Leary came to teach," Marge explains, "I would know my lessons. I wasn't even looking at the music. I was just playing the lessons. She'd say, 'Where are you, Marjorie?' And I couldn't show her where I was on the page, because I knew it by heart."

In those days, says Marge, "there was no type of work for colored women. You were either a schoolteacher (my sister was a schoolteacher) or a nurse. That was about it." After "hanging out" for a year or so after graduating from high school, Marge decided to try a course in nurse's training. After two and a half years, though, she decided it was not for her. Then came an ultimatum from her brother Charlie. They were not going to have her "hanging out" in the streets, and, as Singleton puts it: "They made me play piano." Since she could read, Charlie offered her a place in one of his bands. "Yeah," she protested, "but I don't execute like the men. Off of ragtime, I can do that, but I can't run all up and down the piano." "All I want you to do is read and play," said her brother, "you don't get in the way of the instruments, just play the music as is." Marge started working with the bands, and stayed with the organization for four years.

"I don't call them the 'good days,' says Singleton. "To me they were just like any other day. Only thing I wanted to do was get that check, make the money for playing so I could give it to my mother. I called the *good* times when I was going to a good party with the teenagers. Trying to play and cut each other on the piano! Marcella [Kyle] and I, and them boys. That was fun for me. But after I started working with my brother, I couldn't get to the parties. I grieved about that, 'cause I was working every night and they were having parties and having good times."

During the years Marge played with her brother's band, St. Louis was a ragtime city and its influence was widespread. Jelly Roll Morton was playing for the silent films in the nickelodeon in East St. Louis, and would spend the intermissions with Charlie Creath and the uncle of the boy who originally taught Marge the ragtime. "Oh, boy," she says, "you had to use that left hand. That's the St. Louis style. When I was with the band, they'd let me take a chorus. I was never a fancy piano player, but played with harmony and the proper notes and had a pretty good left hand. And I could play the *blues*. I was noted for my *blues*." (Despite her modesty, Doc Randall, who heard her in his California club when she sat in with Zutty in the forties, claimed she had "the best left hand that came in there.")

In the early twenties, Singleton says, her brother's bands were getting "all the work among the white and black in St. Louis for dances and all of that," sometimes supplying as many as four bands a night. In each band the piano player was a woman, because "the best piano players in St. Louis were women." In fact, she says, there wasn't one St. Louis man who could play piano by reading music. Women were the piano players and they were also the leaders. "When Charlie had his band, none of the boys in the band led the band. I led the band; I stomped off for them, yes sir. In fact, I rehearsed the band. Charlie didn't leave that to any of the horn players. I was the leader of his band—*my* band. It was his band, but I was the leader."

Most of the time, the bands had five or six pieces and never more than seven. Players, male and female alike, got ten dollars a night, top salary. "Charlie had the number-one band. Sometimes he'd take four jobs he couldn't make, but all they wanted him to do was come in and blow the blues and go to another job," leaving the band under the piano player's direction. One of the reasons he appointed the women leaders, Singleton reveals, was that it was the leader's job to collect the money and pay off the band. That way, "the men couldn't steal any of the money. He trusted the women."

Marge also worked as "sort of a secretary" for her brother. Working out of their house, she would book the bands as the calls came in. "Whoever wanted to hire the band, I'd have 'em to come and give their deposit and explain to 'em that Charlie had a band that night but would make an appearance sometime. And then I had to put the band together, because we could get any musicians we wanted. We had no rehearsals, just get on the stand and play. And always carry music. They all had to read. Not really arrangements, just stock arrangements [i.e., printed arrangements]."

Marge was not present on any of the records made by Charlie Creath and his Jazzomaniacs (the group made half a dozen sides for Okeh between 1924 and 1927). Her brother "didn't allow any of the women to play piano [on the records]. He would make head arrangements and teach them to the men who couldn't read music, 'cause they had a heavier touch and he thought they sounded better on the record." Marge did, however, attend the first record date Charlie made, for Jesse Johnson of Okeh Records. "I just wanted to see them record," she said. "Used a big microphone in front of the band. I could have [played]. Charlie would have let me play, but I wasn't interested. In fact, I was not interested in piano playing the whole time I was playing. That's why I was glad to get out of it professionally. I never was interested in it for myself. I liked to hear good piano, but for myself, I had something else to do. Of course, if we got any new music, I would practice all day at home, new numbers and all, because I considered it a job to help my mother."

In 1924 Marge became the first and only woman to play on the Streckfus Steamboat Line in St. Louis. "The Streckfus people were funny to work for," recalled Pops Foster, bass player who worked on the boats for many years. "You played music to suit them, not the public. As long as they were happy, you had the job."[63]

Some of the jobs were one-nighters, but one time Marge took the boat to dry-dock in Iowa. "I cried. I didn't want to go. I didn't wanna leave home," she remembers. Bribed by her brother with the promise of a trip to Chicago, however, she finally relented, and eventually enjoyed the trip up the river. "They didn't like me at first," she says, "because they didn't wanna see any woman playing piano, and they were always up by the piano to see if I was playing right." But it never bothered her. "I didn't care about anything in those days. All I knew, it was a job. And I made the whole season."

Says Singleton in retrospect, "It wasn't a hard job; it was a nice job, very nice." The band played every night, from eight to twelve, earning room and board plus forty-five dollars a week—big money in those days. However, she admits, "I was afraid all the time on the boat, because my room was right down by the captain's bedroom and the boys were way upstairs and I was always worrying as to whether the boat was gonna sink, and when they went through the locks, that was a sight to see—the boat go up over the water!" On board, Marge was protected by her brother and the other men in the band, all of whom she says were like fathers to her, but this was not only because she was a woman. On the steamboats in general in those days, writes Ross Russell, "Bandleaders, usually older than the sidemen, acted as heads of their musical families. Discipline was strict; drunkards and agitators were weeded out and discharged along the way."[64]

The floating orchestras on the Streckfus steamboats also played for one-night dances, and in 1923, when Pops Foster played with the one Charlie Creath band remaining on the steamboats, he recalled that on a Saturday night "the boats were so crowded . . . the crew and the band would go on the back of the boat so the insurance man wouldn't count us in the limit of 500 people. Sometimes they'd get 700 or 800 people on the boat. It would be so loaded the least little wave would wash over the deck."[65]

"You had to be on *that boat*, you had to *hit*, at eight o'clock," says Singleton. "Nobody came late, and at twelve o'clock the boat was back on the dock. They called it the 'levee camp.' There were swinging-door saloons, and you could hear the blues and ragtime piano playing. Women hardly went *in* 'em. No indeed—they were rough. When we got off *that* boat, and I had to go to East St. Louis, my father was waiting for me when the streetcar stopped to see that I got home safely. He had to go to work in the morning, but my mother got him up and dressed, and he met me at the streetcar."

While she was playing with her brother's band, Marge met drummer Zutty Singleton, who had come to St. Louis to play with pianist/calliopist Fate Marable's band from 1921 to 1923 and then gone back to New Orleans. Charlie Creath had told him that if he ever wanted to work in St. Louis again, to let him know. When Singleton wrote, Charlie sent for him, and when he returned to St. Louis, he and Marge started "goin' together." A short time later, when he decided to go north to Chicago, the mecca of New Orleans musicians at that time, Marge went north with him. "I didn't want Zutty to leave St. Louis without me, so I went with him, which broke my brother's heart. He never got over that. And, like I say, from then on, it was Zutty and I. We finally got married. We had to. Our people didn't approve of me goin' to Chicago with him, not bein' married to him. We only did it to satisfy them, because we were happy just the way we were."

When the pair arrived in Chicago, despite the number of New Orleans musicians who offered Zutty work, he could not get a regular job for three months because of union regulations. Marge had joined the black union in St. Louis ("It wasn't integrated then," she says) and in Chicago forfeited her membership in order to bring home a salary while Zutty was waiting out his time. "There was another little band that didn't belong to the union who wanted me to play with their band for my brother's name. They said, 'Charlie Creath's sister who played with him,' and I joined with them and made a living for us for about three months. And as soon as Zutty got a regular job, I stopped playing with them, and the union, they threw me out because I was playing with a scab band. But I could have gotten back in. I didn't want to."

Singleton says she did not miss the life of a professional musician at all. She played to be "sociable" at parties—an unpublished rag of Scott Joplin's ("on the order of 'The Maple Leaf Rag' ") and her famous blues. Zutty encouraged her, but never pushed her to play. "He wanted me to be happy," she says, "and he *did* make me happy, all through the years. I had a full life, and *fond* memories of Zutty. But I was happy not to have to play professionally. I was sick of being around *men*!

"I always went around with Zutty when he had a band or was rehearsing a band, and he'd say, 'How'd it sound, Marge?' " Often she helped out at rehearsals. On a European tour, she showed one piano player how to use his left hand, St. Louis style. "He was practicing this modern style. I said, 'You don't play like that with a Dixieland band. Use your left hand.' In fact, I helped them in their rehearsals before they went on the road. I went with Zutty to the rehearsal down at the Vieux Columbier. He was going out with Claude Luter's band, and Mezzrow [clarinetist Mezz Mezzrow] was directing. They were playing 'Clarinet Marmalade' and they weren't making the right changes. And I told Mezz, 'That isn't right. It sounds bad. It's definitely wrong. Show the piano player how to make the changes.' " When Mezzrow suggested that the French audiences would never know the difference, Marge retorted, "But I'm going to be on the tour, and I can't stand listening to that every night.

"I'm a stickler for harmony," Singleton says. "That is one thing I want to hear—the proper harmony, whether you're executing or not! Make it right on the piano. The piano is really a lead instrument, you know. . . . I showed them how to play some changes in 'Sweet Georgia Brown,' because they were playing by ear, you know—head arrangements. So it did come in handily."

Singleton's piano playing also "came in handily" on other occasions. Once when a piano player canceled out at six o'clock on a Sunday night, she was able to save the job. "Zutty couldn't get another pianist. I said, 'I'll go with you.' And he was playing for some gangsters in Chicago who owned a club. [Zutty said,] 'Oh, you can't play, you haven't been practicing.' I said, 'I'll go with you!' I got my wristband and put it on, because in those days I had a left hand. I put my wristband on and played with them. They wanted to hire *me*, the guys! They wanted to hire me! Well, the piano player came to work the next night, and Zutty said, 'It wasn't so much your piano playing; they liked you. They were after you.' You see, couples—I don't think we'd have been together had I continued to play the piano, because there's only one star in the family, and Zutty was the star."

From 1941 to 1951 the Singletons lived in California, where Zutty appeared in the films *Stormy Weather* and *New Orleans* and worked with many combos, including Nappy Lamar's at the Club 47. "On Sunday nights I'd go to work with Zutty and spend the evening there—meet movie stars and all," Marge recalls. "And I'd play a few sets with them.

I was still pretty good then, because I had a piano and I could practice every day. And it was kicks for me. I loved it, especially if the horns were good." Around this time, she had also started studying Chopin. "If there's such a thing as reincarnation," she says, "I'd like to come back as a concert pianist; that's my desire." Zutty encouraged her to take lessons, but Marge's answer was, "No, I'll learn what I can, and what I can't, I won't."

Marge's training running the Creath office in St. Louis also served her well when it came to handling Zutty's business affairs. "I'd tell Zutty, 'I'm so tired!' I said, 'Listen, man, I'm almost as old as you are,' and he'd say, 'Yeah, but you can walk faster than I can and you can do this and you can do that.' I don't think Zutty was in Local 802 [the New York union] over three times in his life. I was up there doing all his fighting and battling, and paying taxes and everything. I was doing it all myself. I did it *all* for him—everything. I handled the musicians. It was his band, but I was always behind the band. I sure was glad when the Morris Agency signed him up in California, but still, every time he went to [their] office in Beverly Hills, I had to be with him." And, as the musicians knew, if anything went wrong, "Zutty wasn't gonna be bothered. They'd come cryin' to me. I could always straighten things out. But I didn't mind it, because that was my life. . . . I love music. I still like to get out and hear bands. That's my life. Music is my life." Still, she has no desire to play. "I can't play anymore at all. My hands tremble on the piano. . . . Everybody begs me to play. If I *had* it to do, I could practice for a while, but I don't have it to do, thank God."

In 1970 Zutty Singleton became ill and had to retire from music completely. Marge, who had become interested in Science of Mind and Christian Science, was able to take care of him and be with him until his death in 1975. "I think that's why I go on as well as I do," she says. "It's all in your mind. Independence. You have to do for yourself. That's my religion. They told me at the hospital they weren't going to be responsible for [Zutty if I brought him home]. I said, 'I'm taking him *home.*' This room was just like a hospital room, and he spent his last days at home, and *happy,* where I could be with him.

"We had a nice life . . . had so much fun together. . . . I don't *regret* having been a professional piano player, and I admire all women who can play. I don't know, we talk about this movement. I have always been a free woman. I've always done what I wanted to do. I don't dig it at all. We knew nothing about this feminism and women's rights and all. I *always* had my rights. As I said, if I wanted to do anything, I would discuss it with Zutty, and he'd end up saying, 'Well, it's up to you, Marge,' 'cause I could do it if I wanted."*

* Marge Singleton died in New York on January 5, 1982.

Lil Hardin Armstrong
(piano/leader/composer)

Piano player, composer, leader of big bands and small combos, soloist, guiding force in the early career of Louis Armstrong, Lil Hardin Armstrong was a "romping pianistic spirit" and singer whose expression "ranged from literal lyrics to burbling, happy murmurs," wrote John S. Wilson.[66] She lived in Chicago most of her life, and stayed active musically, with intermittent lulls, up until her death during a concert in that city in 1974.

"I was just born to swing, that's all," a newspaper article quotes her as having said ("Born to Swing" was also the title of a tune she recorded in 1935). "Call it what you want, blues, swing, jazz, it caught hold of me way back in Memphis and it looks like it won't ever let go."[67]

Lil Hardin Armstrong had an opportunity few women—or men—in jazz ever had: She was able to talk about her life on an LP record. It was titled *Satchmo and Me,* and on it, she covered the years from her childhood through 1932, when she and Louis Armstrong separated and she made plans to go ahead on her own—as she puts it, to "get back into the music business,"[68] although she had never really been out of it.

Hardin was born in Memphis, Tennessee, on February 3, 1902. Her father died when she was two years old, leaving Lil and her mother, Dicie. At six Hardin began to study organ, learning to read music but using her fingers "any way she wanted." By the time she was eight or nine, she was playing for church and school and little marches. At home, she had heard little jazz: Her mother hated popular music, and both she and Lil's grandmother considered the blues vulgar. (In fact, when a copy of "The St. Louis Blues" was discovered in Hardin's possession, she was beaten with a broomstick.) But already her leaning toward the music was apparent. "I was supposed to be the organist for the Sunday School, and one piece especially I remembered was 'Onward, Christian Soldiers.' I might have known I was gonna end up in jazz, because I played 'Onward, Christian Soldiers' with a definite beat . . . and the pastor used to look at me over his glasses, you know, but I didn't know I had that beat. I had it, but I didn't know it was gonna be jazz."

When Hardin was fifteen, her family moved to Chicago. She had already completed two years at Fisk University, and in Chicago she got her first professional job, playing music at Jones's Music Store on South State Street. She was hired as music demonstrator at three dollars a week, and, to assuage her mortified mother, told her she had only taken the job in order to learn all the music. By the second day, however, she had learned everything on the counter. Said Hardin, "I didn't know how long my job was going to last, so I just got busy and learned all the music."

The teenaged Hardin, who looked only about ten, was becoming quite popular in the store and was soon being billed as "the Jazz Wonder Child." It was at Jones's that she would encounter one of her most significant early influences: Jelly Roll Morton. One day he came in and started to play, attacking the keys with his long, skinny fingers, "beating out a double rhythm with his feet on the loud pedal. I was thrilled, amazed, and scared," Hardin recalled.[69] When he got up, she remembered, he looked at her as if to say, "Let that be a lesson to you." "And it was a lesson, because after *that* I played just as hard as I could . . . and to this day, I am still a heavy piano player."[70]

The famous session did not really end, however, until Hardin sat down and played some classics—Bach, Chopin, and "The Witches' Dance"— and, supposedly, it ended with her still the winner. But, she said, from then on, her style was different. "I had learned all the popular things, and I started adding my own stuff to it and playing loud." Preston Jackson, who heard her at the store, testified that "she could swing, I mean swing, no ragtime."[71]

Jones's Music Store not only sold music but also doubled as a booking agency, and it was through Mrs. Jones that Hardin got her first jobs outside the store. The first one was with the New Orleans Creole Jazz Band. When she asked what key they were playing their first number in, they told her, "Key, we don't know what key. Just when you hear two knocks, start playing." "So I just hit everything on the piano," she remembered, "so whatever key they was in, I would be in it, too. Oh, after a second I could feel what they were playing, because at that time I don't think they used over four or five chords. In fact, I'm sure they didn't."

Hardin then went on to work with the New Orleans Rhythm Kings, beating out New Orleans jazz for three months before her mother discovered that she was working in a "nasty, filthy, dirty cabaret." (Because Hardin was making twenty-five dollars a week plus twenty dollars a night in tips, however, the "Hot Miss Lil's" mother was soon persuaded to be reasonable, and allowed her daughter to keep on working, although she came around herself each night to call for her at ten minutes to one.) From there, Hardin went into the Dreamland, the fanciest club in Chicago, and then into the Royal Gardens to join the great King Oliver band, doubling after hours at the Pekin. "I must admit that from a musical standpoint," she said, "jazz didn't mean anything *too* much to me. Maybe it's because I was as young as I was and I was interested in the money. . . . By the time I was with King Oliver, I was making almost a hundred dollars a week. That was a lot of money then. No taxes. My mother didn't take any money, nothing. You know, just buy ice cream and clothes."

By 1922 Louis Armstrong had come from New Orleans to join King Oliver, but, Hardin said, she never paid much attention to the individual musicians. She liked the "thing as a whole." In fact, when musicians from Paul Whiteman's band started to show up in front of the bandstand to listen to Louis, she used to wonder who they were and what they were listening to. "You see," she said, ". . . they used to talk to Louis and King Oliver and Johnny [Dodds, clarinetist], but they would never say a thing to me—never a word—so naturally I didn't know who they were."

Eventually Hardin, who knew the city well, began to show the new-comer, Armstrong, around, and the two soon became fast friends. When Oliver confided to her one day that Armstrong was actually better than *he* was, Hardin began to listen to his trumpet playing more seriously. And when the band made their first historic Gennett recordings in 1923, she began to understand that Oliver was right: Seeing Louis placed 12 or 15 feet from the recording horn—much farther away than any other member of the band—she realized that there was, indeed, something special about his strength, technique, and tone. "I commenced to feelin' sorry for him," she said, "but he was good and people were trying to keep him back, you know. And that's a bad sign, when you start feeling sorry for a man."

Hardin married Armstrong in 1924, and shortly after some of Oliver's other band members left, she encouraged her husband to do likewise and strike out on his own. Armstrong went first to Ollie Powers's band in Chicago and then to Fletcher Henderson's in New York. Dissatisfied with the attention he was getting there, Lil organized a job for herself back at the Dreamland and planned to have Louis hired at seventy-five dollars a week, with billing as "the World's Greatest Trumpet Player." When the manager balked and said no one had ever heard of him, Hardin answered, "Never mind about him. They know me and they'll come in."

"I feel that if it wasn't for Lil, Louis would not be where he is today," Preston Jackson said at one point.[72] "She inspired him to do bigger and better things." When Armstrong began to record his Hot Five and Hot Seven sides, Hardin acted as pianist and musical director. On the dates, they were told how many numbers were to be on a session, and they would write the required number. "Most of the tunes Louis composed, Lil would write the music to," Jackson said. "Louis would play the melody, and Lil would write it down as fast as Louis played."[73]

The Hot Five, Hot Seven, and Lil's Hot Shots recorded nearly fifty tunes between 1925 and 1927, and titles composed by Hardin include "My Heart," "You're Next," "I'm Gonna Gitcha," "Dropping Shucks," "The King of the Zulus," "Skid-Dat-de-Dat," "Jazz Lips," and "Lonesome Blues." "It wasn't the style during the King Oliver days for the pianist to play many solos," Hardin said. "Sometimes I'd get the urge to run up and down the piano and make a few runs and things, and Joe would turn around and look at me and say, 'We have a clarinet in the band.'" But, when Hardin did solo, she was a fine player, and her work can be heard on "My Heart," "Gut Bucket Blues," and "Cornet Chop Suey," and on "Georgia Grind" she sings with Armstrong. The rest of the time, according to Jackson, she would "lay those chords four beats to a measure and solid, just like the doctor ordered."[74]

Hardin had also been studying at this time, and in 1928 she obtained a teacher's diploma from the Chicago College of Music, as well as a postgraduate diploma from the New York College of Music in 1929. In '28, too, she had a small band of her own, which worked around Illinois and Indiana. Freddie Keppard was a member, as was Don Pasquale, who recalled that the band was hot and always in demand.

In 1931, following Louis's great homecoming success in New Orleans, Hardin and Armstrong decided to separate. Of those early years, Hardin said: "I encouraged him to develop himself, which was all he needed. He's a fellow who didn't have much confidence in himself to begin with. He didn't believe in himself. So I was sort of standing at the bottom of the ladder holding it and watching him climb."[75] Hardin then returned to Chicago, and continued with her career.

Lil Hardin Armstrong came back into the Swing Era, and the Depression, just as she had come into the twenties: talented and on her own. (Unfortunately, no spoken records document her story after 1932.) During the thirties, she led two all-woman units, one of which was called the Harlem Harlicans and included Dolly (Jones) Hutchinson on trumpet, Fletcher Henderson's wife, Leora Mieux, on trombone, and Alma Long Scott, Hazel Scott's mother, on reeds. A third band was all male and lasted from approximately 1933 to 1935. Originally the outfit had been violinist Stuff Smith's and was headquartered in Buffalo. Smith, who was used to a six- or seven-piece group, was having trouble keeping the larger unit together, and one day an agent approached the band members and asked whether they would be interested in leaving Smith and going with Lil Armstrong. George Clarke, who played tenor sax with the band, recalls, "Well, the whole band quit Stuff and went with Lil. But we said, 'We don't know Lil, so we want our own leader.' He would collect the money and pay us off and be in charge of the music, and Lil would just front the band. So he agreed to that. And then when Lil came and we went to work in the Vendome Hotel in Buffalo, we all fell in love with Lil, and we were sorry that we had selected our own leader, because we liked Lil so well."

Jonah Jones and Clarke were with the band at the Vendome when Dick Vance came to join them. "It's been a long time, and I've played in a lot of bands," says Vance, "but I still think about it as one of the best groups I ever played with." Jonah Jones says the same: "It was a great band, one of the best I've ever worked with—and that's saying a lot."

Hard times, both men agree, can be partially blamed for the band's lack of success; more than that, they feel, it was lack of proper management. The band was being handled by Louis Armstrong's manager, and Lil was being billed everywhere as "Mrs. Louis Armstrong." "They had a very tiny little 'Mrs.' and a huge 'Louis Armstrong' on the placards for advertisements," Clarke recalls. The band also featured many of Louis's tunes, and Jonah Jones was billed as "King Louis II." Some customers, in fact, actually thought Lil was Jones's mother and Louis his father. "I thought that was a big thrill at the time," he says, " 'cause I loved him at that time and I tried to do everything like him. Then, as I grew up, I found out that this is self-expression music, and you're supposed to express *yourself.*"

Lil did some of the arrangements (her big songs were "Brown Gal" and "Ol' Man Mose") and fronted the band, wearing slinky white gowns, a top hat, and curls and wielding the baton. Often the unit would pick up jobs when other bands had to cancel, or would get a job here and there, earning thirty-five dollars a week or five dollars a night, "which wasn't *too* bad in those days, you know," says Jones. "Depression things were cheap, but not that cheap.

"I don't know how she kept us together as long as she did," adds Jones, " 'cause you got a bunch of guys like that, you have to handle 'em, you know. It just so happens that we were a nice bunch of guys that didn't get drunk and didn't not show up. These guys were all together, and what we wanted was to get somewhere. We all had the same idea: to play good. And we thought that playing good would make us get somewhere. But I found out later that it's the people behind you, you know. They push you. 'Cause I played in a lot of bands, and I've never had a band play as good as Lil's did together." The men in the band, he says, would have even worked cheaper, just to stay together, if it meant more work.

What the outfit needed was a location or hotel job that would have given them the sort of radio exposure the Ellington, Lunceford, and Calloway bands got. But Lil's band, for some reason, was never taken seriously enough. "I could never figure that out," says Jones. "And she was so nice, you kinda feel more sorry for her than anything else, 'cause you knew she was trying. The bread was short as it was, you know. It was '35. But we just hoped that we could get somewhere and play. But they [management] just didn't try hard enough for it."

In 1935 the band broke up for good, and Lil Armstrong went home to Chicago, again to strike out on her own. Well known there and able to get work, she gave up the idea of having a big band. "I think she gave it up because she just found it disheartening herself, because they didn't do nothing," Jones says. "See, we *knew* we had a great band, *she* knew we had a good band, and then after that, I think she just stopped bothering about it."

By 1936 Lil Armstrong had become the house pianist at Decca, and between 1935 and 1940 was making records under her own name with a band that included, at different times, Chu Berry, Buster Bailey, Joe Thomas, Wellman Braud, Jonah Jones, and Manzie Johnson. They recorded such titles as "Murder," "Born to Swing," "Lindy Hop," "Harlem on Saturday Night," "Brown Gal," "Doin' the Suzie Q," and her own "Just for a Thrill" (which twenty years later became a big hit for Ray Charles). She also worked for long periods of time at Chicago's Three Deuces and other clubs. Intermittently, she taught French, music, and piano, and ventured into enterprises unrelated to music. In 1949, articles appeared in the Chicago papers about her South Side atelier, where she designed and made clothes, a skill she had discovered in 1941 at a WPA sewing class. Among her creations was a cocktail gown called "Mad Money" and a "check and double-check coat" (IJS), and it was well publicized that Louis Armstrong got his clothes from her, including the midnight-blue tux he wore as King of the Zulus at Mardi Gras. At another time, Lil Armstrong had a restaurant in Chicago, which George Clarke remembered hearing about. "It seems like the menu was made up with musical terms, and they had things like Bebop Black-Eyed Peas, Swingin' Ham Hocks, High Note Corn Bread, Arpeggio Salad—I don't think it lasted very long."

In 1952 Lil Armstrong made a European tour, did some recording abroad, then returned to Chicago, where she continued to play, limiting her work in later years for reasons of health. (Her 1962 television appearance on "Chicago and All That Jazz" is a classic and can be seen on jazz-film programs.)

In 1971, six months after Louis Armstrong died, the city of Chicago decided to pay tribute to him and asked Lil to play at the concert. At that outdoor program, held on August 27, halfway through one of her numbers Lil Hardin Armstrong collapsed and died of a massive heart attack. She was sixty-nine years old.

"Lil was the type of person who was always in on something, and nothing disturbed her," George Clarke recalls. "She didn't dwell on any setbacks or adversity. She just went from one thing to another immediately, and with new vigor and new vim and great enthusiasm."

"I don't know," says Jonah Jones. "I thought this was a most wonderful woman."

Dyer Jones and Dolly Jones

(trumpets)

In 1926 trumpet player Dolly Jones made her only recording, "Creole Blues," with trombone player/bandleader Al Wynn. Long before that, her mother, Dyer Jones, had been known as one of the great trumpet players of her day. "She was playin' before Louis Armstrong ever knew what a trumpet was," says pianist/guitarist Ikey Robinson, who knew both Dyer and Dolly in Chicago in the early twenties. Dyer was playing what Robinson calls "old-time jazz horn," more like the style heard before Louis Armstrong came along and revolutionized the music. She had also taught her daughter as well as the young Valaida Snow.

Drummer Tommy Benford met Dyer Jones when he and his brother, Bill Benford, ran away from Jenkins's Orphanage as young boys before 1920. "That's about the first lady I worked with in my life," Benford says. "I run away from the school, then we met on the circus—Hurtig and Seamon's. This was in Charleston, South Carolina. She was playing lead trumpet in the orchestra. She was the only woman at that time. We were just in the pit. We played for all the acts. She was a young woman . . . Doll was about thirteen or fourteen years old, something like that. Dyer had a big name in those days, yes she did. A lot of people knew her and a lot of people wanted her. She was one of the great ladies of the trumpet . . . oh my God she was wonderful. That lady, she used to hit so many high notes, a lot of the guys in the band wanted to know where she got 'em from. Man, she was something else . . . and Dolly was right behind her."

By 1929 Dyer Jones was in New York, working with Sammy Stewart's band at the Arcadia Ballroom on Broadway. Ikey Robinson was also in the band. "He got Dyer as an attraction for a woman trumpet player to be playing with the band," says Robinson. "She was outstanding. Any time you take a band like Sammy Stewart's and feature her in New York, she's got to be outstanding, because we didn't have nothing but good musicians in our band—people like Sid Catlett, 'Big' [Charlie] Green, Johnny Dunn." There were three trumpets in the band, and Jones "just sat up there and played everything we played. And she could hold down first chair."

Even though Dolly Jones had learned trumpet from her mother, her principal inspiration was Louis Armstrong. "I think she was more dedicated than the men that I knew playing," says Doc Cheatham, who knew her then, "because she knew everything about playing everything Louis played, and that takes a lot of time. And she had swing—feeling and swing—just the same as Louis did. She must have spent days and days, every opportunity, listening to Louis. You had to do that if you wanted to play anything like him. She lived with that horn. Every time you'd see her she had that horn. That's all she would talk about. She studied that instrument just like I never say anybody."

Also known as Dolly Hutchinson and Dolly Armenra, Jones worked with Irene Kitchings's band in Chicago in the early thirties, and in Lil Hardin Armstrong's all-woman band as a star attraction. Louis Armstrong "remembered her as great," Stanley Dance recalls, and Helen Oakley Dance remembers that "Fletcher Henderson's musicians always said she was terrific. She used to sit in on jam sessions and hold her own, which in those days was really something for a trumpet player." And Roy Eldridge recounts his surprise at discovering that the powerful trumpet that lured him into a Chicago club one night was being played by a woman. He and Dolly jammed until two o'clock the next afternoon, and, says Eldridge, "She really worked on me!"

While there was always work around Chicago for Dolly Jones, life at that time was hard for female instrumentalists. "They really didn't accept women players back then at all," Doc Cheatham says. "Everybody loved her playing. The men just took over back in those days, that's all. It was very hard for a girl player. The life was hard. Stayin' up all hours of the night and socializing after work, never getting to bed—that'd take a toll on anybody. And that's what they were doing back in those days: hangin' out, goin' home when the sun was shining, playing all night. It was rough on a woman. Rough on a man, too. . . . I guess because of being black in those days, she didn't get the opportunity. Being a woman, too. She should have been a big star. Back in those days the black musicians, all of them had a rough time. There were a lot of places they couldn't play. They wouldn't allow them. So then you bring a girl on the scene, a black girl—out of sight! They didn't even give her the respect she was due."

Thanks to independent black filmmaker Oscar Micheaux, a glimpse of Jones in action is preserved in his film Swing (1937). With her name listed in the credits as "Doli Armena," Jones takes off on powerfully swinging solos on "China Boy" and "I May Be Wrong" and clearly shows that she belongs in the front ranks of the music's trumpet players.

Jones continued to work up until the early seventies, when, in poor health, she was still playing in workshops with Eddie Barefield. Doc Cheatham remembers seeing her in those days at the musicians' union in New York. "We have a room where the musicians, on Wednesdays and Fridays, go and pick up a gig. That's where I saw her. Well, she looked all right. She looked the same. And she had her horn with her.

She takes the horn everywhere she goes. Yeah, Dolly was always ready to play."

"Dolly was gut bucket," says Ikey Robinson, "and she was one of the best."

Irma Young

(alto sax/ B-flat soprano sax/ baritone sax/ ukulele/ tap dancer)

Irma Young, the sister of Lester and Lee Young, was raised in the carnival/circus/TOBA tradition and trained to play with the Young family band. After she stopped playing professional horn in the thirties, she went on to work for the next twenty years as a singer, dancer, and comedienne until her retirement from the business in the 1950s. Her daughter, Martha, is a pianist who currently works in the San Francisco area.

Irma Young was born in the early 1900s in Thebedux, Louisiana, and was the middle child between Lester Willis and Lee Young. Their father, Willis (Billy) Young, had studied at Tuskegee and could play and teach all the instruments. For a while the family lived in New Orleans, but by 1919 they had moved to Minneapolis, where they spent the winters and the children went to grammar school. All the rest of the time, they toured on carnivals and circuses and the TOBA circuit with the Young Family Band.

"You couldn't live with our father unless you played music," Lee Young explained. "He had been a professor of music and had taught school and he had seen some terrible things. . . . He used to say, 'My sons will never be a porter; my daughter will never be a maid. You're going to have to learn to play music.' So that was what he had to offer, and you could not live in his house and not play an instrument."

During the carnival season, the family traveled all over the West. During a typical program the band—made up of Lester, Irma, their mother (on alto and banjo), father (who liked cornet best), and cousins—would play on the "bally," the area outside the show where the ballyhoo went on—the pre-show clamor designed to lure in a crowd. Afterward, inside, Lee and Irma would give a song-and-dance rendition of "Does Your Mother Know You're Out Cecilia?" Years later, while Lee stayed at home, Irma and Lester played saxophone with the band. Then, around 1929, in New Mexico, their father began forming a larger band,

and Lee joined it, playing drums. (Ben Webster, playing piano at the time in Amarillo, also became a member of that band.)

From New Mexico, the family moved on to Phoenix, where they would play in a park once or twice a week, then go up to Yuma or Tempe to play dances. In this way they worked their way to Los Angeles, at which point Irma stopped playing saxophone and started singing and dancing, which, she says, was more to her liking.

Despite her personal preference for dancing, however, Irma Young was one of the greatest of the early women players of the saxophone. "She could scare you to death on that alto," says tenor saxophonist Paul Quinichette. "I've sat up and played with her. I heard Irma in 1933. Lester was working with a band named Art Bronson in Denver, Colorado, and she came in to see him, and she was sittin' there jammin'. They had a place they called the Hole, downstairs. We jammed till maybe noon the next day, and Irma was down there playing like mad. She was fabulous. Great musician. She could play chorus after chorus. Fantastic ideas in her mind, all the time."

As for her sound, Quinichette says she and Lester "sounded like each other, only she was playing the alto and he was playing the tenor. A lot of those saxophone players, in those days, big tone—baaah—you were on top, like Coleman or Ben [Webster] or Hershal [Evans]. They just did it completely different, up a little higher . . . free, flowing . . . and said don't get down and stuck in the mud."

After quitting the horn, Irma Young appeared in various shows in the California area—including *Mikado in Swing* and *Lucky Day*—did a comedy routine with Napoleon Whiting, and worked with tap dancer Bobby Johnson. Young retired completely from show business during the 1950s and currently lives in California.

"God bless her," says Paul Quinichette. "God bless Irma Young."

During the teens and the twenties, ragtime and jazz also began to influence the world of white entertainment: Tin Pan Alley writers turned out ragtime songs; Myra Keaton, her son Buster claimed, was the first woman to play a saxophone on the stage (though whether her playing approached anything like ragtime or jazz, he did not say); female pianists like Norma Teagarden and Doris Peavey were playing in small male jazz bands; and white all-woman bands were playing hot, syncopated numbers at the close of vaudeville bills.

This new, eccentric, jazzy music was the perfect accompaniment for the postwar rebellion against the Victorian mores and repression that had governed the country prior to the war. Ragtime and jazz symbolized the social and sexual revolution of the decade, and the good-time, speedy pronouncements of the orchestra matched the exhilaration and acceleration of life in general. Popular bandleader Paul Whiteman (who, with typical disregard for the music's true origins and creators, had been named "the King of Jazz") had noted that there was something "peculiarly American" about the new music called jazz. "I couldn't understand it," he confessed. "[I] couldn't get the hang of it, but others were getting it—fat-faced businessmen who had never in their lives listened to any music except cheap, thin, popular tunes; rouged young-old women who had never once heard a real concert. Something happened to them, just as it had happened to me that first night—something that shook off their false faces and made them real and human, spontaneous and alive for once. What on earth was it?"[76]

Whatever the new music was, it was quickly adapted from the authentic versions heard in the speakeasies, sporting houses, marching bands, and fashionable Harlem clubs and cabarets to the commercialism of the white vaudeville stage, where white artists and musicians took it over. Jazz, wrote Mary Cass Canfield in 1927, was a folk art and the only real American art form (although she did not explore or credit its roots in the black world). On the vaudeville stage, she wrote, the music, full of the idiosyncratic, the extreme, and the original, represented to white America a "throwing away of self-consciousness, of Plymouth Rock caution."[77] There indeed, as Canfield said, were the elements of joy, surprise, and eccentricity that characterized the new stage music and to which white Americans responded. But, as she had *not* said, it was for the most part music composed without the heritage of deep religious content and fervor, without the undertones of obliteration and suffering and "censored joys" which, as Mary Lou Williams would point out later, had fused and melded in the black world, giving birth to jazz.

For American women, the decade also brought important changes. In 1919 they at last won the right to vote. The next year, following a long campaign for Prohibition (led by, among others, the Women's Christian Temperance Union), America ratified the Eighteenth Amendment. But, unlike her sisters in the WCTU, who had not shed their "Plymouth Rock caution," the "new woman" of the Jazz Age—the flapper—was ready to rebel. With her quest for independence and the new proclamation of her sexuality, the flapper bobbed her hair, painted her lips, shortened her skirt, drank, smoked, and danced all night in gangster-run speakeasies. She was the sophisticate, the bittersweet "good-time girl" of Dorothy Parker's "Big Blonde." The new industry—the movies—had started spreading the message that if young women were glamorous and exciting enough, careers on the silver screen awaited them, and the introduction of the Miss America Contest in 1921 helped to reinforce the notion that looks and glamor were a young woman's key to upward mobility and success. But, while the "new women" of the twenties thought they were sporting their new-found independence, they were really still Victorian at heart, enhancing their appearances and playing out their roles in the old quest—the search for a man. As long as women were still believing and trying to live up to the sexual myths they had been taught about themselves, there would be little release of their creative energy, proclaimed anarchist/writer and free-love advocate Emma Goldman, who maintained that "sexuality was a driving creative force within each person."[78] Goldman and a few others understood this in the 1920s; most of the rest of the world did not.

During the 1920s, then, playing hot, syncopated "jazz"—the music associated in the public's mind with cabarets, nightclubs, and houses of prostitution (one of the only places where black and white could mingle in those years)—was clearly not considered part of the white woman's "proper sphere" of activity. But, in the more "acceptable" settings of hotels or theaters in America and Europe, particularly during and after World War I, this music—or some distilled and popularized version of it—was what many white female musicians found themselves playing.

With the advent of World War I, women, in general, had been freed from the limited range of "female-only" jobs that had been open to them before. In the world of white music, this meant that classically trained female musicians were working the hotel-dinner-music and/or the later jazz shifts for dancing. And, like the music or not—for many serious female musicians disdained the slightly disreputable jazz—it was because of their employment in the world of commercial jazz that they were able to make economic and political strides that female musicians had never made before (while the black women who had helped to originate the music were still struggling in the tent shows and the TOBA theaters).

In 1919 writer Edith Lynwood Wynn noted that the war had been a great help to white female musicians. "Possibly some hotels cut down their force and employed women because they were cheaper," she wrote. "But the women themselves have forced their employers to pay them men's wages because the women can and do play as well as men." (As far as women in other jobs or professions were concerned, only two states enacted equal-pay legislation in 1919, and it would be twenty-five years before another state would add such legislation to its statute books.) Female musicians, however, not only circumvented the wartime scarcity of teaching jobs and concert work by taking hotel jobs *with* equal pay; they also enjoyed union protection, good contracts, and clauses that said they could supply a substitute if they had a chance to play a concert engagement. Finally, said Wynn, because they were working in hotels, these women would not be exposed to "as dangerous an atmosphere as the chorus girl or cabaret singer."[79]

For all the women who believed that, as propriety and myth maintained, they did not belong around the "dangerous atmosphere" of chorus girls, cabarets, speakeasies, or authentic jazz, there were others who were genuinely attracted to the beat and feeling of the music, and who pursued it with dedication and serious musicianship. They found work as pianists in small combos, or as instrumentalists on stages, on radio stations, or in hotels.

"That's when the business really started," says trumpet player Jane Sager, who began playing in the early thirties but remembered the vaudeville stage of the twenties. "With vaudeville, they had what they called 'flash acts,' and then at the end they'd open up this big curtain and there was this big, flashy girl band, and they'd play about two or three or four *hot* jazzy numbers, and they'd be a great way to close the show."

Sager remembers some of the top white women's bands of the twenties: The Bluebelles, organized in Indianapolis in 1926, toured as a unit show and flash act; the Eleven Bon John Girls (1929–1931) played top theaters all over Europe—the Palladium in London, the Wintergarden in Berlin, the Moulin Rouge in Paris—and the Palace in New York; Babe Egan and her Hollywood Redheads started in the twenties, as did the Ingenues, and both groups lasted into the thirties. But the top women's band of the twenties was Bobbie Grice and her Fourteen Bricktops.

"They were absolutely great," says Sager of the Bricktops. "They were the Sweethearts of Rhythm of their day." They had a stage band and a dance band. "The jazz band was a great band," Sager recalls. "I mean, they *swung*. They sounded just like any male band you ever heard. You could go out of the room and just listen to them. You wouldn't know they weren't male."

"The act holds everything—music, color, pep, jazz, sex-appeal, novelty, and showmanship," one theatrical weekly proclaimed.[80] "Each girl doubles or trebles on some instrument and does it expertly," said another. "They registered a decisive show stop in a tough fourth spot," said a New York paper, "doing it twice in quick succession." Grice herself, reported the *San Francisco Bulletin*, "not only swings a baton with the abandon of a Ted Lewis or Paul Whiteman, but sings and dances as well."

By the end of the twenties, American life and trends in entertainment had changed radically. The Depression had closed down countless theaters, and *The Jazz Singer*, the first "talkie," put an end to silent films that needed live orchestral accompaniment. Many of the women who had worked theater and stage jobs during the twenties found themselves out of work. Nevertheless, dedicated pianists like Doris Peavey and Norma Teagarden continued to play for many decades to come, while other instrumentalists worked through the Depression and the Swing Era, as the music increasingly became a part of the mainstream of American life.

Doris Peavey

(piano/organ/accordion)

On the cover of *Eddie Condon's Scrapbook of Jazz* is a 1922 photograph of Hollis Peavey's Jazz Bandits. The sixteen-year-old Eddie Condon is seated next to a dark-haired woman holding an accordion. "I always figured that she was usually the best musician in the band," said Hollis Peavey recently of his late wife, Doris. "You can include me in that, too. I think she was better than I was."

At a time when few white women were making careers in jazz, Doris Peavey was one of the pioneers in the field. Unfortunately, as the Jazz Bandits never had a chance to record, none of her work has been preserved.

Doris Peavey (née Yenney) was born in Oskaloosa, Iowa, in 1895. She grew up hearing mostly church music, classics, and semiclassics, and accompanied her father, singer George S. Yenney, whenever he performed. She also played piano for parties at West Waterloo High School, and studied piano at the State Teacher's College in Cedar Falls, Iowa.

According to Hollis Peavey, Doris's family had entertained hopes of a classical career for their daughter, but at that time there was "no market" for it. The classics survived more or less by "donation" then, he says, and jazz and popular music meant (usually) a salary at the end of the job. Doris's first professional work was with a trio (piano, violin, and cello) that played dinner music from time to time at the Russell Lamson Hotel, where Hollis Peavey heard her around 1916–17.

Hollis M. Peavey had himself been a professional musician since before World War I. A tenor saxophonist, he had led a band that played the dance pavilion in Electric Park in Waterloo, Iowa, and also played for the Lamson Hotel dinner shift. When he was drafted, the outfit disbanded, and Peavey wound up in the 163rd Depot Brigade in Des Moines. As soon as he was discharged, he put together a band to play the Waterloo Armory, and in 1919 Doris joined the unit. A year later they were married.

"We worked, played the Christmas jobs and the New Year's Eve parties and so forth, and then we decided to take a honeymoon trip to Houston, Texas." Driving down from Iowa in an old Ford in the days before there were paved roads was an unforgettable experience, Peavey says. So was the music the Peaveys would encounter down in Texas: It opened up their ears to jazz and gave them their first real experience playing improvised blues.

Hollis worked with different bands for about three or four months in the pit of Houston's Orpheum Theater. Doris was not working steadily then, but from time to time she would sit in on the job with Peck Kelly, the legendary Texas pianist; he and Jess Stacy were among her greatest influences. (Hollis attests to the fact that she had a good strong left hand: "She worked on it.")

It was in this atmosphere of Texas jazz and blues that Hollis decided to work without a violin in his band in the future. "We really started the jazz band from the excursion to Houston," he says. "Houston had wonderful musicians." The Peaveys returned to Iowa to start their new band, and in 1922 they heard about Eddie Condon. Hollis acquired him for his Jazz Bandits, and Doris, whose talent Condon praised in his autobiography *We Called It Music,* taught him chords and modulations on the banjo. She did not play the instrument, but, having perfect pitch, could tell by ear whether Condon was correct or not.

"That first summer," Condon recalled in his *Scrapbook,* "we covered 12,000 miles in the back seat of Peavey's car." Hollis confirms that, over the years, his unit did cover the country pretty well. Jobs might be on beer farms, at the dance pavilions in Wisconsin, at doctors' dances in Minnesota, in hotels, theaters, or even barns where the money raised went to paying off the mortgage. Over the winters, they headquartered in Syracuse, Winnipeg, or St. Paul, usually taking an apartment or staying in a theatrical hotel ("where the dog acts were," says Hollis), and Doris, an integral member of the troupe, weathered the cold and all the out-of-tune pianos.

Doris Peavey's musicianship was superb, says her husband; she as well as the rest of the band could "usually read most anything and fake." Among her favorite tunes were "Smoke Gets in Your Eyes," "I Know That You Know," and "Bye Bye Blues," and she was featured on accordion doing "Jazz Me Blues" and "Yes Sir, That's My Baby." She could also sing, but, says Hollis, "didn't practice it very much. In those days we didn't have a P.A. system, and to shout over a band would have taken leather lungs," he explains (indirectly paying tribute to the blues queens). She did appear on stage with the band doing skits, and occasionally she and Vera Phippen, who played piano, organ, and trombone, teamed up on piano for a number or two.

Unfortunately, the Peavey unit never recorded. "We started down to Indiana one time, when the Gennett record company was there," says Hollis, "but something happened and we didn't get that far." They did do radio broadcasts, however, playing all the dance music on KKY, the government-owned station in Winnipeg, where Doris's piano playing brought admiring mail.

In 1928 Peavey's Jazz Bandits left Canada and settled in California, where they continued to play (mostly at weekend lodge dances) until 1960, when Hollis quit music. Doris had by this time taken up the Hammond organ and she continued to work on that, playing in churches in the area until her death on December 26, 1973, at the age of seventy-eight.

Norma Teagarden

(piano/leader)

Since the mid-twenties, Norma Teagarden has played in territory bands, performed as a soloist, led her own groups, and worked in both large and small male bands—Matty Matlock's, Ben Pollack's, her brother Jack's— as well as Ada Leonard's and Ina Ray Hutton's all-woman units. She has taught piano, worked on radio, recorded, spent some years in retirement, and seven years ago returned to the West Coast jazz scene. Critics praise her sensitivity and taste, her "fine stride technique" and "killer boogie-woogie,"[81] and her always solid, imaginative playing in the tradition of the talented Teagarden family. Reviewing her performance at one of the two San Francisco clubs in which she works, one writer noted that she swung "along like crazy, including requests, and still encouraging her sidemen into solo and riff routines."[82] At the other club, she plays solo, "but a lot of fellows come and sit in with me all the time," she says, "so I'm very encouraged in both places."

Since she has come back to the piano, Teagarden has been in constant demand. She is the only female instrumentalist who is consistently asked to appear at the Sacramento Jazz Jubilee, and in 1977 one reviewer wrote: "The greatest thrill for me was seeing and hearing that great lady of the piano, Norma Teagarden. This soft-spoken veteran of jazz can easily convince an audience that there's nothing she can't make a piano do. Her style is light, bright, and utterly delightful."[83] The same year, Teagarden appeared at the Inverness Music Festival, playing a slow blues, a pair of rags her mother taught her, a medley of Bix Beiderbecke compositions, and two pieces by stride pianist Willie the Lion Smith.

Teagarden says she does not want to work too much anymore—"just enough to keep in practice. And I have a lot of fun with it this way. It's nice to be able to play and have the money very incidental. I don't feel it's not nice to have it, but I'm gonna eat and sleep just as well without it. If it's not going to be fun, I don't have to do it, and that's an ideal situation. I never used to be able to do that. Sometimes in the Depression, you know, it was a question of if a job fell through when your rent was due, it was tough scuffling."

Norma Teagarden grew up in one of the legendary families of jazz. Her father played passable trumpet, her mother, Helen, played and taught piano, and Norma, as well as all three of her brothers—Charlie, Clois, and Jack—learned music early. "My mother had a few years of piano lessons when she was a girl," says Teagarden, "and she taught all of us. She could pick up any instrument and play a little bit on it. She would buy an instrument, study it a bit, learn the fundamentals, and then teach us. Mostly, though, she was so busy trying to feed us, about all she could do was to teach us to read music."

Helen Teagarden was also adept at locating instruments in pawnshops: Charlie learned trumpet, Clois ("Cub") drums, and Jack trombone. Norma herself started out on violin and piano at the age of six. "My mother played piano when we were home, and it [violin] gave me something to play, and it gave me a way to be in the school orchestras."

In 1918, when Teagarden was seven, the Spanish-flu epidemic hit, and her father was one of its victims. The family left Texas and relocated in Nebraska. "Then we came back to Oklahoma City. We were sort of in and out of Oklahoma City. We moved a lot." Jack had left home by the time he was sixteen, striking out on his own as a professional musician.

"I guess when you start out as early as all of us did, you learn so many different kinds of music. When you're little kids, you're playing a lot of classics, and I played violin up until I finished high school. All the time, I'd [also] been playing piano around the gym classes for somebody to sing in the assemblies, and Charles and I, we used to go around to all the schools a lot and play, but I got very interested in the piano about the time I finished high school, and I never went back to the violin at all."

Teagarden's first professional jobs began when she was fourteen. Her mother's attitude, she told an interviewer, was, "if you could play, then everything else was just a lot of nonsense."[84] She and her brother Charlie began playing little dance halls and nightclubs in the area. "A few of the musicians quibbled about having a girl for the first time," she told another interviewer, "but I was always well treated, and generally I was spoiled."[85]

In 1929 Teagarden left Oklahoma City and went to New Mexico, where she worked with "a sort of territory band" headquartered in Roswell and played all up and down the state. "Mostly it was one of those little bands that played all those Shriner dances and the Kiwanis, the Eastern Star, the Job's Daughters. There were a lot of those things." These were the Depression years. "I think that's one reason I stayed out there as long as I did," says Teagarden. "Things were so much better in New Mexico than they were in Oklahoma. I had a lot of pupils and I played a lot at night, and my expenses weren't terribly high. I went to New York several times, and I think I got afraid every time I'd go. When I'd get up there, the competition would scare me, and I'd run back down there where it was safe and secure."

In the mid-thirties Teagarden went back to Oklahoma City. "I got to where I had all the work I wanted; there just wasn't any pay to it." Teagarden led her own group seven nights a week when she was working—which, eventually, was "really all the time." She worked in one place on and off for seven years, had a couple of radio shows, toured with the territory band, played for ballet schools, vaudeville acts and in beer gardens, and taught on the side. "I look back on it and I wonder how I worked so hard."

In 1942 Norma Teagarden moved to Los Angeles, and for the first time in years, the whole family was living in the same town. Her brothers Charles and Cub had enlisted, and Norma was leading her own group, touring, and doing record dates. In 1942, before joining Jack's big band, she worked in San Pedro. "It was a real navy town then," she recalls. "Had a lot of shipyards and things, so the nightclubs did real well, and they all had floor shows. This was the largest one I worked in, and Ivie Anderson was there quite a lot of the time. I loved working with [her]. We found out that we both knew very obscure tunes. One of them, I know, was 'Raisin' My Rent.' She was amazed that I knew it, and I was amazed that she knew it. There were several things that we did. She was great."

Long Beach was also a war town. "So many people were based there," Teagarden recalls. "And I had jobs all over the area, and a lot of the soldiers would play with me off hours. So we had some real good bands. . . . Things were tough during the war, because transportation was so bad. You couldn't get gas. Musicians only had 'A' cards, which was low priority. In fact, when I worked at San Pedro, I had to leave the house two hours earlier, and it was only about a twenty-minute drive. It was the way I had to go. And when I got off at twelve—you see, everything had to close at midnight—I got a ride from one of the waitresses to a lonely filling station out in this fog, and I waited out there an hour until the town shipyards got off at one o'clock, and then they picked me up and I got to Long Beach and took an electric train which ran all night, out close enough to my house. When I did that, the L.A. union gave me a union card without [my] having to wait my time out, because they couldn't get anyone from Los Angeles to go down there and play."

In late 1943 Teagarden went with Jack's big band, and stayed with him on the road for about three years. "The stuff during the war was all one-nighters, practically. Bus and train, and the army flew us quite a bit, too. They would fly you to your next job in exchange for a dance for them." This was the grueling camp-hospital circuit and the roadhouse jobs. One page in Teagarden's datebook shows that they covered twenty-one cities in one month. It was precisely this kind of schedule that Teagarden feels discouraged women from choosing careers as professional musicians. "Few women were musicians or wanted to be," she told an interviewer. "It was very hard to be married unless your husband was a musician. I was married to another musician and it was still hard. I don't see the life as appealing to many women."[86]

The life did appeal to Teagarden, though, and she was able to alternate the road with residence jobs. She got a little group together and went back to working in Long Beach and Hollywood, while Jack went out with Louis Armstrong's band. "After about three years on the road," she says, "I was tired, and Mama was alone, you know. She was livin' in my house. So I thought I was needed at home." Back in Long Beach, Teagarden got her own groups together again, first a seven-piece group, then a four-piece combo, which stayed together for nearly a year. Then, in 1949, while she was teaching, she joined Ada Leonard's all-woman band and worked with them for about six months. "She had a hotel-type band," Teagarden says. "We were at the Hilton Hotel in Long Beach for three months and another hotel for about four. She [Ada] had good arrangers, and [they] rehearsed the band. A lot of the girls didn't play a lot of jazz, but they read well and they played their instruments well, so the piano did most of the jazz work. They had a lot of cute little floor-show routines. It was a nice thing. There were about twelve of us."

By 1952 Jack had his own small group, and Norma joined him again. "He had about six pieces, and it was much easier than it was with the big band, because we didn't do many one-nighters. Everywhere we played, we usually stayed at least two weeks, sometimes six, so that made it much easier about the traveling." Then in 1955, in Milwaukee, Teagarden met John Friedlander. They were married about six weeks later out in Long Beach, and Teagarden left the band. "We went back to Milwaukee and I played a few jobs, but not much. And then when I came out here [San Francisco], I didn't really play very much. I had some pupils, but I just sort of dropped it until about seven years ago. I went on a cruise boat to Mexico. Had a chance to go and I wanted to see it. I had such a good time, and I made some friends among the musicians [the ship's band], and when I got back, I started getting offers to play. My husband said . . . well, he felt that I was much happier playing. He told me to go ahead, and since then I've had all the work I want to do."

Teagarden found that, to some extent, breaking into the business was made more difficult by the fact that she was a woman. "When I first started playing, I was working in a booking office in Oklahoma City— that's before I went to New Mexico—and when they called in for musicians, I thought I'd have a good chance to get in that way, but they'd go through all the line before they would take me. A lot of it [also] was that I didn't have a lot of experience. I'd been playing all my life, and I sounded like I knew a lot more than I did, because I knew a lot of flashy solos and things like that. When I came back to Oklahoma City, I got a job with a band that was one of the best little bands I [ever] played with. Everything they did was different tempos and different keys and different everything than I'd ever done before. And I had to really get busy and practice a lot to stay up with them. In fact, for a month or so I didn't think I was gonna be able to, but they were so darn nice about it, and eventually I got it all whipped. . . . And now those kinds of things bother me very little. It just takes experience. You just gotta learn that there's no way to do it if nobody gives you a chance.

"I had an easier time than most people," she admits, "because everybody liked my brothers and my brothers liked *me*, so I think that helped me a lot." Also, as leader of her own groups, Teagarden circumvented the problem of leaders who did not want to hire women; and, as a piano player, she found more work than women—or even men—who played horns. "I've been almost ashamed," she says. "When the Jimmy Dorsey band and my brother Charles first got out of the army, the Jimmy Dorsey band was only working on weekends and they were really scuffling. Real fine musicians like that, and I had more jobs than I knew what to do with just because I played piano."

After her marriage in 1955, Norma Teagarden dropped out of professional life for some time, but in 1963 she and her family had a reunion at Monterey. The next year, Jack died. "I adored Jack," she says. "I guess everybody did. He was an awful sweet guy. And he was easy to work for. . . . I appreciated him giving me a chance to get out and meet so many people."

Teagarden's first recordings were made during her association with Jack's band. In the forties she did several small group dates with Jack on Commodore and Decca, bringing a powerful left hand to such tunes as "Little Rock Getaway," and laying down some nice blues behind Jack's vocal, "Miss Norma, Miss Norma, I like the way you play the blues." The Commodore session in 1944 was the first date Teagarden ever did.

"I feel when I listen to the records," she says of the forties dates, "that I'm much better now. I think I have a lot more confidence in myself. And you know, a long time ago when you made records, it wasn't on tape. Gee, if you messed something up . . . For instance, one time I was on a record session at Decca and I was playing that 'Little Rock Getaway.' Well, the first time I went through it, it had a little flub in it and they didn't say anything about goin' through it again, but the second time I played it perfectly and the trumpet player messed up the part. And by the third time, I was a nervous wreck, and that was worse than any, so they used the first time. By the third time, those engineers and the record bosses were beginning to get nervous, 'cause those fellows [the engineers] cost a lot of money. But *now* if you make a mistake, they just splice it and go on. Makes it a lot easier.

"But I haven't really made any records [with the exception of one made in Holland, and a performance recorded at the Bix Beiderbecke Festival in 1977]. I sent back a check two or three times from a recording company in southern California because I just hate the feeling that I've got to get it done now because I'm getting paid for it." Admittedly, Teagarden says, she does "sort of put off" the sessions. "Little things keep coming up. It's easy to put things off. Things happen in your family, and other things where your routine is upset. I don't know how to excuse my laziness, but I really do feel that I would like to do a better job of it. I keep thinking I need more time."

Audrey Hall Petroff

(reeds/violin/piano/leader)

Audrey Hall began her career as one of Bobbie Grice's Fourteen Bricktops, and went on to work in some of the major women's aggregations of the next three decades. Trained in the classics, pop, and jazz, Hall came into the business at a time when there were few employment opportunities for women in the classical-music field, and she learned quickly that show business offered the only viable option.

Both of Audrey Hall's parents were professional musicians; her father played violin and trombone, and her mother, piano. "In fact, the way they met," she says, "was my father had a ten-piece dance band and she was the piano player. I have two brothers, and when we were kids we had a family orchestra. We used to rehearse every Friday night. So that's where I got my background, you might say, in the pop." Hall's Harmonizers, as the group was called, also used to play professionally. "Dance music," Hall says. "I played for dances on the saxophone, and at the same time I was doing the classical field, playing on programs and concertizing. So I was exposed to both fields of music from quite an early age."

Hall started out on the violin, playing by ear. She began to study at five, took piano at seven, and later studied saxophone. She received a five-year scholarship to the Illinois College Conservatory of Music, which she started attending when she was about nine (she was the youngest one there), and then had a scholarship to the Chicago Musical College. In her circle, however, a girl playing saxophone was a rare thing. "I don't recall at that time that I knew any other girls that were playing saxophone, or playing wind instruments at all. I did know one girl who played the flute. As I recall, I didn't really have many friends. I think that they thought I was strange—that is, my peers, you might say—because I was different."

At sixteen, Hall, who had always wanted to be a musician, joined the Tacoma union and got a job in an eight-piece concert orchestra playing in the lobby of what was then Tacoma's biggest hotel. "I was with them for two years. Then, when I was eighteen, I left home, and I never lived at home again." She left to go to the Chicago Musical College, and when she finished her studies there, she immediately registered with a booking agency.

"I desperately needed a job. I talked to my teacher about it, my violin teacher, and he said he could get me a job teaching at the [American] Conservatory of Music there in Chicago, but he said they insisted on having a man. They didn't want any women on their staff, for some reason. And, of course, in those days, none of the symphony orchestras would take women either, except in the case, perhaps, of a harpist. They thought it spoiled the looks of the orchestra, I guess." (It was acceptable for women to form volunteer orchestras and play for their own enjoyment or for charity, but this still kept them out of the professional arena and on a double standard.)

At this time, there was a stage band called Bobbie Grice and the Fourteen Bricktops playing in Chicago. Hall had heard them once in the theater. "One of their saxophone players was taken suddenly ill and had to leave, and they needed an immediate replacement, and I was it. So that's how I got with that band."

The Bricktops had been formed in the twenties, when the idea of novelty women's bands first hit the vaudeville circuit, and had gone on to become the best female unit of the decade. When Hall joined them, it was late in their career, and she stayed with them for their last two years. "What they tried to do," she says, "was keep up with the current pop tunes as they came out. . . . It was a very entertaining group. They had a lot of gimmicks. Musically it was excellent. They had some strings in the band, and the first violinist was the manager and she usually rehearsed the band. Bobbie Grice was a very dynamic director and a very nice person. The minute she walked out onto a stage or onto the floor to do a performance in a nightclub, the audience was with her."

After leaving the Bricktops in the early thirties, Hall teamed up with a male guitarist. "I played—they call it 'jazz' now; then we called it 'hot fiddle!' And we had a thing going like Eddie Lang and Joe Venuti. [Guitarist Eddie Lang and violinist Joe Venuti had worked together extensively during the twenties.] And we had a program on radio station KMTR in Hollywood. We got a fancy sponsor—Tabasco Sauce was our sponsor—and we were called the Tabasco Twins." They split up after a year, however, because the guitarist felt that Hall's being a woman was keeping him from getting jobs. "We used to get a great many telephone calls from name bands wanting us to join their band, and he always took the phone calls. They'd say, 'We'd like to have you and your brother join our band here,' and he'd say, 'That's not my brother, it's a girl.' 'A girl playing like that?' 'That's right.' 'Oh, I'm sorry, I guess we can't use you, then.' We got that, you see. They weren't interested in novelty; they wanted us to be members right in the band. I don't know *why* they were so against it. Just conditioning. So anyway, we did split up."

Hall then joined another all-woman band—Babe Egan and her Hollywood Redheads—a popular outfit that had already been together nearly ten years. They'd just had an offer to go into the Schubert Theater in New York for six months with a six-month option, and, at the time Hall joined them, were trying to choose between that and a European tour. Egan left it up to the band. "We took a vote and decided to go to Europe," Hall says. Less than a year later, Egan's Redheads disbanded, and Hall began her association with what was to become perhaps the most famous women's band of the thirties, the Ina Ray Hutton Orchestra, which Hall herself helped to assemble. She'd also had another offer: Joe Venuti had asked her to go to Europe with him playing lead saxophone. It was an honor to have been invited to join an all-male band, Hall says, but because she had already committed herself to the Hutton band, she decided against it. "We were in rehearsals already, and I just didn't feel it would be the ethical thing to do."

Hall stayed with Hutton until 1936, and then spent much of the next four years working in smaller women's units around Pittsburgh and Detroit. When the war came, she was living in Los Angeles and busy raising two children. During those years, she stayed in L.A., working with Peggy Gilbert's band and with an eight-piece women's group called the Golden Strings, and by the early fifties she had rejoined Ina Ray Hutton when she formed a new women's band for her television show. Hall also began to do nightclub work with various all-woman combos, and since moving to Tacoma, she has also been teaching.

During the 1950s—the years when Hall was raising her children—she had two offers she had to turn down: One was from the International Sweethearts of Rhythm, the big women's band of the forties, which was going on the road. The other was from the Los Angeles Philharmonic, which had asked her to play first violin. "And I couldn't take it because *they* were going on tour," she says. "How I wish I'd had that offer earlier." It was a difficult thing to turn down, Hall admits. "But I always wanted to do what I felt was the right thing, not necessarily what would be the best for me. I didn't feel it was right for me to go off on tour with a band

and leave my family at home." She's quick to add that she did not interpret that decision as a sacrifice in any way.

Looking back over the past fifty years, Hall feels that certain conditions
have begun to improve for female musicians. She was constantly told,
"Well, we'd hire you if you weren't a girl. Your playing is fine, but we
can't use a girl." "There were bands that said they would have hired me in
a minute if I had been a man instead of a woman. Made no bones about
it. It brought me down every time I heard it." Today the same thing happens, but it happens less frequently.

In jam sessions especially, she feels that things have opened up more
for women. When she was starting out, there were rarely women in on
after-hours sessions. "You couldn't very well go out by yourself and go
to these places. All the jam sessions that I ever went on, it was always
with a bunch of guys. I always managed to latch onto some guy and get
him to take me, and that's the way I'd get there. That, of course, is where
ideas are born, styles develop."

The early years on the road, says Hall, got "pretty tiresome. It's not
my favorite kind of work, either, because you whip together an act and
you're playing three or four hours a day. You're playing the same thing
every day, every week, and if you're not careful, you tend to stagnate.
You aren't learning anything new.

"We used to always say the agents wanted a band composed of sixteen-
year-old girls who had thirty years' experience, and that just about names
it. And you know, men don't have to put up with that sort of thing.
They're judged by their playing. I think it's even that way now. I don't
think *that* has ever changed, and that's why all these gimmicks. The
Bricktops all had red hair. Babe Egan—all had red hair. My hair was
reddish brown, but it didn't look red on stage because it was too dark,
so I wore a wig, and they were not made as well then as they are now.
They were terrible things. They were hot, and you'd perspire, and we
often had to do publicity stunts. We traveled by train; sometimes we'd
get off the train at nine o'clock in the morning and have to go immediately to a store to try on shoes, and to a dress shop and whatnot, and go
to the theater and play four shows, and appear at some club after the last
show—and *all* this time you're wearing a wig. One of the girls started
getting bald spots all over her head, and she left the band because of it!
So I went to a scalp specialist and asked him which was harder on the
scalp—to wear a wig like that or get your hair bleached. He said it would
be much better for your scalp to have your hair bleached, so I started
having my hair bleached out lighter so that it would look red on stage,
and then I finally began getting henna packs.

"So then I was with two bands that had red hair—two years with one
and a year with the other. That's three years where I had to have red

hair. And that isn't all! After I left those bands, I let my hair go back its natural color, and that was when I joined Ina Ray Hutton for the second time. When she saw me, she said, 'What happened to your hair?' because I'd gone from one redheaded band right into the Hutton band, and she was used to seeing me with the red head." When Hall said that she'd been dyeing it, Hutton's response was: "Go out and have your hair made red again. I like it better." "So that's what I had to do," says Hall. "There I was with red hair again—and I don't even *like* red hair, not especially! *There's* your sacrifice!"

Peggy Gilbert

(reeds/vibes/vocals/leader)

Peggy Gilbert has been working in music since the late twenties, when she organized her first all-woman band. She is one of the few *playing* leaders in the business (not just a personality chosen simply to front and sell the band), and has also been one of the most outspoken women in the field, as well as one of the staunchest fighters for women's rights.

Born in Sioux City, Iowa, in 1905, Peggy Gilbert is the daughter of the late John Knectges, violinist and leader of the Hawkeye Symphony Orchestra, which played in theater pits during the silent-film era. Her mother had been a singer before her marriage. Gilbert (who changed her name after she got into the business) studied piano for three years and then started the saxophone and clarinet, on which she had some instruction but was essentially self-taught. From the age of nine, she was reading music and playing piano with her father's string and wind groups, and as soon as she got out of high school, she organized her first all-woman band, which played nightly in the dining rooms of the local hotels and broadcast over station KNWB. Her parents, she remembers, would listen to the shows and then give her tips on how to improve her overall sound and technique.

When an all-woman band called the Gibson Navigators came through town on the Orpheum circuit, it made a strong impression on Gilbert—the trombone player, Fern Spaulding, in particular. "She stood up and played a solo in a baby spot," Gilbert recalls, "and it was the most beautiful thing I'd ever heard. Well, I went to every show, every performance, and I listened to this group and finally got to meet them all, and finally got to work with Fern various times later. I didn't know there were girl bands till I saw them come through on the Orpheum show. That's why I was so fascinated. I thought I had the only one." After hearing the Navigators, however, Gilbert immediately made plans to start a women's band of her own.

During the 1920s, Gilbert had also begun hearing her first real jazz. "I think the first one was the Kansas City Nighthawks on radio. I used to listen to them all night long." She was also influenced by Boyd Senter, and the programs broadcast from Chicago. "It made such an impression that I had to go in for jazz. I loved it from the beginning and had a natural talent and feeling for it." In 1929 Gilbert moved to California, and immediately started to work on the Fanchon and Marco Show. She toured coast to coast and Canada with the unit, and continued to work throughout the Depression, also playing first sax for the "saxtette" that "backed Rudy Weidoft on his Saxophobia idea." Then she went on to organize two more all-woman bands for Fanchon and Marco units, enlisting the help of such musicians as Lionel Hampton and Stan Kenton.

"I got all the girls," she remembers, "and at that time we had to do everything. We had to be the line girls—chorus line—and everything else. We had to dance—and you can imagine some of the musicians, because they'd never danced in their lives, none of us. But they did it. Fanchon believed that you had to be able to do anything 'cause you were in show business. So I got both those bands together, but at that time I was playing in the band. . . . They always had a good front for every girls' band. It either had to be a fellow dressed in evening clothes, in tails, or a really sharp-looking guy or sexy gal." Gilbert, however, preferred to remain a playing leader. "I dropped my horn a lot of times," she says (such as when she had to front the band and M.C. for an audience in a ballroom), "but my heart was never out in front of the band; it was always sitting in there."

Around 1933 Gilbert left the West Coast and returned to Iowa. "I went back," she says, "thinking I was gonna get married to a boyfriend who was also a saxophone player. I thought I'd missed all that, so I went back there, and as soon as I got off the train, I looked at Sioux City and I said, 'Wow, boyfriend be damned! This is it! I can't stand it! So I borrowed his horn and joined Boots and her Buddies.

"Boots dressed in an all-satin riding outfit, with white boots and everything, and the rest of us were so poor that we had to back into the dining room of the hotels where we played because the seats of our pants were so worn. We were playing hotel dining rooms, we were playing ballrooms on a percentage basis. We traveled ten of us in a seven-passenger car [and] we put a seat across the jump seat, a piece of board across there, so we could have nine of us, and then one hung on or sat on somebody's lap, and all of the stuff piled on top. We made one-nighters doing that, and we'd get in and play percentage basis where nobody'd show up the weather'd be so bad, and we'd have enough to maybe buy a hamburger apiece, and go to the next town, sit in the lobby until the rates went on for the day."

After traveling with Boots and her Buddies, Gilbert eventually made up her own band, using most of the women who had been with Boots, and they worked together for the next ten years, with very few changes in personnel. The band was the top women's unit on the West Coast, and it continued to work despite closing theaters and hard times for musicians. In 1934 Gilbert took her band to the Hawaiian Islands, and the six-week tour was held over for eleven and a half months, playing every island.

Back in Los Angeles again, the band played every ballroom and night-club on the coast. "I was a playing leader," says Gilbert, "and had one of the few all-girl bands without a sex-symbol leader who was not a musician." On August 1, 1937, Gilbert's band opened Hollywood's second Swing Concert, and was the only women's band (aside from Harriet Wilson and her Singing Strings) on a program with such groups as the Benny Goodman Quartet and Orchestra, Stuff Smith and his Famous Door Five, Louis Prima and his New Orleans Five, Ben Pollack and his Orchestra, and Les Hite and his Orchestra.

During the 1940s Gilbert worked for a year on CBS's Victory Belles radio show and was also musical director—with an all-woman orchestra —for W-KMPC, Beverly Hills. After the war, Gilbert, like so many other women, suddenly found herself dismissed from much of her work, because, the union insisted, the returning GI's needed their jobs. During the fifties she went to work as a secretary for the musicians' local in Los Angeles, and stayed there for twenty years. She still continued to play, however, doing such jobs as the Ada Leonard television show (Leonard was a popular leader during the forties and fifties), and currently leads the Dixie Belles, the only all-woman Dixieland band among twelve top names in the field. Gilbert has also appeared in numerous films with her bands—from *The Great Waltz* on, she says—but it has always been a "sidelining" situation (i.e., the women appeared, but male musicians actually dubbed in the music). "We were in all kinds of pictures, but we never got to record. The girls could have played it very easily, but they always had the fellows, studio musicians, playing and the girls faking." Similarly, women did not get to do recording dates. "They had no faith in women musicians," Gilbert says.

Peggy Gilbert's 1938 article in *down beat* (see discussion in the next chapter) was one of the most articulate statements about the plight of women in the field during that era. She still writes a column on women musicians, for the *Overture,* the newspaper of the Los Angeles local musicians' union, and she remains very much in the center of West Coast activity. "What can I say?" she asks. "At my age I am very fortunate, and I guess I must be the only seventy-five-year-old jazz tenor player still blowing!"

THE THIRTIES

The 1930s opened under the weight of the Great Depression. The explosive energy of the twenties had burned itself out, and suddenly American life offered harsh new economic realities: In the South, the number of lynchings doubled over the job issue; in Harlem, by mid-decade, there were riots in the streets; and in some states it actually became illegal for women to hold jobs—or, as it was more commonly referred to, "steal a job from a man."

Still, in mob-run speakeasies (which after Repeal in 1933 turned into fashionable watering spots), in cabarets and dingy theaters and the fancy Harlem clubs, at the "Saturday-night functions" and "rent parties" and Kansas City's twenty-four-hour-a-day jam session under political boss Tom Pendergast's rule, a musical network was busy, as Fats Waller had sung, "Spreading Rhythm Around." In some corners of American society, good times, jazz, and the popular new thing, "swing," ruled the world while Americans drank, danced, functioned, and forgot.

Some of the country's black swing royalty went to Europe, extending their domain to the more receptive environment overseas, as black artists and entertainers had been doing for years: Duke Ellington (in 1932), Louis Armstrong (in '33), Florence Mills, Josephine Baker, Bricktop, and trumpeter/entertainer Valaida Snow (who became known overseas as "the Queen of the Trumpet").

At home, meanwhile, white musicians were more than ever attracted to the music the black bands were playing. Benny Goodman, Glenn Miller, the Dorsey Brothers, and Artie Shaw all started to front their own "big bands," but the germinal music and impulse toward expansion had started in the black bands of the twenties—Duke Ellington's, Fletcher Henderson's, Walter Page's, Bennie Moten's, and, later, Andy Kirk's, Chick Webb's, and Jimmie Lunceford's. As these bands increased in size, adding new instrumental "voices" and new possibilities for texture and color, head (or unwritten) arrangements no longer sufficed. With fourteen or sixteen pieces, success depended first and foremost on the rhythm and the beat, on good, tight written arrangements to accommodate what had become sections of instruments—reeds, brass, and rhythm—and on skilled soloists taking improvised or written-out solos. As the newer white bands began to use arrangements by such black arrangers as Fletcher Henderson, Eddie Durham, Mary Lou Williams, Don Redman, Jimmy Mundy, and later Marjorie Gibson, and to learn from them the proper jazz phrasing and attack, they began to get the exposure and publicity the black bands never had, and "swing" became the popular American dance music of the decade. "Swing" became commercial.

By 1934 a new Chicago-based publication, *down beat* magazine, would begin to focus a regular spotlight on jazz, bringing news of its artists and their activities to the American public. Helen Oakley Dance would become one of the earliest *down beat* contributors, interpreting the music to its new audience, and the magazine would, for many years to come, bring attention to some female performers. But its coverage would also reflect the language and attitudes of the day regarding women in the field, and on some notable occasions, articles would actually fan the flames of the great debate: Did women have a place in jazz?

Given the success of the all-woman bands of the twenties, it followed that enterprising managers and entrepreneurs would see the possibilities in further exploiting such bands in the thirties. Some of the popular twenties units remained: the Fourteen Bricktops; and the Ingenues, which, said one writer in *down beat* (April, 1937, p. 22), had a "Gene Krupa in Girls' Clothes, and sixteen women, all doubling from three to six instruments and playing them with amazing skill . . . The versatility of this band is something to rave about."

Countless new bands were formed as well. In 1932, in the Chicago area, Lil Hardin Armstrong led a first-rate all-woman band that included Dolly Jones Hutchinson, Leora Mieux, and Alma Scott. By the mid-thirties two of the best known of the black women's bands had been formed: the Dixie Sweethearts, which worked around the West and Southwest and was led by Mayme Lacy; and the Harlem Playgirls, formed in 1935 by Sylvester Rice, son of territory bandleader Eli Rice. Given one week to put an all-woman band together, Frank Driggs reports, Rice searched the country for the best musicians he could find. The final lineup included such outstanding players as Margaret Backstrum (tenor sax), Ernestine "Tiny" Davis (trumpet), and Jean Ray Lee (trumpet), as well as players from the then floundering Dixie Sweethearts. After woodshedding with the new group (i.e., spending long, arduous hours in rehearsal), Rice and Orvella Moore, piano player with Eli Rice's band, emerged with a good, swinging outfit. In 1938 the Playgirls were still together, with Lela Julius playing trombone and leading the band. "The Bronzeville Beauties have played in leading ballrooms of 44 states," *down beat* reported (December, 1938, p. 45), "and won plaudits of many swing fans who thought no all-girl band could play such solid swing."

The Playgirls provided an important outlet for some of the finest black female players of the day. Indiana-born, conservatory-trained Lela Julius was a first-rate musician who would later work with Eddie Durham's All-Star Girl Orchestra during the forties. "She was a real, real musician," says Durham, "and that was on guitar, violin, and trombone, and could sing. And she was a sight-reader, too." Margaret Backstrum was another top musician and "get-off" tenor soloist with the Playgirls, although she said recently in an interview that she never intended to become a professional musician, but had done it because she needed to earn a living.

One of the best publicized (although least jazzy) bands of the thirties was Phil Spitalny's all-woman orchestra, a white organization that featured Spitalny's wife, Evelyn, and her violin. This group offered subdued, semiclassical selections, and got many of the more comfortable location and radio jobs of the day, including the Hour of Charm broadcast. In Cuba, Concepcion Castro was leading the Anacoma Orchestra; at home, clarinetist Ann Dupont was leading a male band; and L'Ana Webster, who had played tenor with Babe Egan and with Mike Riley and his Round and Round Boys, was also fronting her own male band. She, too, according to *down beat* (May, 1938, p. 19), had "amazed fellow musicians by her talent and arranging ability." ("Amazing" was an adjective frequently applied to women who had talent.)

Ann Dupont's and L'Ana Webster's bands, however, were the exceptions at this time, for most women were restricted to an all-female musical "ghetto" and limited by sexual and racial stereotypes, the roots of which had taken hold centuries before. White bands were often not expected (and not taught or trained) to play as "hot" or "rough" as black bands, while black bands were expected only to swing and play the blues, and nothing very "sweet." (It should be noted that these standards applied to the male bands, as well.) White women, in fact, at this time were not even supposed to sing very "hot"; in 1939 a *down beat* article called "The Gal Yippers Have No Place in Our Jazz Bands" declared that, given the milieu of the jazz "classroom"—the red-light district of New Orleans and dimly lighted gin joints nationwide—"is it any wonder that excluded (as of course she should have been from this environment, which is the only one which could have given the white girl the insight into what went into making good jazz music), she should be so barren of any appreciation of the finer points of playing on an instrument, let alone trying to interpret it."[1]

Despite the prevalence of all-woman bands, however, the individual "woman as musician" remained a subordinate and practically nonexistent consideration compared with the overall look of a band and with the strong commercial appeal of a sexy, usually nonplaying leader up front "selling" the show. Photographs of the day offer blatant proof of the emphasis on appearance, glamor, and sex appeal, particularly when it came to vocalists and leaders. Instrumentalists, though, were by no means exempt. Maintaining the "feminine" image was so important that in one band the brass and reed sections applied Mercurochrome to their lips, because lipstick would have come off while they were playing.

With jealousies reminiscent of the blues queens, leaders themselves often kept their musicians away from the press, safeguarding all the publicity for themselves. That this would be the case, says Audrey Hall, was "taken for granted" by the women in the band, who were just glad to be working. "We all knew we were just sidemen and let it go at that," she says. "We were not stars."

In February, 1938, four years after it was founded, *down beat* printed an unsigned article called "Why Women Musicians Are Inferior." "Outside of a few sepia females," it said, "the woman musician never was born capable of sending anyone further than the nearest exit." As reasons, the writer cited variations on the standard themes that had kept women out of many professions: Women were, "as a whole, emotionally unstable" and "could never be consistent performers on musical instruments"; they would never really blow on brass or reeds, for fear of looking unattractive; they had only a few short years of playing experience behind them, while men had a centuries-old musical heritage (although jazz, it neglected to mention, had only been around for a couple of decades); they did not have the "time, ambition, or patience"—or the economic motivation—to woodshed. The writer also reiterated the old notion that only piano and strings were "empathetic instruments more in keeping" with the temperaments of women, concluding, "If more girl drummers had cradle-rocking experience before their musical endeavors, they might come closer to getting on the beat."

This attitude, presented in a musical microcosm, reflected the prevailing thought and popular late-thirties psychology which accused women of suffering from what Freud had labeled "masculinity complexes" if they felt the desire to aspire to anything outside their traditional roles as wives and mothers. Essentially, this was yet another convenient piece of male-devised psychological manipulation which served to "keep women in their place."

On the same page, Rita Rio, leader of one of the most successful white bands of the day, took issue with the arguments against female musicians, citing the fact that her band members had endured successive nights and days of rigorous travel and one-nighters. In addition, she said, because women were by nature more "aesthetic," they were more likely to offer a "warm, vibrant tone," rather than the "masculine sock so often emphasized by our men bands." That this "sock," or driving quality, was defined as innately masculine was also part of the sexism that worked against women, who, according to some, were not supposed to possess such qualities as drive, aggression, or power. Women could be "good for girls," or they could "play like men"—in one case, being forced to forfeit musical wholeness for the sake of maintaining their "feminine" image and charm; in the other, having their "unexpected" musical excellence cancel out their sexuality. At the bottom line, this deeply ingrained system of back-handed compliments and trade-offs also worked to keep women segregated as professional novelties or oddities, relegated to a small, relatively uncompetitive corner of the marketplace, still safely "in their place"—or at least out of a male musician's place.

In the April, 1938, issue of *down beat*, Peggy Gilbert responded to the charges in an article entitled "How Can You Play a Horn with a Brassiere?" "*They* put that headline there," Gilbert says. "I was *incensed*." The article, despite its inflammatory title, did bring support from female readers all over the country. "All kinds of girls that read *down beat* were writing me letters and saying, 'Get with it. Stick with it, Peg. That sounds great.' "

Gilbert's article covered the catalog of unfavorable conditions female musicians had to endure, from the psychological effects of being hired for extra-musical reasons alone, to being asked to smile with horns in their mouths, to the "dead end" of the female musical ghetto. "Men have always refused to work with girls," wrote Gilbert, "thus not giving them the opportunity to prove their equality. . . . A great many musicians have highly complimented my band saying it was as good or better than their organizations, but if the question of actually giving us an opportunity to establish our equality arose, we should immediately be relegated to an inferior plane and given the form answer A: 'It's not being done.' "

As for woodshedding, Gilbert said, "it would be fun if we could see there was anything to be gained by it—other than personal gratification. However, even you should agree as an artist that that is an admirable motive in itself. Oddly enough, Father, they [women] take just as much pride as men in their work, and they woodshed as much as men and perhaps more because of the obstacle of prejudice to be overcome and because of the harsh criticism fired at them from all sides such as that in your article. As for the point you noted that women are not compelled to support themselves, we urge you, with apologetic banality, to go West, young man. Evidently you haven't gone further in that direction than Chicago. Now, in California, it's different. The women support the men—as well as themselves."

The message that one had to "play like a man" to really "make it," says Jane Sager, was all-pervasive and understood by women players during the thirties, especially if they wanted steady work. "We were all trying to be like this band, and be like him, be like that, that we were kind of stereotyped. The bands that were making it big were the bands that were different, and we didn't know that. The first thing they'd say to you is, play like so-and-so, play like Coleman Hawkins. That's what they did to you." Sager remembers that, during her early years, she spent more time imitating her idols, Roy Eldridge and Bunny Berigan, than she did discovering her own style, and in general, women were not encouraged to express themselves through their music, but rather to imitate the sounds of the men who were at the top.

For Sager and other serious women players of the era, however, there were musicians—Zutty Singleton, Roy Eldridge, Jimmy Dorsey, Charlie Barnet—who encouraged them to play the way *they* felt. After all, jazz was "self-expression" music, as Jonah Jones said he had learned after spending his early years imitating Louis Armstrong. As young male players began to learn their way, they were able to build an elemental, individual relationship between themselves and the music. In the Kansas City jam sessions, for example, where musicians challenged what Albert Murray called the "bucking bronco" or "wild animal" of the blues, the contest between player and music was itself far more essential than the competition between player and fellow player.[2] Not only did male players have more opportunities to participate in such male-dominated and male-oriented sessions, but the prospect of future forums and recognition encouraged them to carve out an individual voice and mastery of the music, while women were rarely, if ever, given such incentives.

But, if the jam session was the intimate, after-hours, "musicians-only" place where the male musicians "stretched out," learned, and grew, it was also the place where women like Audrey Hall, Jane Sager, Betty Sattley Leeds, and Ernestine "Tiny" Davis could do the same. It was to the smaller clubs, the after-hours clubs, usually the black clubs, that these women went to hear Lunceford's alto man Willie Smith, or Roy Eldridge, or Zutty Singleton, or, in Tiny Davis's case, the roster of Kansas City jazz giants of the thirties. And it was there, where they were always welcome with their horns, that they went to play and jam and break out of the confines of the bandstand and the "image," to experiment, develop their own styles, and really start "to cook."

Ernestine "Tiny" Davis

(trumpet/leader)

Ernestine "Tiny" Davis was one of the most well known women to come onto the jazz scene during the early thirties. She came out of Memphis as a teenager and began her professional life in Kansas City. She then went the route of the all-woman bands, first appearing with the Harlem Playgirls and later, for nine years, as a featured attraction with the International Sweethearts of Rhythm, the most popular women's band of the forties. Following that, she led her own six-piece unit, Tiny Davis and her Hell Divers.

Davis eventually settled in North Chicago, working in clubs with a four-piece band that included her daughter on bass. Davis still works, playing an occasional wedding or union job, and in Kansas City in 1980 she was part of the Women's Jazz Festival's tribute to the Sweethearts of Rhythm. "It was almost forty years we ain't seen each other," Davis says. "It was really just like a family."

Ernestine Davis (nicknamed "Tiny" by Anna Mae Winburn because of her large size) is jovial, succinct, and to the point when she talks about her life. "I went to Booker T. Washington High School, and I started blowing the trumpet when I was about thirteen years old. I was the only girl in the band at that time. That was way back there in the year of 1926, I guess."

Davis was one of five sisters and two brothers. No one in the family played an instrument. It was in school that she first got interested in playing: "I just saw the band, I saw the trumpet, and I went home and told my mother I wanted one, and she got it for me." (No one, she says, not even the members of the all-male thirty–forty piece orchestra, thought it strange that a girl had picked up the trumpet.) Davis received her only musical instruction in school, where the principal taught all the instruments. "Just had to practice, that's all . . . about two or three hours a day, at least try to get in. I'd get up on toppa the barn at home and *blow.*"

The orchestra mostly played band and march music, Davis recalls, and as there wasn't even a Victrola at home, during her early years she had very little exposure to any of the blues singers or to jazz. "I was too young. I wasn't interested in the blues singers. Later on, yes, I did see Ma Rainey and Mamie Smith," she says.

"I just happened to wind up in Kansas City, and that's where I started to play. I started to working in a nightclub up there. I was gettin' two dollars a night, you know, and playing around, and then you'd hear different musicians all around Kansas City." Davis knew other women on the scene, like pianists Mary Lou Williams, Julia E. Lee, and "Countess" Margaret "Queenie" Johnson (later to record with Billie Holiday), with whom she would sometimes work. Generally, though, she sat in with the men. "You worked *all* the time. It wasn't like it is now. Even when I would travel, the same night I'd come back home I'd go to work, there was so much work there."

At jam sessions, Davis recalls, she learned to play just by playing.

"You had to play all the tunes and things, and I'd be with the fellows and jam. At that time . . . things never closed in that town. You'd go to another club or go down to the club where Count Basie was playing. We'd go down there when we got off work." There she would find Basie, drummer Jo Jones, musician/arranger Eddie Durham, blues shouter Big Joe Turner.

Louis Armstrong was Davis's greatest influence in those days. "Loved him," she says. "I would listen to his records when I was in high school. When I picked up the trumpet, I didn't know anything about him; but afterwards I'd get his records and play with him. I still do. I do his 'Mack the Knife' just like he does."

Around the mid-thirties Davis left Kansas City to go on the road with the Harlem Playgirls, one of the new black all-woman bands that had been formed. "We had a swingin' band," she says. "It was really swingin'. We toured all over, on a bus. Pretty rough, but when you're young, going out, you're enjoying it." After one year with the Playgirls, Davis left to have a baby. "And then I didn't go back to 'em. I think it was about '39, and I got with the Sweethearts of Rhythm."

Writer/arranger Jesse Stone was bringing new, experienced musicians into the Sweethearts and he wanted Davis, who immediately became one of the features, doing such numbers as "Jump Children," "I Can't Get Started," and "Harlem Nocturne." Davis had not had any particular aspirations to play with a big band, she says, but it was an experience she thoroughly enjoyed. "See, I'd be out there in the front, and that band, I'd hit a note—da-doo-*dee*—and the band'd be swingin' behind me . . . Really terrific." (Flo Dreyer, a trumpet player with the Sweethearts during Tiny's tenure, says of Davis: "She was just a riot—a lot of fun, a good jazz player, and comical"; Stone, who also coached the band, remembers Davis as the band member *least* interested in being coached.)

Davis stayed with the Sweethearts for nearly ten years, and in 1947 went out with her own small group. The sextet included Texas-born Bert Etta "Lady Bird" Davis on saxophone and Ruby Phelan on drums. "We played the Apollo, and I played on 42nd Street in New York," says Davis. "We played all over. Joe Glaser, he was booking the Sweethearts, and then he booked me when I started my little group. We went to fourteen islands—Puerto Rico, Jamaica, Trinidad . . . A real nice little group, entertainin' group. I was an entertainer as well as a trumpet player."

Eventually Davis and her Hell Divers broke up, too. "I just got tired of traveling, and I went down and worked in Chicago for about six years, on Worth Street in Old Town. That's when I had about four pieces. A steady gig . . . You got to work entertainin' the people. Makin' them happy—that's the main thing."

Given the ups and downs of the business, and the fact that she had

three children to raise at the same time she had to manage life on the
road, Davis might easily have turned away from music. But even during
the hard times, particularly in later years, she says, she never thought of
laying off or doing something else. "Oh *no*," she says. "No no no. Never
done nothin' else but blow the trumpet."

Valaida Snow

(trumpet/vocals/violin/piano/leader/dancer)

On the Broadway stage, Ethel Waters was triumphing with "Supper
Time" in *As Thousands Cheer* and portraying Hagar in *Mamba's Daughters;* Clara Smith was still working on the TOBA circuit, earning thirty-
five dollars a week—and "glad to get it," Clyde Bernhardt recalls;
Blanche Calloway, Cab's older sister, was singing, dancing, and doing
splits "all the way across the stage"; and the Whitman Sisters—Bert,
Essie, Alice, and May—were starring in and running one of the classiest
black troupes of the day, and helping to train many talented young
black entertainers.

Valaida Snow, one of the most popular attractions of the decade, had
started on the stage in the twenties, and made her name not in the all-
woman bands but as a stage and cabaret performer. By the thirties, she
was far more appreciated as a trumpet player in England than she was
at home, and was one of the earliest women to pioneer jazz around the
world and win international recognition as a solo instrumentalist. It has
been suggested by Mary Lou Williams that if Snow, a strong high-C
player, had concentrated on the trumpet alone, she "could have been
one of the greats on the instrument."[3]

Valaida Snow was born in Chattanooga, Tennessee, around the turn
of the century. Her sisters, Alvaida and Lavaida, were both singers.
Snow learned trumpet from her mother, who taught all the instruments,
and, according to drummer Tommy Benford, also studied with Dyer
Jones.

Snow's career began in 1920 in Pennsylvania and Atlantic City, the
resort town that had been the pre-World War I mecca for the best black
musicians and entertainers. By 1922 she was living in New York, working at Barron's and in Will Masten's revue, and in 1924 she made her
Broadway debut as Manda in *Chocolate Dandies*. She was cited by
one critic as a "thrilling young woman," and along with Lottie Gee,

"carried the female honors for the show" (LCL-T). That same year, leading the band for the first act and playing solo trumpet in *Rhapsody in Blue,* Snow starred along with Ethel Waters in the show *Rhapsody in Black.*

In the late twenties Snow began a long series of tours that would eventually take her all over the world. She made her first trip to Shanghai in 1926, and would later visit such places as Hong Kong, Rangoon, Cairo, Bombay, and Tokyo. In 1928, however, she was back in Chicago, where Earl "Fatha" Hines caught her act at the Sunset—and later described it to Stanley Dance:

"In her act she had seven different pairs of shoes set out in front, and she'd do a dance in each of them—soft shoes, adagio shoes, tap shoes, Dutch clogs, and I don't know what else, but last of all Russian boots. She'd do a chorus in each, and on the tap number she tapped just like Bojangles. Louis Armstrong had a fit when he saw her. 'Boy, I never saw anything that great,' he told me. She broke up the house every time." Snow also occasionally pitched in as producer and director. "She was so talented," Hines recalled. "She always knew what she wanted and nobody could fool her."[4]

When Snow left the Grand Terrace in Chicago, she went to England to appear in *Blackbirds of 1934.* (Actor Joseph Attles, who worked with her over there, remembered her at the time—glamorous, smartly dressed, and driving a purple Mercedes.) Arriving in London just after Louis Armstrong's first spectacular visit, Snow was an immediate sensation. British writer Brian Rust has described the way "the Queen of the Trumpet" (also billed abroad as "Little Louis") took the city of London, both because of the excellence of her playing and because it was such a novelty to see a woman blow a horn: "Her stage presence and brilliant musicianship captured London's theatregoers, who were amazed to find this slender, shapely girl capable of the sort of jazz trumpet that had hitherto been the prerogative, in their minds at least, of such as Louis Armstrong and Nat Gonella."[5] Ikey Robinson had described Snow's trumpet as "melodic" and "refined," while writer Jeff Aldam noted one month after Snow's death in the fifties that her style during the *Blackbirds* days was "on the beat, swinging powerfully, broad-toned and with a most unfeminine vibrato."[6]

In 1935 Snow returned to America to work in Los Angeles with her husband, dancer Ananais Berry (of the Berry Brothers). She continued to tour, also appearing in three films, *Take It from Me, Irresistible You,* and *Alibi,* this last a French film in which Sidney Bechet also appeared. Then, in 1941, while working in Europe, Snow was taken prisoner when the United States entered World War II. In an article written in the fifties, manager and producer Harrison Smith gave an account of Snow's harrowing experience in Europe:

"Prior to World War II, while [Valaida Snow was] appearing with

Chevalier in Paris, Americans were warned to leave France because of a threatened Nazi invasion. In Copenhagen, while she was doing a concert, leaflets were dropped from the sky, proclaiming, 'This is now Germany.' Unable to get a passport, she and many other Americans were hauled to Wester-Faengle concentration stockade. All of her belongings, including $7,000 in traveler's checks and a gold trumpet presented to her for a command performance by Queen Wilhelmina, were confiscated. Prisoners were given 15 lashes by whip each week. Ill health reduced her weight to 68 pounds. By an exchange of prisoners, she returned to the U.S. in 1943 on the S.S. *Gripsholm*."[7]

"Probably," speculates Doc Cheatham, "Snow saved her life by being a great entertainer."

In 1943, after regaining her mental and physical health with the help of her new husband, manager Earle Edwards, Snow went on with her career, making her first appearance at the Apollo that same year. In 1945 she moved to California and continued to work in the United States and Canada, where she was a great favorite. Snow died in 1956, after suffering a stroke.

Ina Ray Hutton
and Her Melodears

In 1934 Irving Mills, recognizing the commercial potential of a good all-woman swing band, decided to back one. With the powerful Mills organization behind them, Ina Ray Hutton and Her Melodears went on to become the most popular women's band of the decade. Audrey Hall, who had played with the Fourteen Bricktops and Babe Egan's band, was a member of the original Melodears, many of whom she helped bring into the organization.

"I had a little notebook that I took names down in," she says, "and when I was traveling, if I heard that there was a good girls' group playing, I'd look them up and listen to them, and if there was somebody I liked very much, I'd take the name and address and enter it in that little book. And I did that all across the United States as I traveled. So, when they got this bug about Ina Ray Hutton—there was really a lot of money back of it when it was first organized—where were they going to get their musicians? I got out my little book, and we got them from all over the United States. Many times they were just small combos and, of course, nobody knew of them." (Hall, like a number of other women who worked on the road, confirms that many talented women who could be heard in small local settings undoubtedly never had the chance to leave their hometowns.)

After the band was chosen, Hall remembers, Ina Ray Hutton was selected to be the leader. Born in Chicago in 1916, Hutton had started as a child tap dancer in a Gus Edwards revue, then gone on to Lew Leslie's *Clowns in Clover,* George White's *Melody,* and the Ziegfeld *Follies of 1934.* She was not a musician—for the first few months, Hall set the tempos for the band, while Hutton held the baton—but, when the Melodears opened in 1934, Hutton was the epitome of the 1930s female bandleader. Glamorous, sexy, and extravagant, "the Blonde Bombshell of Rhythm," as she was known, "spelled box office forward and backward," according to *Variety,* and set the standard for the stereo-type of the female bandleader. In some places, policemen had to sur-round the stage as Hutton danced and gyrated to the music. Her six costume changes a night were famous, and her seams were double-stitched so they would not give way during a performance. Her silver foxes, sex appeal, and savvy were equally well known, and magazine articles also touted her keen business instincts.

The original Hutton band included such excellent players as trom-bonist Alyse Wills (who played over twenty instruments and had toured the world with Tommy Dorsey); pianist Betty Roudybush; trumpet player Estelle Slavin; reeds player Audrey Hall; and tenor saxophonist Betty Sattley. With their tight swing arrangements by pianist/composer Alex Hill (who had also arranged for Fats Waller, Andy Kirk, and Benny Carter), the Melodears were practically an over-night success. While most female musicians of the day never had the chance to record, the Hutton band—with Irving Mills behind them—was unusual in that it did. Two recently reissued recordings—the up-tempo "Wild Party," featuring a gruff baritone sax solo by Betty Sticht, and the "jungle"-genre tune "Witch Doctor"—show the unit's smooth, rhythmic section work around this time.

By 1936 the band had reorganized, and eventually Eddie Durham was called in to manage and arrange for the outfit. Some of the original members had left, but others, like Alyse Wills, stayed on. "She had international perfect pitch," Durham remembers. "She'd go down to the dressing room and give everybody a note. They wouldn't have to tune by no piano. They'd tune by her voice. She was a *great* musician. She was the first trombone player, then she helped to pick the others." Wills also helped rehearse the section, which included Jessie Bailey and Fie Hesser.

Of pianist Betty Roudybush, Durham says, "She was about one of the best I could get at that time on the piano, who could play solid like Mary Lou Williams and those people. She was a pro." "She was so good," adds Jane Sager, "her choruses were written up in *down beat.*" (Roudy-bush's influences, *down beat* reported, were Fats Waller and Earl Hines, and although her hands were only three inches across, she was able to reach the ten-note span necessary for stride piano because of "stretching exercises done patiently and consistently over a period of years."[8])

Marian Gange was on guitar. "I was teaching her guitar," recalls Durham (who had made the first electric guitar). "But in those days I wasn't teaching them the get-off solo work so much as teaching them rhythm, teaching them to be an anchor personality with the instrument." Betty Sattley, who had been with the band earlier, also came back. "Betty was the outstanding personality," Durham says. "She was there playing second tenor and hot tenor. . . . That's the way the band stacked up. Lined the band up to be strong."

After three weeks of rehearsal, the band went into the Paramount Theater in Newark and then prepared for the Paramount in New York. While they were getting ready to open, says Durham, the unit was sent to upstate New York for a preview. "Duke Ellington came. They sent him up and lots of guys like that come up to see what they think the future of that band was." Durham (who always stood in the wings giving the band the tempo, while Hutton made her entrance later) opened up with a hot number, the show went on, and then came the critical response. As Durham remembers:

"They said, 'Well, everything was fine, but I didn't think I'd live to see the day when I'd see girls fannin' hats and wavin' their horns and stoppin' a show like that.' And they said, 'Well, what *you* think, Mr. So-and-So?' Course Duke Ellington, he always went along with everything as it was, he said, 'Well, I think it's *great!*' And they said, 'Well, I was expecting to come in and see the girls walk out, and I thought the opening was gonna be "A Pretty Girl Is Like a Melody," ' and Ina Ray, she said, 'I wanna sound like Benny Goodman and Basie and everybody else.' And they said, 'Well, I don't think it's nice for those girls to be playin' like that.' That's the only way they would have bought it— sayin' 'Open up the show with "A Pretty Girl Is Like a Melody." ' I must have opened up with 'Tiger Rag' or something!"

Once the band hit the Paramount, however, it played the big time all the way down the line. (The Hutton band of this period can be seen in the film *The Big Broadcast of 1937*, and such shorts as *Accent on Girls* [1936] and *Swing, Hutton, Swing* [1937]). "The things they did was fantastic," Durham says. On one program at Madison Square Garden that featured about twelve bands, Durham asked Hutton to find out where Count Basie was on the program and to use her influence (of which she had plenty) to have the Melodears put on just ahead. When Hutton closed her set, the band played all the Basie numbers, with the Basie solos.

"They played 'One O'Clock Jump,' and I had numbers in there like 'Jumpin' at the Woodside' and 'Out the Window,' " Durham recalls. "Everything that was on the record with Basie that they were gonna play, that band, Hutton's, played it. The girls were wavin' their hats like [trumpet player] Harry Edison, and he ran out of the dressing room half dressed up on the stage, and they all come out and they didn't believe it. Today if you do it, you'd have trouble, but those guys, man, they felt great hearin' those girls play their solos. That's the way that band played, just the same as the boys. They had to. I trained 'em down like that."

In an interview given at the time she led the second band, Ina Ray Hutton talked about the subject of women in jazz:

"For some reason, the formation of a girl band today is regarded by everyone as an unusual achievement. It is true that the formation of any kind of a successful band is quite a job, but I am very happy in the realization that I am a member of one group which has played its way into a state of popular approval—and with that approval expressed 'financially.'

"Jazz is here and in swing, presents a formidable job for anyone to put over correctly. But putting it over is well within the capabilities of the fairer members of the human tribe, and wherever music goes when it develops away from swing, the girls will have little trouble accompanying it."[9]

By 1939, however, Hutton was no longer associated with the Mills Agency, and could no longer make a financial success of the all-woman band. She disbanded it and put together an all-male unit, the press reporting that she was "tired" of female musicians. The male band, critic George Simon noted, had "several good jazz musicians . . . played well, if usually too loudly," held audiences with "its good dance music,"[10] and lasted till the end of the war.

During the early fifties, Hutton brought a more commercial fourteen-piece all-woman band to the relatively new medium, television, starring for several years on her own weekly hour-long program on WKLA in Los Angeles. Hutton also appeared fronting an all-woman band in the 1955 film *Girl Time*, but she never again reached the prominence she had enjoyed during the 1930s, when she and her famous Melodears were one of the top bands on the circuit.

Betty Sattley Leeds

(tenor saxophone)

When Betty Sattley joined the Ina Ray Hutton band for the second time, she was the one Eddie Durham featured, because, he said, she was one of the few white women really playing "get-off" tenor. "Sattley was something else," Jane Sager remembers: "She was a tremendous ad-libber. She could just put that tenor in her face and close her eyes and go all night. And she blew around. She was with some men's bands, too." Sattley was also one of the few women to have her own trio on 52nd Street during the forties.

Betty Sattley was born in a small Illinois town, population 700. "They had a professor of music that came to each town in this county one day a week. Our day was Monday, so we got one music lesson a week." Her first instrument was a C-Melody saxophone (between the alto and tenor). "I picked it out of a Sears catalog. My father said I could have any instrument I wanted, and I wanted that long thing with all the wooden mallets. I couldn't say that [the word *xylophone*], so I said 'saxophone,' and he got me one, and that was my first horn."

Sattley's family were all musical. "My father formed a band with the four of us girls. My sister played drums. One played bass, the next one played trumpet, and I played sax, so he got a piano and that was it. I played when I was nine or ten. We went to all the towns around Illinois, the coal-mining towns, and they had the Saturday-night dances, and I think the gigs paid all of two dollars a night or something."

Sattley also grew up listening to records: Fletcher Henderson; Duke Ellington; Andy Kirk ("That's where I first learned of Mary Lou, and Dick Wilson on tenor. I liked him. And Chu Berry—oh my God, that was my idol!").

Sattley then "kinda went to high school and kinda didn't," because she went on the road. "As a matter of fact, I came to New York when I was thirteen to join a band called Babe Egan and her Hollywood Redheads, appearing in a Broadway revue with Thelma White, leader of another all-woman band." The show carried a comedian, an acrobat, and a line of chorus girls, but the written band parts left little room for improvising.

By 1935, however, the Ina Ray Hutton band had sent for Sattley, and she joined the outfit in Toronto. She stayed for a year, then quit (over the firing of another musician), jammed around New York, and eventually rejoined the band. By this time, Eddie Durham was writing the arrangements. "It seemed to me like Eddie wrote the whole book for me," she says, "whether it was a ballad or a jump tune, the whole book was like for me, with a little trumpet now and then to break it up. The *biting brass*—I loved it! I guess that's why I love Basie, 'cause it's reminiscent of Eddie."

With the Hutton band, Sattley remembers, the music was "a ball." "I think she could stand up to any man's band—that was the way people talked in those days—except there were certain weak links in the chain, which there is in any band, but with girls it's harder to cover it up and harder to replace. If she lost a really good, good musician, it was very hard to replace her; whereas with the guys, you just go out and get another one."

By 1939 the Hutton band was breaking up, and Sattley, who had married tenor player Charlie Leeds, moved to New Jersey. Leeds was playing with Louis Prima at the time, and when he left to go overseas, it was his wife who took over his chair with the band, "saving his seat," as she puts it. (Prima told her that he'd keep her until he found a 4-F who could play better sax.) When Sattley did eventually leave Prima, she took a trio of her own into the Ha Ha Club on 52nd Street. (Whenever any of the clubs refused to advertise her as "Little Bit"—a name she had been given because she was 4' 11" and weighed 110 pounds—she insisted that they bill her as "Miss Leeds" instead.) "Dizzy and Bird and Don Byas and Erroll Garner were the relief band at the Spotlight," she recalls, "and Stuff Smith was across the street, so it was a real jam session all the time. Except that I was not into bop. I didn't play bop at that time. It was strictly the Swing Era, like Vido Musso, Charlie Leeds, that kinda stuff."

After giving up her own trio, Sattley joined Estelle Slavin's group, the Five Brunettes, for a brief time. "We played at Columbo's in Philly, and it was good money. I was still with her when Charlie got home in '45, and then everybody's husbands came home and she disbanded, and I started playing club dates around Elizabeth, Newark—weddings and that kind of thing. After the second baby—he was born in '55—I guess I played about five more years, but that was about it. About 1960 I quit. Couldn't get a baby-sitter I could trust. I'm one of those nervous [mothers]—if they have a cough and I have to leave, I call in every hour to see how it is, and if the phone's busy, I think she's talkin' to her boyfriend—and by then I was gettin' older, so I figured it was about time I quit and stayed home." Sattley was also not a fan of the rock-'n-roll that came in in the sixties, and she says she "got turned off from music completely. I didn't even want to hear jazz, except Basie with Sinatra singing 'Pennies from Heaven' or something." In retrospect, she says she had a "guilt complex" about admitting that she missed the music once she quit the business. But "Yeah," says Sattley, "I missed it tremendously."

Like Jane Sager and Audrey Hall, Sattley agrees that jamming was where musical freedom really lay. "They took you for your music instead of your color," she says; but she did get her share of sexism. "They almost clenched their teeth when they'd [men] congratulate you or give you a compliment, although some of them were really knocked out. Today, for example, kids come up to my children [both of Sattley's sons are professional musicians] and say, 'Who do you study with? How do you play that lick there?' They didn't ask us, I imagine, because we *were* women. 'Cause I would have been more than happy to tell them what little I knew."

Estelle Slavin

(trumpet/leader)

Estelle Slavin was one of the members of the original Ina Ray Hutton Orchestra and has also led her own small combos and male bands. In the 1960s she retired from music to work as an interior decorator.

Estelle Slavin started playing trumpet when she was in junior high school. "My father taught me," she remembers. "He was a musician in Europe when he was young." In New York, he worked as a tailor. "He had a dry-cleaning establishment on the Lower East Side, and we lived there till I was about maybe nine. I was born in Connecticut, but I went to P.S. 60 [in the Bronx]. I used to play in the band there, and then I joined somebody's grandfather's German band, and I learned a lot there, playing all the operas and classical music."

Slavin never intended to become a professional musician, but, in her last term of high school, she had an offer to join the Ina Ray Hutton band. While some families were opposed to having their daughters take off from school and go out on the road, Slavin's family's response was just the opposite. "I was the one that didn't want to go on the road," she says. "My brother forced me into doing that, because I had this very good offer. So I went to the rehearsals and I met all the girls, and I didn't know any of them except the drummer at the time." The music, she says, "was just very natural to me. I don't know why, but it was. I just liked Jimmie Lunceford's band and a lot of the black guys' bands, and I just had that inborn. I can't say I learned it from anyone."

By the early forties, Slavin had started her five-piece group, 'Stelle and the Brunettes, which included Marlene Gray on alto, Ceal Zirl on bass, Rose Gottesman on drums, and, at various times, Mary Tadler on bass and Betty Sattley on tenor. "We had all these head arrangements I used to make," says Slavin. "I don't know how I did it, but I did it. I never wrote a thing down. I wasn't good at writing. So I gave each girl her notes and she memorized 'em, and they were really good, especially the first group. We played all the ballads and all the up tunes, and all the musicians, they just couldn't get over us. We were way ahead of our time." In April, 1943, one reviewer wrote about a rehearsal: "It seems pretty clear that girl bands are creeping out of the novelty class, getting more respect from musicians and fans, and bigger and better jobs. This outfit, fronted by 'Stelle on trumpet, is entitled to all that."[11]

"I think we were a bunch of jerks to not have done better, even," says Slavin. "All the guys from bands used to come hear us when we were in Philly. They came from the theaters. They couldn't believe it, because we were pretty hip, you know, and the arrangements were good." Slavin believes bad management was responsible for the band's not doing as well as it might have. After some of the original women were replaced, she says, the group became "more commercial. The band was more danceable. And then after that I got a little disgusted, because I couldn't have the same sound as the girls with the head arrangements."

Slavin was still working in the fifties, but then the women started leaving the band. "Some got married, and then it kind of broke up." She continued to work till the mid-sixties, first fronting a New York-based all-male band "that didn't really go anywhere," then another male band in New Jersey. "The band wasn't as good as the band I had in New York," she says, "but there were possibilities. If it had stayed together, it could have been really great, but then the big bands started dying out, and so I gave up.

"Then I played a couple of club dates, and that's when I really gave it up completely. I went on a job and I had a terrible time with the drummer. And the piano player was playing all wrong chords—one of those things. It was a pick-up band. That night I came home and I said, 'No more. That's it. If I have to play with guys like that, I don't even want to play.' Because I was very serious about my playing, and if I couldn't work with a good piano player and a good drummer, you know, what was left? So I just gave it up and that was it. And I had studied interior design all the time I was playing, so that was the thing I went into very wholeheartedly, and I've been with it ever since. It's my second love, you could say. And it's a form of art."

While she was playing, Slavin was sometimes called "the Female Harry James." She says she admired Roy Eldridge very much, too, but never consciously tried to copy anyone else's style. "I just played how

I felt, and it came out. It's so long ago that when you talk about it, it seems so strange now. I can't believe it myself. I used to like to play very pretty ballads or bop—I guess that's what they called it then. And the guys used to come and they were fascinated. I don't know how I did it. I just did it."

Jane Sager

(trumpet)

There's only one way to play music, and that's with authority—it doesn't mean man or woman.

—Jane Sager

One of the most outspoken and active women in jazz, Jane Sager played major roles in the all-woman bands of Rita Rio and Ada Leonard, as well as in the International Sweethearts of Rhythm, and the Victory Belles. She has also held Bobby Hackett's chair in Katherine Dunham's band, and played with the bands of Charlie Barnet and Johnny Richards.

Born in Green Bay, Wisconsin, Jane Sager started playing violin at the age of six. By the time she was ten she was appearing on a radio show playing Mendelssohn, and as a reward, her father bought her a bicycle. "I went out and got hit by a car right off the bat," she says, "and the back wheel of the car ran over my left hand, so you can imagine how much violin I could play." When Sager saw a girl at a high-school concert playing a cornet—and using her right hand to press down the buttons—she went down to the Moose [Lodge] Hall, which had advertised lessons and horns, and picked up a Tonk horn. "The only other one that had an old horn like that was Louis Armstrong," she recalls, "and they were the worst horns you ever heard." Sager took it home and practiced until she literally "fell over."

"I could play 'Come to Jesus' and make it swing," she remembers, and when the local jazz trumpet player got hurt in an accident, Sager was the one asked to work in the ballrooms on the lakes around Green Bay, playing all summer alongside the fathers of the kids she went to school with. "My break was that I worked with nothing but boys and men in my school band. There were a few girls that played good, but mostly this boy and I had our own little band in high school, and I just knew how the fellows worked, and thought I had to be the same way."

Sager went on to Stevens College in Chicago, where she got her degree in violin, and then on to the American Conservatory of Music. "I studied from the first [-chair] trumpet player in the Chicago Symphony Orchestra and Roy Eldridge at the same time. My studies consisted of the Three Deuces till seven A.M., and I used to sit in there, and oh, it was the end, you know. That's where I got to play with Art Tatum. I just had to play that horn, that's all there was to it."

When Sager first arrived in Chicago, she says, she "didn't know there was such a thing as a girl musician. When I got into Chicago, I got into these girl bands, and I thought, wow, here's another chance to play with girls, as well as men." But, as Sager discovered, it was not as easy being accepted by male musicians in Chicago as it had been in Green Bay. "I'll tell you where you'd notice it: When you went to audition for a fellows' band, you'd walk up to the bandstand and they'd look down their noses and they'd think, 'Oh, God, here comes a girl.' You felt just like ice was thrown over you. But you'd get in there and you'd prove yourself to them, and they'd be marvelous to you. You had to prove yourself, though, and you had to do another thing: You had to put them at ease. For instance, one of the things I'd do after I got in there, if I missed a note, I'd quickly call that four-letter word out, and the fellows would say, 'Hey, she's a regular! She's not a silly girl! She's just like us.' And that's what you had to establish."

The first show Sager was on was out of Chicago and was one of what she calls the "cheap unit shows" that came in after the Crash of '29. "What they had was a line of girls and a juggler and a comedian and a sexy girl tap dancer, and then finally the band would do some numbers. But the band was not only being the flash act, the band had to play the whole darn show, which was marvelous experience for all of us, and we traveled and played all the big theaters."

Then, in the mid-thirties, after Ina Ray Hutton's band made such a big hit, Rita Rio "came along as competition," and Sager had a chance to join that outfit. The band had two books, one for dining rooms and "one for out there in the dance halls, where we could *whip* it up." Rio tap-danced and sang, writhed and twisted for her audiences, and once (in Scranton) it got so bad, Sager says, "they called the law in. She was wild, absolutely wild." Rio, whose theme song was "La Cucaracha," did her special numbers, including an imitation of Cab Calloway's "hi-de-hi-de-ho," and the band had arrangements by musicians like Charlie Barnet and Fats Waller (who also used to rehearse the group). By the early forties, Rio gave up life on the road and, as Dona Drake, tried to break into films.

"We used to run up against the Sweethearts back in those days," Sager recalls. "That's when I met Tiny Davis and Pauline [Braddy]. We would go and hear them if we could get there when our jobs finished, and if they were off, they would come by and see us." The women never got a chance to jam together, though, says Sager, because one group would always be on the bandstand. And when the job was over, "we'd be off and they'd be going to another town, or they'd be off and we'd be going to another town."

Sitting in with male musicians was a different story. "Of course, I sat in with every black band you could imagine. I used to go into Harlem and sit in in all the famous clubs—Dickie Wells's, the Silver Dollar . . . And I sat in with fellows like Lips Page, Rex Stewart . . . In fact, if I found a black band anywhere, that's where I headed, because that's where I got my real kicks. I mean, white bands are great, too, I love 'em, but I'll tell you, in those days when you'd get in these little clubs, you'd find three, four, five pieces, a tight black combo, and you could get to sit in with them, you'd just soar. They were much more receptive than the organized male white bands."

Making that scene, says Sager, was not a difficult thing for her as a woman—"not if you had a horn and proved what you could do. We never thought of anything but just we were musicians. If you could blow and you had a soul, that was it. I went everywhere, and as long as I had my horn under my arm, you couldn't be treated with more respect. People don't realize how close we were, the black and white musicians in those days. Finally, Benny Goodman broke down the color lines [see Helen Oakley Dance], and things began to happen more and more. . . . We were all kind of segregated in a sense, as musicians. We were just so dedicated to our music, we'd play all day and all night. It wasn't an exclusive club. We were just forced to be. The kind of life we lived, the kind of hours we kept, traveling all day in a bus, playing all night, traveling another day, and then finally sacking out in a hotel for a few hours—how many people love that kind of a life? I've got news for you: I'd turn around and do it over again."

When the Rio band broke up, Sager joined with Ada Leonard, a glamorous ex-burlesque queen who had also turned to fronting an all-woman band. The first date was to be in Chicago, and Sager helped to organize the group. "I remember staying over at Ada's apartment, staying up all night going over tempos and showing her how to lead. She got it very quickly." Sager gave the cues off the end of her trumpet, and Leonard's All-American Girls went on to become one of the highly successful units of the forties, playing top theaters, USO shows, and army camps.

When Sager's run with the Leonard outfit ended, she relocated on the West Coast, where she started to play with the Victory Belles on radio and also got the job she says was one of the highlights of her career—playing in the Johnny Richards Orchestra. "They were looking for a trumpet player," she remembers, "and I went over there and they made me sit *all night* to audition. They auditioned about three different guys in front of me. Finally, late at night, I was mad—seeing-red mad—and I went on that bandstand and he put me on these lead arrangements that were, oh, they were like the stuff they play today, that start out on high-C sharp and go up to F's and F sharp. He did that to me because I was a girl, and I knew it. So I did it. I was mad and I could do it; I knew I could.

"Then I started blowing the jazz chair, and he'd call out to me, 'Aren't you tired?' I'd say, 'Am I supposed to be?' I said, 'If I was tired, I wouldn't be trying out for this job, would I?' So the final was 'Body and Soul.' That was the old tune they tried all the jazz musicians out on. And I had a friend down there that counted eight straight choruses, slow, slow pace, trying to wear me down. Finally the gig was over. It was about one-fifteen, and I went up on the end to the cadenza and ended on a nice high E flat. And he looked at me and said, 'My God, you're not supposed to be able to do that! You're a girl.' I said, 'See? You've listened to the propaganda.' So he said, 'You've got the job.' But do you know, for the first two or three weeks when I played in that band, he'd come up to me and say, 'Aren't you tired?' And I'd say, 'No, I'm not tired. If I was tired, I wouldn't be sitting in this chair, would I?' I said, 'I don't understand, Johnny. We people train the same way that the men do, and if you cut the mustard, what difference does it make?' He said, 'You're right, Jane.' "

The war years were rigorous and demanding for musicians, not only because travel was so difficult, but also because people's daily schedules and routines were altered. For musicians like Sager, it meant added hours of playing, accommodating the swing-shift dance, from 2:00 A.M. to 6:00 A.M. "You know, when they had all the aircraft plants going, those people had to go out, too, and have a good time. I played ten and a half hours a day," she remembers. "Then I found out the guys were laying bets on how long I'd hold out, 'cause I was a girl. And of course, thank God, I held out for all of it. But what you go through! They plant a seed, and you'd think, 'My God, why are they saying that? Am I not supposed to hold out? Maybe I won't, then. That would be horrible.' "

"No man or woman ever played as great a lead as you just played for me," one conductor told Sager after she'd finished playing a wartime job; whereupon she asked him for a job on the staff.

" 'Oh, Jane,' he said, 'I can't do that. The fellows'll be coming back from the service, and they won't allow a woman. These men have been in the service, and I have to give them their jobs back.' And there I was. What could I do? He said, 'They've got families.' So I said, 'Well, I've got myself to support. I've got to live, and I've worked and trained myself, and you tell me this [that she played a great lead] and then you tell me you can't hire me just because of my sex.' He said, 'Well, that's the way it is, Jane. I can't help it.'"

At the Orpheum, when she wanted to play jazz and second trumpet, Sager recalls, the answer was more concise: "You're a girl. I can't use you. Period. Shut up."

Near the end of the war years, Sager also had a chance to join the Sweethearts of Rhythm. "That was the greatest, I think, of all the girl bands . . . and I've been in some of the best. Maybe a couple out here on the coast that were equal with them, but for a dance band that just got in there and *swung* and had that beat—well, when we were at Club Alabam, Jimmie Lunceford was in there every night and he tried to take the whole brass section. And Louis was there every night." Sager had taken the place of trumpet player Jean Starr, who had left to join Benny Carter's band. "I never had so much fun in my life. I never played with a group of people that were so dedicated, so wonderful. When they had intermission, a lot of them were sitting there with pad and pencils studying harmony, modern harmony, chart writing. Those were dedicated kids."

By the fifties it had become too expensive to keep the big bands going, and Sager worked with the new all-woman band Ina Ray Hutton was forming. She also taught, played with Charlie Barnet, and got Bobby Hackett's chair with Katherine Dunham. In 1964 she became part of a group called the Frivolous Five, which lasted until 1970 and featured five women playing and doing comedy. Sager still teaches three days a week, and loves having the chance to pass along the knowledge she has accumulated after fifty years in the business.

"Every outfit that she was ever with that I happened to be connected with," says Peggy Gilbert, "she was never afraid to speak up. Believe me, she's the one that stuck her neck out every time, to really fight for what was due. Women were intimidated. There weren't very many women musicians that I can think of along the way that really had the courage to get up and face anybody and really talk, because when they did get a good break, they were so glad to have that break, and so happy about the whole thing, they'd let anything go by. They'd work night and day. They were afraid to say anything. But Jane was such a fine musician, she could get by with it."

As for Sager, she says she is delighted with women in jazz today: "Amen. Heavy applause. Go to it."

❖   ❖   ❖

During the thirties, women all over the country continued to work as pianists and pianist/singers. In New York, Hazel Scott had started out playing in her mother's band and "swinging the classics" at Barney Josephson's Café Society Downtown; out west, Edythe Turnham was leading her family band; Una Mae Carlisle, protégée of Fats Waller, was singing and playing piano at home and abroad; and in Chicago, Cleo Brown had been discovered by Texas Guinan and become the rage of the city before going on to New York, Hollywood, and a Decca recording contract.

In Kansas City, the all-day, all-night jam session continued. When Andy Kirk and his Twelve Clouds of Joy were laying off, Kansas was their home as well, and Mary Lou Williams, pianist/arranger/composer for the Kirk band, was one of the inner circle of Kansas City giants, helping to create the good-time, blues-based Kansas City "school" of jazz. Other women pianists of the day included Julia E. Lee, Rozelle Claxton, Edith Williams, Juanita Bolar, "Countess" Margaret "Queenie" Johnson (who replaced Williams in the Kirk band for a short while), and one woman whom Williams remembered simply as "Oceola."

As usual, Mary Lou Williams was ahead of her time. Musicians would get together after regular jam sessions, Father Peter S. O'Brien has written, and ask her to play what they called "zombie"—new and "out" harmonies and "chords she says were 'modern,' even 'avant-garde,' as those terms are used concerning jazz today."[12] The compositions and arrangements Williams brought to the Clouds of Joy were also something new—"something a little different," Andy Kirk remembered. Known then as "the Girl Who Swings the Band" (also the name of one of her tunes), Williams helped in great measure to establish the musical identity of the Clouds of Joy.

When "Froggy Bottom" and "Corky" were released (both composed and arranged by Williams), reviewer Sinclair Traill noted that they showed "to good effect her ingenious scoring talents. She is quite definitely the only woman pianist in the jazz business who is on a par with any of her masculine rivals" (IJS). Soon Williams was scoring for other big bands as well—the Dorseys, Louis Armstrong, Benny Goodman ("Camel Hop" and "Roll 'Em"), and Jimmie Lunceford ("What's Your Story, Morning Glory?"). In addition to the records she made with the Kirk band—playing such compositions as her own "Little Joe from Chicago," "Walkin' and Swingin'," "Steppin' Pretty," "Corny," "Messa Stomp," "Isabelle"—she also recorded with small units from the band. One session, *Six Men and a Girl*, also featured Kirk tenorist Dick Wilson.

In those days, "even the women piano players had a little hard time," Eddie Durham recalls. "Mary Lou Williams didn't have a hard time, but she was one of the pioneers who broke in people knowin' that a woman was a great musician. Mary Lou really brought the jazz on in,

Edythe Turnham and sister Frances, third and second from left.

Edythe Turnham's Dixie Aces. Back row, left to right: Floyd Turnham, Sr., Frank Pasley, Edythe Turnham, unknown (bass horn). Front row, left to right: Happy Johnson, Teddy Buckner, Charlie Saunders, William Griffin, Floyd Turnham, Jr., Floyd Eddie Wilson.

Lil Hardin Armstrong leading her mid-thirties band. Top row, from left: Milt Robinson, Paul Butler, Johnny Washington, Sylvester Turpin, Jimmy Sherman. Front row, left to right: Jonah Jones, Sleepy Tomlin, Henry Clay, Luke Stewart, Al Williams, Al Gibson, Teddy McRae, George Clarke.

The Bluebells, 1926.

Bobbie Grice and the Fourteen Bricktops. Audrey Hall is directly to right of Grice.

The Bon John Girls, 1930.

Mary Lou Williams, 1938.

Mary Lou Williams with Andy Kirk (to left of vibes) and the Twelve Clouds of Joy.

Pianist Cleo Brown.

Marge Creath Singleton.

Babe Egan and her Hollywood Redheads. Audrey Hall is second from right, behind bass player.

Ina Ray Hutton's brass section. Top row, from left: Althea Connelly, Ruth McMurray. Front row, left to right: Estelle Slavin, Kay Walsh, Elvira Rohl.

Helen Oakley Dance.

Sweethearts leader Anna Mae Winburn.

Vi Burnside with three members of her late-forties group. Flo
Dreyer is second from left.

Publicity photo of the 1941 Sweethearts unit. Top row, left to right: Ina Bell Byrd, Helen Jones Woods, Corinne Posey, Evelyn McGee Stone (with baton), Edna Williams, Nova Lee McGee, Sadye Pinkey. Bottom row, left to right: Grace Bayron, Alma Cortez, Judy Bayron, Pauline Braddy Williams, Amy Garrison (with clarinet), Johnny Mae Rice Graham (piano), Bernice Rothschild, Sweethearts tutor Vivian Crawford (holding tenor), Willie Mae "Rabbit" Wong.

The Sweethearts en route to Europe for their 1945 USO tour. Standing, left to right: Maurice King, Helen Saine Coston, Johnny Mae Stansbury, Vi Burnside, Margaret "Trump" Gibson, Ina Bell Byrd, Helen Jones Woods, Anna Mae Winburn, Evelyn McGee Stone, Jean Travis, Rae Carter, Tiny Davis. Kneeling: Roz Cron, Mim Garfield, Grace Bayron, Pauline Braddy Williams, Johnny Mae Rice Graham, Willie Mae "Rabbit" Wong.

Eddie Durham's All-Star Girl Orchestra. Top row, left to right: Edith Farthing, unknown (drums), Edna Williams, Jean Starr, Nova Lee McGee. Bottom row, left to right: unknown (piano), Mildred Jones, Marion Freeman, Alma Cortez, Ellarize Thompson, Helen Scott, Sammy Lee Jett, Jessie Turner, Lela Julius (former leader of the Harlem Playgirls), Eddie Durham.

The Prairie View College Co-Eds, ca. 1944. Top row, left to right: Elizabeth Thomas, Jewel Simmons, Margaret Grisby, Helen Cole, Doreathea Williams. Bottom row, left to right: Nelda McDonald, Bobby Jean Nunn, Melba Wren, Bert Etta Davis, Flores Jean Davis, Clora Bryant, Ernest Mae Crafton, Bernice Payne, Argie Mae Edwards, Marcella Gauthier, Marion Davis, and director Will Henry Bennett.

I'm tellin' ya. But then, they recognized Mary Lou Williams as a great musician. Before that, a lot of people didn't care about women."

Another outstanding musician of the twenties and thirties was pianist/leader/composer Irene Kitchings.

Irene Kitchings

(pianist/leader/composer)

Irene Kitchings lived and worked in Chicago during the years of Prohibition and the Depression. Solo pianist and leader of her own hot combos through the early thirties, Kitchings retired after she married pianist Teddy Wilson and moved with him to New York around 1934. After their marriage ended, she did not come back to the music as a player but as a composer, collaborating on all but one song with lyricist Arthur Herzog, Jr., and producing such classics as "Some Other Spring," "Ghost of Yesterday," and "I'm Pulling Through."

Everything she wrote, says pianist Jimmy Rowles (who titled one of his albums *Some Other Spring*), even the lesser known of the dozen or so songs she produced after the mid-thirties, were "gorgeous." (Rowles had first discovered Kitchings through the Teddy Wilson recordings of her tunes—"Some Other Spring"; "This Is the Moment," with a Ben Webster solo on the first chorus; "What Is This Gonna Get Us?") "She was *tough*," he says. "I think she was one of the best. I wish they would resurrect her music. Her songs are very special. They're *inside* songs. They make your heart ache. That's what she was—she was a heartache writer."

Born in Marietta, Ohio, Irene Kitchings's early training came from her mother, who taught her piano. At thirteen she moved to Detroit to live with an aunt, and by the time she was eighteen she was living in Chicago and was an integral member of the jazz scene of the late twenties. Her first jobs around the city were as solo pianist. "Irene was my favorite when it came to piano players," Ikey Robinson says. "We used to have jam sessions together. When the joints would close up, we would all meet." In those days, says Robinson, the bands relied on a "rhythm beat" on the piano. "And to plug them chords out, you had to hear that piano beatin' them chords out for the musicians takin' solos and things. Irene, she could play with anybody, because you could hear her when you turned a corner to go into a joint. She was heavy-handed, like a man.

She could swing, and she could play anything. She sounded like Louis playin' trumpet on a piano. Yep, she made the same stuff Louis made. She was good."

Eventually Kitchings had her own band and went into the Vogue with it. The personnel included such top musicians as Budd Johnson (tenor sax), Walter Fuller (clarinet), and Dolly (Jones) Hutchinson (trumpet). "Irene was the pioneer of the women that could play and had talent as a composer and had an all-male band out in Chicago," tenor saxophonist Paul Quinichette remembers. "Irene was the first woman and the greatest of them all. She knew how to handle the men, and she was also a composer and writer." Most of the popular female bandleaders of the day, he says, were glamorous "baton-wavers." Kitchings was an exception. "She knew the *music* part of it." Kitchings was writing at the time, Quinichette recalls, but "just numbers in the band, not the classic tunes she would later produce.

"Al Capone loved her," says Quinichette, "and so she worked all the time. Actually, she had a lot of experience there, and in those days it was rare for a woman to have an all-man band, 'cause most musicians thought, 'Well, we don't want a woman to lead us.' But they respected her because she knew what she was doing."

When the Vogue was raided, the syndicate went to work on a new club for Kitchings, and in the interim she joined with Kathryn Perry (later Mrs. Earl Hines) and Eloise Bennett to form an act called the Three Classy Misses. The piano, violin, and vocal trio worked in the Sunset and at the Café de Paris (where Ethel Waters was the headliner), and soon Kitchings had taken a new band into the Cottage Café. By 1931 she had married pianist Teddy Wilson, and when the new Vogue opened, she went in with an enlarged band, which she told Helen Oakley Dance was one of the best she ever led. Kitchings continued to lead the band during the first two years of her marriage, and Callie Arter, a close friend, remembers her playing at the World's Fair in 1933.

That same year, Benny Carter came through Chicago, and offered Teddy Wilson a chance to go to New York. "Great as the musicians were in Chicago," recalls Callie Arter, "they didn't seem to get anywhere particular. They had to come to New York." But, if New York offered promise to Teddy Wilson and other Chicago musicians, for Kitchings the move meant retirement. "From that time on," she told Helen Oakley Dance, "I gave up performing. My mother-in-law disliked my working in public places, and Ted's career was more of a concern to me than my own."[13]

By mid-1935 Wilson had become a part of the new Benny Goodman Trio and had started recording under his own name, using a young vocalist whom his wife would befriend and always remain close to— Billie Holiday. However, despite her husband's growing reputation, Irene Kitchings was not as happy in New York as she had been in Chicago.

Writing home to Callie and Ann Arter (Callie's mother), she said that for blacks, New York was "a joke" compared to Chicago. "As you know," she wrote, "Harlem is very large and thickly populated, but all the business is run by the white man and the places, I mean everything except the restaurants here all have white help. Groceries and all." At another point she wrote, "It is very lovely and all but if you ask me, I would rather be sitting in the open air camp tonight playing pinochle with Callie and Ann."[14]

Very soon after Teddy Wilson's career began to take off, the Wilsons' marriage came to an end. For Irene, the breakup was a devastating blow. The period that followed was a time of difficult transition, and it was Benny Carter who helped to pull her out of her despair. Recognizing her great gifts as a writer, and appreciating her unusual sense of harmony, he encouraged her to write. Then Billie Holiday introduced her to Arthur Herzog, Jr., who had collaborated with her on her own "God Bless the Child," and Herzog began, as he says, "to equip her music with songs." Their first published song was "Some Other Spring," which Billie Holiday was the first to record. (Later it would be recorded by Teddy Wilson's big band, Benny Carter, Art Tatum, George Shearing, Charlie Byrd, Carmen McRae, Dakota Staton, and others.)

For the next five years or so, Kitchings would continue to write and bring her music to Arthur Herzog. It was a tragic time in her life, and "of course," says Callie Arter, "that music was just pouring out from her heart." When he received the music, Herzog never made any changes. "This is very unusual between collaborators," he says, "but I don't think I ever asked her to change a note. Anything she wrote, I could put words to, and that doesn't happen very often. Everybody asks a songwriter, how do you go about it? What comes first, the words or the music? There is no answer, and usually, if it's a collaboration, you beat the thing out, you compromise. But in her case, everything she wrote was all set when I got it. She'd simply play it for me, give me a lead sheet, I would write the words, and that was it."

The last tune they wrote together was "I'm Pulling Through," written around 1940. By then Kitchings had become ill and gone back to Cleveland, where her aunt took care of her. "When she got on her feet," says Herzog, "she wrote a tune for her aunt and asked me to give it words. That's the song 'I'm Pulling Through.' It wasn't written commercially, but about two years later, Billie found it and recorded it.'"

During her stay in Cleveland, Irene Kitchings met Elden Kitchings, the man she would marry and live happily with until her death in the mid-seventies. Afflicted with Eale's disease, her eyesight deteriorated over the years, but she continued to lead an active life. She learned to play the organ, which had been a gift from her husband, and played and sang in church, where she teamed once again with Kathryn Perry, this time in the church choir. She also often played and sang her songs for friends.

During the Chicago years, Irene Kitchings had been one of the few women to succeed in what was essentially considered to be a man's world. She had been highly respected by the musicians, and rewarded by the reigning syndicate in big ways—a seven-room house, furniture, a grand piano. Although she gave up her own career in the mid-thirties and did not again take up the challenge of performing, her talent nevertheless reasserted itself during her years of greatest sorrow. "Her musical streak came out in composition," says Helen Oakley Dance. "Whatever unhappy bouts she would have would finally come out in a song. She didn't even sit down to compose or hope that she would publish. It was just one of those things that happened."

As the Big Band Era got under way, female singers began to replace the male vocalists who had sung with America's popular bands prior to 1929. Countless numbers of attractive young women were ushered onto American bandstands by bandleaders who knew that they would draw a large male audience; it was not long before the stereotype of the girl band singer—"chirp," "warbler," "thrush"—emerged.

"Mostly when the bandleaders were looking for girl singers," recalls Helen Oakley Dance, who herself had had a brief stint as band singer, "they were quite relieved if they got girls who didn't sing maudlin, if they were just *clean*—but what a thing to have to settle for."

During these formative years of swing and big-band music in America, however, a number of important and well-respected female vocalists did get their start as band singers, among them Helen Ward (with Benny Goodman), popular singer Lee Wiley, Helen Forrest, and the dynamic and compelling Lena Horne (with Noble Sissle and Charlie Barnet). And a handful of innovative and revolutionary female voices rose to actually define the Swing Era and create altogether new styles, harmonies, and textures in jazz.

In 1931 the New Orleans-born Boswell Sisters scored an overnight sensation at New York's Paramount Theater. Raised on a combination of Mamie and Bessie Smith, Caruso and the classics, the Boswells virtually revolutionized three-part harmony. With their inspired phrasing, advanced harmonies, starts, stops, colorations, and choice of top jazz accompanists (whom they wisely allowed an unusual degree of musical freedom), "no singing group had such a hand in shaping our popular music as the Boswell Sisters," wrote one reviewer in the middle forties.[15] After producing such hits as "Heebie Jeebies," "Shout, Sister, Shout," "Roll On, Mississippi, Roll On," the trio retired in 1935, when Vet and Martha married. Connee Boswell continued to perform until the seventies, and died in 1976.

Mildred Bailey was another of the early, influential singers as the music shifted from the blues to swing. Part Coeur d'Alene Indian, Bailey joined Paul Whiteman's band in 1929. Whiteman already had a male singing trio, the Rhythm Boys (Harry Barris, Bing Crosby, and Al Rinker, Bailey's brother), and when Mildred was added to the unit, she became the first female vocalist to join a big band. "In Mildred's heyday," wrote one reviewer, "a jazz singer was a rare and precious thing; at one point, when Bessie Smith had fallen into obscurity and Billie Holiday and Ella Fitzgerald were not yet on their way, she was almost the only real jazz singer of any prominence."[16]

In 1934 Bailey left Whiteman to join her husband, vibraharpist Red Norvo, in creating some of the most innovative music of the decade. Norvo was leading a ten-piece band organized around Bailey, and "Mr. and Mrs. Swing," as the couple were nationally known, were producing music far ahead of their time. "As was probably inevitable," one critic noted twenty years later, "the public did not fully appreciate it. Their band was one of the real milestones of modern jazz."[17] (On record, Bailey and Norvo can be heard on such tunes as "When Day Is Done," "Someday, Sweetheart," "I've Got My Love to Keep Me Warm," "Bob White," "Weekend of a Private Secretary," and "Don't Be That Way.")

Bailey sang with a barrelhouse beat, flawless phrasing and diction, and a light, high voice that seemed incongruous with her large size, and she recorded with some of the finest jazz musicians of the day. Writing about her in 1950, Studs Terkel drew a parallel between Bailey and bluesman Leadbelly (Huddie Leadbetter): "They shared a zest for living, a casual giftedness, and above all, hope. When Mildred sings the blues, the big idea is, 'I'll snap out of it.' "[18] The next year, Bailey was dead at age forty-four, never having fully received the acknowledgment she deserved as one of the vocal pioneers of jazz.

Two years after Bailey joined Paul Whiteman and the Rhythm Boys, singer Ivie Anderson joined the Duke Ellington Orchestra in Chicago and became the first female solo vocalist with a big band. Already a seasoned performer when she joined, Anderson would stay with the band until 1942, and would always be remembered by both Ellington and her public as the Ellington vocalist of all time. While other singers might have drowned amid the sea of Ellington growls, mutes, dazzling slides and slurs, Anderson fit into the vocal spot perfectly, giving it importance and impact, setting herself and her material apart from the texture of the band with her cool, disengaged, slightly ironic, slightly comedic delivery.

Anderson never made any records under her own name (with the exception of two 1937 dates, one of which produced "All God's Chillun Got Rhythm," the song she sang in the film *A Day at the Races*), and because she was such an integral part of the Ellington band, she was often given less attention than other female vocalists. An album of all her work with the band was released in the early seventies, and provided what John S. Wilson called "the definitive portrait of one of the true originals among jazz singers."[19] Her versions of "Stormy Weather," "Mood Indigo," "Solitude," "I'm Checkin' Out Goombye" (with Ellington drummer Sonny Greer's repartee that made their act such a hit), and the theme song of the decade, "It Don't Mean a Thing (If It Ain't Got That Swing)," showed the full range of her presentation with the Ellington outfit.

In 1942, due to illness, Anderson left the band. Every singer since, Duke Ellington wrote, had tried, though none had ever managed, "to prevail over the Ivie Anderson image."[20] Anderson continued to work on the West Coast, also running her popular restaurant, Ivie's Chicken Shack. She died in 1949.

In 1935 another singer made her entrance, and went on to become an institution in the world of American music, what one writer called a "legendary American reference point, like the Yankees in their prime."[21] Ella Fitzgerald's pure tone, her assured, swinging sense of rhythm, her virtuoso steeplechase scatting, and her deep, rich ballad delivery were entirely new to thirties audiences and they loved her. Discovered during an Apollo Theater Amateur Night show, Fitzgerald (who once said that Connee Boswell had been her greatest influence) was hired by bandleader Chick Webb, and her career became a top priority of the Webb organization. Fitzgerald's hits, beginning with her own swing nursery rhyme, "A-Tisket, A-Tasket," followed by "I Found My Yellow Basket," "Flat Foot Floogie," and "My Last Affair," brought the Webb band the commercial success it had never had before. When Webb died in 1939, Fitzgerald continued to front the band for two years, turning down numerous other offers. With the advent of World War II, however, keeping the band together became impossible, and in the early forties Fitzgerald struck out on her own.

Hailing from Louisville, Kentucky, Helen Humes also worked as a band singer in the 1930s. (Her first recordings, however, had been two blues, which she made in the late twenties.) Humes worked with Count Basie's band from 1938 to 1942, withstanding all the one-nighters and rigorous six-month tours. While Jimmy Rushing handled the blues and original songs, Humes did the pop tunes and "pretty" songs, her clear voice riding over the swinging Basie aggregation. During the mid-forties Humes got side-tracked into rhythm-and-blues with her hit on "He Baba

Leba," and R&B became her musical focus for nearly a decade. By the 1950s she had returned to jazz, and in 1961 recorded an excellent (and recently reissued) album on Contemporary. In 1967, however, she retired to Louisville to take care of her ailing mother, and took a job in a munitions factory for a short time. An appearance at the Newport Jazz Festival in 1973 heralded a triumphant return to jazz for Helen Humes. On blues, ballads, or jazz tunes, wrote Nat Hentoff, in the notes to her 1974 album, *Sneakin' Around* (Stash Records), Humes "keeps focusing simultaneously on what the song itself says while also curving phrases and swinging with inventive, often subtle, gusto." One of the authoritative, "get-off" singers in jazz, Humes died in September 1981.

Of all the singers who came to prominence in the thirties, one was the most original, the most innovative of all. Bessie Smith and Louis Armstrong had been her two greatest early inspirations. Billie Holiday often said, in fact, that when she sang, she approached the music not as a singer, but as if she were playing a horn. She tried to improvise, like Lester Young or Louis Armstrong, and always made the tune her own. (Lester Young, a personal and professional friend who had a special musical rapport with Holiday, once talked about the records they had made together: "Sometimes I sit down alone and listen to those old records, all by myself. It sounds like the same two voices, and two of the same mind."[22])

From the first, Holiday's voice and style were new to thirties audiences. She presented the Depression public with a cool, unemotional delivery, but, unlike Ivie Anderson, Fitzgerald, or Bailey, Holiday always projected her own vulnerability into her material, from the coy, upbeat early tunes like "Twenty-four Hours a Day" or "What a Little Moonlight Can Do" to her own "God Bless the Child" or "Billie's Blues."

Holiday, who worked briefly with the Basie and Artie Shaw bands in the late thirties, continued as a single through the forties and fifties despite her tangled odyssey through drugs, heartaches, courtrooms, and hospitals. "With her, the whole thing was total instinct," says Helen Oakley Dance, who knew Holiday well. There was her exotic, "get-off" phrasing; the difficult intervals made with no formal knowledge of harmonics; her special "signature" slur at the end of her tunes. "She was never happier than when she was singing," Dance recalls. "That's when she was unburdened and at *ease*."

In 1959, at the age of forty-four, Holiday died, in the hospital and under arrest. Her life has been explored in a full-length biography, *Billie's Blues*, by British writer John Chilton, documented in her own autobiography, *Lady Sings the Blues*, and was also the subject of a major motion picture that actually had little to do with the facts or texture of her life. Like Bessie Smith, she was mythologized in death as she had never been in life, and became, as Dan Morgenstern wrote, the symbol of "the sufferings of her race, sex, and profession."[23] The essential truth about Billie Holiday, he also wrote, was her final "triumph in her art." Betty Carter expressed the same thought in her song, "Don't Weep for the Lady."

Like Mildred Bailey and many other jazz women of the decade, Holiday, as charismatic as she was, never scored the commercial success she wished for during her lifetime. One woman who did receive commercial acclaim in the thirties was Maxine Sullivan; but, as Sullivan reveals, there were two sides to the story of overnight success.

Maxine Sullivan

(vocalist)

Maxine Sullivan was one of the star vocalists of the Swing Era. Known as "the Lady Who Swung the Scotch" and "the Loch Lomond Girl," she was catapulted to overnight fame with the release of her 1938 recording of a swing version of "Loch Lomond," and, as a result of its success, she says, was typed with folk material for many years thereafter.

Despite a number of retirements starting in 1950, Sullivan is currently extremely active as a vocalist, and, on standards, pop tunes, or blues, is still noted for her impeccable diction, musical integrity, simple, understated delivery, and what one reviewer called the "clear-bell lyric quality" of her sound.[24] A resident of the South Bronx, she is also involved in local politics, and owns and runs The House That Jazz Built, a community center dedicated to the memory of her late husband, stride pianist Cliff Jackson.

Maxine Sullivan was born in Homestead, Pennsylvania, a community in which her grandmother had been one of the first settlers. "Those were the days," she remembers, "when in order to sell Victrolas, companies gave away about a hundred records in order to get you to buy the machine. So we had quite a selection, although when we got our phonograph, it was before the so-called 'race' records came out, because I know that we had recordings of some of the popular white singers. Marian Harris [a white vaudeville artist who also sang blues], [singer] Frank Crumit, and people like that. Most of the records at that time, I suppose, were light opera, operetta." In 1920 "Crazy Blues" came out, and then followed the whole slew of blues women. "I heard them," says Sullivan, "but I wasn't into that kind of bag, because the records were sort of *double entendre*. That wouldn't be the kind of thing we'd be singing around. I like to feel that I was influenced more by Ethel Waters than by any other."

Sullivan's father played mandolin, and her uncles played banjo, violin, and tenor and sang barbershop harmony. "I just sang all the time, I guess," says Sullivan. "In school . . . in the glee club. And I do remember when I was going to junior high school, we formed a little trio—two boys and myself—and we used to book ourselves out to the other classes, so we were doing our circuit in school there."

One of Sullivan's uncles was drummer in Lois Deppe's band around 1922. (This was the band in which Earl Hines was playing piano.) He didn't care for drums, and "he especially didn't like *playing* the drums," she remembers, so he went back to Homestead in the late twenties and formed a group of his own, the Red Hot Peppers. "I used to go along with the band," she says, "and they'd let me sing a few songs."

Sullivan says she never made a conscious decision to be a singer. "I suppose that when I started doing these gigs, I considered myself pretty much in. That is, I was too far in to turn back. . . . Before I started tagging along behind the band, I had different little odd jobs, waiting tables and things like that, but Homestead was a very small town and there were few opportunities there, even in the clubs. Now, downtown Pittsburgh was jumping, but the singers that were tops were those gals with these big voices. I mean, they could stand in the middle of Yankee Stadium and you could hear them all over the place. . . . My handicap was that my voice was just a little bit too soft, and I wasn't into the repertoire that most of the singers were into. I wasn't exactly a blues singer."

Sullivan's break came in 1936. A woman pianist who knew her uncle was working in the Benjamin Harrison Literary Club in downtown Pittsburgh, and told Sullivan to come down for an audition. "It was just my size," Sullivan recalls. "The club had eight tables." There was another singer in the place, however, and Sullivan had to go through a probationary period. At the end of a week, Sullivan saw the manager and the piano player huddled in conversation, and prepared for a dramatic exit line, only to discover that she'd been hired at $14 a week. "I said, 'Well, if you have that much confidence in me, I'll be here for a long time.' So I was at the club for a whole year, which was a long time, and I saved my money."

While Sullivan was working at the club, Gladys Mosier, pianist with Ina Ray Hutton's all-woman band, told her she ought to come to New York. She did soon after, and Mosier made an appointment for her with musician/arranger Claude Thornhill at the Onyx Club on 52nd Street. "We auditioned . . . on Wednesday, and I went to work there on Friday," Sullivan remembers. "Pretty fast, you know. They said it couldn't be done.

We did it. And, of course, it was at the Onyx Club that Claude made the arrangement of 'Loch Lomond' for me, and that just about did it."

While Sullivan greatly admired the style of the swing singers of the day, Thornhill and Mosier (who had become her personal managers) recognized the need for a different presentation for her. "I imagine that's one of the reasons why Claude selected 'Loch Lomond' for me," she says. "Because if I had continued with the style, I would probably have been a second Ella Fitzgerald or Billie Holiday, which wouldn't have led to very much. With my material and the sort of low-key treatment, it set me apart as an individual. . . . Of course, for years I was *stuck* with the folk material, you know. But it didn't hurt a bit."

For the record date, Sullivan received twenty-five dollars and no royalty arrangement. "In those days, I guess I was lucky to even get a record date," she says. (Prior to making "Loch Lomond," she had recorded "Gone with the Wind" and "Stop, You're Breaking My Heart," songs she only recently discovered had been released.) The John Kirby quintet was also getting started at that time, and Thornhill chose them to make "Loch Lomond." After the success of the record, Sullivan and the quintet did more work together.

Sullivan's first inkling that the song was causing a stir came when CBS's Saturday Night Swing Club played it and Detroit station manager Leo Fitzpatrick cut it off the air because he considered it sacrilegious to swing a traditional Scottish song. "But that went over with a thud," says Sullivan, "and CBS put the Saturday Night Swing Club on the stage at Loew's State, and I went on as featured vocalist."

The success of "Loch Lomond" plus the dearth of standard material due to the ASCAP strike combined to keep the Kirby unit moving in the direction of swing arrangements of classics, as well as of rumbas, congas, jump numbers, and minuets. And the classy combination of Sullivan and Kirby—who by then had married—was drawing a nightly crowd of high-society patrons into the Onyx. "When I first came to the Onyx Club," Sullivan remembers, "he [Thornhill] was very particular about anybody photographing me, because, well, at that time it still wasn't the easiest thing in the world for a black artist to reach that particular stature. And, of course, you realize that I did not start in Harlem, I started right on the Street [New York's 52nd Street], and the Street wasn't that integrated at the time, let's face it."

Following the success of "Loch Lomond," Sullivan was in demand. Although her salary went up, for five years she was under contract to Mosier and Thornhill, and after legal complications ensued, her earnings were held in escrow in lieu of settlement. "At the end of five years I was free again," she says, "and I have never signed up with anybody since."

In 1939, two new fronts opened up to Sullivan: stage and screen. In the theatrical extravaganza *Swingin' the Dream,* a swing version of *A*

Midsummer Night's Dream, she played the part of Titania, queen of the fairies. "I guess that was because of the type of material I was doing," she says. Some of her hit songs were given new lyrics for the production, and "Darn That Dream," written especially for her to sing in the show, went on to become a jazz standard. That year she also made her Hollywood debut singing in *St. Louis Blues,* and appeared with Louis Armstrong in another film, *Going Places,* which introduced the song "Jeepers Creepers." She and Armstrong, she recalls, repeated the song at the old Cotton Club Downtown. "They projected on a paper screen a scene from *Going Places* in which Louis and I did 'Jeepers Creepers,' I in a maid's uniform and Louis in his grooming attire. And, at a certain point, we came through the paper screen and came down the sides and that was the opening of the Cotton Club show."

As the Kirby band became more and more popular in the early forties, Sullivan and Kirby found themselves becoming "very independent of each other," and in 1941 they divorced. (Kirby died in 1943.) "In fact," says Sullivan, "one of the reasons we had to separate was because he was on the road going in one direction and I was on the road going in another. . . . The only time we were really affiliated as a team was when we had the radio show, 'Flow Gently Sweet Rhythm.' "

After the breakup with Kirby, Sullivan did a short road stint with the Benny Carter band, covering twenty-three states in six weeks, and came home with increased admiration for singers like Ella Fitzgerald and Helen Humes, who withstood for so long the rigors of the one-night jobs. Over the next fifteen years, Sullivan continued to work on her own, and after the job with the Carter band, she went into a long stay at the Ruban Blue, an exclusive supper club in New York. Tired of the exploitation and commercialism of the business, there she had a chance not only to do current popular music but also many of the standards and songs she loved. "I've always taken pains to select what I would consider the best of standards and music that had the potential of lasting, instead of just being an overnight-success-type song and the next year you wouldn't hear it." In the commercial mainstream, unfortunately, there was often no choice. There were years that saw very few new Sullivan recordings, when she simply would not "go along with the program." "I wasn't under contract to any of the major companies," she says, "and they weren't particularly interested at the time; they never *were* interested in my doing anything except the so-called folk material."

One album, cut with Ellis Larkins in 1947, broke through the typed material. On this album, in Sullivan's estimation, were some of the best things she'd ever done—"and they did not include songs like 'Loch Lomond' and 'Molly Malone' and 'If I Had a Ribbon Bow.' " But the recording industry was suffering from a wartime shortage of materials, and when the disc jockeys began to play the record on the air, Sullivan recalls, "the needle just skated all over the disc."

In 1956 Maxine Sullivan added another dimension to her musical personality: She started to study the trombone.

That year, she went to Hawaii to work in a club. "A lot of the girls that were in Ina Ray Hutton's band lived in Hawaii." One of the women had bought a sixteen-room hotel and turned it into a club. On the top floor was a room called "The Clouds," where Sullivan was working. On Sundays they had jam sessions, and one day a woman who had played trumpet with Hutton's band showed up. "She sang a few songs and then she played the trumpet," Sullivan remembers. "So I said, you know, that's a good idea, because a singer, after you've sung a couple, you've heard them all."

By this time, Sullivan had married stride pianist Cliff Jackson, and when she returned to America, she told him she wanted to play a horn. "But I was afraid of the trumpet at the time," she says. "I figured reaching for those high notes, my eyes would pop out. I was thinking about what kind of instrument could I get. I wasn't gonna be bothered with a saxophone, that's too many fingers, and I didn't wanna play the slide trombone, because at that time there was a girl playing the trombone [Lillian Briggs, who had joined a rock group]. So I remembered that Billy Eckstine, when he had his orchestra, played the valve trombone. I told Cliff, 'Next time you're down at Manny's [music shop], find out if he's got a valve trombone down there.'"

The very next day, Jackson went to Manny's, picked up a valve trombone for sixty-five dollars and brought it back wrapped in newspaper. "Vic [Dickenson] was staying here at the time, so Vic gave me a mouthpiece, and I took a few lessons with Vic. Cliff had a friend who was a trumpet player—his name was Branch—and I took lessons from him. I didn't have a case; I carried it in a Gravy Train bag. I practiced like mad."

Finally, at a festival on Long Island, Sullivan unveiled the trombone and played "Do You Know What It Means to Miss New Orleans?" "John Wilson wrote it up," she says. "He said I played the valve trombone like I sang, but he wished I'd stick to singing!" Undaunted, in 1968, when Sullivan went to work at Blues Alley in Washington, D.C., she took the trombone with her. "The horn was bigger than I was, practically," she says, and "seemed to be gettin' bigger all the time." So she asked the owner of the club to bring her a flugelhorn. "The guy brought two to the hotel. I didn't even have nerve enough to try 'em out. I said, 'I'll take it. Gimme one of those.' Finally, I took the flugelhorn out of the case and I went to blow: Nothing happened. I couldn't imagine what was wrong with it. I didn't realize that you had to oil it, you know. So, I played around with it a couple of days until I got some notes goin' for me. And I practiced. But then the flugelhorn's kind of large, too. . . ." At last, in Connecticut, Sullivan discovered an instrument of the right proportion: a pocket trumpet, which she also plays now.

"One of these days I'm gonna play a whole solo and maybe I can prove that I can play the horn a little bit," she says. "I've got a little way to go yet. I'm not into the high register yet. I'm still practicing my middle-register tones, you know. . . . I'm not as brave today as I was twenty years ago, when I went out there and played 'Do You Know What It Means to Miss New Orleans?' on the valve trombone. I'll do it one of these days. But I should really practice, get at least one solo under my belt. If I could, I'd like to have a little group to come into The House That Jazz Built, and we'd rehearse every once in a while."

The House That Jazz Built is headquartered in a South Bronx building that Maxine Sullivan bought in 1956. It is supported by its membership and various grants. "It took us a little while to arrive at a formula," says Sullivan, "because, to be frank, when we started out, I had no idea what I was doing; it was just an idea. And of course, in the beginning, it was a lot of my own money that went into fixing the house up. But then it's my own property; I had to do this."

Nineteen fifty-six was also the year Sullivan first retired from show business. She had just come back from Hawaii and had celebrated her twentieth anniversary in the business. "So, I figured, you know, what am I gonna hang around for and be a has-been? I was tired, too. I did a lot of variety, vaudeville, and clubs. . . . And then, I became ill, too. I had to go to the hospital. And I guess the body had *had* it for a while."

Sullivan took advantage of her retirement to get involved with the community. Her daughter had just entered junior high school, and she brought her energies to the PTA ("We had a really swingin' PTA," she says) and to the local school board. She was still working on her trombone in the late fifties, and as for missing show business, she says she enjoyed "being part of the overall situation" of parenting and community activism. In 1968, however, Sullivan was lured down to the Washington, D.C., job at Blues Alley, and slowly found herself moving back into the world of jazz, touring with "The World's Greatest Jazz Band of Yank Lawson and Bob Haggart," doing stints at the Riverboat with Bobby Hackett, and making numerous appearances around the country. She also began recording again, and in the early seventies did an album of Shakespeare songs arranged and accompanied by Dick Hyman. "This kind of simple, self-contained art singing is the closest thing to Lieder singing Americans have ever developed," said a *down beat* reviewer, "and Maxine is one of our few but most successful exponents."[25]

*   *   *

Looking back over her career, Sullivan is content. "There's a possibility that I've just been naïve enough to not let it faze me," she says. "I've always looked at it from the standpoint of, this is something I wanted to do, and I felt I was gonna make it one way or the other. As I said before, I never made a whole lot of money. The years when I would have been making money, I owed it all out. So, I wound up being able to *survive* and earn a decent living for myself . . . but I'm still living in the house that I bought in 1945, and I'll be there, you know. . . .

"I never thought of myself as a great singer, or a great *anything*. But when I listen to things like 'Gone with the Wind,' and especially since I heard 'Stop, You're Breaking My Heart,' I think I was a pretty good singer. I didn't dare think that way in those days, because in my estimation Ella Fitzgerald and Billie were on a throne, so I would just consider myself one of the lucky people in show business that had a break. . . . I didn't feel that I was competing with anybody, and then too, as I said, my material put me in another class. I never knew how the other singers felt about me, but I knew how I felt about them. I admired Mildred Bailey, Thelma Carpenter, Helen Humes, all the girls, because we were all swinging in those days.

"And, of course, since I've been back, I've done a few jazz concerts, appeared at some of the festivals. I've made some albums, and I'm havin' fun. I'm busier than I was, you know, when I was busy. And year before last—it ran up until last year—I got involved in a musical on Broadway. It was off-off Broadway to begin with, and I wound up with a nomination for a Tony Award for my performance in *My Old Friends*, so, looks like I'm back in business to stay."

Helen Oakley Dance

(writer/producer)

Despite the fact that jazz was beginning to reach a wider audience during the thirties, the music and its artists were still struggling for respectability and acceptance in the world of music. Helen Oakley Dance, who worked with some of the most eminent names in the field—Duke Ellington, Red Norvo, Fletcher Henderson, Benny Goodman, Mildred Bailey, Chick Webb, the Bob Crosby Band—was instrumental in gaining exposure for the music and making it more accessible to the general public.

❋   ❋   ❋

Helen Oakley Dance was born in Toronto, and was the only member of her family, she says, who possessed an "innate feel" for jazz. In those days, record shops would send around a dozen selections at a time for families to play and keep the ones they liked, she says, "and I distinctly remember as far back as when I was eight years old being the only one who would single out such people as Hannah Williams of the Williams Sisters. Those two could *sing*; they were exciting. Occasionally, there would be some very early King Oliver or perhaps early Henderson, which the family said was 'terrible' but which I singled out right away. Then, as I grew older, I would consciously try to find these records, and by then you'd be going to dances, and there would be Romanelli's Orchestra and things like that, and you'd get an opportunity to talk to musicians. That way I began to determine who was playing what instrument, and I became familiar with Louis Armstrong's sound and with Earl Hines. Then I started listening to the Hines broadcasts from the Grand Terrace, and those of Claude Hopkins from New York. I was fast developing an exclusive taste for this kind of music. I could identify people like Goodman in early records just from listening, but I really didn't know anybody who knew anything about jazz. Still the music soon took precedence over everything else."

As fast as she could, Dance came to America, going first to Detroit, then moving on to Chicago, and ending up in New York. In Chicago, one of the first people she met was Glen Burrs, who was just beginning a publication called *down beat*. "He would stand himself around the corner from the musicians' union and he would hand out these sheets," says Dance. "It was really nothing about jazz; it was just a music sheet. We met, and right away I sold him the idea, 'Get something in there about somebody worth hearing.' And so I started writing. . . . A lot of musicians were really bitter because what they were doing was not recognized, and they couldn't go to work for any kind of money anywhere, because none of the straight musicians would hire them. So this was my idea—to focus a spotlight on this kind of musician. Also, I started to work as a free-lance writer for *The Chicago Herald and Examiner* and that gained some exposure for these musicians, too. . . .

"There was no respect whatsoever for jazz musicians. Straight musicians didn't even recognize the fact that they were talented, or that what they were doing was difficult. Well, obviously, my entire intent was to do or say whatever was going to work to get them an ear. So I would tie that up with my more general background, which gave me an idea of what people would listen to or be interested in reading about. I tried to write in a way that would register with laymen."

Dance also realized the importance of getting active public support behind jazz, and with a group of young, well-known Chicagoans, she helped to form the Chicago Rhythm Club, which she also headed. One of the first things she did with the club was to plan the now-legendary

Benny Goodman concert at which the Goodman trio (with Teddy Wilson
and Gene Krupa) appeared for the first time in public. The "Let's
Dance" broadcasts had finished, and Goodman had gone to the West
Coast. The first trio recordings (made in July 1935) had caused a sensation, and Dance decided that the trio should be featured with the band
at the Congress Hotel. Goodman, she recalls, "was very leery then of
presenting a black musician, but I talked him into bringing Teddy Wilson
from New York, arguing that the trio would be like an intermission act.
He finally agreed, and I sent Teddy the money for his fare. The trio's
performance was, of course, an enormous success. This was actually the
first real jazz concert in the United States (although Duke Ellington had
given one in London in 1933). It predated the Carnegie Hall concert, and
it was the first time black and white had been presented together in
that way publicly."

Dance followed up the Goodman success with concerts by Duke Ellington and Fletcher Henderson, and had begun producing recording sessions
in Chicago, including one with Paul Mares' New Orleans Rhythm Kings,
as well as some dates with Jabbo Smith and a mixed band. By this time,
however, Dance had also decided the time had come to move east. Very
much involved with the Duke Ellington organization ("As far as I was
concerned, nothing was as great as this," she says), she went to New
York to work for the Irving Mills office, and on her lunch hours studied
trumpet with Maurice Grupp. (During World War II, she did a stint
with the Women's Army Corps Band.) Dance began writing for a Mills
house organ edited by Ned Williams (future editor of *down beat*) and
when Mills brought out Variety and Master records, Dance became A&R
(artists and repertoire) woman for the cheaper label, Variety. "And, of
course," she says, "that was exactly what I'd wanted to do always."

The recording venture started with what Dance calls "the first sort of
public jam session. It was really a party for everybody that meant anything, and I had the delightful role of hostess and, having invited everybody that I loved to hear, it was tremendous. Ellington, Goodman, Chick
Webb, Artie Shaw, and Ella Fitzgerald were there. Basie had just come
to town. I was able to use a great many [of these people] for a number
of small groups. Frankie Newton's, for one, was very successful. . . . I
used Cozy [Cole] on drums whenever I could, and Clyde Hart and
Billy Kyle. I'd have the Palmer Brothers sing, and I had Lips Page also
doing gorgeous vocals, and Tab Smith and Ed Hall, and a whole lot of
people. This worked out quite well. Naturally, there weren't the sales on
these kinds of things, but it was the second label, and I could get away
with things while they were busy doing 'Twilight in Turkey' and whatnot with Raymond Scott on Master. Then I had more of a free hand to
do what we all wanted to do. It was terrific, to be able to use Chick on
drums under another name, and so on.

"Then I sold Irving the idea of forming a small band inside the Ellington band. I *always* had the idea of small bands. This was a great thing to do, to get the *great* guys together, a few of them, so that they could stretch out . . . and inspire each other. The whole idea was to take advantage of the idea of recording to arrive at summits that you wouldn't be able to get to in any other way. . . . You take Ellington's band—where are you ever gonna hear *enough* Johnny Hodges? So, you get a small band. And, of course, Duke knew right away. Duke saw. He said, 'Good, we'll form bands around each of them . . . we'll make all that many more records, we'll make all that much more music.'

"Wherever my heart was, I wanted to do some work there and do some good for the outfit," says Dance. She had worked for Mildred Bailey and Red Norvo, had brought the small-band idea to the cooperative Bob Crosby band, and had gone from the Mills office over to Moe Gale's in order to work for the Chick Webb band. "It just hurt me terribly that Webb had all that terrific talent and had never got to the top. And, of course, nothing was needed, really, but management and some creative thinking."

It was while she was working for Webb that Dance introduced the famous Battle of Swing. "There'd been battles for years," she says. "The bands would battle each other on the road and at the Savoy and so on. But it had never been promoted as a public event and so, of course, the Savoy was the ideal place, and it was home for Webb. So I put on that battle between Benny Goodman and Chick Webb, and it was a sensation. Thousands of people turned out. They had mounted policemen all over the pavements, and pictures in the daily press, and it was very, very terrific."

Following this success, Dance staged one more contest—the sensational 1938 battle between the Webb band and the Basie band, newly arrived from Kansas City—after which she went back to work for Ellington briefly. Receiving word that her brother had been reported missing in action, she departed to spend part of the war years in the OSS assigned to secret operations in the North African division. Three years later she went to England, where she married writer/producer Stanley Dance, whom she first met while recording for Irving Mills.

Helen Oakley Dance continued to write or work on broadcasts "occasionally," but, for the most part, she says, was "too busy raising a family to do other work. And I didn't return to writing really until we eventually settled in the United States in 1959. And after that, for about eight or nine years, until three out of the four children were grown, I was too tied up to write much. I did occasional pieces for the *Saturday Review*, wrote liner notes, some book reviews, and usually contributed a chapter here and there to the series of books Stan had begun." (Today, Dance is engaged in essentially the same kind of work.) She also assisted on the albums her husband produced for British Decca, RCA, and British Columbia, and began work on a biography of jazz/blues guitarist T-Bone Walker.

"Naturally, in my case, it was a surprise to a lot of musicians that I succeeded in working in the field, and that my critical essays were published under my name and were evidently found acceptable. But I had the best of influences, because Irene Kitchings and Billie Holiday were my closest friends." (Dance also includes as her chief inspirations Duke Ellington, Louis Armstrong, Chick Webb, Fletcher Henderson, Coleman Hawkins, Johnny Hodges, Cootie Williams, Earl Hines, Count Basie, Lester Young, Benny Goodman, Ben Webster, Sidney Catlett, Davey Tough, Jack Teagarden, T-Bone Walker, and Jay McShann.)

"The affinity with jazz which has determined my life was not inherited. It was a gift. In my writings and in everything else, I have been aided first and foremost by instinct. Studying music later broadened me, but for perception you need to be able to rely on your ear. For the record, I was never really career-minded. My priorities were reversed, because I wasn't that hungry for gold. All my feel was for the music and the people who played things you wanted to hear."

THE FORTIES

In 1941 America entered World War II, and in a radical about-face from the Depression years, when women who worked were accused of "stealing" jobs from men, women were now called upon to fill many traditionally male roles. Practically overnight, Rosie the Riveter dominated the industrial scene, and during the war years nearly 6 million women (36 percent compared with 25 percent in prewar America) held paying jobs.

Women worked both day and night shifts running the machinery of the wartime economy (even Lovie Austin was working as a security guard in a defense plant) and still held down the domestic front. Even Hollywood—now catering to a predominantly female civilian audience—began to reflect the new roles women were taking on. Actresses like Greer Garson (in *Mrs. Miniver*), Bette Davis (in *The Corn Is Green*), and Joan Crawford (in *Mildred Pierce*) portrayed courageous, hard-working, quick-thinking women in both domestic and professional settings. The music and entertainment industry, too, opened its doors to women, hiring them to replace the men who had been drafted or had enlisted, as well as to entertain the vast new GI audience. Betty Sattley Leeds replaced her husband, Charlie Leeds, in Louis Prima's band; Gracie Barrie took over a band-leadership spot for her husband, Dick Stabile (but was reportedly worried about "the practice of newspapers in stating that she had taken over . . . 'for the duration.' "[1] Barrie had signed a five-year contract, she said, and would continue to lead a band, war or no war); and, in Philadelphia, *down beat* reported, women had "crashed studio bands for the first time, with the first mike maestro succumbing to a skirt."[2]

Even as women entertainers and musicians replaced men, touring armed-forces bases and hospitals around the world, they still could not escape being stereotyped as decorative, sexy, morale-boosting objects that really had no serious place in jazz. The forties creation of the "pinup girl" was rivaled by *down beat*'s offer (April 15, 1944, p. 2) of the "kiss autograph" of a popular dance-band vocalist with every issue; an item on an all-woman band, the Swinghearts, noted that, after making a 1,500-mile jump between jobs, perhaps the "weaker sex" was not so weak after all;[3] and another writer yet again defended the exclusively male dominion of the music by presenting "The Lowdown on Two Kinds of Women"— "those who don't like jazz music and admit they don't and those who don't like jazz music but say they do . . . Good jazz is a hard, masculine music with a whip to it," he declared. "Women like violins, and jazz deals with drums and trumpets."[4]

In the world of jazz, meanwhile, swing had reached maturity. In New York, a small group of musicians dissatisfied with the music's limitations had begun to experiment with a faster, more harmonically complex, less "good-time" music that had been given the name of "bop." At the forefront of the movement were Charlie Parker, Charlie Christian, Dizzy Gillespie, Thelonious Monk, Bud Powell, Kenny Clarke, Sarah Vaughan, and arranger Tadd Dameron. In explaining bop, Dameron once said, "It's as if you had two roads, both going in the same direction, but one of them was straight with no scenery around it, and the other twisted and turned and had a lot of beautiful trees on all sides."[5]

Mary Lou Williams, as usual, was leading the way along the scenic route. In 1941 she left the Andy Kirk band, retired to Pittsburgh briefly, and then worked with Duke Ellington for six months, during which time she arranged "Trumpet No End," her version of "Blue Skies," for the Ellington band. She then settled into a long residence at Café Society in New York. One of the earliest supporters of the controversial new music, she opened her uptown apartment to the boppers, who often spent days and nights there, working at her piano and asking her advice. "It was still like the thirties," she once told Whitney Balliett. "Musicians helped each other and didn't just think of themselves."[6]

Williams also composed and recorded some of her own most important work during this decade. On the two-record set *Mary Lou Williams, The Asch Recordings (1944–47)*, she had complete freedom: She played solo piano, as well as in combination with such artists as Bill Coleman, Al Hall, Dick Vance, Frankie Newton, Don Byas, and vocalist Nora Lee King; performed her own compositions—"Lonely Moments," "Froggy Bottom," "Roll 'Em," "Little Joe," "Carcinoma," and others—some with new arrangements; and also recorded standards. *The Zodiac Suite*, her first extended work, was composed in 1945 and performed at Town Hall; the following year, Williams scored part of the piece for the New York Philharmonic and performed it with that orchestra in Carnegie Hall, in the first meeting of jazz and the symphony.

In addition to the Asch recordings, Williams also went into the studio as leader of some all-woman trio and quintet sessions. The various dates included Bridget O'Flynn on drums, June Rotenberg on bass, Marjorie Hyams on vibes, Mary Osborne on guitar, Vivian Garry on bass, and on one date, a bassist listed as Bea Taylor, who in actuality was bassist Billy Taylor. Williams did a "Waltz Boogie," and on "Hesitation Boogie" and "Boogie Mysterioso" she brought to the music her distinctive phrasing and touch, as well as a darker, more lyrical feeling than was generally associated with the eight-beat-to-the-bar boogie form.

When the Mary Lou Williams trio (with Hyams and Rotenberg) appeared at Carnegie Hall in 1947, one headline proclaimed, "Fair Sex Cops Honors at Concert." "There are undoubtedly soloists their equal in each instrument," the reviewer noted, "but very few who in a public performance would stick so closely to playing good jazz, rather than displaying dazzling techniques and learned tricks."[7]

Yet, despite Williams's prominence and acknowledged stature in the field, in some cases even *she* could not escape the clichés of the times—most notably when she worked with other women. When she, O'Flynn, Hyams, Garry, and Osborne appeared on the radio program "We the People" in 1948, the group's name, O'Flynn read from her script, was "The Suffragettes of Swing," because, she explained, "we dared to compete with men." Then came the familiar kitchen metaphor (which some writers are still invoking today), informing listeners that "not since Phil Spitalny's all-girl orchestra had a group of women banded together to prove that all jam isn't made in the kitchen."[8]

That same year, Williams recorded some experimental bop pieces—"In the Land of Oo-Bla-Dee," "Tisherome," "Knowledge," and "Shorty Boo"—with trumpet player Idress Suleiman and bassist George Duvivier. Even as her own music expanded and grew, Williams always retained elements of her early musical roots. She never adhered to one particular style or school, but instead drew upon her own resources to supplement contemporary thinking (and vice versa). In 1948 she told one reviewer, "Right now, I've got chords way ahead of bop" (LCL-M).

Even though swing had ceased to challenge some of the musicians themselves, it continued to please the public. In the early part of the decade, all-woman big bands were on the increase, as small units started to augment to full size in efforts to cash in on the wartime big-band "shortage." The trade papers ran ads seeking female musicians for bands all over the country, from New Mexico to Connecticut, South Carolina to Michigan. Some women went right from high school into big bands; some bands, like the predominantly black International Sweethearts of Rhythm, the all-black Prairie View College Co-Eds and the Swinging Rays of Rhythm, came directly out of universities or schools. A band like Eddie Durham's All-Star Girl Orchestra—made up of seasoned pros—was playing as well as the best male swing bands of the decade, while big white

bands like D'Artega's or Joy Cayler's, were limited in their ability to
swing, but always included an attempt at it somewhere in their repertoire.
These bands also gave women with a feeling for improvisation and jazz
a chance to get some big-band experience before going on to more
authentic swing bands or combos.

By 1943, while such all-black bands as the Darlings of Harlem and the
Prairie View Co-Eds, and such all-white ones as Ada Leonard's All-
American Girl Orchestra, were just being formed or continuing to work,
some booking agencies were cutting down to smaller, more economically
feasible groups. Estelle Slavin, who had started out with Ina Ray Hutton
in 1934, led her own quintet, 'Stelle and the Brunettes, managed by the
William Morris Agency, and their work was well reviewed in *down beat*.[9]

Other women had opportunities to work in formerly all-male bands.
In 1941, when trumpet player/vocalist Billie Rogers joined Woody Herman's band, *down beat* noted that she was "the only girl musician" in
America who was a regular member of "an otherwise all-man big-name
band." "Women musicians are a good drawing card for any band,"
Rogers was quoted as saying. "Even though they may not play as well as
the men, as the war continues, there will probably be more female
musicians playing with bands, especially if they can double as vocalists."
She also addressed the issue of why women were not taken seriously as
horn players, and her comments reflect the prevailing myths and attitudes
of the day, so widely espoused that they were given lip service not only
by critics of women in the field, but often by the women themselves. One
reason Rogers cited was the familiar "lack of physical stamina." The second was the fact that most women looked forward to settling down and
"usually [thought] of their careers as a premarital state. I certainly don't
intend making this my life's work," she said, "and most of the other girls
I know feel that way, too."[10] Clearly, for women at this time, career (or
art) and family life were considered so mutually exclusive that the
pressure to sacrifice one for the other went unquestioned, at least in this
instance. Despite Rogers' comments, however, she was still leading her
own all-male band in 1944, she later played in Jerry Wald's orchestra, and
she was still on the scene to start another all-male postwar band, which,
unfortunately, as Frank Driggs notes, "had less luck than her first and
disbanded in 1950."[11]

As individual female instrumentalists began to gain greater visibility
and audibility in the forties, they also began to record more, as various
small combos were put together in "pick-up" situations (i.e., brought
together for the date). There were the Mary Lou Williams all-woman
trio and All-Star dates; the powerful Philadelphia-born pianist Beryl
Booker solo and trio dates (with June Rotenberg and Bridget O'Flynn);
and other sessions (recently reissued), presenting such players as Edna
Williams, violinist Ginger Smock, Marian Gange, L'Ana Webster, Jean

Starr, Vicki Zimmer, Rose Gottesman, and Cecilia Zirl, playing standards
as well as tunes with such titles as "Seven Riffs with the Right Woman"
and "A Woman's Place Is in the Groove."

Despite the enormous contribution women had made to the jazz world
during the war years, once the war was over, the male-club atmosphere
returned to the entertainment business, as it did to many other professions
and industries, and women, once again accused of stealing jobs from men,
were systematically streamrolled out of the way. "By the end of 1946,"
Carol Hymowitz and Michaele Weissman report in their history of American women, "two million women had been fired from heavy industry."[12]
Metronome started a gratis employment service for musicians coming
back from the war, and noted that while top leaders had been struggling
with "inferior musicians,"[13] a new "soldier jazz harvest" had come in,[14]
and *Metronome* was ready to help distribute the crop. The program provided assistance to male musicians whose careers had been interrupted
by the war, as well as to young male musicians who had matured during
their service stints and now were ready for work; female musicians, meanwhile, who had been paid and praised for their competence up until then
were suddenly let go and out of luck. Some women who had started out
in the prewar years were used to the closed market, but those who had
started working only during the war years were rudely awakened to the
realities of the jazz world during peacetime.

The excellent vibes player Marjorie Hyams began her career in the
1940s, playing with Woody Herman, George Shearing, and Mary Lou
Williams and leading her own groups at 52nd Street's Hickory House.
One of the most highly touted and well-respected musicians on the scene,
Hyams retired from the business when she got married in 1950, and has
remained absent from the world of professional music ever since. In an
interview that appeared on a 1978 album that reissued some of her work,
Hyams shed new light on some of the reasons women like herself, and
undoubtedly many others, opted to give up their careers permanently.
"Only in retrospect," she said, can you "see the obstacles that were put
in front of you. I just thought at the time that I was too young to handle
it. But I see now that it was really rampant chauvinism."[15]

The most popular of the all-woman big bands of the forties was also one
of the great swing bands of the day. Founded in 1937 at the Piney Woods
Country Life School for poor and orphaned black children, the International Sweethearts of Rhythm (which eventually included Mexican, white,
and Oriental women as well) was a unique phenomenon not only in jazz
history but in social history as well.

The International Sweethearts
of Rhythm

In 1910 Laurence Clifton Jones ("the Little Professor") came to Piney Woods, Mississippi, twenty-one miles south of Jackson, and started the Piney Woods Country Life School. In exchange for their education, students participated in "work-study programs," doing farm work, going out with the Cotton Blossoms (one of the many touring religious vocal groups), or participating in some other school-sponsored program, their earnings going to the school.

By 1937 the success of some of the all-woman swing bands inspired Jones to add a jazz band for girls to the school's music program. This band would tour, play for dances and football games, and act as another fund raiser for the school. Musician Consuella Carter put the band together and trained the young women, and as they traveled more and more widely, their potential became apparent. Trumpet player Edna Williams came in from Iowa to act as musical director, and Nebraska-based Rae Lee Jones (no relation to Laurence Jones) was brought in as chaperone and manager.

The International Sweethearts of Rhythm, soon the school's primary fund raiser, continued to tour nationally and, after a successful 1940 debut at Washington's Howard Theater, made an appearance at New York's Apollo Theater. The "all-girl mixed orchestra had come to town unknown," *down beat* reported, but "had all of Harlem talking" before they left.[16] The lineup included Edna Williams and Nova Lee McGee on trumpet, Helen Jones on trombone (she and Williams were singled out as soloists), Ellarize Thompson and Willie Mae Wong on alto and doubles (second instruments), Gracie Bayron and Alma Cortez on tenor, Johnny Mae Rice on piano, Judy Bayron on guitar, and Pauline Braddy on drums.

One year later, the Sweethearts severed their connection with the school. "Eighteen girls of Piney Woods School band quit the school," *The Afro-American* reported (May 3, 1941), "took the school bus and, pursued by highway police, fled through seven states to Washington and freedom." (They made this decision, it said, when they learned that eight of their members who had been traveling for three years with the band would not graduate.) A second school band, the seventeen-piece Swinging Rays of Rhythm, replaced the Sweethearts and went on to tour nationally on behalf of the school, but it never reached the national prominence of the Sweethearts.

In Arlington, Virginia, outside Washington, the Sweethearts moved into

a ten-room house and began polishing up for the "big time," woodshedding under the tutelage of some of the top arrangers and music directors
in the business. The first coach called in was Eddie Durham, whose
playing/composing/arranging credits already included the bands of Bennie Moten, Count Basie, Glenn Miller, Jimmie Lunceford, Artie Shaw,
and Ina Ray Hutton. Durham remembers going down to Washington to
to hear the women play. "I wanna rehearse ten days," he told the backers
after he heard them. "I said, 'I may not get but two numbers, but they're
gonna be numbers.' I changed people around on different horns. . . . If
you're weak, I may give you one note that would stop a house. We
started at ten in the morning and quit at nine at night, and I got the 'St.
Louis Blues' and a couple of other things. 'Sundown'—that's a number
you might hear 'em talk about. And [I] trained 'em to sing and everything, and then I taught 'em the little choreography I wanted with their
horns—not dancing, but how to come in with their horns and do things."

Not only did the Sweethearts play good music, Durham recalls; they
also had fabulous gowns, spectacular lighting, and great effects. "When
they'd come out, Nova Lee McGee played a solo—Taft Jordan used to
work with her a lot—and she could play beautiful. She'd be playing a
solo in a spotlight over here, and they'd blacken all the stage, and while
the stage was black, the five saxophones would move down to the front
in the dark. You wouldn't know they were there."

After the trumpet solo, the five sax women were spotlighted while they
first sang a chorus and then brought out their horns. "But it wasn't *over-
loaded*," Durham says. "It wasn't too many notes. It was something with
little ditties in it, and it was beautiful. Then a lot of guys went to the box
office and wanted to see Mr. Schiffman [owner of the Apollo]. The musicians wanted permission to go backstage to see what boys' band was
back there playing, see how this thing is done. 'It was pantomime, they
gotta have a band back there,' they said. 'Ain't no girls can play like
that.'

"I worked with them awhile, and I started not getting along with
management. I couldn't stand by and see them take money like they were
takin'. We played the Apollo Theater again, those girls got thirty-two dollars a week [approximately half of union scale, Durham says], and I
said, 'Well, what did they [management] tell you?' 'Well, we gotta have
money to pay for the bus [the Sweethearts had a live-in bus complete
with berths, air conditioning, and bathrooms], we gotta pay the mortgage
on that home [in Arlington].' And I didn't tell them they didn't have no
home. The man [their backer] owned that home. He gave them that home
just to live in, but they didn't buy it."

After Durham left the band, two other coach/arrangers were brought
in in succession: Jesse Stone and Maurice King. Seasoned professionals,
such as the popular East Coast tenor player Vi Burnside (who had
played in Bill Baldwin's all-woman band), trumpet player Tiny Davis,

guitarist Roxanna Lucas, and alto saxist Roz Cron, were also brought into the band.

"In the very beginning," says Jesse Stone, "they [the Sweethearts] were very young. [Their ages ranged from fourteen to nineteen when they first left the school.] Most of the work was ensemble work. Then Helen Jones, she developed as a good solo trombone player [in the Dorsey style], and Pauline [Braddy] developed as a drummer, and these things happened gradually. . . . When I came in, they started playing for dances, and that's when they started developing individually, 'cause when you play for dances, you got to play solos and whatnot, and it was different from the stage work that they did. I think Roxanna Lucas set a standard or a pattern for the rest of the girls to study. When they found that she was so serious about learning to read and all, then I finally got them to fall in, come in individually. I used to teach them one at a time."

After a highly successful European USO tour in 1945, the Sweethearts underwent a succession of major personnel changes. Due to that, poor management, and the illness of Rae Lee Jones, the unit finally disbanded in the late forties, although other versions of the band continued under the leadership of longtime Sweethearts leader Anna Mae Winburn. Some of the women—Roz Cron, Vi Burnside, Tiny Davis, Toby Butler, Roxanna Lucas—remained professionally involved with music, while others retired to marry and raise families.

In Jesse Stone's evaluation, the Sweethearts made a "bigger and more lasting name than any other female group in the country." On their recordings of "Jump Children"—with Tiny Davis shouting the blues as the chorus of women's voices answers in the call-and-response pattern— "Sweet Georgia Brown," "Tuxedo Junction," and "Slightly Frantic," one can hear the deeply swinging quality of their music and the clean, even work of the sections (and, on "Georgia Brown," Vi Burnside's tenor drive). Stone remembers seeing their fans standing in the rain outside Detroit's Paradise Theater one time when it rained for a solid week, waiting to get in to hear the band. "Four abreast, all around on Woodward Avenue. I've never seen a bunch of people stand out for Duke Ellington like that," he says. "I really *didn't*. I never saw them do that."

Pauline Braddy Williams

(drums/vocals)

Pauline Braddy Williams started with the Sweethearts of Rhythm at the Piney Woods Country Life School and was the group's original drummer. She left the band in the early fifties and worked in small combos until the late sixties, when she moved to Washington, D.C. She has not played since then, except for her appearance at the 1980 Women's Jazz Festival in Kansas City, where, as part of the tribute to the Sweethearts, she accompanied Evelyn McGee, former vocalist with the band.

"I always miss it," Braddy says about the music, "but I think I've gotten a little used to it now." Afraid she would "never be able to keep up anymore," at Kansas City, she says, "it was just natural, like I had just stopped playing and got a drink of water and went back. . . . [Evelyn] was doing 'I Cried for You,' and with my old-fashioned beat, we swung."

Reeds player Fostina Dixon, who began her career in 1973, was also at the tribute, and says of McGee and Braddy, "They were swingin' harder than anybody at the festival!"

Pauline Braddy was born in Mississippi. "My mother's people went to that school [Piney Woods], and before them, and it went all down. . . . Nobody ever mentions it when they talk about black history. It was Laurence Clifton Jones who started the school. Well, he was not a militant. He didn't get into civil rights and that kind of stuff, but it was a gorgeous place, and it did so much for so many poor blacks in the South. It usually ran on donations, people from 'up north,' as they called it. A kid could go to school and didn't have to pay anything. You worked your way and they taught you something. It's a great thing."

The brass band had about forty girls in it when she was there, but not too many boys; she played the clarinet. "Then Mr. Jones decided maybe he could have a girls' jazz band. One of the teachers, Consuella Carter, was a great musician. She taught every instrument there was, and she was really the one that started the band out after Mr. Jones decided that he might want to try out the girls playing 'swing music,' as we called it in those days. And he wanted to know from her, did she think the girls could play. So, she picked the ones, the saxophones, the trombones, and whatnot, from her big band and rehearsed them. She played the cornet and led the band. We used what they called stock arrangements; we bought them and they were already arranged."

Most of the girls' early inspiration, she says, came from records. "We had never heard [live] bands [very much], you know. I think the first big band that we heard was when Professor Jones took a bunch of the girls to Memphis, Tennessee, to see Louis Armstrong. We were little kids. We had records, too, and we weren't supposed to have them, 'cause it was a religious school. We used to hide the records . . . and play them on those old windup things. It was usually Count Basie and Andy Kirk and all of the old black bands, the swing bands. You weren't supposed to play it [swing music] and you weren't supposed to dance. When we started the band, we were kind of like outcasts from the rest of the girls.

"I got the drums by accident," says Braddy, whose heart was set on the alto sax. "They always said I had a good sense of rhythm. When the drummer that they had dropped out, they said, 'What are we gonna do for a drummer?' They said, 'Pauline's a natural.' I cried. It was all right for *her* to play, but who wanted to play drums? So, I was stuck with it, really."

There were few female drummers at that time to serve as models, Braddy remembers. There were the women with Spitalny and D'Artega, "but I didn't know them. I didn't even meet them. There was nobody to look up to." Of the male drummers, she says she liked them all—Big Sid Catlett, Jo Jones, Ben Thigpen, Gene Krupa. "I just wanted to play. I never thought that there wasn't many girls that played." Nor did she think of music as a career. "In those days, the kids weren't as smart as they are today, I don't think. You didn't have any idea of what was a career or what you wanted to do. What you were doing was fine—at least that's the way I felt, 'cause I never even realized that we were supposed to be famous until it was all over. 'Did you know you were great?' [people asked me]. I said, 'No. I know I played. That's it.'"

By the mid-forties the Sweethearts were at their peak. The quartet within the band (including Anna Mae Winburn, Evelyn McGee, Ina Belle Byrd, and Pauline Braddy) recorded a version of "Blue Skies" arranged by Jesse Stone for the armed forces, and Braddy also did a solo recording of one of her specialties, "Drum Fantasy." "It was a fabulous thing," she recalls. "You painted the sticks with that fluorescent stuff, and the cymbals and the rims, and then they put on black light. I played with white gloves. It broke up the thing all the time. That was the first time I ever heard myself playing a solo." The Sweethearts also made some movie shorts while they were in New York, filming early in the morning and then making their first show at the Apollo at 11:45. "Seven shows a day, and even then you couldn't get in." The band, she says, was enormously popular among blacks, but hardly known at all by whites.

When the Sweethearts came back from Europe, "the best band broke up. Most of the girls got married. Their husbands took them out or they just quit or whatnot. I was with the band until the fifties, and then I left and they were still together. Anna Mae had them." After retiring for about five years, Braddy went back to playing with small groups in New York—a trio with Edna Smith and bassist Carline Ray, another with George Bucher and Eileen Chance, as well as with various duos.

Throughout her career, Braddy says, she has encountered the typical prejudices against women—the "Oh, no, not a girl" attitude (until they heard her play); the attitude that women "should stay home and learn to cook and all that kind of stuff. They still pull that, I think, the men. And even 802 [the New York musicians' local], when we went to transfer from 710 here in Washington, they didn't change the letter heading. There were quite a few women in 802 and they still used 'Dear Brother' and 'Sir' with the letters. Kind of insulting, I thought. They never recognized you as being anything. And there were a lot of bands, you know, men that played and were considered great, and we were better than they were.

"In our time, by seeing girl bands, I think that kind of motivated a lot of the kids. They would play hooky from school to come in the theater, and they would have to turn the lights on and put all the kids out, and every little girl either wanted to play drums or piano or trumpet. We had quite a few girl musicians after a while. But now you don't see any girls much. In some places, they [the schools] go back to the roots of jazz, but you ask a kid around here, they don't even know a band from the thirties. . . . I think it helps to hear about the first girl this and the first woman to play piano and the first one that they let do so-and-so, because it's always been hard."

One reason for the Sweethearts' great success, Braddy feels, was that, unlike the black women's bands that went before them, they presented and maintained a certain image and discipline. "We laugh at them [the rules] now, but I think they were great for that time. You couldn't go out with a guy if he didn't have on a shirt and tie and jacket. You couldn't dance with one if they didn't have on a tie. People dressed up then. When you hit New York and Washington and Chicago and L.A., you dressed up if you went downstairs to get a pack of cigarettes. You dressed because everybody was watching. We had seven different gowns . . . seven different pairs of slippers that went with those gowns, and you weren't seen on the stage unless you were just so. It was bad in those days for girls if you weren't just so, and we had all those rules and things, and Mrs. Jones would chaperone us, so it was protection. And it was good for us. Mrs. Jones would have died if she saw something in the paper that she didn't know about. She would have had a fit.

"See, we used to sneak off and go to places. Like we sneaked up to the Savoy and went to those old jitterbug dances. . . . I remember one time, Willie Bryant ran us out of the Elks' Club. We had gotten our cigarettes and our rum and Coke—we didn't know anything to drink— and we were being grown-up. And the lights came on, and he was emceeing the show, and he looked down and said, 'Excuse me, ladies and gentlemen, I see some of my children.' And he came and ran us out of the club. We didn't get to see the show. He knew we weren't allowed there, and the people were *laughing!* And he put us in a cab to the Theresa Hotel, tipped the cabdriver, told him, 'Don't leave till they get on the elevator.' And you're trying to be grown-up! We tried; it never worked. We were a bunch of little nutty kids."

Evelyn McGee Stone

(vocalist)

Evelyn McGee Stone was the original vocalist with the International Sweethearts of Rhythm. She retired in 1947 to marry and raise two children, and did not reappear on the music scene until the sixties, singing and playing drums with her second husband, Jesse Stone, one of the first teachers and arrangers for the Sweethearts. In 1980 Stone performed in the tribute to the Sweethearts at the Women's Jazz Festival in Kansas City.

Evelyn McGee was born in Anderson, South Carolina. "A product of the Depression," she says. "A very painful time in my life which I can't seem to forget. I remember the school would sell candy, boxes of candy they'd give the children to bring home and sell, and I'd eat up the whole box, and my mother'd beat the hell outta me, 'cause she didn't have the money to pay for this candy. And yet, it was survival for me. . . . Even when I was fourteen I was still goin' barefooted, you know. If I had a good pair of shoes, it was special to go to church with or something. And working very hard, fifty cents a week, washing clothes—just the whole dirty bit—I did it as a child, and experienced this poverty of not having any breakfast, lunch, and dinner many days during the week. Going to school hungry, coming home, nothing to eat."

Although she was never a member of the choir, McGee did belong to a quartet and sang at church, on the radio, and at "all the funerals." She also remembers hearing the blues women when she was a child. "I can see them crankin' up the old Victrola when I was a little girl. I didn't know who they were, because at that time we couldn't afford records, but we could go to our friends' homes, and they would play these records—you know, the Charleston and all that. We were just kids dancing all of these dances and listening to the blues and Bessie Smith and all these people. But today I realize that we were listening to the pioneers and we didn't know it."

Nor did McGee know anything about the International Sweethearts of Rhythm before they came to a community center in Anderson, when she was nineteen. She had never heard of any of the women's bands at all. "I didn't know about *anybody*. I was just another black child in the South, coming out of the abscess of the Depression and glad to be alive. And when they came there and played that night, it rescued me. It makes me want to cry, really. They rescued me. I can't forget it."

The night the Sweethearts played in Anderson, McGee recalls, "one of

the influential black people [W. I. Peek] asked Mrs. Jones, the manager of the Sweethearts, to let me sing, and she did. And would you
believe I left that night with that band? They came to my house, and my
mother came out on the front porch with a lamp in her hand and wanted
to know who it was, and Mr. Peek told her what they wanted. It was my
senior year in high school and I hadn't graduated and my mother wanted
me to stay in school, but it was a chance for me to escape the drudgery
and the poverty of this existence. And knowing that I had this talent as
a child, she wanted to see me get a break. So my mother let me leave
that night.

"I had a cardboard box that I put my clothes in, and I left that night
with the understanding that Mrs. Jones would see to it that I continued
going to school. They did bring in a tutor. Her name was Vivian Crawford, from Akron, Ohio. We had to go to school every day, with our
books and so forth. It didn't last that long, because as we progressed we
became well known and didn't have time to go to school. We were performing and we had to sleep. But Mrs. Jones made us drink a quart of
milk a day, and we had Eddie Durham and Jesse Stone, Maurice King,
all of these people—some of the best—who got to organize this band."

When McGee joined the Sweethearts, they were a group of closely
chaperoned teenagers practically fresh out of school. At first, trumpet
player Edna Williams wrote some original things for the band, and then
Eddie Durham came in. After Durham, Jesse Stone came in, essentially
as a teacher. "He taught them more or less how to read orchestrations,"
McGee recalls, "and that's when the girls really started developing. When
Maurice King followed Jesse, Jesse had laid the groundwork for him
musically. All Maurice had to do was make arrangements, and the girls
would go out there and play."

Jesse Stone had also helped to strengthen the band by bringing in
more experienced musicians—Tiny Davis, Vi Burnside, Rae Carter, Amy
Garrison, Marjorie Pettiford (sister of bassist Oscar Pettiford). "All these
people came in years later," notes McGee, "after we had established a
name for ourselves, but they were much better musicians, which solidi-
fied what we were trying to do and made it a *great* girls' band. A lot of
these women are dead now. Tiny Davis is still alive. She'd get out there
and blow that trumpet just like Louis Armstrong. I mean, it was great."

A typical bill might include such stars as Etta James, Redd Foxx,
Slappy White, perhaps the Nicholas Brothers or Billie Holiday. Sometimes there would be all-female bills—the Peters Sisters, Moms Mabley,
the Edwards Sisters, Holiday, the Sweethearts. "We were *somebody!*"
McGee says. The band would open the show with a number, play between the acts, and feature Tiny Davis on trumpet, Vi Burnside on tenor,
or Evelyn McGee singing "Candy," "I Understand," or "Rum and Coca

Cola." "Those old torch songs reached the people, and they loved it. As the singer with the band, I felt honored, because this was my chance in life to express myself from my childhood. To be able to sing and walk out there, and to hear people scream before I even opened my mouth . . . Wow! Made me feel *good!*"

The Sweethearts were not only pioneers in music, McGee adds. "Most of these girls from Piney Woods School were southerners," she explains, "but when Mrs. Jones took over the band and we started traveling all over the United States, and especially in the North, they started bringing in other nationalities, and would you believe, how dare we have the gall to travel throughout the South with Jewish girls, a Chinese girl, Irish girls?" (The white women would wear dark makeup, and some nights, McGee recalls, local police would stand in front of the bandstand for hours, trying to distinguish blacks from whites.)

"That's where the 'International' came from—all kinds of people. But in music, the language is universal. There is no prejudice. It's all love and harmony and we speak the same language, with singing and with horns, and that's where it's at. The Sweethearts of Rhythm defied all the traditions and we got away with it, and we were proud of the fact that we could do it, and we got a taste of what freedom was really like. We had people of all nationalities screaming for us."

In 1945 the Sweethearts made a year-long USO tour of Europe, and when the band returned to the States, McGee left to marry a man she had met in Germany. Up until the European tour, Mrs. Jones had been handling the women's money, paying them minimal salaries and supposedly putting the balance of their earnings into the Virginia house that represented security for their future. The army, however, paid all the women directly, and by the end of the tour, McGee had managed to save over $5,000. "When I came back," she says, "I proceeded to think that I was rich. I didn't even get a job. Sometimes I would call up and have my lunch sent up! I'm rich! But I finally got an envelope that had some eagle wings on it with a dollar in its mouth: I had drawn out all of my money! But I *did* buy my mother a fur coat—that was one of the good things I did out of that money. We were unmercifully taken advantage of financially. But I think all the girls were just as naïve as I was at the time. We didn't think too much about the money; we were just so happy to be able to have the curtain open up in any theater and to have people scream at us, and *we* were great."

Having been hurt by her own father's desertion of the family at a time when she needed him, when McGee's first child (a boy) was born, she was determined to devote herself to him. "I wanted to be the mother of that baby that I had, and I stayed home until he was three years old. I couldn't afford it, but I stayed there, then put him in nursery school and got a job as a receptionist." When her son was ten, her second child, a daughter, was born.

After her children had grown up, McGee started singing again with Pauline Braddy, and one of their demos reached Jesse Stone, who remembered McGee immediately. "You've still got the voice," he told her. "It's a little rusty, but I'll work with you." Stone came out of retirement to work with her in the Jesse Stone Duo. McGee was divorced by this time, and in 1966 she and Stone were married. "I had fallen in love with him in the forties, anyway," she says, "long before I knew my husband. I always had a crush on him. So it was meant to be. . . . For ten years we worked together as a duo and he *made* me play the drums, which I became good at. I was petrified at first, because I didn't think that I could play the drums." (With rock coming in, said Stone, there would have been little work for McGee as a stand-up singer, so she "had to do something else to get paid.") The duo retired in 1978 and then attended Kingsboro Community College for two years through Local 802, working toward B.A.'s in music.

Memories of her difficult childhood in the South still affect McGee deeply. "I'm proud to be able to talk about this thing that happened, because there are a lot of musical geniuses in the South who don't get the opportunity to express themselves the way I [did]. Here, at fifty-nine years old, I'm still crying over something that happened. I think the suffering part of it made me a better person, a more humane person. 'Do unto others as you would have others do unto you.' I live that way; I don't just talk about it."

These are the same feelings that lie at the heart of her singing. "Sometimes around the house, I can start singing 'Sometimes I Feel Like a Motherless Child,' or 'Swing Low, Sweet Chariot.' I get so wrapped up in it, and it's usually when I'm by myself that I'll start singing these songs. If you're a human being, you get the feeling inside of you, because it just touches the soul . . . it makes me *think*. You think about the *pain* of it all . . . the *pain* of it all. But, thank God, I think better days are around the corner."

Helen Jones Woods

(trombone)

Helen Jones Woods was one of the original Sweethearts of Rhythm and remained a member until the unit broke up, ten years later.

An orphan, Helen Jones was raised at the Piney Woods Country Life School and was the adoptive daughter of Laurence C. Jones. At the age of ten, she began to play the baritone sax so that she could join the forty-five-piece all-girl marching band, and later, after trying but rejecting the violin, she switched to trombone in order to play with the Sweethearts.

When Woods was growing up, she remembers, few records by black artists reached the school. She can remember hearing Bert Williams comedy routines, but, oddly enough, her father had mostly Paul Whiteman records. They also had access to a radio. "I used to stay up late at night listening to all the different bands—Benny Goodman, Tommy Dorsey, Guy Lombardo. At that time, I can remember Benny Goodman was just getting started, and I liked Tommy Dorsey 'cause he was playing 'The Song of India.' And Fletcher Henderson, I enjoyed him. We didn't hear too many black bands in those days. They weren't on the radio much." She also remembers hearing about Ina Ray Hutton's band and seeing Phil Spitalny's all-woman orchestra. Then, sometimes in the summer, she would go to Chicago to hear Duke Ellington and Ivie Anderson at the Orpheum Theater. "The train ran right by our school, and you could go overnight for about fifteen or twenty dollars." Band director Consuella Carter often saw the shows in the cities and brought back material for the girls to work on.

As a youngster, Jones says, she had no ambition to become a professional musician. "My ambition was to get away from the school. See, I was an orphan, and my only goal was to get away from there. So music was my way. I played with the band, so when we left the school to go on our own professionally, I just followed the group. There wasn't any *choice*. . . . When we moved to Washington, D.C., we met a [wealthy] man there [Al Dade], and he put us up in this house and bought us a bus and things like that."

One reason for the Sweethearts' immense popularity with black audiences, says Jones, in addition to the band's swinging music, was the fact that for the first time it offered a new image of black women in entertainment. "Because really there wasn't but one group of black women at the time—the Cotton Club chorus line—and then there were the black women singing blues and things like that. A lot of them were kind of heavy drinkers, so I think really the impression was that it was an awful hard life for black women. I think this was one of the things that made us become so popular among everybody—among the blacks: to see a bunch of black schoolgirls, we had chaperones, and we had to be neat and clean, we had curfews, no drinking, and things like that."

Jones's greatest experience with the band was the European tour, playing for the Fifth and Seventh armies (the black units). "But there were a lot of Germans that came to hear us, too. They were intrigued seeing women musicians, and especially a number of black women musicians, 'cause they had their own perception of black people at the time, due to what Hitler had told them. But really, to me, that was quite a learning experience."

When the band came back from Europe, many of the women retired. Anna Mae Winburn stayed, and so did Helen Jones, who explains: "I had no place to go, you know. I had to stay." The Sweethearts went from seventeen pieces to about ten, and at this point, says Jones, "nobody really cared. We really didn't have anybody like Motown to promote black artists . . . and I think really they [management] felt that maybe if we did become kind of popular, we might go out of their hands. They invested as little as possible, but they expected as big a reward as possible. This is one of the reasons of their downfall."

In 1947, not even earning a living from her work with the Sweethearts, Jones married and left the band, following ailing Sweethearts manager Rae Lee Jones to Omaha. "I really hadn't planned to stay out here," she says, "but I got stranded, and I stayed here all this time." Woods played with a small all-male group for about four or five months in a local nightclub, but, for black musicians in Omaha at that time, work of any kind was extremely sporadic. "Of course, if you played organ or piano or sang," she says, "you got more." Jones had also started raising a family, "so I stopped paying my union dues and I just stopped playing."

At that time, she did not miss it at all. "To me," she says, "I thought the whole scene was a bad experience. I was very poor and I didn't have anything, so I just thought, well, gee, I've wasted my life. I should have been going to school, getting a degree, and learning to do something so I could have made a decent living. . . . Then, later on, I realized that really it was an education within itself. Traveling and seeing the world *is* an education."

Helen Jones and the rest of the Sweethearts never viewed themselves as pioneers, but, at the 1980 Women's Jazz Festival in Kansas City, they found out they really were. "We were so pleased and thrilled," says Jones, "to think somebody remembered us!"

Helen Saine Coston

(reeds)

Helen Saine Coston was another of the original members of the Sweethearts of Rhythm. She was with the band from its earliest days until 1947, when she left to marry and settle in Chicago.

Born in Tennessee, Helen Saine had taken piano lessons and learned to read music between the ages of ten and thirteen. When she got to the

Piney Woods Country Life School in 1939, she joined the marching band playing clarinet, and when a spot opened up for a saxophone player in the Sweethearts, she switched instruments and joined the band. "It was always an honor around the school," she says, "if you played well enough to go into the jazz band. At that time, Johnny Hodges [with Duke Ellington] was popular and sort of the alto saxophonist we all tried to imitate. We didn't come *near* him."

When the band started touring professionally, they would often tour with other bands—Fletcher Henderson's or Jimmie Lunceford's—with each group playing half an hour at a time. "All those musicians in those bands were helpful to us," she remembers. "But there were as many musicians that didn't help us as there were that did. I suppose it was male chauvinism. But there were musicians we approached that didn't offer anything."

Once the band was on the road, the coaches were available for help, as well. "We rehearsed practically every day," Saine recalls. "We would get into a town twelve o'clock in the day, and we would probably have a rehearsal at two, from two to four, then play, say, from eight to twelve or nine until one." Some of the women in the band, she says, were extremely conscientious about their playing, and "really thinking about possibly playing later on. They practiced a lot. And there were some that considered it for the moment and maybe didn't put as much into it."

"When we would go into a town, I would go into the music stores," says Saine, "and look through the music and a lot of saxophone books. When I think back, if we had had some real good teachers [for each instrument], we probably would have made more progress than we did. Once we were on the road, whoever happened to be traveling with us just turned out to be the teacher. Now, sometimes if we were in a town where we were gonna be staying at least more than a month, a lot of us would try to find teachers and take some lessons on the side, and if we knew musicians in that particular town that would offer private lessons, we would do that. Other than that, all we did, well, we helped each other—as much as we *could*.

"Some of the first arrangements we had, the arranger would select maybe the person who could play best to take the melody or the solo, and the saxophone section would have a very *simple* background, something with a few halftones, but it wouldn't be too difficult. We really were learning on the job, and you could see the improvement in the band. And when we left the school, we started picking up seasoned musicians who had been playing for many years, and that helped the band. Not only did it help the band; that really helped us."

Musicians like Vi Burnside would take the sax section aside and work with them alone, Saine recalls: "If it didn't sound just right, she would say, 'Wait, I'll show you,' and we would stay there until we got it. But all of those seasoned female musicians that came in were very helpful, because they usually came in as a soloist, in a featured place."

Most of the time, the women in the band felt they were never treated fairly or adequately by the press. "I think they considered us a novelty act," says Saine, "something filling in for the guys who were overseas, a passing fancy. They never did really cover us well. Vi would get pretty good write-ups [but] Tiny didn't get the credit she deserved. . . . We were just sort of ignored."

In retrospect, Saine says, those years with the Sweethearts were among "the best years" of her life—"not financially, but the work and the music were fulfilling in themselves. At that time we were traveling with the band, we had a matron with us, and she didn't allow us to do *anything*. We *had* to be getting a big kick out of the music."

When the band came back from Europe, Saine left, went to modeling school in New York for six months, and then moved to Chicago, where she married and retired from the business. But, says Saine, she missed it. "Yeah, I really did. I dreamed about it. I still dream about it; I really do."

Anna Mae Winburn

(leader / vocalist / guitar)

Anna Mae Winburn fronted the Sweethearts of Rhythm from 1941 until it disbanded in the late forties. She continued to keep smaller Sweetheart units on the road until the mid-fifties, when she retired from professional music. Winburn's career began nearly a decade before she joined the Sweethearts, however, when she sang and fronted bands around the Midwest.

Anna Mae Winburn was born in Tennessee. Everyone in her family, she recalls, was musically inclined. "They could all play the guitar, the harmonica. We children loved to sing. My father and mother loved to sing, and we used to have family group singing when we lived in the country in Tennessee. Then we migrated to Indiana—a town not too far from Louisville, where I'm living now."

Winburn's career began when she entered a talent contest at the Isis Theater and won second prize singing one of Ethel Waters' songs, "Lovey Joe," accompanying herself on guitar. (The Hoosier Hotshots came in first.) From there, Winburn got a job on station WOW out of Fort Wayne, singing songs like Cab Calloway's "Minnie the Moocher" with a white studio band. She loved blues and rhythm as well: "They tell stories about our people and I can relate to them." She also got work singing in clubs, doing Mae West songs like "Kisses Sweeter Than Honey" and "Lovin' That Dallas Man." "I used to sing these songs and I wore these satin gowns that was cut on the bias, that fit real snug, and I tried to dress like her and act like her—you know, anything to sell. Kept you working."

During her early years in the business, Winburn also spent some time in Chicago, working in the penthouse of the Grand Terrace Ballroom, while Earl Hines was downstairs. "I worked up there on tips alone, and I had four numbers in my repertoire: 'Did You Ever See a Dream Walking?', 'If It Ain't Love,' 'Shanty Town,' and 'Red Sails in the Sunset.' I could play those songs on my guitar, and I had two evening gowns, and I'd walk around the tables and people would stick money in the guitar, and that's how I made my living.

"My mother had died. We had a big family. I took my little brothers and sisters and put them around in different families, and my sister come and give me a hand, and I just had *nerve* to get out and try to do something, because I wasn't prepared for a job in an office and things. I didn't get to finish high school, so I had to think of something, to use what little talent God had given me and try to do something with my life."

Around this time, Winburn moved on to Indianapolis, and also changed her name to Anita Door. "Spanish!" she says. "If I passed for Spanish, I could get more work. I worked the Chateau Lido in Indianapolis, two black boys and myself. They were dancers there, and I was the singer. That was in the early thirties. I wasn't even twenty-one then. 'D-o-o-r'— that's the way I spelled it, and they accepted it! And I didn't speak any Spanish at all! And the lady that owned the club, she was very kind to me. I was so dumb and backward at that time!"

Winburn had also organized a male band with instrumentation that included spoons, bass fiddle, tenor guitar, and clarinet, and worked all around Indiana. When Red Perkins came through with his orchestra, he offered Winburn a chance to organize a male band out of Omaha. "I had been married when I was fifteen," says Winburn, "and I left him because it wasn't a success, and I went to Omaha, Nebraska. I thought I was going to a place where cowboys roamed the street and everything, but I found that it was quite a nice city. They had a lot of big bands booking out of the Middle West then [1935]. I started fronting a band that belonged to Lloyd Hunter [Lloyd Hunter's Serenaders]. They said I was vocalist with the band, but I fronted the band. In those days, orchestras didn't sell unless they had a front to sell the band, so I was the commercial part of the band. When I started directing the band and singing, then we started getting bookings all around Nebraska, those open-air pavilions."

Winburn stayed with the Serenaders until the war broke out and the men began to be drafted. (At that time, her salary was $35 a week, while the musicians made $1.50 or $3.00 a night.) In need of another band for her, Winburn's manager sent to Oklahoma City and got the band that had formerly been the famous Kansas City Blue Devils, and this group was billed as Anna Mae Winburn and her Cotton Club Boys. "Charlie Christian was in the band," says Winburn. "Oh, it was a terrific bunch. We were really settin' the West on fire."

Winburn was working small jobs with her band (which was about to get "disenchanted," she says, "because there wasn't too much money being made"), when the owner of the Dreamland Ballroom told her to come out and listen to a group of young girls from Piney Woods, Mississippi, who were playing for a local dance. "So I went to hear this band, and they were a bunch of little kids. But pretty. They made a beautiful picture." The owner of the Dreamland suggested to Sweethearts manager Rae Lee Jones that she hire Winburn to front the band, and shortly afterward Winburn received a one-way ticket to Washington.

Winburn joined the band in time to appear at the Apollo in 1941, where she remembers singing "I Got It Bad" and "I Cried for You." "Mr. Schiffman [owner of the Apollo] would stand in the wings and watch me," she says. "And he told me, 'Anna Mae, when you go out on stage, go out smiling, look at your audience, start at the top balcony, captivate your audience, look at them and smile, then take your eyes down to the bottom balcony, look from one side to the other, and go into your number.' Well, I listened to him, and it worked. So at the Apollo Theater they put me in front of the band, and that's when I started directing the band. And the band continued as the International Sweethearts of Rhythm under the direction of Anna Mae Winburn."

When the band broke up after its European tour, Winburn, who had gotten married again, stayed with the outfit and searched out new musicians from all over the country. Vi Burnside stayed with the band, and Winburn reorganized it, calling it Anna Mae Winburn and her Sweethearts of Rhythm. In 1953 she cut the group down to eight pieces, then tried to have a big band again, and finally, a few years later, disbanded the unit altogether.

"And in the meantime, I'm havin' children," says Winburn. "I had four babies in five years. I stayed on the road with all of my children up until the last one, and that was my baby Rita. I had to get off then. I had a nurse to take care of them out in Jamaica, Long Island. As soon as I would have 'em and I was strong enough, I'd hit the road again. It wasn't an easy job at all. But they're all grown now."

Says Winburn of the Sweethearts, "They never got the recognition they should have had. I thought—this is my own opinion—that male musicians resented girls really that could play. They would never give them credit. They would say, 'Oh, they're just girls.' And I really don't think that the office that was booking the Sweethearts and the publicity people behind them gave them the publicity they deserved. That band did *so* much to break down prejudice in the South. They never got any credit for that, because the girls went through so many things in the South that have never really been told. To have to put dark makeup on the girls' faces, try to disguise them as mulattoes . . . and we were chased by the police, we were put in jail. I remember one time in Annapolis, Maryland, we were playing a high-school prom there for some of the black kids. They had rented that auditorium, and the people were so prejudiced, they started a fire in the basement under the bandstand, and Pauline [Braddy] had to snatch her drums out of there and set 'em on the street.

"At that time, the publicity agent . . . would take advantage of that, and publicize *that* to draw crowds at the Apollo Theater. And I do remember that we broke all records at the Regal Theater in Chicago, because of publicity—but it was the *type* of publicity they gave, that these were poor little orphan girls, nobody cared for them, they came up from the school, without mothers and fathers. People were standing in line and they had baskets of food they wanted to bring to the kids, and things like that. But they really never gave us the credit for what they contributed to jazz. Great pioneers in that field, and we really paid our dues.

"There's so many great women singers and musicians. They even paid with their talent. You take people like Billie Holiday. Exploited, and never got the credit that she gets now. She's legendary. Bessie Smith, and the things that she went through. When I saw those girls [the original Sweethearts] in Kansas City [at the Women's Jazz Festival] it was just wonderful to see how they picked their lives up and went on. They still love music; all of them do. Even Mr. Carter sent a telegram. I think he recognized it. And the contribution that the girls made to soldiers overseas, the joy. We volunteered to do that, and it was not easy for us to travel under those conditions during wartime. We went right at the end of the war, but Germany was still torn up, and to travel like soldiers, in those big old vans, with no food, eating K rations, sleeping on the floor sometimes . . . I think it's worth mentioning.

"I don't think the public has any idea about the background of what women musicians and singers have gone through. They just look at them as something pretty to look at onstage, and don't understand what they really did."

Eddie Durham's All-Star Girl Orchestra

When Eddie Durham left the International Sweethearts of Rhythm, he immediately went on to form another women's band, Eddie Durham's All-Star Girl Orchestra. "That band was great," recalls saxophonist Lorraine Brown, who worked with it for about six months. (Brown also played with the Sweethearts and both played with and helped to organize the Darlings of Rhythm.) "It was a pleasure when we were playing. The women were very professional—the most professional group of women I've ever seen."

Recently Durham talked about the excellent musicians in the band, and the reason for its breakup as soon as the war was over.

Generally, says Eddie Durham, there were from eighteen to twenty-two women in the All-Star band, all of them experienced, first-rate players. "These were musicians with reflexibility and phrasing and volume and pianissimos and everything. Always kept two extra trumpet players. Always had about five to six, keep trainin' 'em, keep 'em on hand. In that particular band, it was hard to use weak musicians. The trombone section could play as well as I could."

The trombone section consisted of Lela Julius, former leader of the Harlem Playgirls and member of several other bands, Jessie Turner, and Sammy Lee Jett. Jett was a good soloist, Durham says, who had a fine jazz tone and could also put over the blues. One Durham composition, "Sliphorn Jive," called for the section to play a high note. "It's a gliss [glissando] thing," Durham explains. "If you miss, it's too bad." Durham himself would walk out onstage and play the note with the trombone section. "And they tried to write it up and say the girls wasn't makin' the note, that it was just me makin' that note. That's how close we sounded together." From then on, he would still come out onstage, but he would drop his trombone when the women hit the note. "And that stopped that, 'cause every trombone player there could get that high C. Many boys' bands couldn't hit that high C. You'd find maybe one trombone player in each of them that could."

In the trumpet section, Durham had Flo Jones, and at one time he had Dolly Jones (Armenra), Edna Williams, Jean Starr, and Nova Lee McGee. "Those were the four best trumpet players that I knew, except for Tiny Davis," Durham says. "Jean Starr could tear it to pieces. [She] could play anything that Dizzy could play on paper, by sight, and had the top range. And Jean Rae Lee, she was a high E flat, with a big, broad tone. Those girls could reach up to C. That's why they was able to play Ella Fitzgerald's music, Butterbeans and Susie. Any act you put up, that band could play."

Starr, who had also been featured with the Sweethearts, had toured as a solo for many years and later played with Benny Carter's band. "They booked her [as a solo act] behind Louis Armstrong all the time," Durham says. "Everyplace, she played two weeks behind him. She played the trumpet, she could sing, she was a great dancer." Because she *was* so excellent, Durham adds, her standards were high. "She wanted everybody to be as good as her. She wanted that section to hit like Basie's or Benny Goodman's. She considered herself equal with anybody, could do whatever they did—anyone." Starr eventually left the business, but she did have a chance to record on a small group all-woman date in the forties.

In the reed section, Durham had Ellarize Thompson, Margaret Backstrum, and Alma Cortez, all three of whom had played with either the Sweethearts or the Harlem Playgirls. Backstrum was one of the best tenor players around, male or female, Durham recalls, and Thompson was a "pro" as well. "She was playing flute, alto sax, clarinet, and violin, and was a sight-reader." Cortez played baritone sax and was also a sight-reader. "She could sit down in Lunceford's band and play baritone parts right off the sheet, anything he had in his book. She could sit down in Hampton's band and play the baritone part better than the guy could play—read it fast on that baritone. That Spanish tongue, that has a lot to do with it. Anybody that speaks fast languages can execute fast."

During the war years, things were hard for all the bands, male and female. The road was virtually dead, with gas rationing and bans on pleasure driving (which also included the buses carrying the bands). For the black male bands, unless they were the top names, like Ellington, Basie, or Hines, there were few opportunities for theater or location work, since that went to the often inferior white male bands. Durham's All-Stars, however, had a sleeper bus and permission to ride all over with it, using it for their commercial jobs six days a week and giving the armed forces one day. "That come through from Mrs. Bethune," Durham recalls (Mary McLeod Bethune, founder of the National Council of Negro Women). "She had to get the permission from Mrs. Roosevelt. They delivered the bus to Washington, D.C. It would sleep twenty-one, single and doubles, and I had a private compartment and an office." The bus also had a priority from Washington, so it could be driven anywhere. "You could drive it on the Capitol grounds if you wanted to," says Durham.

The band toured seventy-two army camps in Canada, and Durham kept it going for the duration of the war. He had by then helped to put over one hundred women into the musicians' unions in New York and Washington, and remembers that he changed piano players about twenty-two times. "Couldn't change too many horns," he says. "You had to keep what you had. But the piano players sometimes was weaker. That band was strong."

When V-J Day came, Durham was in Oakland, California, on a location job at Sweets' Ballroom. "Played one week and canceled the other week," he says, " 'cause they [Frank Schiffman, Earl Hines, and others] called me up and told me to disband. 'This is V-J Day, and we gonna do wonders with boys. They're all coming out of the army. Give the girls a vacation. You can reorganize if you want to.' " Durham immediately disbanded the All-Stars and headed back to New York, giving each woman a week's pay and drawing on a $1,000 donation he had asked for to take them all back to their homes.

"I took the bus to everybody's home and stayed for a couple of days. I carried 'em to Las Vegas, carried 'em to Reno, Nevada. I carried 'em out to see all the events, anything their hearts desired on the way in, and dropped everybody home on the way out. The money was flowin' like water. The All-Star band was in the money. Could draw and play. We played opposite Louis Jordan right there [in Oakland]. Hamp come one night. You couldn't wash those girls away, though. They knew all the novelties, too. That was some band."

After Durham returned to New York, he trained singer Jean Parks to take over fronting the All-Stars, and within several months, the formidable women had been reassembled as Jean Parks's All-Girl Band. Durham continued to travel with the unit as manager, and the band did theater tours with such stars as Ella Fitzgerald, Moms Mabley, and Butterbeans and Susie. Unfortunately, it disbanded less than one year later, when Jean Parks became ill.

This was the last female big band Durham was involved with, and by the end of the forties, the era of the big bands, male and female, had started drawing to a close.

The instrumentalists who follow were all active during the decade (and after). They are representative of the fine female musicians who worked in big bands, small combos, and the recording studios.

Clora Bryant

(trumpet/composer)

Trumpet player Clora Bryant began her career in the early forties with the all-black, all-woman Prairie View College Co-Eds, formed at Prairie View College in Texas. One of the most respected trumpet players on the West Coast, Bryant has worked in big bands, show bands, small combos, mixed bands, and all-woman groups. She began composing in 1975—a suite titled *To Dizzy with Love*—and has won two NEA awards for composition and performance. Bryant has also raised four children, often taking them on the road with her: "It takes both of them for me to be fulfilled," she says, "but, between the trumpet and my family, that's it."

Clora Bryant was born in Denison, Texas. "There was no TV then," she says, "and I grew up listening to the radio. They had a lot of big bands comin' on, like Tommy Dorsey and Harry James and Charlie Spivak, and I grew up listening to these guys, and Louis Armstrong. We'd buy all the records, and when they'd have dances in my hometown, my dad would take me to see people like Jimmie Lunceford, Basie, and Duke. He wouldn't go in the hall; he'd stand by the window with me on his shoulder, and that's the way I got turned on to this particular kind of music. At that time it was swing."

When Bryant was only two years old, her mother died, and she was raised by her father. "I'm very proud of the job he did," she says. "He wouldn't let me go out at night [though,] and I wanted to go to the football games. So [when] my brother went into the army, he left his trumpet at home, and I just picked it up and started playin' on that, 'cause I was determined to get in the marching band. I taught myself scales and everything, and then I had a teacher in school."

As soon as Bryant started playing the trumpet, she says, "there was nothing else. My dad wanted me to play the harp, but I knew the trumpet was it." By the time she was a senior, she was in the school dance band, playing mostly prom dates in Oklahoma and little towns around Texas. "When I got ready to graduate and go to college, I'd gotten a scholarship to Oberlin and Bennett, but Prairie View College in Houston had an all-girl orchestra, and that's where I went."

The Prairie View Co-Eds was another of the black women's bands popular on the black circuit. "On weekends we'd go out and play places like Houston and Austin and San Anton' and Port Arthur and Corpus Christi, and then that summer [of 1944], the first summer I was in school, we did one-nighters up and down the East Coast and ended up in New York at the Apollo. We traveled in three station wagons. It was hysterical, now that I think of it, and we had a chaperone, and this lady must have been about three hundred pounds, and we were forever havin' flats. She was so big, she kept busting the tires."

The Co-Eds had sixteen women at the time Bryant played with them. "I was playing first [trumpet] and the solos, too, at that time. Now they switch, and the second trumpet player plays the solos mostly, but at that time whoever had the endurance played. I practiced so much— well, in a small town you had nothing else to do, and Dad wouldn't let me go out with boys, so I'd just sit up and practice all the time. So I've always had a strong embouchure." Mostly the band played stock arrangements of the hits of the day, such as Basie's "Jumpin' at the Woodside," Woody Herman's "Woodchoppers' Ball," and Harry James's "Back Beat Boogie." One of the other outstanding women in the band was alto player Bert Etta "Lady Bird" Davis, who later played with Tiny Davis's small group. "She had a Charlie Parker sound on the alto," says Bryant. The tenor and bassist were also very good, she says, "but not too many of the women stuck it out."

Like the other women's bands, during the war years the Co-Eds played army and marine camps and navy bases. They also played the Howard Theater in Washington, the Royal in Baltimore, the Apollo in New York—the "chitlin' circuit"—and a lot of one-nighters. "I'm tellin' you, it was something. You know, like that was before the integration bit, and you went through these changes sometimes, up and down the road, tryin' to find a place to stay. Yeah, we paid some dues. The Sweethearts, they traveled in their own bus. They didn't have to go through that kind of thing, 'cause when they'd pull into a town, they could just live right there in that bus."

When Bryant left the Co-Eds two years later, she transferred to UCLA, since her family had moved to California. For a short time before the semester started, she played with the Sweethearts, but her father put his foot down about her traveling with them and even insisted that she come home between shows. A year later, Bryant left school and started working, taking a job as an upstairs maid for a famous Hollywood actor. "I'd never done anything like that before," she says. "My dad would never let me do anything [like that], you know, he thought that was so degrading." After working for a very short time, Bryant says she "couldn't stand it," and by the late forties she was again playing trumpet and also doubling on drums with various women's groups all over the country. She worked behind Billy Daniels when he first went out to Hollywood, and also with the Darlings of Rhythm, which, like the other women's bands, did one-nighters and armed-services bases. None of those groups, however, was as stable as the Sweethearts, says Bryant, and because of their big turnover, none of them had "as much on the ball."

In 1947 Bryant heard Dizzy Gillespie on a radio broadcast from Billy Berg's, and at that point began what she calls "the most important part of my life. Everybody can tell you I'm a Dizzy nut. I'm his disciple from one end to the other. When I first heard him in those days, I was comin' home from school or whatever, and I'd turn the radio on and listen and leave it on, listening to that broadcast from Billy Berg's. That's where Dizzy and Charlie Parker were. And I heard this music and I couldn't imagine what they were doing. I'd never heard anybody play trumpet like that, and the saxophone, playing so many notes. I said, 'What is this?' And every night I listened to the broadcast and I tried to understand. Then when I found out they were recording, I started collecting Dial records [one of the early bop labels]."

In 1948 Bryant went back to L.A. and got married, and her first child, a son, was born in 1949. "After he was born, I went back to work, and I'd take him backstage so I could nurse him. And I went out to Bakersfield and Fresno with him a couple of times. And the first time I took him to Las Vegas, he was about nine or ten months old and just beginning to walk. I couldn't take him to work at this one club, but I'd rush home in the breaks, 'cause I didn't live too far, and nurse him and go back to work. It's been some fun days, I tell you. I did the same thing with my daughter and my last two kids. I'm tellin' you, I took them everywhere. Like I said, one without the other is not it. My family and the horn— they belong together, the two of them together."

While many women in jazz were dropping out during the fifties to raise their families at home, Bryant was beginning what she considers the most important period in her growth as a musician. There were jam sessions all over L.A. then, and while her husband, bassist Joe Stone, was playing with T-Bone Walker, Pee Wee Crayton, and Jimmy Witherspoon, for her, she says, "it was bop and jazz all the way . . . always had work, when I wasn't havin' babies. At that time there was such good camaraderie. I used to go to all the jam sessions. But that's when you could walk the streets. Sometimes I'd just walk from one club to the other all by myself. I'd go everywhere by myself, because my husband was usually on the road, traveling with the band or something, and I'd go and just jam. And I'd be the only girl that would get up.

"A lot of the good musicians were still around, and there was a different kind of feeling among musicians. They don't have it now. They tried to help you. You'd woodshed together, and you'd sit down and listen to records. Like Lee Morgan, when he was with Dizzy, he and a lot of the guys, we'd hang out together. They'd come over to my house, I'd fix breakfast, we'd sit up and listen to Dizzy records and Clifford Brown records, and we'd analyze things, what he's doing here, man, you know. We were *listening*. It takes talent to listen. And that's what most kids don't do nowadays. They hear. They've got to turn it up so loud they can't do anything but hear."

In the early fifties, Bryant had the distinction of becoming one of the first jazz women to appear on television, when an all-black, all-woman quintet, the Sepia Tones (with Vivian Dandridge as vocalist), went on the air in California. The program lasted only six weeks, however, since sponsorship was not forthcoming. On another program around the same time, Bryant played in a racially mixed band, but letters of protest to the station, she remembers, quickly put an end to that.

In 1957, Bryant went into the recording studios and made *The Gal with the Horn*, the only album she ever did. The record, made in one day for the Mode label, also featured Bryant on vocals. Mode did not last very long, however, and, says Bryant, by the time she returned from Canada one year later, the album was unavailable and the company had closed. (Eventually, Bryant had to order a copy from a dealer and pay fifteen dollars for it.) By 1959 in L.A., she says, things were "kind of rough." Not much was happening for her, but late that year she got a booking in Denver and from there began to work in Las Vegas, where she spent much of the sixties working behind such artists as Damita Jo, Harry James, and Sammy Davis in the film *Pepi*. For two years she also worked with Billy Williams's band, playing "only the best places" all over the country.

Bryant left Williams's band in 1964 and for the next two years did an act with her brother, actor/singer Mel Bryant, working on the road. When her fourth child was born, she decided she wanted to stay home and "do my own thing." She free-lanced through '74, but the jobs were few and far between, and then she was laid up by an accident through '75, at which time she had also started to compose.

After thirty-three years, Bryant has gone back to UCLA to get her B.A. "I'm motivated," she says. She goes to school full time and works on weekends, having taken over Blue Mitchell's chair in Bill Berry's big band. She has also applied to graduate school and hopes eventually to open a private school that will teach the basics while focusing heavily on music. "You have to teach kids how to listen. That's what I'm tryin' to do with my kids. My son likes to play rock and stuff, but I make him sit and listen to jazz." Though fellow musicians have been trying to convince her to get some exposure outside L.A., the recent focus on women in the field, she says, has brought her hardly any recognition at all. "I've never been the type of person to push myself, and the things that I've done, nobody knows anything about."

To Bryant, the most important quality in music is "swing." "To me, getting to play with a big band again was it. Just since I've been playing with them, so many people want me to play with their group. The whole thing that they've lost with jazz and bop is they forget that it started with swing. It was finger-poppin' and it moved. So when I'm up there playing, that's what I'm thinking about. With Bill's band, I do an impression of Louis and I do an impression of Rose Murphy, so there's a top voice, really high, and Louis is down low. Everybody gets into the thing, and it's a good setup for them. I like it when people get involved, because if I'm going to hear music, I'm gonna get involved. But that's the way I was raised. When my daddy would put me on his shoulders standing outside the dance hall, he was a very demonstrative person, too, and he would listen and he would be talkin' about this, and my ears were like antennas, and he'd be jumpin', and I'd be jumpin' on his shoulders, and I can remember that. That's the way it started, feeling the music and listening to the music. I get so involved I'm getting carried away. But that's the way it is. Music is my life."

Fagle Liebman

(drums/arranger/vocals)

Fagle Liebman worked with D'Artega's all-woman orchestra, Ada Leonard's band, briefly with the Sweethearts, and for over thirty years with the Flo Dreyer Quintet (and later Quartet). Liebman currently lives in Florida, where she owns and runs a bookstore and, on weekends, still plays drums in a quartet with Flo Dreyer.

Fagle Liebman was born and raised in Brooklyn. She never played the drums in school, she says, but "used to play things in the house. I hit tables and all that kind of thing, but of course nobody noticed it. In those years, the parents didn't think that if they had a daughter she was gonna be a drummer. Today if the kid hits a table, the mother goes out and buys him a drum set. My parents worked, so when they'd come home and there was damage on tables and pillows and stuff, they would bawl me out, but nobody said, 'Hey, this kid's got talent! Let's get her a teacher!'

"I loved jazz," says Liebman. " 'The Make-Believe Ballroom' . . . I loved *only* jazz; this was the only thing I listened to. I knew everyone's solo, I knew everyone's licks, I knew all the lyrics. I was a real hip little kid. . . . My first drum thing that ever happened to me in my life was when I went to see Benny Goodman at the Paramount—me and zillions of others. And when I saw Gene Krupa, something just happened to my insides. I was never the same after that. It was like an emotional trauma. In that era he was, I think, every male and female drummer's idol, or was the cause of their awakening. Also, I had a sister who was seven years older than me, who took me to the Apollo every Wednesday when I was a young teenager. So when I was twelve and thirteen, I had already seen Duke Ellington—everybody that played at the Apollo—and that was a tremendous influence. I was fortunate that my two sisters before me also loved jazz. There was always jazz in the house, and record players that we wound up."

Liebman's professional life began during the summer between her junior and senior years of high school, when she auditioned for a job with an all-woman quartet playing on the "borscht circuit." "As I look back," she says, "I can only say that I was led by some unseen force all the way, to get to this point." She had managed to save twenty-five dollars for her first drum set, expressly for the audition, and got the job, having told the pianist she was an experienced drummer.

"After I was up there," says Liebman, "it was about six weeks, and I called Teddi [the pianist] aside, 'cause I couldn't stand this lie. I used to play with records—that was about it. I called Teddi aside and I told her the truth, that I had only been playing real drums for the six weeks. Of course, they didn't believe me—but then they did. And it was really a wonderful story as I look back, because I loved it so much; just my absolute *love* for it kept me going. I didn't even have a high hat [cymbal]. One of the guests—an ex-trumpet player—he bought me a high hat and taught me how to use it. And so this is how it started. I was with that group. We worked a summer job and then we worked a winter job in the Jewish resorts. I never went back to school to finish. There was no way I could go back to school and be away from it once I got the taste of it. It just happened so fast, my mother never knew what hit her. There was no discussion—is Fagle leaving town or is Fagle not leaving town? Fagle is a drummer, and she's *gone*."

Liebman's next job was with D'Artega's twenty-three-piece all-woman band on a USO tour. At this point, she had still had no formal study and could not read music. ("Watch me," D'Artega told her; "you don't have to worry.") "Eventually," says Liebman, "whatever girl I could grab on the band and say, 'Teach me this, teach me that,' I learned that way. I learned to read chord symbols almost self-taught. . . . I think at that time that if somebody had said, 'Look, I'll finance you completely,' I don't think I could have gotten off the road and away from bands to do it. I was making it with what I had, and I was too young to know the value. Later on, with the quintet [Flo Dreyer's], when we would go on locations that lasted a year, a year and a half—and we had many like that—I would always take piano lessons, and I had the self-discipline. But I didn't have it then. I was having too wonderful a time."

D'Artega was a "great arranger," says Liebman, "but he didn't feel jazz at all. We did one jazz number—'One O'Clock Jump'—and then I wrote everyone's jazz choruses. Actually, I sang the choruses and D'Artega would write them down. I'd write a tenor solo, once even a solo for xylophone. . . . The band wasn't noted for its jazz. So this was our one attempt, and it always frustrated me. I used to lean over my high hat when we'd be playing 'One O'Clock Jump,' and I would sing things to myself to sort of move myself so I could get through this thing, which was like walking through mud with boots on. This one time it was the most incredible thing, I must have been singing to myself, and all of a sudden I looked up and I'm the only one playing! This was in Cleveland, in a theater. And I looked up and D'Artega was looking at me with this look, and the band, some of them were standing up, some of them were sitting down. They thought we'd changed the arrangement and didn't tell them.

"It was unbelievable that this could happen to someone that hears everything like I do. I so closed myself out that I didn't hear twenty-two other girls stop playing—if you can believe that. And from then on, D'Artega never trusted me. He would come right under my nose on the last chorus and say, 'We're going out.' Of course, it never happened again, but it was the talk of the town for a long time amongst the band. He called me in his dressing room afterward. He said, 'What happened? What happened?' I said, 'I do not know. I was out of it, that's all.'"

D'Artega's band traveled from New York to Savannah and all the way to California, the full orchestra playing theaters at night for the servicemen, and a smaller unit playing hospitals in the afternoon. They spent three months in Hollywood, where they made one film, *You Can't Ration Love,* and began to work in civilian theaters.

When the band reached Indianapolis, Ada Leonard's all-woman band was playing at the Indiana Ballroom, and Liebman went up to hear them. "I saw those two trumpet players up there [Fran Shirley and Norma Carson] and I said, 'I should be with them.'" Leonard, who came to hear D'Artega's band, had been told by a friend about Liebman and, after hearing her, was also convinced that she should be with them. Eventually Liebman left D'Artega to join Ada Leonard's band in Philadelphia. "I loved D'Artega," she says. "Those violins, and a harp— I thought I was in heaven. I only left because I wanted to play more jazz."

"The Leonard band," says Liebman, "was the first really thrilling musical time of my life, because that was all jazz. We played a few Mickey Mouse things, but for the first time in my life there were girls on that band who played and felt like I did. [Arranger Gene Gifford] made us play things that were way over our heads, and we rose to the occasion. The book was unbelievable. It was a man's book. The band was on fire. There was no ego problem or anything like that. We couldn't wait to rehearse, to see what Gene was gonna give us next."

The Leonard band spent most of its time on the road, and finding rehearsal time was sometimes difficult. "I would have to say that there were times when we were so tired that we literally thought we were gonna die," says Liebman. "Once on a train we were so tired—we hadn't laid our bodies down on a bed in I don't know how long—that we put newspapers on the floor and lay on the floor of the train. And we would dream of baths and showers. And, of course, a week in a theater or something was like heaven. One-nighters, it was very rough. But if you wanted to play, that's what you had to do at that time. For me, there was never any question, ever. If it came with the package, then I bought the package. I had to play to breathe and that was it."

After Liebman had been with the band for three and a half years, Leonard disbanded, and Liebman joined the Sweethearts of Rhythm. It was around 1947; Mrs. Jones was ill, and many of the original players had left. Eventually the Sweethearts broke up, too, and Liebman left the splinter group she'd been playing with in Columbus, Ohio. Then, in 1950, she met trumpet player Flo Dreyer. "That was the beginning of the Flo Dreyer Quintet," she says, "which was *the* highlight of my life. And it stayed that way until six years ago, when the band got off the road and we stayed in Miami. Nothing stopped us. We played together [with no changes in personnel during the first nine years, and only two between 1959 and 1965]. It wasn't that anyone was *great*, but we were such a tight unit. It was everything I ever wanted. It was totally organized, totally disciplined, and everyone got to play what they liked to play. Even if we didn't like a tune, we played it so that we liked it. [Liebman was the group's arranger.]

"We were very consistent in our rehearsal schedule, and we were always producing. You have to have some kind of team that somehow thinks alike in most ways, to have anything successful. And all the girls in the band, they wanted to play music." While it was relatively easy for men to move from band to band, Liebman says, such was not the case for women. "We sort of had to stick together. Where were we gonna go? We needed each other. And so this was a good feeling, that we needed each other.

"I can tell you, we never once had a moment in our career together, either one of us, where we ever had a desire to become famous and make it to the top. All we wanted to do was work and be good. It never crossed our minds to make records. We worked in a lot of little towns where we were big stars, and we got tremendous satisfaction out of being in these towns on long locations. Christmas would come, and they'd bring us fruitcakes, and we'd go to their homes for dinner. It was that kind of a life. And we all loved the family life. In fact, we hated big cities, because everything was a hassle in a big city.

"Right now we are in a local band. But we still have our little book. We play for two acts, and it takes two hours, and then we play two little dance sets and go home. They love us as a combo. We're still good. We're still a unit. We all read and play great for the shows. I love to play for shows. Next to jazz, it's my absolute favorite. I love a juggler, an acrobat—I love all that. It's fun for a drummer."

As a player, Liebman says, her strongest point has always been her beat. "You either have it or you don't. I didn't rush; I didn't slow down. I wasn't a great big technician that could take a twenty-minute solo, but when it came to keeping time and pushing a band, I have to say I was as good as anybody. . . . The whole thing with me is the piano. If that's right, the bass and piano, everything's right. I had to hear the chord changes. Although I loved to express myself as a drummer, I really don't think I thought like a drummer; I thought more like a piano player. If I worked with a bad piano player, my life wasn't worth living. The piano player had to play the right chords. Without that, I was so miserable that I think if I liked drink or drugs, I probably would have gotten hooked. But I was fortunate that I didn't like either one of them.

"Your inspiration comes from the people you're working with and your audience. We always loved our audience. The feeling comes from the people you're working with, and the harmony that generates, and you have this great self-confidence when you walk onstage. You know your arrangements are there, and your wardrobe is right, and your group is there, and you all know there's not gonna be any accidents. You go out there and you do it, and the people dig it and that's your reward. And you go home and you can't relive that night again; you gotta start all over. We were just little pipsqueaks, but we had that pressure, too. You gotta go out 'cause you want 'em to love you—that's the whole thing. And if it can come off with any sort of consistency, you're very fortunate. The consistency comes with the group being together a long time, and the rehearsals. Even on a bad night, that *you* know is bad, the audience doesn't know it, because you have the thing going. That consistency has *got* to be there or you ain't nothin'."

"I've been very blessed," says Liebman. "There is no doubt in my mind that it was God's plan that I should be a drummer."

One of the greatest rewards of her career, she says, was the fact that she was eventually able to take care of her family. "I moved them all down to Florida, bought my mother all new furniture, bought her a home, and all the things I wanted to do, 'cause she had worked so hard all her life. And she had a good old age because of it, without any worries. So I was able to do that just from playing drums.

"I used to think, when I got on the stage in my early years as a drum-

mer, I used to think that *everyone* out there in the audience was jealous
of me, that they wanted to be where I was. That's how thrilled I was at
the beginning of my playing, and the feeling was incredible."

Flo Dreyer

(trumpet/valve trombone/leader)

Flo Dreyer played with various all-woman big bands, including the
Sweethearts of Rhythm during their peak years, and for nearly thirty
years has led her own small units. Now living in Miami, Dreyer currently teams with drummer Fagle Liebman and two male players in
a quartet that works on weekends.

Flo Dreyer was born in Indianapolis, Indiana, on the outskirts of the
city. "My father was a very big influence in my life," she says. (Her
mother died when she was four.) "He was a very in-depth man. He had
invented many things. He built race cars and he had many medals for
racing motorcycles as far back as in the twenties, and some of the
records still hold, racing sidecars.

"My dad had this cornet that he had gotten when he was thirteen
years old, and that was at home there. When they started giving lessons
in the school, I took that to school, and that's the story of my life, practically. If he would have played saxophone, I would have been a saxophone player. [The cornet] was the only thing available. I still have it;
it's the one I started on. And I remember I was so proud of it I used to
carry it to school without the case so everybody could see it.

"My teacher used to go to sleep when I was takin' my lessons, so that
tells you how much I learned. Actually, I used to come home and write
down the fingerings. For the trumpet, you know, there are three valves.
I would write down 'one,' 'two,' which would mean the first and second
fingers, and learn that way. So I learned to play more or less by ear,
because my teacher, at least the first one I had, didn't teach a thing."

Soon Dreyer was playing in the school marching band. "I was the
only girl trumpet player, and I played lead right away—I made *sure*
of that. I practiced hard enough so I could get the first chair, which
seemed to be a thing that was necessary for me. . . . Harry James used
to have a fifteen-minute program on the radio every night [in the early
forties] and I remember I couldn't live unless I heard that. I think that
my ears first opened to the jazz world there."

By the time she was thirteen Dreyer had gotten her first professional job, with Belle Sharp and her Flats, playing dances and the USO Hall. Sharp and most of the other women in the band were attending the university and were quite a bit older than Dreyer. "Then, when I was fifteen, there was a big girl band that came to town, to the Indiana Ballroom, and that was a very big place," Dreyer says. "Name bands used to work there all the time. I remember even asking Les Brown for a job once. I figured I could do it, and I had a lot of nerve; I don't think I have that much nowadays." Dreyer asked Joy Cayler, too (it was her group that came to the ballroom), if she could play with her band. "She didn't let me play that night, but then I got a telegram from someplace down south. They were on a USO tour—I think it was Monroe, Louisiana —and I joined her. I took the bus there [on July 4, 1943]."

"She was up there with the best of them," Dreyer says about Joy Cayler (who was booked by Joe Glaser). "It was just a swing band. I wouldn't say that there were any jazz players in it." Still, Dreyer was seeking out jazz wherever she could. "After I got with Joy, then I really started diggin' jazz. The V-discs. I collected many of those, and I really liked that, and then, of course, the arranger that was with Joy was very up to date, and he leaned towards jazz a lot." Even though she had no formal study, she was drawn to players like Cat Anderson and Cootie Williams. "It always thrilled me to hear the high notes or the growling tones they'd get. Not too many white musicians really turned me on as far as jazz."

Essentially Dreyer remained self-taught. "I had taken a few lessons at a music school in Indianapolis, just on my own, but the actual playing experience was where I learned the most. I was never a great technician, but had a very, very good range and feel, so that carried me through a lot, and I had very good chops. When I was with Joy, I got on a kick that every town we would go to, I would hunt up a trumpet player, and I think I took a few lessons from every trumpet player in New York, just to find out what the different methods were. Then, I used to think how to strengthen my diaphragm, and in Joy's band, I used to tell somebody to stand on my stomach and I would move it up and down. I always tried to use logic, and I still do when I don't know something. I usually get where I want to go, one way or the other. And then a lot of it is just plain spirit. I mean, you have to kind of psyche yourself up to it, and then you just attack the note with guts behind it and it comes out."

Dreyer stayed with the Cayler band for four years, touring Japan twice, China, the Philippines, and all of the United States. During the second Japan tour, she decided to leave the band and join the Sweethearts of Rhythm. "The main reason I made the decision was, the Sweethearts said they were gonna go to France, and I wanted to go to France, to Paris. P.S.—we wound up in Paris, Texas. I never did get to Europe with the Sweethearts. I was with [them] about two and a half years."

Dreyer had first heard the Sweethearts play in 1942 and been thrilled. "That was my first exposure to black girl musicians. There were a few small groups here and there, but that was the first real swing thing that I heard. I would venture to say that when I was with [that] band, I think it was the peak—for two reasons. First of all, when you keep goin', you're building all the time, and then, they did have good arrangements." It was also the period of the great soloists, like Vi Burnside and Tiny Davis. Dreyer was playing lead trumpet, and found her experience in the Cayler band a great asset. "When you're playing a jazz chorus, you just do whatever you want to do, but some time or other you gotta come back to reality."

When Vi Burnside left the Sweethearts, she did so with plans to form her own small group, and Dreyer was one of the musicians who went with her. She stayed with the Burnside Quintet for a year (1949–50), mainly working on the East Coast, doing one-nighters and week-long jobs in theaters and clubs. Burnside, she remembers, was a huge attraction. "They billed her as 'formerly with the Sweethearts,' so she was gettin' it from two sides there. Mostly the group played original numbers, and most of the time used head arrangements."

Then, in 1950, Dreyer had an offer to take an eight-piece band of her own to South America. For the next two weeks, working nights with Burnside on the road and traveling to New York by day to rehearse, she got the group together, and went down to Caracas. The band, which included Pat Selkin, Betty Rosner, Myrtle Young, Marge Kewit, Toby Butler, and Shirley Moore, did so well in South America, they extended their stay by three months. When Dreyer returned to the States, she decided the group was too big and reduced it to a quartet, which was easier to book and more certain of stability.

In order for Dreyer to keep on working, she says, she had to have a group of her own. "You couldn't go out and do a single as a trumpet player," she says, and as for trying to join male bands, it never occurred to her. "I didn't know any. I just did whatever I thought of at the time, and I guess that's what I thought of at the time. . . . At first we played jazz. We didn't have any written material at all." When Fagle Liebman joined the band, they started to have arrangements. "Then we got it down to a system and it really worked much better, because it was clean cut, and we rehearsed, and everything was just perfection. Of course, we could still take solos and everything in between, but the overall presentation was excellent."

"I really didn't plan it," says Dreyer. "That's why I feel like I've been led, and I've been protected. And that's the way I always believed— that there's a time and a place. And [my life has] satisfied me. I look back on it and I'm happy with it.

"Unfortunately, the times have changed, and the musicians you know change, and then, not bein' able to just raise a new bunch, work 'em in and what have you . . . you get locked into a city like Miami. [Dreyer has gone into the real-estate business in recent years, but still practices every day and works on weekends.] Actually, I'd just like to be playin' my horn every night, and bein' a musician."

Norma Carson

(trumpet)

During the forties, Norma Carson worked with Ada Leonard's band and, later, with the Sweethearts. In 1951, she was the subject of a feature article in *down beat*, and in 1954, she was on a record session that was released as *Cats vs. Chicks*, which also included such players as Beryl Booker, Terry Pollard, Mary Osborne, Elaine Leighton, Corky Hale, and Bonnie Wetzel. Her instinct for phrasing and her strong, appealing tone are evident on her solo on "The Man I Love."

In 1952 Carson married musician Bob Newman, and although she continued to work as much as possible, she found more and more of her time devoted to raising her children. Carson currently lives in Pennsylvania and has recently been working on the horn again, hoping to come back to playing.

Born and raised in Vancouver, Washington, Norma Carson was first attracted to the trumpet when a family friend brought one to the house. Her father, who played cornet, taught Carson and her sister for about a year, and then she went on to more advanced study. "I was very much into classical music," she remembers. "I never even thought about jazz way back then. . . . I was inspired from the time I began because I had an excellent teacher and a wonderful conductor in high school. Our town was very musical and would always provide for us [the concert band] to go all over the place. I just knew I was gonna be a musician from the time I was pretty young. There were quite a few girls in the band, but none, to my knowledge, kept it up. They just did it for the fun of it."

Carson started working in little bands around Portland, Oregon, and then was called to go on the road with Ada Leonard's band. Fran Shirley, an excellent jazz trumpeter, got her the job. "I thought I was a lead player," says Carson. "I never even thought of taking a [jazz] chorus. The thought terrified me. Then when Fran left to go with Charlie Barnet and there was nobody to fill her shoes, and they said, 'Norma, you're gonna have to play some jazz,' I said, 'Oh no I'm not. I can't do that.'

And I remember the first night I stood up and tried to play, I was so scared my knees were knocking.

"I hate to say it," Carson says, "but she [Ada Leonard] dressed us in ruffles and stuff. There were some good-looking girls in the band, but she had to be the one that stood out. They had these strange-lookin' pink dresses with ruffles down the front all the way to the floor. We didn't like them much. And ironing all those ruffles was murder. On a suitcase— that's the way you do it on the road. We had to take care of our own stuff."

The women, says Carson, were exploited and underpaid, although they never knew it until they began to talk to male musicians. " 'What? You mean you're getting X amount of dollars?' the men asked. [The management's] attitude was, well, there are plenty of other girls that would like to take your place. I remember, though, once another band called me up and wanted me to join. The manager was right around the corner and he overheard my conversation, and the next day I got a raise."

After Carson left Leonard's band, she worked on 52nd Street for a while and then, around 1949, joined the Sweethearts of Rhythm. "That was the band where I started to venture out a little bit," she says. "I got my phrasing together, and I had a lot of great friends on the band. It was just a ball. There was a certain closeness there that taught me a lot—about swinging, about life, about a lot of things that are very important to me now. It was a great time in my life." The women had a chance to jam before and after jobs, Carson recalls, and someone always had records along, so there were chances to listen, as well. "That lasted only about seven months, though, and then the owner died and the manager became ill and [the band] just sort of fell apart."

Following her stint with the Sweethearts, Carson worked with Vi Burnside's Quintet and later went into Café Society Downtown. In 1951 Leonard Feather featured her in a *down beat* "Girls in Jazz" column (April 16, 1951, p. 3) with the headline, "This Chick Plays Like Navarro" (trumpet player Fats Navarro), and in 1954 she made the *Cats vs. Chicks* date. "I was terrified," she remembers, "lemme tell you, 'cause there were some very, very good players on that thing—Lucky Thompson, Clark Terry . . . Well, the girls played by themselves and the men played by themselves, and then we did a thing together ["I Can Do Anything Better Than You Can," a challenge number between the men and the women]."

In 1952, Carson says, she "got married and started having babies. When my oldest daughter was little, just a baby, we had a jazz band in Philadelphia. We played quite a bit there. Then we had a gig down in Atlantic City. Actually, my jazz days were very short, the time that I was able to play with no family. I managed to play anyway. In fact, I played till I was seven months pregnant with most of my kids. I regret, in a way, that I couldn't put in more time." Carson and her husband eventually moved to Pennsylvania, and as her children grew up her work schedule diminished. "But I learned to accept the fact that I wasn't gonna have all that much of a career. I wasn't free to go on the road; I wasn't free to even go into New York anytime. I just felt very grateful that I had as much as I did. That's my first and only love, you know. Music is *it*. And classical music is still very dear to my heart. I fool around with the piano, although I never really studied."

In the 1951 *down beat* article about her, Carson was quoted as saying that working in all-woman bands sometimes forced her to play with musicians who were not always as serious about the music as she was. Today, she still feels that was true. "They were just havin' a good time. Well, I did, too, but they played a little while and then just forgot about it." She also feels that, as a woman, she had fewer opportunities to jam. "I never had near as much playing in sessions as I would have liked to. That's where you really get to know your ax and changes and all. That's what gives you the experience. You can know every tune and every change, and unless you experiment with it, nothing will ever happen. And listening to records a lot also gives you a lot of experience. You might not be an innovator like Bird [Charlie Parker] was, and might not arrive at your own way entirely, like he did, but you're more apt to arrive at your own way of playing from hearing a lot of people. I never wanted to be an imitator. Maybe there's some flavor of somebody else that you've been influenced by more than others, but I think that what really makes a good player is when you can have everyone's influence. That's a part of your whole musical experience—to be able to play, you know, with that flavor, but still, your own soul comes out.

"Tone has always been very important to me. That's what I loved about Clifford Brown. I loved Miles's tone, too, which was totally different. Tone is very important, and sound. Funky sound, too, not just a pure trumpet sound, you know. That's all part of our emotions, anyway. Funk and even anger, and the whole gamut of emotions. It's good to let it all hang out.

"It's sort of an instinctive thing that I feel I have, and other people I've talked to, that you know when you've played well. You know inside, deep inside, what you're capable of. Not that you would hit some kind of an ultimate and say, 'That's it, I'm cool now.' Not that, 'cause there's always more to learn, there's always better to play.

"I'm really thrilled about practicing now. I'm going through some very discouraging days, because I go through a thing where my lip swells and then I have to put my horn down. I'm so anxious, because every time I put my horn down all these years—like when I lost my little girl with the malignant brain tumor, I didn't play for a long time, and when I came back and played, it was so different, because I was different. I had gone through something. And now it's been six years since I've played. I can't *wait* to see what's gonna happen.

"I refuse to play until I really feel that I'm ready. I don't care how long it takes, that's the way it's gonna be this time. I'm being more positive right now. Sometimes I'm completely bummed out. And then I really give myself a talking to, and I say, 'It's got to be worth something if you want to do it.' It's very frightening when you think of all the people that have been with their axes all these years and I haven't. I've been a part-time musician. Not in my *heart* I'm not; I've been right there all the time! But it is kinda scary. And it doesn't happen overnight."

June Rotenberg

(bass)

June Rotenberg has had a dual career as both a jazz and a classical player. She was a member of D'Artega's band briefly, was on Mary Lou Williams, Beryl Booker, and Marjorie Hyams record dates in the mid-forties, and, in addition to playing Broadway shows, has appeared with the St. Louis Symphony, performed in Mostly Mozart and Casals festivals, and in both of New York City's opera houses.

June Rotenberg was born in Philadelphia. She began to play the bass when she was thirteen years old, using money her father gave her for piano lessons to study bass instead. It was "a whole year before anybody found out," she says. "And then when I decided I really wanted to be a bass player, my sister, who was a fine pianist, was very encouraging. She was teaching and she paid for my bass lessons for about a year."

Rotenberg's first teacher was with the Philadelphia Orchestra. "A typical Spaniard, you know—macho type. He wasn't about to see any women being bass players. And he was not encouraging. None of them were, actually. And there weren't too many women around. When I graduated from high school [Rotenberg was only sixteen], I came to New York. Found some money on the street and came to New York and took an audition to get a scholarship here with the National Orchestral Association from the Philharmonic.

"Actually, I started playing jazz, or whatever it was, because I needed to make a living when I was a student. But I became very interested, certainly, and I got to know many of the fine jazz players and spent a lot of time on 52nd Street sitting in and all that stuff. Sid Weiss [bassist] used to let me sit in all the time on Monday nights. He had a bass with a diamond-shaped F hole. He let me play on it, and it was a marvelous instrument."

Eventually Rotenberg met a number of musicians from the Duke Ellington band, including Ben Webster, who was still with the band then. "He was very, very wonderful," she recalls, "because he used to take me uptown to sit in and to listen after the job, and took very good care that nobody ever molested me or anything. I got to play with everybody. There used to be these places, you'd go to a sub-basement or something and it was *packed*. At four o'clock [A.M.], that's when everybody started to arrive after their jobs.

"It was a good beginning. It was nice to have been among the first, too, because there weren't that many girl bass players around. I just wanted to play and hear good stuff, and there was good stuff around. It was a very creative time. It was better than any ear-training class or any counterpoint class or anything I ever took. And actually, I think you need that. Most of the kids don't have a chance to do that today, just go out and play."

Before moving to New York in the early forties, Rotenberg had heard Ina Ray Hutton's band at the Earl Theater in Philadelphia, and she had heard Phil Spitalny's band, but had never worked in any big bands at that point. Later on, in New York, she declined an offer to join Spitalny's band, worked for four or five weeks with a big band made up of male and female players, and did a long USO tour with D'Artega's outfit during the war. They played "every camp and port and ship and everything else," she recalls. The arrangements were good—"for that time," she says. Mostly "you played for 10,000 guys. Played the hospitals. It was rough. Didn't make any money. I think we got eighty-five dollars a week or something. That was without per diem."

Most of her work at that time, Rotenberg recalls, was in small jazz units rather than bands. "We had a six-piece group [that] worked on 52nd Street. Lenny Bernstein used to come in. He lived across the street then, upstairs. People like that would come in to hear us. It was fun. But it wasn't a living. The first real, what I would call good jazz that I played was with Ben Webster, and Mary Lou, and with Pres [Lester Young] and so forth." (After proving herself on two or three choruses, Rotenberg remembers, Lester Young "finally turned around and acknowledged my presence. But he was so marvelous, it didn't matter.")

Both Ben Webster and Mary Lou Williams were living at the Hotel Cecil at the time. "I remember the first time I met her [Williams]," Rotenberg says. "She was writing an arrangement for Benny Goodman— you know, on the bed, in this tiny room up there at the Hotel Cecil. Imagine a woman doing orchestral arrangements! It was marvelous! She was really a first in everything. Then we began to work together. We worked a couple of little jobs. Bridget O'Flynn and Mary Lou and I played together—just a week here, a week there. Times weren't good. It was very difficult for girls. We began to play some of the jazz concerts. They had jazz concerts in Carnegie Hall, and I think we did two of them.

But the thing was, there'd be a couple of big bands on concerts like that—Billy Eckstine's or maybe Duke's band—and when we would play, the boys in the band, you would hear the drummer helping out behind us. It was like, the little girls, they can't make it on their own. They didn't do it with any malice or anything, but I think it was typical of the attitude at the time. . . .

"The big experience was the recordings, because it was a chance for women to make music sort of on an equal basis with men." (Rotenberg's strong, solid bass can be heard on "Hesitation Boogie" and "Boogie Mysterioso," with Mary Lou Williams, and "Don't Blame Me," with Beryl Booker.) *The Girl Stars in Jazz*, the album that included Williams's and Booker's groups, sold out, says Rotenberg. "They just had two printings and they didn't print any more. And I never understood that, because it sold very well. I can't even get one. I don't even have one." Despite the success of the album, however, the women did not continue to record together.

At the time the recordings were made, Rotenberg was spending six months out of the year playing with the St. Louis Symphony. In New York, she had been sitting in with Art Tatum five or six nights a week and going to after-hours sessions uptown. In St. Louis, nothing like that was going on, and what was going on was difficult to get to. "There was no mixing of the colors there," says Rotenberg. "It was a Jim Crow town then. But you could sneak over to the black section sometimes. They had separate cabs, even, so they would come in a black cab and take me over to hear something. But I didn't do any jazz playing there."

In 1950 Rotenberg began playing at the Casals festivals. "From then on," she says, "I didn't hang out so much uptown, because I was going to Europe every summer." In Europe, though, she continued to play jazz whenever she could, sitting in at clubs like the Vieux Columbier before the festival started, and she also began to study solo bass. At the time she played the first festival, the jazz records were out, "so a lot of people in the symphonic, longhair field knew about them, including pianists, particularly Leon Fleisher and Billy Kapell, who was still living then." One night Rotenberg accepted an invitation to play with a protégé of George Shearing's at Honeysuckle Johnson's, a club in Montparnasse. "And sure enough, all the piano players came in," she remembers. "All these bigshot piano players, longhair, and they saw me there! They were screaming and carrying on! I was ashamed! They said 'Nothing to be ashamed about'! I did a lot of playing there," Rotenberg says of those early days in Paris. "Just running around playing in the caves. They were just dives then. I was just a kid."

In Europe, Rotenberg found herself more welcome on the jazz scene than she had been in America. If there was any prejudice against her because she was a woman, it was quickly overridden by the fact that she was an American who had had experience playing with some of the giants of jazz. "Oh, they loved it," she says, adding that "at that time European players had no beat . . . no sense of humor in their playing. I felt like a big star because I knew what I was doing."

When she returned from the first Casals Festival, Charlie Mingus called her downtown to ask what Casals was like. "What can I tell you?" Rotenberg answered. "He opened my eyes."

"Actually," she says, "I think that's what gave me more incentive to go back into *music*, instead of just being in the music *business*. I was solo bass there, and I had a lot of chamber music to play. We did one hundred recordings for Columbia there. Every morning we started eight-thirty to rehearse, and by ten we were recording. And I did three of those festivals with Casals. So I felt that I was an artist, and I didn't want to just play in some terrible place, or stroll tables or anything, and that's the kind of thing that was open.

"After the jazz thing kind of died, and before I got into the Broadway shows, I was doing club dates for a while, too, and you know, it's demeaning. I made more money than I ever made in my life *then*, but it's just ridiculous, so I gave the whole thing up. I would like to play with people that I would choose to play with. I don't want to just play with a piano player, either, although that's a marvelous thing for a bass player. You play a lot of solos and stuff. I don't think that's my style. I don't know. I haven't done it lately. I'd rather play an opera at the Met."

Rotenberg has also done a great deal of studio work. She agrees that women have to play better than men on these dates, because more is expected of them. "And to be treated as an equal, you better be very good," she says. "If you go on a recording date now, you better be excellent. I do a lot of that work, and I can tell you, it's nice to get the residual checks, but it's also a murderous thing to go in there and be the only girl on the date."

After Rotenberg came back from the first Casals Festival, she did two more seasons with the St. Louis Symphony. "Then I didn't want to go there anymore, either. I came back to New York and stayed here. And I'm not sorry. I should have stayed here from the beginning. But imagine a girl seventeen getting into a major orchestra on bass. It was a big thing. And I was very happy. I loved playing with symphony orchestras. That's the thing I like best, really. But that's *really* the feeling of jazz—if you have good ensemble, good chamber music, that's what it is."

Bridget O'Flynn

(drums)

Originally from California, Bridget O'Flynn went to New York in the early forties and was active in the jazz world until the early sixties. Described by June Rotenberg as a "very innovative drummer," she worked with small combos led by Mary Lou Williams, led her own groups, worked in a variety of other combinations, and appeared on the Mary Lou Williams Trio date. After the death of her young son, O'Flynn dropped out of professional music, and since then has lived in New York and worked outside the music field.

Bridget O'Flynn was born in Berkeley, California, in 1923. When she was thirteen, she heard Fats Waller on the radio, and that was the beginning of her love for jazz. "I got a couple of whisk brooms and I started playing on the old Atwater Kent. I couldn't *stand* that marvelous beat without trying to play with it."

Her mother, she says, herself a classical pianist, thought she was crazy. " 'What the hell's the matter with you?' she asked. And I said, 'Oh, I don't know.' How do you explain these kinds of things to people?" (Years later, O'Flynn recalls, her mother finally understood. "Had I known," she told her, "I would have sent you to school, I would have given you lessons. It never occurred to me that a *woman* [the emphasis is O'Flynn's] would play a rhythm.")

After discovering Fats Waller, O'Flynn next discovered Duke Ellington and Ivie Anderson. "I used to go to sleep with her records on," she says. Then, at some point, O'Flynn wound up at a school for girls. "Whenever they don't know what to do with kids that are incorrigible, they box them in and lock 'em up, so they put me into the Alameda Girls' Training School, and this is where I got my first idea. I think I was about fifteen or sixteen years old, and I said, 'I'm gonna be Doc Jazz and you're gonna be my Pills,' and we had a little orchestra that we formed, and I played the drums, not knowing anything—not a damn thing except a beat and rhythms! So that was the beginning of that."

O'Flynn had started out in school playing by ear, but then began to study formally with Henry Adler. Other musicians she encountered also gave her tips along the way, and taught her how to listen: Lionel Hampton, Lee Young, Harry "Sweets" Edison, Dale Reed, Lloyd Reese. By 1939 O'Flynn had landed her first job, playing with Sally Banning's all-woman band in San Pedro. Doris Burg was on saxophone—"one of the most marvelous female saxophone players I ever heard," O'Flynn recalls. Later on, O'Flynn played with a big all-male band, led by Sally and George Banning, where she was featured with the chorus girls and also on the drums. Eventually she also had her own all-male big band. Married at the time to one of the musicians behind the venture, she had no difficulty "breaking into" the big-band business, she says. "He [her husband] saw the dollars and cents in me, so he took over the management and organization."

When the war broke out, many of the band members went into the service, including O'Flynn's husband, and the band broke up. O'Flynn went to New York to establish herself in Local 802 so that when the band came back, they could start to work on the East Coast. Seven of the men were killed overseas, however, and by the end of the war, O'Flynn, whose marriage had ended when her husband returned, was alone and working in New York on her own.

At first O'Flynn began to find work in different clubs, "little dumb grooves," as she calls many of the jobs. Then one night she was playing at the Club Boheme when Mary Lou Williams, then appearing at Café Society, came in. O'Flynn had always wanted to work with Williams, and eventually she did, becoming part of the Williams all-woman trio that recorded "Hesitation Boogie," "Humoresque," "Boogie Mysterioso," and "Waltz Boogie." In an *Esquire* review (September 1948, p. 117), Herbert Kubly called O'Flynn a "female Krupa"; but, for the most part, the side women on the date—O'Flynn and June Rotenberg—were rarely given the credit they deserved. Critic Barry Ulanov, for instance, mentions the sides and credits Williams's brilliance, but neglects to give the names of the side women on the date.[17] "This is one of the most painful things in my life," says O'Flynn.

By the mid-fifties O'Flynn was doing a southern stint with one of the small groups that had broken off from the International Sweethearts of Rhythm. After only three weeks, however, she left, disillusioned by the racism that made it impossible for women of both races to work openly together playing music, and was ready to quit the business for good. Writer Henry Miller encouraged her to stay. "You don't put down your instrument," he told her. "In my case it's a pen; in your case it's a drumstick. Don't put your instrument down."

In the early sixties, however, O'Flynn did quit. With the passing of such musicians as Charlie Parker, Billie Holiday, and Lester Young, and with her increasing distaste for the compromises, insults, sexism, and racism that existed in the jazz world, the music business was something she no longer wanted to be a part of. Although she has not performed for the past twenty years, she still goes to hear the women she used to work with. Sometimes, however, she does not go back to talk to them. "Too painful," she admits.

Recently O'Flynn has begun to think about playing again. She would especially like to work with the "right vocalist," one "who really has something to say. I think I'd be absolutely perfect, because I know what they're saying and would feed them." As a drummer, O'Flynn has always favored brushes in her playing, and considers herself a "sensuous" drummer, more into the ensemble sound than into soloing, more "laid back" in her approach than aggressive. "I used to talk to people," she explains. "If it were a vocalist, and they had something to say, and they'd go 'uh,' I'd go 'uh-huh'—talk to them while they were playing."

"I've seen all the old-timers go back," says O'Flynn about the contemporary scene. "Kind of encouraged me," she adds.

Rose Gottesman

(drums)

Rose Gottesman, whose actual playing career lasted under three years (while her sitting-in career lasted almost five), was a member of the Estelle Slavin Quintet, and also played on small-combo record dates with Mary Lou Williams and the All-Stars, as well as with the Hip Chicks— Jean Starr, L'Ana Webster, Cecilia Zirl, Vicki Zimmer, Marjorie Hyams, and Marion Gange. "I was quite willing to be the kind of drummer in the band who wasn't a soloist but who could back the soloists so that they played better," Gottesman says, and tunes like "Striptease" and "Popsie," recently reissued on an anthology album of women in jazz, show her crisp, supportive playing in a small-group setting. "This was actually after I had stopped playing," says Gottesman about the '46 and '47 record dates. She was called in by Leonard Feather to do the sessions, and while they were "fun," she says, the "pick-up band" circumstances were not ideal. The women had never worked together before, and had very little rehearsal time before recording. "I think they [the records] were pretty good," she says in retrospect, "but I don't think they were that accurate [in representing each woman's top level of playing]. I wasn't relaxed, and I imagine maybe some of the others weren't relaxed, either."

Rose Gottesman was introduced to jazz in the mid-thirties, when her brothers started taking her to the Apollo Theater. "One of my brothers brought some drumsticks home and a practicing pad, and that's how it all started. He showed me whatever he had picked up, and then I learned a lot from the fellows at school." (James Monroe High School in the Bronx, where Gottesman played in the marching band.)

Gottesman says she "never could have done it" without her brother. "He was the one who thought I had talent, and encouraged me, and would take me downtown to sit in or take me to Harlem to sit in. I never could have done that on my own, because this was the thirties and girls just didn't do things like that. He guided me and trained me like a prizefighter. He saw that I listened to the proper bands, and whatever he couldn't explain to me, he would take me to hear."

Gottesman was mostly influenced by the black musicians, she says. She sat in with the Savoy Sultans, Lucky Millinder, and at the jam sessions on 52nd Street. Along with drummer Jo Jones, she also cites Cliff Leeman (with Charlie Barnet) and Gene Krupa as early inspirations. "Everybody was very encouraging," she remembers. "Now I'm nervous about it, because when I used to sit in, I didn't know how many bars I was supposed to take. I always thought those things were spontaneous. Actually, I was unstudied. I did most of my studying afterwards. But of course, I had the confidence of youth. I had gone on the Apollo Amateur Night. My brother pushed me into that, too. I sat in with Jimmie Lunceford. And I won that night."

Even though people were encouraging, Gottesman found it difficult to actually get started working. "Nobody came up with a job—that's what made it rough." The big bands, like Phil Spitalny's (which was not playing jazz) or the Sweethearts of Rhythm (which was always on the road), were not her "thing," says Gottesman, and finally, after "poking around," doing club dates and other small jobs, she joined Estelle Slavin's Quintet, where she did what she considers to be her best work. "I think we were a little ahead of our time," she says. "We would have done much better if we had come along with TV and also if we had had the proper handling. We weren't a big band and so we were thrown in with cocktail units, and of course, that can be a little rough, too."

Gottesman's last job with Slavin was in the summer of '45. She was married the same year to musician Irving Lang. "I had two kids. I didn't think about anything else," she says. "Well, I felt that eventually, when my children got older, I might work. I knew I couldn't travel. I knew music would have to come second, but I didn't actually expect to quit. One of my little girls needed me at home, and I just stayed home . . . because my child came first. And that's why I never got back. I had no intention of quitting. My husband didn't expect me to and neither did my brother. As a matter of fact, they're encouraging today, but I couldn't get back. I'm fifty-eight going on fifty-nine. I'm in pretty good shape, but the music business has gotten along fine without me. . . . I have some drums. My brother has some, and maybe every two or three years I try to play. I have no problem keeping time, but if they give me four bars, I'm terrified. Had I continued playing, I would have continued studying, because drumming became much more intricate and it advanced quite a bit. I knew exactly who I would have studied with, but I would have really had to work hard to keep abreast."

During the years she was working with the Slavin group, says Gottesman, "there were probably hundreds or thousands of female musicians scattered throughout the country, but because we weren't all in the same place, we couldn't work together. In our combo, there were only five of us, and we had one bass player; if there were three fine girl bassists in town, they had no groups to work with. And you're only as good as the group you work with. . . . You had a lot of women who fooled with playing jazz. They didn't really work at it, or they thought because they filled a sweater, they could get away with less practicing than a guy. There weren't that many that really took it that seriously or loved it as passionately as others.

"It's been almost forty years, but I whistle or I hum sometimes, and I remember most of our little arrangements. They're all in my mind."

Lucille Dixon

(bass/leader)

Lucille Dixon, who began her career in 1941, started out with the intention of pursuing a life in classical music. As she soon found out, for a black woman in the early forties, that possibility was out of the question. "At that time in New York City," she recalls, "I think there were only three recognized girl bass players." Dixon was one; June Rotenberg and Natalie Clair were the others. "June was the first woman bass player ever to play with a major symphony—she went with St. Louis—and Natalie Clair went with Cleveland. And naturally, me being black . . ."

The classical world might not be open to her, but Dixon knew that the jazz world would. She went on to become the first female bassist with a name male band, leader of her own big band (which stayed in residence in a New York club for twelve years), one of the first black booking agents, a symphony player, and manager of the New World Symphony. The mother of three children and a student of business management and orchestra management, Dixon has also been involved in politics, from the NAACP to the Urban League to Concerned Musicians, a group she organized in 1969 to work against discrimination in classical music.

Lucille Dixon was born in Harlem in 1923. Her father was a Baptist minister, and her mother, who had always loved music, taught her to play the piano. Musician "Specs" Powell and his family were friends, and at seven Dixon began to study piano with Powell's teacher and eventually to play in her father's church.

When Dixon got to high school, she decided that she wanted to play clarinet. "My mother had just bought my brother a used saxophone, and I admired the saxophone. I heard that everybody who played clarinet could play saxophone." A new teacher in charge of the orchestra, however, needed a bass player and, as Dixon says, "conned" her into it. "Truthfully, I didn't take it seriously until she asked me to try out for all-city orchestra. I went down and I didn't even think I could make it. In fact, they used to rehearse at this high school on 14th Street, and before going back for the audition, I listened to the orchestra playing—I'll never forget it—Overture to *Rienzi*, and I said, 'Oh, my God, I can't play that.'" Dixon made the audition, however, and the leader took her in on one condition: that she take the music seriously and study. "After that," she says, "I really went all the way. Then I really fell in love with it, because I said, 'Here I am performing with a group of people.'"

By the time Dixon was attending Brooklyn College, word reached her that the newly formed International Sweethearts of Rhythm were looking for a bass player to make a summer tour with them. Dixon auditioned and got the job, fully intending to return in the fall and pursue the classics. "After about the first week, the manager came to me and she said, 'Gee whiz, we know you're playing all the right notes, but even if you play a wrong one, you have to smile.' That was very disillusioning, because to me, music always came first, playing the correct music. And this is one thing I find against the girls' bands—I don't say it holds true today, but at that time it did: More femininity is projected, more so than what is being played. And when she told me that, I realized that what I was playing on the instrument came second. I had to sell myself." After working with the Sweethearts for two months, even though she had begun to learn to play "by ear," says Dixon, "I realized that that wasn't what I wanted."

In 1943, realizing that the classical field was going to be virtually impregnable, Dixon thought of getting a job with Phil Spitalny's all-woman orchestra, but, says Dixon, she couldn't even get an audition—Spitalny's band was all white. Dixon put the situation to her teacher, Fred Zimmerman: "Fine, I could go to Juilliard, I could study, I could be well qualified to play, but would they let me in?" Knowing the answer, she decided at that point she would pursue a career in jazz. "Because I've seen it," she says, "where a lot of black talent, they stick to their guns about staying in classical music and they wind up doing nothing. That's why sometimes, I say, something works against you, but in the end it works in your favor. That's why you have a lot of black musicians who are capable of playing jazz and of playing classical, too. Many times when I was playing with the community orchestras up here, I'd leave a concert, then I'd go on to a Latin gig and they'd say, 'Well, how can you change?' "

Another incentive that helped Dixon make the change in 1943 was the fact that an opportunity had come up to work with one of the greatest of the big-name bands, the Earl Hines band. Hines was adding a female string group, but had had no intention of getting a female bass player, Dixon recalls. "But it so happened that Jesse Stone became his arranger, and since I'd worked with Jesse and the Sweethearts of Rhythm, he said [to Hines], 'Well, this girl can cut it, don't worry about it.' So then [Hines] tried it out." The band also had the excellent Roxanna Lucas on guitar.

"It opened my eyes," says Dixon. "I said, 'Well, I'm gonna be one of the fellows.' There were little things. It seemed like the women wanted special favors. For example, we were playing in the theater, and a comedian usually comes on 'cause it's a variety show. Earl had made arrangements for the girls to go off while the comedian was on. Well, the fellows had to stay out there. So when I didn't go off, Shorty McConnell, a very good trumpet player, said to me, 'Well, baby, go off, you're a woman.' I said, 'No, I'm a musician. I'm with you.' So I had to find ways for the men to accept me as a musician. Plus, there was another thing, too, which I'm a stickler for, and that is, being a woman, naturally you have fellows, say if we go out, they want to buy you a drink or something like that. If I'm with the fellows I'm working with, if they buy drinks, I buy drinks, too. And this is years back, and I didn't feel funny about it. They were making the same amount that I was, and at the end of the night, I wouldn't want somebody to say to me, 'Well, you know, we treat you like a woman, so therefore . . .' I don't feel that women should expect anything. I'm talking about how many years ago—forty years? That's the way I felt. And to me, it never took away from my femininity. I think it worked well, because I've always had the respect of the musicians."

"Up until about five years ago," says Dixon, "I thought I had two strikes against me—being a woman and being black. Then I realized I had *three* strikes: I was playing a man's instrument." She says she could feel the cool attitude when she walked onto a job with her bass. "Then, after I play the first set, I get smiles. It isn't like the guy who walks in with a horn and right away they welcome him and say 'Hi,' and then if he's bad, they'll put him down. I get put down first.

"With my instrument, I know today if I played a lot of solo bass I could do an awful lot. I mean, I could be projected as a soloist. But in my era, coming up, I was always working with big bands, and there a bass player had very little opportunity. Being a woman, I was more concerned about rhythm. I never wanted them to say, 'Well, the bass is light because a woman is on it.' So I really concentrated on my rhythm and tried to be very solid."

In 1945 Dixon left the Hines band. She had married musician Gus Chappell, and that year their first child was born. The family settled in New York, and in 1946 she founded the Lucille Dixon Orchestra. When her son was three years old, she and her husband separated, and Dixon continued to work. But, after a two-week job in Washington when her second son was nine months old, she came home to find that he no longer recognized her, and, she says, "that was the last time I went away."

Determined to stay and to keep the group she had worked with in Washington together in New York, Dixon became her own agent. "I always went to booking agents, and they always said, 'No work.' So I decided to book the band myself, and I started going to the different clubs. I was able to get in a couple of small clubs. Then I went out to Astoria, and then I got the job at the 845, which at that time in the Bronx was one of the biggest clubs. It had all the big names going." Dixon's band was hired to replace a vacationing band, and stayed there for eight months. After the 845, the band opened at the Savannah Club and stayed for twelve years. The outfit included such top players as George Kelly (who also did many of the arrangements), Tyree Glenn, Taft Jordan, Fats Navarro, Buddy Tate, and Sonny Payne, with Dixon on bass. "I've always felt very bad for the black musicians," she says, "because most of our good black musicians had to stay on the road. This is why I really pressed to try to stay in town."

During the time that her band was at the Savannah Club, Dixon remarried, and in 1954 she went to Panama for two years with her husband. It was there that she had her first chance to join a symphony—the National Symphony of Panama. When she returned to the United States in 1956, Dixon kept her own band together for four more years, and in 1960 began to work such engagements as Radio City Music Hall, the Boston Women's Symphony, the Ridgefield Symphony, and the Scranton Symphony. In 1965 she became the manager of the Symphony of the New World, an orchestra she formed in order to give young musicians a place to work. Nine years later the symphony disbanded, and Dixon began to work at the Elmsford Dinner Theater. In 1980 Dixon and the theater celebrated their fortieth production, and also added a second piano to the trio of drums, piano, and Dixon's baby electric bass. In this job, where the shows run for two weeks, Dixon makes it a point never to memorize the show, because she doesn't want to get "rusty" on her reading. When the show is over, she may go to a local club to sit in and jam, but at this point in her career, she considers the theater the ideal job. It is close to home and it is steady, and, says Dixon, "I like the idea of working steady."

Melba Liston

(trombone/composer/arranger/leader/vocals)

In 1980, after nearly a decade in the West Indies, where she created the African-American Division of the Jamaica School of Music, Melba Liston came out of retirement to start her own group, Melba Liston and Company. The group, whose personnel has included Sharon Freeman, Erica Lindsay, Dottie Dodgion, Britt Woodman, Phil Woods, Fostina Dixon, Carline Ray, and Chessie Tanksley, has been enthusiastically received both at home and overseas, and Liston's distinctive arrangements have made for some of the most exciting and invigorating sounds in jazz today.

Since Liston started out in the business in the early forties, she has played with and created arrangements for bands led by such top names as Gerald Wilson (early forties), Dizzy Gillespie ('48–'49, '56), Randy Weston (sixties), Quincy Jones ('60), Johnny Griffin ('61), and Clark Terry, as well as for the Buffalo Symphony (1968).

"We finally talked her into coming out of retirement and playing," says Dianne Gregg, president of Kansas City's Women's Jazz Festival, which in 1978 brought Liston back to America. "Now she has her own band and has gotten back to performing. That's one of the things we're most proud of in our whole festival career. If we don't ever do anything else, we're happy with that."

Melba Liston was born in Kansas City, Missouri, in 1926, and spent the first eleven years of her life there. She says she was too young to have heard much of the live jazz that was rocking the city in those years, and the closest she got to music was the player piano, church, the radio, and friends of the family who would come by to play and sing. Her grandfather, she remembers, loved Cab Calloway, and "things that were swingin'," and the day she got her trombone, she says, she sat out on the back porch with her grandfather until late at night, picking out "all the little things I knew. I was playing church things—'Deep River' and 'Rocked in the Cradle of the Deep'—folk things, things of that nature," she says.

In 1937 Liston moved to California, and that was where she became more interested in jazz. She learned to read music "more from singing in glee club in school than on my instrument," she says, "but I met some young musicians that were working in the youth band from the playground—Parks and Recreation Department—under Mrs. Alma Hightower, who was [alto player] Vi Redd's great-aunt. After school we would go to the playground and she would work us in theory and harmony, scales and stuff like that, and we would play stock arrangements, and she put this little big band together. We played at the YMCA, dances, churches; we'd play on street corners and pass the hat and all that kind of thing. The boys would steal all the money, 'cause the girls weren't allowed to pass the hats, you know.

"I would say from twelve until I was sixteen I was with her, and she taught us quite a lot. She made us sing, dance, do clapping exercises, recite poetry, do minstrel kind of comedies, and the whole bit of show business. She was a marvelous woman. She had been doing this earlier in the WPA program, and when that closed down, she just kept doing it as a hobby. It seems as though she turned out several generations of musicians. When she saw somebody she thought had talent, she would take extra time with them. She played drums, saxophone, and piano. She could just about make it over any instrument, but her main instruments were drum and piano."

When Liston turned sixteen, she and Hightower's daughter and pianist Alice Young all graduated from high school together and headed straight for the musicians' union. "We couldn't wait until we were sixteen," she says, "to join the union and start working professionally." All through school, Liston had been more concerned with reading and writing music than she had been with playing or soloing. Her teachers told her she was "destined" to become an arranger, and often they gave her special exercises writing ensembles and working on orchestral scores. An only child, Liston enjoyed the solitude of writing and creating music. "My mother used to call friends of mine and ask them, 'Would you please come and see if you can get my daughter out?' I moved my piano into my bedroom and set up a workshop in there, and I would stay there, come out to eat, then go right back in, pile up tons of music paper, and I can do the same thing now."

Liston's first job after high school was in the pit band in the Lincoln Theater. "Bardu Ali was the director. He used to conduct Chick Webb's band. We got to play for some very good acts. There was a stage show with Dusty Fletcher, Pigmeat Markham, and we sure got good experience there for a year and a half."

When the Lincoln closed, nearly the entire band moved over to arranger/composer Gerald Wilson's band and began working in nightclubs. "Then I started writing and copying for Gerald," Liston says. "He was a fine arranger, and so I studied and learned a lot from him, and then he, in turn, introduced me to everybody: to Dizzy, to Basie, to Duke, Bird—everybody. So I was welcome in their company, and that was kind of a blessing. I just floated along from one set to another, which the youth don't get much chance to do nowadays. I was very fortunate to get in before the big-band era died out."

Liston made some early recordings with the Wilson band, and during the late forties also cut some records with Dexter Gordon, a close friend from their school days. "When he got his record date, he said, 'Come on, Mama'—I think they were callin' me Mama already back then, 'cause I used to fuss with them about smokin' their cigarettes or drinkin' their wine—and they'd come and get me when something was goin' on, and I would play little gigs with them. I was scared to go in the studio, though, because I didn't really hang out with them when they were jamming and stuff. I was home trying to write, so I didn't have that spirit on my instrument as improvisational person. I was really very shy. I really didn't wanna make that record session. I don't know which was worse—makin' it or trying to persuade them to leave me *out* of it. I'm happy for it now. I'd rather not *hear* it, however."

In 1948–49, Liston had also worked with the Gillespie band that included John Coltrane and John Lewis. When the group disbanded in 1949, Billie Holiday, about to start a southern tour, hired Gerald Wilson as musical director and Liston as assistant director and arranger for the big band. "I think we were stranded longer than we worked," Liston remembers. "It was kinda mean there after a while. She didn't draw good down south. We sat in the bus for days in Charleston, South Carolina."

When Liston sings, people sometimes tell her that she sounds like Holiday, but if the Holiday influence is there, Liston feels it is more in her choice of tunes, her feeling, and her approach than in anything else. "I think *she* sounds like a horn player," she says of Holiday, "'cause she sings like Louis Armstrong. They kind of use their throats to sing. I don't have her range or her exquisite diction. The phrasing is like an instrumentalist's, so I think that's where the similarity is."

By the time Liston returned to California, the big-band era was on its way out. "We started working with seven pieces, and I had to start learning how to stand up and jam all night, and I didn't like it." Then one day, on the spur of the moment, Liston decided to take the Board of Education exam, passed, and was immediately called in to work. "My mother was so thrilled," she says. "My family was trying to get me out of the business anyway, and I wasn't anxious to get back on the road again, so I said I'd try it." Liston worked for four years at a job in the evening school and looks back on it as a good experience. "I had to learn how to talk to people, and that helped me quite a bit. When I left there, I was a little more secure within myself."

During this time, Liston had continued to work on her writing but not on her horn. She even quit the union for a year or so when she was working for the Board of Ed and had gotten married. "I was trying to do those kinds of *ordinary* things, but it didn't work too well and we broke up, my husband and I, and then I started easin' out with my horn, took weekend sessions and stuff, and the guys said, 'Uh-oh, there's Melba with her horn. She's single again.' I tried marriage three times, and every time I tried marriage, I would put the horn down and just be *wife*. Then the next time they'd see me with the horn, they'd say, 'Uh-oh, there goes number two.' So that's what happened there. I got rid of the husband, quit the job, and picked up my horn."

In 1955, shortly after Liston quit her job, Dizzy Gillespie sent for her to join him on a State Department tour. "I was copyist and just flunkie," she says. She also did arrangements on "Stella by Starlight," "Annie's Dance," and "My Reverie"; but, even though she had the respect and admiration of many of the best musicians, there were still problems she had to face because she was a woman and not known to everyone in the band.

Liston talked about some of the problems in Gillespie's autobiography: "You're on your own out there. If you're gonna be in the band, you must carry your own luggage and be self-sufficient, and the only way I could survive is that I was young and strong then, and I was self-sufficient. So when I showed them that I was not gonna be a burden to them, you know, everything was cool." When she first got to New York, she "heard some comments about, 'Why the hell did he send all the way to California for a bitch trombone player?'" Once they got into the rehearsals, however, and started playing her arrangements, "Well, that erased all the little bullshit, you see. They say, 'Mama's all right.' Then I was 'Mama,' I wasn't 'bitch' no more."[18]

After the Middle East tour with Gillespie, Liston began a period of great activity and creativity. In 1959 she joined the Quincy Jones big band for a European tour with the show *Free and Easy*, and in the early sixties did arrangements for a Johnny Griffin album, *White Gardenia*, a tribute to Billie Holiday. At the same time, she also began to arrange for pianist/composer Randy Weston, contributing her ideas to his albums *Little Niles* (written for his children all in three-quarter time), *Blues to Africa, High Life, Uhuru Kwanza*, and *Tanjah*.

"I'd been writing the ballads and stuff all the time, so here was a chance to do some African rhythms and stuff like that. I was thrilled. [Of] all the music I've written (aside from the ballad things), I really enjoyed his compositions the best. He leaves me free. He doesn't tell me what size orchestra, who or what. He just gives me the composition, I tell him what I've done with it, and we just go ahead."

In the early seventies Liston went to visit Jamaica and wound up staying for five and a half years. "The government decided that they wanted this other division in pop and jazz [for the Jamaica School of Music] and so I had to start it. The administration didn't really love the idea; they didn't like the idea of these poor little pickaninnies comin' on their campus, 'cause this school was really for the wealthier kids." Liston and her students (who knew nothing but reggae) "hung in there," though, and now, she says, there is hardly any musical institution in Jamaica that doesn't have some of her students.

In 1979 Carol Comer and Dianne Gregg, the women behind the Women's Jazz Festival in Kansas City, began pleading with Liston to come back for the festival. "I didn't wanna come," says Liston. "I said, 'I can't sing, I haven't played in years.' They wrote, they called, they sent telegrams. That was in March, and I didn't even have a winter coat. But it went down all right."

The festival appearance was followed by a concert at the New York Salute to Women in Jazz, where, playing and singing standards, Liston quickly reestablished herself as a compelling and exciting performer. Boston followed New York, and Liston finally said to herself, "Oh, my goodness, if they're gonna keep me doing this thing, I have to get my own group, 'cause I don't like this jam session with strangers all the time. That's when I decided if I'm gonna be back here, if I'm gonna play the horn, I'm gonna write some arrangements and I'm gonna get a group together, so when I go out, I know what I'm gonna play and how it's gonna sound. And that's the main reason why I started the Company."

Her band, says Liston, is basically "just a swing band. I write in the tradition, bebop and swing and jazz, and a little out, but not too far." The repertoire includes material by Duke Ellington, Miles Davis, Fats Waller, Patti Bown, Mary Lou Williams, and Liston herself. Always Ellington-inspired, even from her earliest years when Ellington trombonist Lawrence Brown was her chief influence, Liston says that she still learns from Ellington's scoring all the time. "I usually sort of meditate on it for a long time, and get an idea or a plan in my head, and then I will go to the keyboard and work at it, and search for moods and colors to give the feeling of whatever the story is that I'm trying to tell."

One of the things Liston strives for in writing harmony for the horns is to make each instrument's line individually interesting and affecting. "Being a section player, I got real bored in the old days just playing straight down from the trumpet, that kind of vertical thing, so whenever I wrote something, I always tried to make the lines individually beautiful so the player could put more feeling into it. Even when I was in the school band, I used to not play the trombone part. I played the baritone part or the cello part or something, because they had the moving lines that I loved. So I try to make all the parts sort of free and special. Melodic.

"It hasn't become so popular yet," says Liston, who still has to do her own copying to save on expenses. "Looks like I have to stay out of the country to keep working. Maybe somebody'll hear it one of these days. I had trouble with the orchestras playing it, too. They're so accustomed to all the reeds playing this way, and all the trumpets playing this way, so when they get my arrangement, the saxophone might be playing with the trombones, this one might be playing with the trumpets, and the mixture slows things up. Every now and then I get some kind of funny remarks from the dudes—'Why can't you write like everybody else?'—but then, after they get used to it, they find out that they like it very much.

"The horn has always saved me from any sadness. Anytime I need a lift, the trombone takes care of me. I'm not so good to it as it is to me. The trombone set me up for an arranger, and then when I'm writing, I forget the trombone. But then when things get dull, I go back to the trombone, and it saves me again."

Mary Osborne

(guitar/vocals)

Mary Osborne has worked with her own groups, toured with male and female bands, and appeared with the major all-woman small units of the forties, as well as with such musicians as Coleman Hawkins and Charlie Shavers. In the early fifties, she began to do extensive studio work on radio and to record widely. Married to trumpet player Ralph Scaffidi, and mother of three, Osborne has lived in California since 1958, where she has been both teaching and performing, appearing in such jazz concerts as the Newport Guitar Explosion, with Marian McPartland at Concord, and with her own four-piece group at local California clubs. "Music," says Osborne, "is my life."

Mary Osborne was born in Minot, North Dakota, in the early twenties. "When I was about four, I was playing the ukulele and tap dancing and singing, and my dad used to bring home every type of string instrument for me to play—mandolin, banjo—and I started taking violin lessons when I was in the first grade, and played in the orchestra. When I was about nine years old, my dad got me a guitar for Christmas, and I started playing guitar."

Until she was nine, says Osborne, she thought everybody in the world was a musician. "My dad had several bands. One was what they called a ragtime band for those days—about six men. Then he had a square-dance band, which I was practically weaned on. I think I spent every night of my life taking a violin lesson from my father, and then afterwards we used to practice. Well, that's where I learned to fake on guitar. My dad played in all the sharp keys, and I learned to fake on guitar by playing the hoedown numbers with him." With another of his bands, Osborne played the banjo.

"My first singer that I really cared about was Perry Como," says Osborne. "Then, as far as jazz, my very first musician that I was just thrilled with—late at night I'd listen to the radio and hear this live broadcast from the Blackhawk restaurant in Chicago—was Red Norvo with Mildred Bailey. I thought, 'That's great!' I didn't know what it was, didn't even know the word 'jazz.' I just knew that I liked what they did."

By the time she was twelve, Osborne was appearing on local radio twice a week singing standards of the day and accompanying herself on guitar. She was also playing rhythm guitar in her father's band. Her career began in earnest, though, when she joined an all-woman trio led by Winifred McDonnell. "That's really how I happened to get into the music business. McDonnell was a musician/schoolteacher. Mary Wood, a bass player, was going to college in my hometown. We got together and started working in Bismarck. It was a very fine trio: Winifred played piano, Mary Wood played violin and string bass, and then myself, doubling on guitar and bass, and we all sang." Eventually the group was augmented to include a saxophone and, later, another violinist and bass player.

"I always thought [McDonnell's management] was amazing," says Osborne. "She did everything by mail. She'd find the name of a place in a magazine and she would contact them. She was very professional. We had great pictures taken, she made demonstration records, we had beautiful clothes, and she was very big-time-thinking. Musicians were very attracted to our trio, because they recognized the musicianship. Whatever we did, each person, you could hear the quality. All of us could sing solos. I was the pop singer, Winifred was the ballad singer, and then Mary Wood had a very good range; she sang the harmony parts. It was strictly good music, and it also swung."

One night while Osborne was appearing in a cocktail lounge in a Bismarck hotel, some musician friends told her about a group playing at a pavilion called The Dome. "They said, 'You have to come out and hear this guitar player. He's tremendous.' There was a sixteen-piece band up there [the Al Trent band] and I hear this great jazz, and I kept waiting to hear the guitar player [Charlie Christian]. They said, 'That *is* the guitar player'; I thought it was a tenor saxophone. The only electric guitar I'd ever heard before was Hawaiian guitar. That used steel guitar and that was electric. I've never forgotten the sound and the impact that [Charlie Christian] had on me."

The very next day, Osborne went out and bought her own electric guitar. "It appealed to me," she says. "That was the starting point for me playing. They happened to have one just like [Charlie's] in our local music store, that original Gibson electric guitar. I knew chords and I used to play chord solos and things, different syncopations and all. I never went off the melody for a long time; I just played the notes in the chord, and from then on I was an electric-guitar player."

One night she heard Charlie Christian playing guitarist Django Rinehardt's solo on "St. Louis Blues." "I was just young enough and interested enough to not be shy about asking him." When she mentioned the solo to him afterward, he said, "Somebody in this place knows to listen to Django Rinehardt besides me," and began to let her sit in.

By 1940 all three women had decided to marry, and the McDonnell trio broke up (though all of them continued to work in music). "I've often said it was a unique position that I was in," says Osborne. "I was *very* lucky, and my husband was very instrumental. There wasn't a time that he ever heard of anything happening about guitar that he didn't say, 'Gosh, call Mary.' He was my benefactor."

From 1940 to 1942, Osborne worked (sometimes with Scaffidi) in the bands of Dick Stabile, Terry Shand, and Bob Chester, and once, when she got tired of the one-nighters, she accepted an offer to join a commercial all-woman band on a long winter job in Florida. She also worked with violinist Joe Venuti, and was, in fact, the first guitarist to be associated with Venuti since Eddie Lang's death, in an automobile accident, in 1933. "I was very complimented that he hired me," Osborne says.

Then, in 1942, when her husband went into the armed services, Osborne left New York for the duration of the war. When Scaffidi came home in '46, they returned to New York, and Mary immediately set about forming her own trio. "I had Sanford Gold on piano and Frenchy Cauette, and we were at Kelly's Stables for a long time." It also marked the beginning of a busy recording period for her. With her own trio she recorded "Mary's Guitar Boogie," "You're Gonna Get My Letter in the Morning," "Wonder Where's My Man Tonight," and "The One I Love Belongs to Somebody Else." She also recorded with Coleman Hawkins, Charlie Shavers, Jerry Jerome; with the Beryl Booker all-woman trio on "Low Ceiling," with June Rotenberg on bass; and with the Mary Lou Williams All-Girl All-Stars. On all of these records, Osborne displays the driving, assertive playing that she was noted for.

In 1951 a *down beat* story on her reported that she had settled down to being a housewife;[19] but, just one year later, she was back in the studio working on the Jack Sterling radio show, beginning what she considers the most productive ten years of her career. "That's when I studied guitar," she says. "I really did a lot of different things. I learned to read music on guitar more extensively than I'd ever done before. The very short time that I studied with him [classical guitarist Alberto Valdez Blaine] I feel was the most rewarding thing that ever happened to me. It just opened up so many things."

As for the aggressive, swinging quality of her forties work, Osborne says, "Well, I give all that credit to just being in there playing." By the fifties, she says, "It was *serious* then. I had to really buckle down and do some hard reading. I was lucky; I got exposed to some awfully fine jazz people. With my earlier playing and training, there was no work attached to it at all. And, of course, I'd listened to records all my life. Harmony and things like that were just a natural thing with me." In the studio, however, "it was strictly confined to stuff that I had to play that someone else had written—and that is the greatest training in the world."

Osborne's current group includes her husband on trumpet and her son on bass, and features what she calls "traditional jazz." As for combining career and family so successfully, Osborne says, "I couldn't have done it without my husband being a great person and cooperating in every way."

Of her playing today she says, "I think I'm a little more mellow now." On the album *Now's the Time*, recorded with Marian McPartland, Dottie Dodgion, Lynn Milano, and Vi Redd, Osborne has more room to "stretch out" than she did on the earlier records, and "Sophisticated Lady" is a showcase for a richly textured Osborne solo. "I look back at the records that I made then and I'm amazed that I played that well. But, as I said, there wasn't a day when I wasn't playing in some club. And all the big, great jazz piano players—how can you go wrong? It had to rub off. But I feel now that I've become more broad and a better guitarist all around. Teaching, too, teaches you a lot.

"When I think about my life, I really feel I've had a charmed life. That's because I've done exactly what I was born to do: I wanted to be in music and I was. I was blessed with some terrific parents who were both music-oriented and encouraged me in every way, and I met a terrific guy who also encouraged me. If it had been anything different, I'd be a different story. I got to do everything I wanted to do, and I'm ending up still doing exactly what I want. I'm still in music, and I'll stay in it until—*until*!"

Carline Ray

(Fender bass/guitar/piano/acoustic bass/vocals)

Carline Ray was trained as a singer and pianist, is self-taught on guitar and Fender bass, and is currently studying and performing on acoustic bass. She has worked in small jazz combos and big bands, done recordings, been on radio and TV, sung as chorister, backup vocalist, and band vocalist, and been an educator and musical director. On vocals like "Danny Boy" and "Unchained Melody" the special, haunting quality of Ray's voice (with its three-and-a-half-octave range) transcends one's expectations of the human voice; on Fender bass, her strong, solid playing and rich acoustic sound have earned her the admiration and respect of artists in all genres of the music.

Ray has spanned the generations of jazz, working with such names as Erskine Hawkins, the International Sweethearts of Rhythm, Duke Ellington's band under the direction of Mercer Ellington, Sy Oliver's band (where she is the only female musician to date), Skitch Henderson, Mary Lou Williams, the Big Apple Jazzwomen, Aerial, the Alvin Ailey Dance Company, and Melba Liston and Company and the hit revue *Jerry's Girls* (in which she plays acoustic bass). She has also served as musical director for the New York Salute to Jazz Women, and has inspired many other women in the field to "stay out there and show them how it's done."

Carline Ray was born in New York City in 1925. Her mother was born in the Hell's Kitchen district of the city in 1889, and her father, a Tuskegee graduate, went to New York to attend the Juilliard School of Music. He graduated the year Ray was born. "He would have been the first black man in the New York Philharmonic, because Walter Damrosch asked him to join the brass section, but he needed more substantial employment. I was coming along that year, and at that time the Philharmonic didn't have a year-round schedule, just a few weeks a year." Ray's father went to work, instead, for the U.S. Post Office.

Ray grew up hearing all kinds of music. During World War I, her father had gone overseas with the famous 369th Infantry band under the direction of James Reese Europe, and he continued to play with the band when they returned to New York. "He used to take me to all the brass-band rehearsals when I was only three, four, five years old," Ray says. "And I used to listen to the radio a lot. I always had a good ear— I could pick out things and play them on the piano—but I couldn't read until I started studying in junior high. I was always singing, too, but I think I started really seriously in junior high school, because I belonged to all the glee clubs."

In September 1941, Ray entered Juilliard at the age of sixteen, and stayed for five years, adding a year to the program when she changed her major from piano to composition. (She, Ellis Larkins, and Enola Laws, Ray notes, were the three black students in the graduating class of 1946.) Ray's career in jazz began while she was still at Juilliard, when Edna Smith, a bass-fiddle major at the school, asked her if she wanted to form a group. "It happened to be all female," says Ray. "We weren't in the union at that time, but we were bold. Edna was the aggressive one, and she would go out and get the jobs. I was playing piano; she played the bass. I think the first job she and I had together was playing at a taxi dance hall, located on 47th Street and Broadway. It was called the Parisian Dance Hall, and I think we were the first females in that [otherwise all-male] band. In taxi dance halls, the music had to be continuous, because the more tickets the ladies collected, the more money they made. They used to call them ten-cents-a-dance halls. Before we got there, the guys would have to get up one by one, so that the music could continue, but we got them to let us have a complete five-minute break. The owner loved to hear me sing 'Stardust'—that was his favorite tune—so we said, 'Well, if you wanna hear "Stardust," you have to let us [all] off for five minutes.'"

The guitarist in a later group often didn't make rehearsals, and one day Smith said to Ray, "Every time we rehearse at your house, I see a guitar up on top of the closet in your room. Why don't you ask your father's permission to use it and see if you can play a few things on it." "I started fooling around on it," Ray says, and about three months later, she took it on her first union job. "I joined 802 as a pianist," she recalls, "and I had to play a little Beethoven, a little Bach, and a little boogie-woogie, believe it or not. We gigged around for a while, and we got with an agent named Nat Nazarro, who used to be in the Brill Building and had acts like Chuck and Chuckles, and Buck and Bubbles, so I got a chance to meet a lot of those guys, and he used to book us around.

"One day we were coming from his office, and Edna was carrying her bass on her back. This gentleman came up to us and said to Edna, 'Excuse me, don't I know you?' So Edna said, 'Well, I'm sorry, mister, if you're not a musician, forget it.' We were walking to the subway, and he said, 'No, I'm serious,' and he introduced himself. He was musical director of the Sweethearts of Rhythm and his name was Maurice King. He said, 'I'm looking for some girls to replace some people who are leaving the band.'" They took him back to their agent's office, and by summer of 1946 (after her graduation from Juilliard), Ray, Smith, and pianist Jackie King had gone into the Sweethearts of Rhythm as new members of the rhythm section.

Ray had heard of the Sweethearts, she says, but had never actually heard them play. "They used to come up to the Apollo," she recalls, "but in those days I didn't go to the Apollo. In fact, I didn't start going to the Apollo until I started working there, because I was a student and I really didn't have money to go anyplace that much. Actually, most of my running around was coming down to Carnegie Hall. I lived in Carnegie Hall. I used to go to see all the fine pianists there—Rachmaninoff giving his last recital there in 1943, Artur Rubinstein . . . Then too, Edna and I used to go down to 52nd Street. A lot of times we would go down on the Street with our books in hand; we didn't even go home in between. I was soaking up *all* that stuff. That's how I got to meet Art Tatum, Billie Holiday, Sarah Vaughan. And every Monday night I used to go to jam sessions at the Hollywood around 133rd Street and Seventh Avenue. They used to have a session there for pianists, and a lot of the old stride pianists would come out. Of course, Art Tatum was the king, so he'd be the last one to go up and play. And I even had the distinction of saying that Art Tatum played for me to sing one night. I think I sang a Gershwin tune. When I got through, Art said to me, 'Did I play all right for you?' I said, 'Are you kidding?' That's something I'll never forget! Art Tatum played for me!"

Ray stayed with the Sweethearts as rhythm guitarist and featured vocalist on such production numbers as "Night and Day" and "Temptation," and then went on to join the Erskine Hawkins band as the band vocalist. "This was in February '48, and I stayed with them for one year. I was the band vocalist, but I used to take my guitar out on the road with me and play in the section so that I wouldn't just be sitting up there doing nothing while the band was playing. I didn't do any recording with the Hawkins band, because that year the record ban was on and there was no recording at all, unfortunately."

After leaving Hawkins, Ray, again playing piano, joined Edna Smith and Pauline Braddy (former drummer with the Sweethearts), and the trio worked around New York. Then Luis Russell, noted Panamanian-born pianist and bandleader of the thirties and forties (and also Ray's future husband), got the trio a job in Town Hill, a Brooklyn club that he was managing. The booking was for two weeks, but the group stayed six months. "We wouldn't just be playing jazz; we would be singing and doing a lot of specialty material," Ray says. "Back in those days—I hate to use the word 'novelty,' but I guess we *were* a novelty because we were good on our instruments. We were not just women who held our instruments; we were actually playing them and sounding good, if I do say so myself. Back in the days when the Sweethearts of Rhythm were first around, they probably more expected the women to sit up there and look pretty rather than really actually produce anything. That's what made these bands that did make it unique, because the women were really playing well, as well as looking good."

It was also on this job that Ray first played the Fender bass, often picking up Edna Smith's instrument early in the night while Smith took over at the piano. Ray says she would play the "things she always wanted to hear from the bass" whenever she was playing piano. The customers approved and increasingly asked her to continue throughout the evening. Frank Anderson, a Panamanian pianist working with his group in the back room, would also let Ray sit in on Fender bass, and as a result of that Town Hill meeting, she had a chance to work with his outfit over the next twelve or thirteen years. "That band featured a lot of Latin music, so I got my chops up in Latin music, in calypso, and in jazz," she says. "The band used to play a lot of the gigs around in Manhattan, a lot of cotillions, social clubs, and a lot of the West Indian carnivals, especially up in Harlem and Brooklyn. The people would dress up, make their costumes, and they'd have a contest. That was the West Indian side of things."

During this time, Ray had also gone back to school, attending the Manhattan School of Music from '54 to '56 and receiving a master's degree in voice. The same year she got her degree, she married Luis Russell, and their daughter, Cathy, was born. "Unfortunately," says Ray, "my husband and I were only married for seven and a half years before he died."

Throughout the sixties and seventies, Ray continued to work in a great variety of contexts: singing with the Scuola Cantorum (and with every other noteworthy choral group in New York), in a group with pianist May Tatum at the '64 World's Fair, and later with Skitch Henderson, Alvin Ailey, Mary Lou Williams, Mercer Ellington, and Melba Liston. She also decided, at the end of the seventies, to study acoustic bass. Through New York's Universal Jazz Coalition's Salute to Women in Jazz, Ray had learned about the National Endowment for the Arts, and in 1980 applied for and won a 1981 grant to study the instrument with bassist Major Holly.

"After playing Fender bass for so many years, I wanted to study string bass because I wanted to be a complete bass player. So I said, 'Well, it's never too late for me, even at this late date in my life, to learn to play string bass.'" Her approach to the instrument is "a little different" from her approach to Fender bass, says Ray, "but even before I started playing string bass, my mental attitude toward my Fender bass was to make it sound as much like a string bass as possible. Because of my influence from Ray Brown [her major influence on the instrument since the forties], I always wanted my bass playing to have a nice, big, fat string-bass sound."

To Ray, the most important elements of being a good bass player are listening to section mates, "having your own time clock within you and being able to hold your own rhythm" without needing to have a drummer on the job, knowing a lot of tunes, and being able to play the right changes in any key. "I'm called on a lot of jobs because of the fact that I can play anything, and I can play the right changes, and I can play in any key. There are a lot of bass players that can't do that. I can operate very well in a lot of different situations, and I have had experience."

With one of the most eclectic and diverse careers of any musician in the field, Ray finds her time more and more devoted exclusively to jazz. "Choral work has really dwindled to a devastating degree," she says, "so I'm glad that I have my jazz, which I'm really devoting full time to nowadays. In fact, Mary Lou [Williams] made me promise to spend more time in jazz than I was at one time, because I used to do so much choral work that I was half and half. But now I'm more jazz than choral. I feel now that there are many exponents of the classical European music, so I feel that I should stay with my jazz and keep that out there. That seems to be a never-ending uphill battle. But I'm gonna make it my business to keep the jazz out here, and perform as much as I can, wherever I can. And I'm gonna help to keep Mary Lou's music alive, too."

In the past, says Ray, "it was just a matter that a lot of women were not taken seriously, except those that joined big groups and traveled around. All of a sudden now, they're beginning to take women seriously, but I would just rather be taken seriously as a musician, and the fact that I'm a female—I just happen to be female, that's all."

During the forties, Mary Lou Williams remained, in Duke Ellington's term of highest praise, "beyond category," an original and innovative voice in jazz. Hazel Scott was captivating film and club audiences with her dazzling keyboard combination of jazz and the classics; Connie Berry was playing solo piano in the clubs; Rose Murphy was playing intermission piano at the Famous Door but gaining greater fame with her high-pitched, highly stylized vocals; and Nellie Lutcher's piano playing and murmuring, melismatic vocal style made hits out of her tunes "He's a Real Gone Guy" and "Hurry On Down to My House." (Lutcher had started out playing in family and territory bands in the 1920s.) At the Hickory House, Adele Girard was playing harp with a group led by her husband, Joe Marsala, and the gifted pianist/vocalist Dardanelle was working with her own trio; and in 1946 an English-born pianist arrived in America to work with her husband, cornetist Jimmy McPartland, and his group. With her taste and keen sense of harmonics, Marian McPartland soon set out with her own trio, and has been at the forefront of the jazz world ever since.

In 1946, too, another pianist, Philadelphia-born Beryl Booker, was beginning to gain recognition, working with bassist Slam Stewart. On her mid-forties trio recordings with June Rotenberg and Bridget O'Flynn (made under Booker's name), as well as on her later recordings with Don Byas (when her trio included drummer Elaine Leighton and bassist Bonnie Wetzel), Booker showed herself to be a forceful, authoritative, and swinging player. In 1952, the headline of a Leonard Feather profile (*down beat*, April 4, p. 8) would speculate "Beryl Best Since Mary Lou?", yet when Booker died in 1980 at the age of fifty-six, she had never received the attention or acknowledgment she deserved.

The women who follow represent the widely diverse contexts in which pianists worked during the forties.

Dorothy Donegan

(piano)

In the early forties, Dorothy Donegan wowed the Chicago public and press. Trained in the classics as a child, she went on to become one of the sly, wry, unpredictable, hard-playing heavyweights of jazz. However, because she also entertains—with her wiggling, her distinctive singing style, her "show-biz" antics and leopard-skin or sequined gowns—she has often been denied her rightful recognition as a major jazz artist. "Her reputation as a lounge entertainer," John S. Wilson once wrote, "has virtually buried the fact that she is potentially the greatest jazz pianist playing today."[20] After hearing her in New York in 1980, Wilson praised her simplicity, sensitivity, and "almost subliminal sense of swing" in what he called a "dazzling performance that incorporated Miss Donegan's genuinely exceptional talents as a jazz pianist and her ability to go from subtle brilliance to a pre-gut appeal that rocks the house and moves normally sedate audiences to cheers and whistles."[21]

Donegan is also one of the strongest piano players around. "Well, I do have that incredible stamina and power," she admits impishly, "and great pyrotechnics and technical skill. But I lead a clean life and I get a lot of rest and I don't smoke or drink or use any narcotics. And I go to Steinway Hall and practice my classical things on those good pianos. I guess a musician is an athlete in one sense, in the fact that you have to get rest and stay in shape. . . . Sometimes people say, 'Well, she plays like a man.' I say, 'You mean a *heavy* man.'"

Dorothy Donegan was born in Chicago in 1924. She began to study when she was six, and at eight, had lessons, first with Alfred Simms and then Sterling Todd. "I've always had that power," she says. "When I was eight years old, I used to play baseball. I used to bat the ball over the fence on the South Side of Chicago. I think God gave me something a little extra."

As a child, Donegan says, she practiced in order to avoid housework, and by the age of ten or so she was ready to start working professionally. She began playing as church organist and at fourteen got her first paying job, working at a club called the Hi-Jinx. She also played for house-rent parties. Her first big engagement was at Costello's Grill in Chicago, which "was unheard of then," she says, "because there was segregation, and you weren't supposed to work downtown." When she put her pocketbook down on the piano and played, she remembers, the audience consensus was unanimous that she be hired.

In 1942, at the age of eighteen, Donegan cut her first records, four piano solos, and she continued playing in Chicago cocktail lounges, swinging the classics and specializing in boogie-woogie. It was her mother more than anyone else, she says, who helped, listened, and appreciated her talent. "She would make me dress nice, and she'd always tell me to put feeling in my music. Sometimes it gets technical, [just] a barrage of notes. I get redundant, I think. Sometimes I play with more feeling than others."

In 1945, Donegan recalls, "I was in Chicago . . . and I was suggested for this picture, *Sensations of '45*, so they brought me out to Hollywood— my mother and I; I was chaperoned then. They had these directors, musical directors, symphony directors, to listen to me and to evaluate my talent, and they said, 'Oh, amen,' and we made the picture. They put a dark Egyptian [make-up] on me to make me look darker than I actually was, and then they put me in a scene with a male pianist, and they had us playing back and forward at each other. Then, after the picture ended, they said, 'If you don't come back to New York with this picture, you will be blackballed.' I said, 'Well, I got something else to do.' They just threatened me like that. So I came back to Loew's State with the picture."

In New York, Donegan continued to record, making records for Continental, Jubilee, and Decca. "Oh, I made a hundred sides for Decca," she says, "and then somebody put [them] on the shelf for a hundred and fifty years, and then they sell [the masters] to another company and put me with all the rest of the women pianists. They put us all together like a supermarket full of goods. So, I guess to get out of that, you have to just make your own [records]. They like me in Europe a lot, and America will buy you after you've been accepted in Europe."

"When I was coming up in '41," says Donegan, "black people didn't get a chance to play with the symphony. They just had one Marian Anderson and one Paul Robeson. Today they have an André Watts, who's doing classical, but there should be encouragement for the rest of us. And there should be many black women playing.

"Now I've gotten a chance to play with the symphony, so I have to keep on studying so I can devote [more] time to the classical. I'm not going to withdraw from jazz entirely. I'll play 'Tenderly' and a few light jazz things, but I would not stress the entertainment part of my act. I would go classical and light jazz, with a lot of embellishments in it, floral patterns." In the meantime, says Donegan, "if you're going to entertain, you have to use the hip-shaking, too." As far as the criticism of her on-stage antics is concerned, she says, "The critics out there don't pay your bills. You're not there as a concert artist, you're there to entertain—as long as the talent for playing is there."

Generally, Donegan prefers to solo, but she also likes working with a rhythm section. "They don't all like to work with me," she says, "because they say I work them too hard. Each time I come up with something different, it blows their minds—'What is this woman coming up with now?'

"Sometimes I'm fighting, you know. I always have control, but sometimes my creative juices are on more than others, and then the mix just comes out perfect. And sometimes it doesn't come out perfect. But usually it does. You can tell. Everything you touch turns to music. And other nights it's a *chore* and I wanna *cry*. Well, you're not on all the time, I guess. Two married people, every night they make love, some nights are gonna be better than others. When you feel great, you just play great. And if you have love, you send it out and you get it back in return. That should be it, you know."

Art Tatum, more than anyone, has been Donegan's idol. "He came to my house for the first time in 1942," she says, "and then we would have cutting sessions. Well, he was the greatest jazz pianist I have ever heard, now, then, and yesterday. I guess he was the Horowitz of the jazz field. So I try to play like him. I guess I do him with the hip-shaking," she quips. "A little hip-shaking never hurt anybody."

Donegan's playing, she feels, is becoming more "polished and coherent." "But I can't forget the fiery things, you know, the applause-getters . . . 'Bumble Bee' and things like that. I like applause. I think everybody wants to be loved and appreciated."

Much of Donegan's time now is spent in Europe and on the road. "I'm used to being alone. I'm not a party girl and I don't go out. Usually some people will invite me to dinner and I may go. . . . The worst part is packing. Looks like I take too much stuff on the road."

Donegan worked for two weeks at the Sheraton Centre Hotel in New York in 1980 and was told that she broke attendance records during her appearance. "Said they never had so many calls," she says. "I said, 'Well, why am I gettin' all this attention? I been playing the same old stuff for years.'"

Sarah McLawler

(piano/organ/vocals)

Sarah McLawler knew at the age of seven that music was her mission in life. Trained in the classics and jazz, she started her career in the Chicago of the early forties, working as a single and also as leader of some of the

finest all-woman small combos of the day. The groups included some of
the excellent musicians who had been with the all-black big bands, the
Darlings of Rhythm and the Harlem Playgirls. By the 1950s McLawler
was working as a duo with her husband, violinist Richard Otto, in an
association that would last nearly until his death in 1979.

An exceptionally tireless and dedicated entertainer, McLawler is also active in organizations that range from the Negro Actors' Guild to Eastern
Star to the Universal Jazz Coalition to the Baptist churches where she
plays, teaches, and leads the women's day choir. Since 1975, she has
worked in and around New York City, appearing with her trio at such
clubs as Joe's Pier 52 and the Pan Am Motor Inn, and with a larger
group, the Big Apple Jazzwomen, at numerous concerts and festivals.

Sarah McLawler was born in Louisville, Kentucky. Her father, a Baptist minister, was founder of Mt. Linden Baptist Church and a scholar
who tutored in Latin, Greek, and Hebrew. Her mother (who died when
McLawler was ten) came from Cameron, Texas, and was "a great gospel
singer, a great musician, and active in the church." She and McLawler's
father had met at the National Baptist Convention. "My roots are in the
Baptist Church," says McLawler, "which I'm very proud of."

"I remember one day," she says, "I was listening to the radio and I
guess I was about six or seven years old. It just dawned on me that I
could see the notes. I just understood the music. I told my mother about
it, and my mother said, 'Well, then you should have music lessons, because no matter what talent you have, you should have the proper
training.' And I remember telling my mother, 'No, no, no, I see the notes.
I know the notes. I don't need music lessons.' And sure enough, when I
got to the piano, I could pick out the notes. And I'd say, 'If I play in this
key, I must not play that key, because it won't sound right.'"

McLawler started playing by ear for her father's church Sunday school,
and the minister of music, Mrs. Vesterine Slaughter, quickly offered to
teach the child for fifty cents a week, "which was a lot of money then,"
McLawler recalls. "Thanks to her, I got very good early basic training.
She made a tremendous impression on my life. It was through her I got
what technique I do have. I remember many times I used to skate
through. I hadn't practiced and was trying to play it by ear, and she
would stop me and say, 'You know, that was not written!' So that was
the beginning of my improvising."

Blues and jazz also played a large part in McLawler's early life. "I was
the regular teenage fan," she says. "I had my idols—Ella Fitzgerald,
Count Basie, Duke Ellington. I would cut their pictures out and put them
on the wall." During her last year in high school she became more seriously interested in jazz. Her family had moved to Indianapolis, and
McLawler, an honor student, had won a scholarship to Jordan Conserva-

tory, where she was studying pipe organ. There she met a musician who began to teach her the structure and "inner workings" of jazz. Her first playing experience was with the Jean Pope orchestra, where she also started to learn about orchestrations. And at a place called the Sunset Terrace she first heard Charlie Parker, Fletcher and Horace Henderson, Gene Ammons, and Billy Eckstine, as well as the Harlem Playgirls, the Darlings of Rhythm, and the International Sweethearts of Rhythm.

When McLawler's scholarship ran out, she moved to Chicago. Her sister, a songwriter, lived there, and her brother-in-law worked as a chef in the hotel where the Earl Hines band was playing, with the young Sarah Vaughan as vocalist and pianist. "I used to sneak around there," McLawler remembers, "and they would chase me out. But I was fascinated by the music; I wasn't interested in the seamy side of entertainment."

Chicago proved to be a great starting point for McLawler, and it became her base as she traveled between there and Fisk University, where she had won another scholarship. When that ran out, she continued to study under John Work and Arthur Crowley and also played weekend jobs with a band made up of musicians from Fisk, Vanderbilt, Tennessee State, and Maharry Medical School. Back in Chicago, she would spend her nights at the Regal Theater listening to the Sweethearts and next door at the Savoy, where all the great bands and singers appeared.

"And I would listen, listen. And finally I got a job on State Street, playing right downtown doing a single. At that time they had music early in the afternoon, like at one o'clock. On State Street they had the theaters—the Chicago and the Oriental—and they had all kinds of cocktail lounges. That's how you got your apprenticeship. You worked these little places. I know I made a few boo-boos," she says of her first club dates, "but I was just a kid, and they would tell me, 'You got talent, you're young.'"

For the next couple of years, McLawler continued working on the North Side, and eventually wound up back on the South Side, on 63rd Street. "While I was playing there, two girls came in. [One of them was the drummer Hetty Smith.] They had played with the Darlings of Rhythm and they spoke to me about forming an all-girls' group, because all along 63rd Street [there were] quite a few bars and cocktail lounges and they all had bands. I said, 'Girls? I don't know. I have to think about it.'"

McLawler was skeptical, not only because she had never heard the women play, but also because she'd been happy working as a single. Dorothy Donegan and Hazel Scott, both singles, had impressed her, and she wanted to develop her act along those lines. However, when she heard that the job was at the Blue Heaven, a beautiful new club on 63rd and Cottage Grove, she agreed to take it, and after the first rehearsal, any doubts she had about the quality of the women's playing were quickly put to rest. Margaret Backstrum, the sensational tenor player with the Harlem Playgirls and Eddie Durham's All-Star Girl Orchestra, was in the group, and another of the women had just come off the road with the Darlings of Rhythm. McLawler remembers saying, "Well, why haven't other people been doing this? All we've had is the big bands with the girl musicians, and no small jazz groups have come out. That's really where you show your musicianship. 'Cause if you can play in a small group, then you show that you can really play your instrument."

This group marked the beginning of a long period during which Mc-Lawler would work with excellent all-woman small combos. When they left the Blue Heaven the group split up, but soon afterward McLawler got a call from Hetty Smith and guitarist Roxanna Lucas and joined them in a group that went to work as the intermission band in a new Detroit club called the Frolic Bar, where the headliners were stars like Sarah Vaughan and Dinah Washington.

When this group split up, Smith asked McLawler to take the band. "I told her I didn't want to be bothered with any band. They said, 'We need to keep girls working; they're giving girls a hard time.'" The problem, says McLawler, was not that female musicians weren't getting work, but that they weren't getting adequate *recognition* for their work. "We wanted to be recognized in *down beat* and the trade magazines. We weren't getting it and we didn't think it was fair. We wrote letters— 'How about mentioning the girls who are doing great things?'—'cause there were girls doing great things, but it never happened."

McLawler did form another women's group, with Lillian Jones on drums, Vi Wilson on bass, and, after Backstrum left, Lula Roberts on tenor sax. This new group, the Syncoettes, stayed together from 1948 to 1953. In 1949 Hetty Smith joined them, and remembers that they were "always in demand for one-night stands and nightclubs." In Chicago, they were the house band at the Savoy and getting top publicity all over the city. Their repertoire included tunes by Lester Young, Gene Ammons, Stan Kenton, show tunes, and some then-avant-garde Latin numbers. McLawler was also featured on a number of Billie Holiday vocals, "because Billie was very hot at that time," she says. In 1950, the group also had a hit with "My Whole Life Through." "We were ahead of our time," McLawler says. "We would experiment. We tried to be an entertaining group, along with being a good musical group." The women sounded good and they looked good, "and we worked some very good rooms behind that," says McLawler. "Whatever was happening at the time, we were up with it."

After a tape of the group playing "The St. Louis Blues" reached New York, the Moe Gale Agency brought them east. They went into the Club 845, and from then on New York became their base, with the Hotel

Theresa their home. "In those days," says McLawler, "the Theresa was *fabulous*. You walked downstairs, you saw *everybody*. On 125th and Seventh Avenue, you could find any performer you wanted to see. After work, we'd all congregate there, two or three o'clock in the morning. There was always something happening on 125th Street. It makes me sad to see it like it is now. I'm glad I got in on that era before it died out."

During the late forties and early fifties, there were a number of all-woman small groups on the scene—Tiny Davis and her Hell Divers, Beryl Booker's excellent trio, smaller Sweetheart units, Vi Burnside's quintet. These groups and the Syncoettes, says McLawler, were the groups that were "really out there"; but the women were still not receiving the serious attention they felt they deserved. "We were getting pretty good jobs, but they just wouldn't let us up there with the other musicians. It wasn't the club owners that much, because they were glad to advertise that an all-girl group was appearing." The male musicians themselves recognized and appreciated the women, McLawler says, but the media and the critics could not be swayed.

McLawler's group continued, but Lula Roberts became ill with spinal meningitis and died. Demoralized by her death, McLawler tried to keep the group going with other fine players, like Jean Davis and Gloria Bell (Coleman), but somehow the new group never "got off the ground." When Vi Wilson left, McLawler traveled all over New York trying to find the right musicians, but at last she gave up, discouraged by the number of women she heard who really could not play. "The girls that I knew, they really knew the instrument," she says. "But most of the girls I came across, they thought just because they were a girl, they could get away with it. And I said, 'It's not like that.' "

Just before McLawler's last group disbanded, they were working in Atlantic City, where organist Wild Bill Davis was also playing. "I was fascinated by the sound he got," says McLawler, "and he was telling me, 'You know, Sarah, there's nobody doing this but Bill Doggett and myself.' And I said, 'You know, Bill, I wanna go back doing a single, and I like the big sound that you get. I'm gonna look into it.' "

McLawler bought herself a Hammond organ and began working with a trio at a small restaurant in Brooklyn. Then she moved to another place down the street. "I started doing a single, playing and singing with the organ, and the place was jumping. It was packed every night." Musicians from Manhattan started dropping by or sitting in—Max Roach, Rector Bailey, Gloria Lynn, Dionne Warwick—and "the place became known as Birdland of Brooklyn." Then one day Rector Bailey told her about a violinist named Richard Otto: "This guy is a genius." "Well, the only genius I know on the violin is Eddie South and Stuff Smith," said McLawler. "So he played over the telephone, and I couldn't believe it."

She and Otto teamed up musically, and eventually they also married. "That's how the organ and the violin was born. We packed that place. Business got so good that the owner bought the furniture store next door, knocked out the walls, and enlarged the place." A drummer joined them, and after a year they went into the Apollo, Birdland, and Basin Street. Once again working as a duo, McLawler and Otto (who had also been classically trained) became "very daring" in the nightclubs, mixing the classics and jazz. "I reached a new plateau when I met Richard Otto," says McLawler. "The organ with the violin was a very unusual thing. What was so phenomenal about that was that we sounded like a seventeen-piece band, because Richard had an ingenuity for getting sound. He was always experimenting with sound."

One of the duo's biggest hits was Duke Ellington's "Flamingo" on their first album, *We Bring You Love*, in the mid-fifties. (Today the album sells for seventy-five dollars.) On it, the organ and percussion create a spare landscape behind the long, quivering lines of the violin, and there is a gentle, deliberate skittishness to the performance. *We Bring You Love* presented the duo in ballads and "beautiful" things, and their second album, *We Bring You Swing*, showed them in a more up-tempo (or "upstairs") vein. On all the selections, the variety of effects, the intensity of sound, the dramatic and innovative approach, and the remarkable responsiveness of the two instruments to each other stand out.

Through the sixties the pair worked all over the "chitlin' circuit," playing "gutbucket things" in saloons with sawdust on the floor, in fancy hotels and supper clubs, and then all over Europe. "We used to take pop tunes, show tunes, and play around with them, jazz them up, and the people got a kick out of them. They'd enjoy that. That's how we could work in the hotels," McLawler explains.

The combination of organ and violin did bring them a great deal of attention, but, says McLawler, it was not always positive—at least not until they'd had a chance to play. "Joe Glaser had booked us into the Apollo Theater with Moms Mabley and a singing group from Detroit," she remembers. "So when I got up there for rehearsal on that Thursday afternoon, [the manager of the Apollo] asked me, you know, 'Where is the band?' And I said, 'Well, there is no band, they tell me I'm playing this show.' I thought this poor guy was gonna have a nervous breakdown, and I understood how he felt, 'cause he didn't know me. And he said, 'Well, what kind of band have we got for tomorrow night?' I said, "Organ, violin, and drums,' and he looked at me. . . .

"I had to rehearse the acts on the piano because the stagehands were not gonna bring this organ down in the basement and then take it back upstairs, so he, this poor guy like to had a stroke. I said, 'I don't know what to tell you. The only thing I can tell you is that you'll just have a sleepless night until tomorrow.' He said, 'Well, at least they could have a *horn* or something—but a violin!' So I said, 'Well, you know, the organ has a big band sound.' And he said, 'What about the violin?' I said, 'Well, the violin is only with *our* act; only the organ and drums is gonna play the show.' They could not believe this. The next morning when we opened the show—we had to open the show, the trio—well, I don't need to tell you. They wouldn't let us off the stage. We got a standing ovation. They called us back and called us back, and then Joe Glaser came backstage and he said, 'Don't be working my stars to death.' The relief on [the manager's] face was unbelievable! And the drummer and I played that show the whole week, and people came in there just to see what the hell was going on."

At a recent concert of the Big Apple Jazzwomen in New York, Sarah McLawler noted, in introducing the personnel, that women have always been treated as "the stepchildren of jazz." Because of this, she has always tried to give as much work as possible to other women in the field. "This is a struggle that started *long* ago, back there with Eddie Durham, even before I got into the professional life. I was glad to see in the past couple of years people like Cobi Narita [founder of the Universal Jazz Coalition] and others have fought to give the girl musicians some recognition. Women's rights is a big thing now. The only women's rights I know is just to get paid for what you do. The whole thing is food, shelter, clothing, whether you're a woman, a man, or a kangaroo. Whatever. I'm just trying to see that people who have talent get a chance to express it."

In the Baptist religion, McLawler remembers jazz was always considered a terrible thing. "I was playing for the devil. My father was wise. He told me, 'We have taught you all we know. Just take God with you. You know how to act. God is everywhere. Use your talent, but don't ever forget God.' And I never did. And I think that's one of the things that kept me together through the disappointments and the negative things that have happened in my life. I just say to help your fellow man and realize that all good things come from God.

"I know who I am and what I'm about and 'I will survive,' as Gloria Gaynor says. I don't have that problem, but I like that motto. 'I will survive.' We all will."

Norma Shepherd

(piano/vocals)

I learned long ago that people take a singing pianist for granted . . .
I think there's so many of us who are so much better than some
of the stand-up singers, but it's hard to get the recognition. It's a
shame that we are at the bottom of the totem pole, because I think
we've contributed a lot.

—Norma Shepherd

Norma Shepherd was born in Washington, D.C. Her maternal grandfather had been a voice teacher, and both her parents played piano,
though not professionally. Her mother played and sang—"home-type
stuff, where we could all sit around and listen or sing along. Religious
music, mostly; not so much gospel, but spirituals and hymns."

"One older brother started out to be a child prodigy with the violin, but
my parents were so poor, they couldn't continue his lessons," Shepherd
says. Her younger brother, an excellent pianist in the style of Fats Waller,
formed his own band, Shepherd's Society Six, when he was only fourteen.
"I learned a lot from him," she says. "Unfortunately, he passed away at
a young age—only thirty-six." Still a third brother played bass and guitar
with Rex Stewart and later at the original Jimmy Ryan's with Wilbur
De Paris's Dixieland. In addition to what she learned at home from her
talented siblings, Norma also began taking piano lessons, as did her sister.

At sixteen, her younger brother left for New York. There were few
outlets for blacks in Washington and few places to work. "That's one of
the reasons I wanted to leave when I was old enough," says Shepherd,
"because I didn't think there was any opportunity there. You had segregated schools, churches, theaters. There was this one theater, the Howard,
and this was part of what guys like Redd Foxx refer to as the 'chitlin'
circuit.' You started at the Apollo and you went to the Pearl in Philadelphia, then you got down to the Royal in Baltimore, and you got to the
Howard Theater in Washington, and that was the end of the chitlin'
circuit. Then right back to New York to wait for your next gig. But those
theaters brought the very best in black entertainment. We would scrape
a little money together so we could get to the Howard on a Monday
night to catch that first show. That was our only touch with the show-
business world.

"My own exposure to any culture at all was in churches. This was
where people like Marian Anderson and Roland Hayes came to sing,

because the DAR refused to let them use Constitution Hall. My teacher, who was well thought of in the community, did a lot for the kids he taught. He used to have these recitals two or three times a year, where the children and the parents were invited and we could get together and communicate. And whenever Marian Anderson would come to Washington for an engagement, she would always have to sing in one of the churches, and he got the tickets and would see to it that we were there. I practically cut my teeth on her.

"I got to know and appreciate and love show people just by going to the Howard Theater every Monday. We went religiously. We went out and we sold garden seed, we did a whole lot of hustling around doing unpleasant chores—mostly domestic—to get the money together to be able to go to the Howard Theater on Monday. We didn't wanna miss that! That was glamour and a touch of New York rolled into one. And this is the way I heard Jimmie Lunceford, Duke Ellington, Count Basie, Erskine Hawkins—all the big bands, all the big singers." (Eventually, her brother came back from New York to join Tommy Miles's house band at the Howard.)

At Dunbar High School, Shepherd, a music major, studied with Henry Grant and Mary Europe, sister of the renowned bandleader and composer James Reese Europe. There were coed school bands, but they never interested Shepherd. "I wanted to play like my youngest brother, and when I graduated from high school, I hoped to go on to conservatory. I was sort of on an ego trip, because I was doing so well with my teachers." Shepherd consistently won all the scholarship recitals given by her teacher, or won a year's free lessons. "Today I don't think I was that good," she says. "I really wasn't absorbing the technique that I should have."

Although her parents had been able to send one brother to Howard University, a conservatory was out of the question for Shepherd. "Kids live in a world of fantasy," she says. "In the real world, I knew my parents were poor and struggling. I just thought by the time I was through with high school, something would happen that I could go on to conservatory. I just thought that I was gonna really get into the classical field."

"In Washington," says Shepherd, "if you couldn't further your education and become a professional person, like a teacher or a doctor or a lawyer, the next step was to become a government worker. Of course, I couldn't see that. I took a number of odd jobs. I did a whole lot of things, because I had to work; so did my sister. We just took whatever was available to make money to help our parents."

"Somewhere along the line," she says, she got married, but as yet hadn't seriously considered a career in music. The marriage ended in divorce two years later and, says Shepherd, "she got sick of the way of life in Washington; it was very limited. You couldn't get a decent job; it had to be as a domestic or some very unsatisfying thing. And one day I got mad. I got tired of being treated like a second-class citizen. I said, 'To hell with this. I can play the piano. I can be independent.' I took a lot of little jobs so I could save up my money, and in the back of my mind I was always thinking about coming to New York and trying to carve out some kind of career."

Shepherd finally went to New York in the early forties. "I have to laugh at this," she says. "I thought I was a *terror* on the piano, and I really thought I was gonna make it that way, but I didn't." As soon as she arrived, several knowledgeable agents advised her to sell herself as a singer/pianist. "And I said, 'Well, I can't sing. I don't know the lyrics to two songs.' And they said, 'Well, lie about it, like everybody else does.' So I lied and they got me jobs. I'd last two nights and get fired. I'd last three nights and get fired. Finally they booked me into the Hickory House, and I was really following some heavy stuff, because they had two great gals there—Hazel Scott, who was a big name, and Deloyd McKay.

"The Hickory House had three bosses, and I got fired by all three. There was always one that would be sympathetic and take me back, and that's where I served my apprenticeship in a way, because I made myself sing. I thought I was terrible, but it seemed to sell. So I wound up singing at the Hickory House fourteen months, and, of course, you make connections and you get the exposure, and little by little I got a foothold."

Eventually Shepherd got a job on 52nd Street, playing at the Three Deuces. "They had giants there—Art Tatum's trio with Slam Stewart and Tiny Grimes, and Ben Webster with his group, so you know that was some heavy company. The owners put me in between them. I was just window dressing. They thought I was young and cute and I'd do to sit up there till Tatum finished his beer or Ben Webster felt like going on." Shepherd was also working as a stand-up singer on a WMCA radio show (where she stayed for two years), and she decided that singing was what she really wanted to do. So, she started taking lessons.

"I was doing very well," she says, "but you can't stay still; you gotta travel, and the road can be awfully rough and depressing, especially for a singer. It's all right if you're traveling with a band or a group, but to be out there as a single, it's a kind of lonely life. It's a disorganized life. You have to do everything yourself. I wasn't making the kind of money where I could have a traveling companion or secretary, like Pearl Bailey or Ella Fitzgerald or Sarah Vaughan. You got to press a dress on a bureau or find a decent place to eat the right kind of food. Every penny you make, you put right back into it or give it to the doctor. Of course, you take it in stride, because this is show business and this is what you want.

"But I ran into a lot of other problems that I just couldn't deal with. At that time, they just weren't ready for me. I didn't fit into any stereotype in looks, in voice, in manner, and this was true of many of my black sisters. I just wasn't a salable commodity as far as some of these owners were concerned. So I just bounced around doing this and doing that and coming back to this and coming back to that. I guess I was naïve enough to say, 'Well, the hell with all of you. I've got talent and I've got looks; I don't need to go to bed with you.' But that ain't the way it was, and it ain't that way now. And so I was just turned off with the compromises. I said, 'Norma, you can play piano and you can always work in New York.' And I sort of settled down. You could say I was a dropout by choice. Before, I'd had people pulling me fifteen different ways, which is the way it is when you become a struggling act."

Shepherd continued to work in small clubs throughout the fifties; the sixties, she says, were "very ordinary"; by the mid-seventies she was back working full time, in an East Side club where she continues to perform for a loyal and enthusiastic following. She is a great lover of professionalism, and credits this to her training as a stand-up singer. She also spends much of her spare time listening to other pianists—Tatum, Oscar Peterson, Erroll Garner, Tommy Flanagan, Ray Bryant. "And I've been listening very closely to a lot of the Duke Ellington piano," she says. "Wow! What piano! Once upon a time I used to listen to music as a whole, or if there was an instrument, like a tenor sax or piano or something, I would just sort of hear that. But now I can separate the whole voicing of it in my ear, and it's great.

"I think the owners who have hired us, I guess they're pretty smart. Maybe they're smarter than we are. They know they're getting two for one. They're getting a pianist and a singer, and some of us are damn good. You've got others who have gotten onto the fact that it makes them more employable if they play the piano and sing, and they can't even spell 'piano,' much less find the chords. They play enough chords to get by, and if the price is right, the owners will hire them anyway and shut somebody out who is really worthwhile. You've got a lot to contend with, but I don't let it bother me. My living has been consistent. As I said, I'm a dropout by choice. I'm not looking to send up no flares, and I know I'll never get rich. But if I can survive—and I think I'm a survivor—that's good enough."

Martha Young

(piano)

Martha Young, daughter of saxophone player Irma Young, has been playing piano professionally since the mid-forties. A school friend and contemporary of alto saxophonist Vi Redd, Young grew up in California and still performs mainly in the San Francisco area. Currently, her two greatest ambitions are to record and to work in Europe and Brazil.

Martha Young's childhood, she says, was "all music." Although Irma Young had quit playing alto sax by the time her daughter was born, Martha recalls hearing her play baritone sax and ukulele. "She even had the changes right," says Young. "She'd best to have 'em right, with Papa [her grandfather, Willis B. Young] listening. . . . I played piano. My older cousins, one played piano, one played trombone, one played trumpet, and the small [kids], like my brother Brownie and the youngest girls, played tambourine, and my grandmother played banjo. Papa played cornet. On Friday we'd have . . . it wasn't considered sessions, it was just a thing of family music." The family played church songs (they were Baptists and played for the congregation on Sundays), as well as songs composed by Willis Young. "Papa wrote a lot for the family," says Martha. "He wrote me 'Martha's March,' and we'd play a lot of [his] things and just have a good time."

At that time, the family was living in L.A., but one important member, Lester Young, was on the road. "Uncle Bubble—that's the family name for him and that's all I ever called him—he didn't live in Los Angeles, because he was with Basie's band and then he was with Jazz at the Philharmonic. The thing of him coming home was always like, there was gonna be a really hot time! I stayed up later when he was in town so that I could be with him." As a child, however, Martha never played the piano for him. "I would freeze at the piano," she recalls. "It was just a thing of him being who he was, and quite naturally, being my uncle, he was just that much bigger to me."

The elementary school Young attended had no pianos, and in order to keep up on her reading, she studied the alto sax. In junior high school she switched back to the piano. (Her grandfather, she says, was a "stickler for the beauty of the women in his family" and did not want her playing the sax.) By the time she was ten she was working professionally, playing for church teas and fashion shows, and once she was in high school she became a member of the school jazz band, playing campus club dances, and she also began to play for school functions. "We weren't making any money," she says, "but we were playing." During the war, she played at the Hollywood Canteen. "It was exciting," she remembers, "young kids seeing all the movie stars and playing for the servicemen."

"I came up in the bebop era," says Young, "and to me it didn't last long enough, so that's where my playing is. I play those tunes they played in that era, only with a different flavor, probably." Young also admires Mary Lou Williams, Hazel Scott, Erroll Garner, Herbie Hancock, and Oscar Peterson for his swing. "That's the way I like to play," she says; "I like it to swing, you know."

Her greatest influence was Art Tatum, always her "number-one man." "It fascinated me to see how he could play, and just be doing that with two hands. I must have been fourteen or fifteen years old, and coming from a musical family, it was very hard for me to slip into clubs like a lot of kids my age could do and not be recognized. [One time] Tatum['s trio] was playing in Hollywood, I think. It was a small club. Quite naturally, he'd start up and do a few trio numbers. Then they would announce that Tatum was getting ready to play solo and there would be *no drinks served*. And you could hear a pin drop. But they don't pay the artist that respect today. I mean, *then* they didn't have to be told not to talk while this man is playing. Automatically you didn't talk, or somebody might hurt you."

Martha Young has never worked outside the music field. "Living up here in this area I'm in now," she says, "I work over at Lanie College for the dance department, and I have my trio and my steady gigs. On Wednesday and Thursday I'm in a beautiful place out here on the Berkeley marina, and then on the weekend I'm over in San Francisco.

"I don't feel that it's necessary to express that I'm a woman musician when you can *see* that I'm a woman musician. There's one thing I get very tired of hearing, and I guess I've just learned to accept and ignore it at this point; it's 'You play good for a woman.'" With most of her male colleagues, says Young, "we just go on and play. . . . My thing in playing is not how many notes I can play. I'm not into running up and down the piano and all that kinda mess. My grandfather used to always tell me that if you play something with a *beat*, the people will enjoy it because they can feel it, and I try to play with all the feeling that I have, to give to the people that have come to hear me. I feel the music and I love the music. I love what I'm doing."

In 1958, a year before he died, Martha finally invited Lester Young to hear her on a job. "I was working in Los Angeles with a group called Johnny Otis, and he [Lester] was here. That was his last performance in America, I believe—the Jazz at the Philharmonic, at the Hollywood

Bowl. I was working the night of the concert, and I finally got up enough nerve where I wanted him to hear me play. So I invited him down and he came, and Johnny let me do a trio thing without the rest of the group. I was sweatin' like a hog! You couldn't believe the water that was running off of me, 'cause he was right there by the stage, at the front table. But I had made up my mind, and I thought I was ready for him to hear me play. And when I got through and I went down to the table, Uncle Bubble told me, he says, 'Well, I've got to find a gig for my niece—*and* me!' And that was the last time I saw him, 'cause he died the following year. That has stuck and helped me to go through a lot of things that I go through in the music business. Somebody that you have some respect for and love can tell you something that'll carry you through life. I'll always remember [what he said that night] as I remember nothing else.

"I'm pushing hard that I don't stop playing. Quite naturally, I get mad, I get frustrated. There are a lot of people that I've heard recorded that I feel I can cut the mustard, too, if given a chance. God, is it ever frustrating. But it doesn't make me give up; it just makes me work that much harder—but I *am* getting tired."

In 1979 Martha Young went to New York for the first time, to be present when 52nd Street was named for Lester Young. "Papa Jo Jones took me around," she remembers. "I was just so excited. He took me to Jimmy Ryan's, and I sat in with Roy Eldridge. I had a ball. It took me a long time to come out of the clouds when I finally came back. My head was altogether different, music wise—not what I was playing, but *how* I was playing. Playing with Papa Jo and Roy, I stayed high off the music the whole time. I'd come in at five o'clock in the morning, which was a gas, and be back up at eight o'clock, 'cause I was only there for five days and I didn't want to miss seeing anything of New York."

"You can't give up," says Young. "I can't afford to. I've come too far, too long. And I feel that I have something to offer. And that is what I have to keep feeling. It's very easy to be negative in the world today, with all that's going on. Thank God for music!"

Jane Jarvis

(piano/organ/producer/composer)

"I learned very early that if I wanted to eat on a regular basis, I would have to forego the precious title of jazz musician," says Jane Jarvis. One of the few women who made an inroad into the production end of the business, Jarvis was a vice-president of the Muzak Corporation from 1963 to 1979 and has worked as a radio staff musician, as organist for the Milwaukee Braves and the New York Mets (BMI gave her an award for her musical contribution to the game of baseball), and as a jazz musician in numerous concerts and clubs. In 1979 she decided to give up her career behind the scenes and return to performing. Since that time, she has appeared with her own trio (which includes George Duvivier and Grady Tate), with such musicians as Roy Eldridge, Lee Konitz, Lionel Hampton, Bob Wilbur, Maxine Sullivan, and Helen Humes, with Clark Terry's big band, Ed Polcer's band at Eddie Condon's, as well as at the Pepsi and the Kool Jazz festivals. In concert, Jarvis is a witty, thoughtful, and imaginative player and will include in her program everything from Ellington to Irving Berlin, from "Onward, Christian Soldiers" to Latin tunes. Says Jarvis, "I like to hear interpolations, improvisations, new thinking."

Jane Jarvis was born in Indiana. Her father wrote commercial jingles as a sideline, and her early musical education, she says, was extremely good. "My first real brush with jazz on a professional basis was when I was a tiny little kid. My parents had taken me to a radio station in Gary, where they wanted me to be the accompanist for a children's program, of all things. I was supposed to play for all the little youngsters that were gonna come in to sing on this crazy little program." Jarvis herself was nine at the time. "All this took place in a hotel that had a ballroom right next to the radio station, so I went wandering in there, where a very famous—*then* famous—jazz musician was playing: Frankie 'Half-Pint' Jaxon. He was a regional musician, very big. So I went up to the pianist and asked if I could sit in with the band. Can you imagine the audacity? Well, they thought it was *funny* that a child would ask, particularly a little girl. So I sat down and played. The band was playing 'Avalon,' and I can remember asking them what key and everything, you know, 'cause it didn't matter to me. And I played and even took a couple of choruses. These fellows, you know, it just knocked them out. I can imagine how I would feel, even now, if some youngster was to come up! So then, having gotten by with that, every time a band would come to town, they'd herd me in there to play with them. That was the start of my jazz career."

Jarvis's first professional challenge came from, of all people, an unpopular Gimbel's floorwalker. Jarvis was playing in the store one Christmas when he approached her, saying, "You can't play 'Stomping at the Savoy,' can you?" When Jarvis boasted that she never used music and didn't need any because she knew thousands of tunes, he challenged her to play 10,000. When she'd gone through all the pop tunes she knew, Jarvis drew on Methodist hymns (which she'd learned from her mother), Catholic hymns (from her father), and even Czerny exercises. People began to bring her lists of songs, and the first recognizable phrase qualified as a tune. If the floorwalker remained unsatisfied and challenged her further, Jarvis made up a bridge (middle section), and in the end she emerged victorious.

When Jarvis was thirteen, her parents were killed in a train accident. "I was terrified when I was a youngster," she says, "because it was really scary times. I had no family, and it was imperative that I had income. There was no place for me to go home to." Winning scholarships, Jarvis continued with her education, attending Bush Conservatory, Chicago Conservatory, and DePaul University School of Music, and she began to make her living through her music. "Even when I was fifteen and sixteen I was writing arrangements; so, if I couldn't play, I'd write for somebody. Also, the fact that I could play organ helped a lot. If I couldn't find a job on piano, there was one on organ. When I was growing up, many of the hotels would have organs in their bars. These are rooms that you'll find trios in now, but then they put in organs, because they only had to hire one musician, and so I really had the pick of these jobs. And then, after my job was over, I'd go out and jam with other musicians to keep my hand in."

In those years, Jarvis was hearing bands like Benny Goodman, Fletcher Henderson, Charlie Barnet, and Lucky Millinder, and she credits pianist Jess Stacy as a strong influence, one who taught her to "lay back" and give the other instruments a chance. She had also taken to the road, playing in hotels all over the country, but she quickly found out that there was little glamor in that life. The places that "tolerated" jazz were often unsavory, and on some jobs, union scale was only nineteen dollars a week, for playing nine to one on weekdays and nine to two on Saturdays. During these early years, says Jarvis, the prejudice was not so much because of one's sex as because of the music itself, and both she *and* the male musicians were equally the victims.

Mary Lou Williams and Norma Teagarden were two of the most important female pianists Jarvis knew of in the Midwest. "There were lots of fine female musicians that played out there," she says, "but they were stylists; they weren't all-around musicians, see, which limited them as to the kinds of jobs they did." For these women, there were no options in other areas of the business, and there were few clubs in which to work. "So their names didn't surface," Jarvis says. "I *know* there must be hundreds of them."

At another point in her career, Jarvis worked in Chicago. She found more women working in that city's community of radio- and TV-studio musicians, but, she recalls, they could be of little help to one another. "There was no way. There were so precious few jobs that if you heard of one, you weren't about to share it, I'm ashamed to say, but that's the truth of the matter. There was nothing to recommend anybody to. Remember, when I took jobs in radio and television, I wasn't taking another woman's job, I was taking a man's job. And the only reason I got them was because I played two instruments well, I could transpose or sight-read anything, and could arrange. There weren't too many men that could do that."

If there was any feeling against her, says Jarvis, it was not overt. "I think they just accepted the fact that I was able to do it. If they could have found somebody else that could have done it better, you may be sure I wouldn't have gotten it."

"Life never lets you completely control what you're doing," says Jarvis, but one decision she did make was to stay away from the all-woman bands. "I wanted to be accepted as a musician, not a female musician, a young or an old musician, not white or black. And I knew that once you got into playing with all-woman bands, you were tagged." She also objected to the fact that the leaders received the publicity, while the women in the band were unrecognized.

In the early sixties, Jarvis moved to New York. She had been with NBC in Chicago and Milwaukee and had been given a courtesy job as rehearsal pianist for "The Tonight Show." Just out of a marriage, with two young children to support, she soon joined the Muzak Corporation, and went on to become one of the leading producers in the industry. "I went through the back door. I became a producer that hired all these people," she says, referring to the many male musicians who would never hire her. "Isn't that wild? If you can't make it one way, you do it another."

At Muzak, Jarvis handled A&R, helped select players for the dates, directed engineers at the sessions, supervised the mix and sequence, and, to some degree, planned the cover material and notes. After sixteen years, she decided to resign and concentrate on her own work as composer and performer. A member of ASCAP (with three hundred recorded compositions), Jarvis also owns two publishing companies, one with her son, drummer Brian Jarvis.

"It would be foolish to say that there isn't still a big task for women to overcome. The jobs in music are limited, and there are more men qualified than there are women, and they're entrenched in the minds of men who are the heads of business and hire men. It's going to take a long period of education. You would think that because there isn't a single recording musician in New York of any stature that hasn't either worked for me or that I haven't been associated with somehow or other, now that I'm playing, I would be very busy in the studios. Such is not the case." Once a woman steps out of her usual "role," says Jarvis, it becomes more difficult to be accepted. "The men are there, and I would only be called upon if there was some kind of hand-holding thing that I could do, a *quid pro quo*, and there isn't. (She is called upon to play the organ, however, and says that women will be called in to play the traditional strings, flutes, or harps, but rarely other instruments.)

"Now I'm situated where I can plan my new career. I don't want to give [anyone] the false notion that I'm rich, because I'm not. But I'm just comfortable to the point where I can really be selective. I'm planning my career just as if it were somebody else's. . . . Somewhere along the line, there'll come a road for me to take. This is the way it has always happened for me in the past. The only difference now is that I'm not waiting for it to happen; I'm planning it. It's an incredible situation to be in, and I'm very happy about it. And I know I'm gonna make it work, 'cause everything else I've done I've made work. There's no reason why I can't do it this time."

In 1943, two of the major new vocalists of the forties started singing with big bands: Newark-born Sarah Vaughan joined Earl Hines; and Dinah Washington began a three-year tenure with Lionel Hampton.

Vaughan, who was also a pianist, "brought to jazz singing a kind of musical literacy which before her arrival was rarely found in singers of her genre," one critic noted at the time. "Musicians admire her for her almost uncanny ability to suggest harmonic changes in a song by inserting subtle alterations of the melody, for her facile phrasing, her silken soprano sound and her startling capacity to reach a high note without apparent effort and hit it squarely and accurately" (IJS). Writing about Vaughan's early years with the Hines band, Leonard Feather noted: "Sarah's own influence as a musician is not to be discounted. Many were the nights when she would sit around at the piano after the dance was over, working out new ideas."[22]

By 1944, Vaughan was working with Billy Eckstine's bop big band, with such musicians as Dizzy Gillespie, Charlie Parker, trombonist/arranger Gerald Valentine, Budd Johnson, Clyde Hart, and Oscar Pettiford. (The first of its kind, within its first six months the band had become the highest paid black band in the country.) After some early record dates—"I'll Wait and Pray" with Eckstine, "Lover Man" with Gillespie, and her own session with Tadd Dameron on "If You Could See Me Now"—Vaughan began to gain recognition when she started working on 52nd Street. By the mid-fifties she had become, and has remained, a seminal singer in the worlds of both jazz and popular music.

Dinah Washington (born Ruth Jones in Tuscaloosa, Alabama) started working as a single after she left Lionel Hampton. "The lusty-voiced young woman with a passion for comic books and tailored suits had come up when America was practically denuded of women blues singers of any stature," *Ebony* reported. "In a brief and bitter ten years, she struggled up from the obscurity of tiny churches and dingy dance halls to her present position as the nation's number one interpreter of the blues."[23]

Washington was touted as the first eligible successor to Bessie Smith, and her rural audiences, said *Ebony*, received her as they did the earlier blues women, "with a fervor akin to worship." By the middle of the decade, with songs like "Blowtop Blues" and "I Love You Yes I Do," she had helped to establish the music known as rhythm and blues and, along with Bull Moose Jackson, T-Bone Walker, and Wynonie Harris, was one of its most important singers. Washington was also one of the few women to run her own booking agency, Queen Attractions. During her later years, she captured audiences with her blues-tinged renditions of pop tunes like "What a Difference a Day Makes," and *Dinah Washington: The Jazz Sides* (EmArcy) showcases the singer doing more jazz-influenced vocals (and also features some arrangements by Melba Liston). As Washington's tempestuous life had frequently been the subject of headlines and news items, so, sadly, was her death: The charismatic performer died suddenly in 1963 from an accidental overdose of sleeping pills and barbiturates.

In 1948 another singer joined Lionel Hampton's band after winning an amateur-night contest. Like Billie Holiday, Detroiter Betty Carter was influenced mainly by the horns. "It was actually Charlie Parker and those guys who really kicked me in my behind and made me move," she told an interviewer. "That music was so strong."[24] With Ella, Billie, and Sarah ("it" when she was coming up), Carter had to search for her own vocal path. She found it, and has been following it so faithfully from then till now that she is considered by many today virtually the only pure jazz singer.

Other voices of the forties were Peggy Lee (with Benny Goodman), Anita O'Day (with Gene Krupa), Jackie Cain (who was singing with Roy Kral in Charlie Ventura's band), Helen O'Connell (with Tommy Dorsey), Rosemary Clooney (with Tony Pastor), Etta Jones (with Buddy Johnson), Buddy's sister, Ella Johnson (who in 1945 was the first to record and score a hit on one of her brother's tunes, "Since I Fell for You"), Helen Merrill, Kay Starr, Margaret Whiting, and Ella Mae Morse.

And then there was another young singer in Detroit—like Betty Carter, profoundly influenced by the music of Charlie Parker. This was singer Sheila Jordan.

Sheila Jordan

(vocalist)

Sheila Jordan takes the risks other singers never dream of. "She scares you at first," said one critic, "when you hear her stretch or bend a note through an octave and a half of variations, until taking it triumphantly to resolution."[25] Said another: "No matter how wild the shifts and turns or how emotional, you are always aware of the keen musical intelligence honed over years of study and practice . . . she is incapable of a false step or a wrong note."[26]

Yet Jordan does not settle for technical subtlety and range alone; rather, she relies upon her instrumentalist's instincts and what Charlie Parker called her "million-dollar ears" to pilot her, to set her free, as she turns songs inside out, taking her listeners to the bottom line of raw emotion. "[Her] ballad performances . . . are simply beyond the emotional and expressive capabilities of most other vocalists," said Robert Palmer (*The New York Times*, October 23, 1980), "and reveal a finely focused intonation and attention to decorative nuance worthy of an Indian raga singer. She can be so heart-wrenching that conversations stop cold, and breathless listeners hang on her every inflection."

Jordan may sing words set to Charlie Parker lines that turn into scat-chorus gold; she may do silken, deeply plummeting ballads, original material by Steve Kuhn (with whom she works in the Steve Kuhn/ Sheila Jordan Quartet), or the poetry of Robert Creeley set to music. The common denominator is (and always has been) her reverence for the music and her refusal to touch any song she "does not feel." It is this tender, searing honesty, coupled with her impeccable craft, that has made Jordan what a third critic has called "quite simply, one of the most daring and highly individualistic stylists performing in jazz today."[27]

Sheila Jordan was born in Detroit. Her mother, only sixteen at the time, married Jordan's father the same night her daughter was born. Jordan was raised by her grandparents in the coal-mining area near South Fork, Pennsylvania; her eleven aunts and uncles, she says, were more like her siblings.

Summerhill (the town where she grew up), Jordan says, was impoverished, both culturally and economically. "There was nothing for young people to do; there was nothing for *old* people to do. They worked in the coal mines or steel mills. Once a year, maybe, they'd have a picnic, you know, but there was nothing else to do. So you'd swim in the sulphur creek, but there were no outlets as far as movies or plays or things like that. We didn't know what that was. My grandfather hunted. He went out hunting and caught deer, squirrel. We even ate porcupine. We grew up very hard. I think that I knew at a very early age one of the reasons I would never stop working at a menial job [Jordan still holds a nine-to-five office job at a New York advertising agency] and struggle for music is because there was a lot of struggling when I was coming up. One thing I promised myself when I was a child, I said, 'I'm never gonna go without regular food, I'm never gonna go without heat, I'm never gonna go without water in my house.' Even though I could survive out in the woods tomorrow, I told myself that if at all possible, I would like to have the luxuries of always being able to have *a* meal, food on the table, and a roof over my head."

The two strongest forces in Jordan's childhood were religion and music. Her grandfather, of American Indian descent, believed in God but not in the church, and her grandmother had been raised as a Catholic, as had Jordan and her siblings. "As a child, I liked the church," she says, "because it was warm. I used to go in there and keep warm in the winter. I used to feel I was a sinner because of never having anything as a kid. A lot of times we didn't have food. A lot of times we didn't have clothing. And seeing my brothers all in the coal mines, and seeing so many people in the town dying from coal-mining blasts—we saw so many terrible things as kids . . . I think the church gave me strength. If I hadn't believed in God, I don't know if I'd have survived. I knew that there was something else out there, and swore I was not gonna become a coal miner's wife."

"We used to always sing," says Jordan. "Singing to us was a form of release from the pain and suffering that everybody went through." She sang at PTA meetings, in local beer gardens (learning pop tunes from borrowed copies of *Hit Parade* or on neighbors' radios), on occasional radio spots, and at school. Because her classmates heckled her so mercilessly about her singing, she finally quit singing there altogether. The church, she says, was the only place where people left her alone—but she was never permitted to sing in church. "In the church, I never felt I would be harassed by the other kids, but they *never* used women singers, young girl singers; they used male singers and an all-male choir. I found that very prejudiced, even as a young kid—very upsetting."

Jordan never studied music formally. "We had mountains, and you could go to certain points on certain mountains and sing and get your echo. I used to do a lot of that; not yodeling—I never knew how to yodel—but I used to love to just hear my voice, sing out and then hear it come back and sing over it. I used to hear birds, too—their whistling. I can still do that, and try to write down the intervals they're singing."

Jordan is sure that even if she had not heard jazz, she would have become a singer anyway, probably singing country; but, at about the age of ten, she made an important discovery. "I had gone to visit my mother in Detroit," she remembers, "and I traded this kid a record. It was a 78, and I think it was Count Basie or Ellington. I took it back to Pennsylvania. We didn't always have electricity, but we had one of those windup Victrolas, and I worked on that thing for days and got it to work. I heard this music and I knew it was special—I just knew it."

During her first year of high school, Jordan left Pennsylvania to live in Detroit with her mother. "That was *very* heavy," Jordan says, "because she had a drinking problem, but at least by going to live with her, I got turned on to jazz. I got turned on to jazz from this jukebox downstairs in the hamburger place"—an integrated establishment, which, says Jordan, was rare in Detroit at that time. "They had all of these fantastic artists: Charlie Parker and his Reboppers, Billie Holiday, Dizzy Gillespie. They even had early Sarah Vaughan—early, early Sarah—Count Basie, Duke Ellington, Louis Armstrong." Of them all, Charlie Parker got to the young Jordan most. "I said, 'This is gonna be my mission in life.' Charlie Parker was like my musical Christ or guru. Through his music, I learned everybody else's music. He took me back to musicians such as Lester Young, Ben Webster, Coleman Hawkins, and Billie Holiday. In later years, after I got to know him, he turned me on to new composers like Stravinsky and Bartok. He turned me on to dance, plays, books, paintings."

Jordan felt an immediate and intense rapport with this music that had grown up in the black world. "I fed from what the music was about. It nourished me spiritually. I started going to black hangouts—that's where the music that I wanted to do was. I would fake my birth certificate and sometimes I would get in. They had the Graystone Ballroom, and they did have an interracial club that did not sell alcoholic beverages where young people would hang out. . . . I always knew the plight of the black person through being poor myself, and I felt a complete acceptance from them. I felt the need to be part of what they were. I wanted to *be* black. I wasn't happy being what I was. I didn't want the cops botherin' me all the time or school principals telling me I should hang out with white students. I couldn't understand that. I started to doubt white people with authority." (When she challenged one of her teachers, she never got an answer, she remembers.) "This was my first introduction into prejudice from the black standpoint. If you were in a car with some black people, they [the police] wanted to know where you were from, where you were born, how old you were, and where you were going. I was constantly down in the police station being searched. They could never believe that here was a bunch of young people hanging out together that loved this music and that were learning from [it]. And I was determined that I wasn't gonna let anybody tell me who I could hang out with. I wasn't gonna live in the kind of world I had lived in when I was a kid."

Soon Jordan discovered two fellow Bird "freaks," singers Skeeter Spight and Leroy Mitchell. "One night I asked them if I could sing with them," she recalls. "I was very, very aggressive and I think I'd had some drinks. We [became] a group then. We never made any money, but we were always sitting in, writing words for Bird tunes. I learned a lot from Skeeter and Mitch. We had one thing in common: We *loved* Bird and we *loved* Billie. We loved that music, and we all loved each other. We were persons, colorless, with nothing on our mind but to educate ourselves and learn this beautiful, beautiful music." In its day, the trio was unique, predating Lambert, Hendricks, and Ross.

"In jazz, my training was through Bird," Jordan says, "because I listened to his music constantly. I learned every line. I learned all of his solos. It was like a precious gift from God for me to hear this music, and the thought of being able to utter just two notes out of a whole thing made me feel marvelous. So I got a pretty good conception of where chord changes were. Yeah, I can hear pretty good."

Right after high school, Jordan moved to New York—and "went lookin' for Bird." She first tried to find him through Duke Jordan, his piano player, whom she eventually married. "I spent a lot of time supporting Duke, or trying to at least, and not doing very much about my own music," she says. "Once I left Detroit, I left the trio, and once I left the trio, I wasn't doing any of my own singing. There was just no place for me to do it. I would sing with Duke once in a while—not often—and I would have sessions at the loft that I got for us on 26th Street in Manhattan."

At the suggestion of Charlie Mingus, Jordan began to study with pianist Lennie Tristano and to attend his loft sessions to hear such players as Warne Marsh and Lee Konitz. The studying ended when her daughter, Traci, was born; two years later, so did her marriage. Jordan hired a baby-sitter and took an office job. "I only worked half a day, because I didn't want to be away from the baby all day. That was just enough to keep my rent paid, and I went around trying to get some gigs in clubs, but it was very heavy, especially as a woman. In the regular bars and clubs, you'd go to the club owners and they'd see a woman so they'd want to make a scene with you, and that's just never been my style. So, unfortunately, I didn't work very many clubs; I would do sessions. Another thing that always bothered me was, if somebody would try to get a gig in a club somewhere, they [the male owners] wouldn't say 'What does she sing like?' [They] would always say, 'Well, what does she *look* like?' "

Finally, Jordan got a job at the Page Three in Greenwich Village. "That's basically where I started working out the music, the songs that I wanted to do. I still sing the way that I did then; it's not changed at all, except maybe it's stronger. I'd always been into scat singing, because when I sang with the trio, we didn't do anything *but* scat singing, and I had the straight-ahead tunes and the swing tunes from when I was a kid. I really worked on my confidence, which I had to get together because I was just so knocked down from a lot of things that had happened to me in the interim."

While she was at the Page Three, Jordan also began to meet some of the musicians with whom she would work later on: Steve Kuhn, Herbie Nichols, Jack Reilly, Steve Swallow, George Russell. When Russell first heard her sing, he wanted to know where she came from to sing the way she did. Jordan took him back to Pennsylvania with her, to the coal mines, where life had become even more difficult because of strikes and the increasing use of oil. Jordan and her grandmother took Russell to one of the beer gardens. One old miner asked if she still sang "You Are My Sunshine," a song she used to sing as a kid. "No," said Jordan, "I don't sing that anymore." "Well, could you sing it now?" the miner asked. "Yeah, let's hear that," said Russell. "So my grandmother went over and played the piano and I sang," Jordan recalls. "And George Russell, after seeing the coal mine and seeing the miners, came back and arranged this twelve-minute musical documentary on 'You Are My Sunshine' for the miners, because he saw they were all out of work and the conditions were very bad."

"Sunshine" was recorded for Riverside Records in 1963, and first released on a George Russell album titled *Outer View*. It "was quite startling when people first heard it," says Jordan of this devastating evocation of Appalachia. In the liner notes to *George Russell: Outer Thoughts* (Milestone), a 1975 collection of Russell's early-sixties work, Bob Palmer comments: "Sheila's three choruses build to a pitch of guileless emotion which is quite unlike anything else in the jazz of the period." Another '63 album, *Portrait of Sheila*, won her the attention of *down beat*, which voted her "singer deserving wider attention." A rave review by Don Heckman praised her singing as the finest since the last days of Billie Holiday, citing her rare ability—on such tunes as "If You Could See Me Now," "Laugh, Clown, Laugh," "Dat Dere," "When the World Was Young," and "Falling in Love with Love"—to "draw her audience into a world that is completely her own, to reach them with an emotional impact that is devastatingly personal."[28] Still, little work followed the recording.

When Jordan left the Page Three, she thought she was doing "pretty well. I figured life was pretty good to me by this point, even if I wasn't working very much. The only bad thing about working in a nightclub steady like that is you're tired and you find yourself getting into the habit of drinking. It starts off with one drink to lift you up; but, after eight years, by the time I left that club I was pretty heavy into drinking."

"I did slip," Jordan says in retrospect. "But I also feel that if I hadn't slipped, I wouldn't know what evils are lurking out there to do a number on me. I've had a lot of strength and I've had a lot of encouragement, but I've never really leaned heavy on anybody. I've worked very hard at being strong."

"I'm not as confident as I want to be," says Jordan, "but it's getting better." (As early as 1963, Nat Hentoff noted that Jordan had always had the ultimate confidence: "refusal to compromise."[29]) With this refusal to compromise, she has maintained her artistic integrity, in spite of frustrating times when she was not getting work. At those times she sang in churches, doing jazz liturgies by such composers as Paul Knopf and Jack Reilly, and she continues to do so on occasion.

By the seventies, Jordan found increasing opportunities to perform her music for audiences here and in Europe, and in 1976, '77, and '80, she was, ironically, once again voted in *down beat* the singer most deserving of greater recognition. In 1979–80 she sang at the New York Salutes to Women in Jazz, and in 1980 she performed at the Kool Jazz Festival.

Jordan works most frequently with Steve Kuhn (piano), Harvie Swartz (bass), and Bob Moses (drums). She does not consider herself a singer with a trio; rather, the group is made up of four individuals who "accompany each other and feed off of each other's musical vibes." Their album, *Playground*, was prepared this way: "I think of this album as one song; it's a suite." Of the album *Home* (Robert Creeley's poetry set to music by Steve Swallow), she says, "This is a whole new direction for me. It's a whole new approach to where the voice can place itself without just making sounds, nonlyrical sounds. I don't think it's ever been done before."

Her music, Jordan says, is also inextricably bound up with her womanhood. "I really admire women. I love their attitude. I love their strength. I love what they've been through and I love the way they support each other. I think of women like my grandmother, who had all of these children, who did all of her wash by boiling water on a stove that she chopped wood to heat, who would get up at five in the morning and start a fire so that she could boil water to put down the pump outside when it was frozen. Now, I don't call that a weak woman.

"But I'm not against singing sad, lost-my-man ballads, because that's also a part of my life. How can I cut off part of my life? I *love* those tragic ballads. I'd love to do an album of just tragic ballads. Nobody would buy it, I'm sure, but I wouldn't care.

"I think that my music—or the way I interpret what I sing—speaks of a woman who's never had anybody but herself. The only things I have are music and my daughter. The music's there and it's a part of me. It's like my arm. It's part of my body. When I go, that goes. . . . I was walking down the street the other day and I said to myself, 'My God, I'm over half a century old, and I've had a lot of bad things happen to me and I've had a lot of good things happen to me, but I know one thing: I've never wanted to be anybody else. That must mean I'm proud of myself. I must be proud of myself as a woman and also as a human being. And I really feel kind of happy today!' And it was nice to feel that way. Maybe a lot of it has to do with the fact that all of a sudden I'm singing a little bit more than I used to. Sometimes I'd wait a whole year to sing. Singing in Europe and churches here eliminated a lot of that tremendous need to express myself. And every year it gets a little better.

"I'll just try to live the rest of my life out as gently as I can. I don't want to get too excited about anything anymore, and I want to enjoy everything I do from now on musically, and just hope that I can keep singing and bringing people pleasure or whatever they get out of it. I don't want to be a star (not that I think I ever could); I just want to do my music. I know that in ten years I'll be sixty-two years old, and when I'm sixty-two I'm gonna get Social Security so I can leave my office job. By the time I'm sixty-two, unless they don't have Social Security anymore, I'll be able to do nothing but music. I'm not goin' anywhere; I'm gonna stay with it. I don't think I'll lose my voice. And I'm open to any kind of music that I can feel—as long as it's jazz!

"There's two things I'm eternally grateful for: that's that I was given this wonderful gift of expression, and that I was given it through a woman's body and mind."

THE FIFTIES

With the end of World War II, American women were once again told that their most important role was domestic. Matrimony soared, the baby boom began, female altruism and self-sacrifice were equated with love, and a return to traditional roles was embraced by everyone in the name of "normalcy." By the early fifties, sex symbols, glamor, and the Doris Day heroine were also a part of the feminine package. "Creative homemaking" was expected to provide enough of an outlet for women's creative impulses, but motherhood was still presumed to be their sole source of true fulfillment. So widespread was this belief that after children had grown, depression in middle-aged women was universally attributed to the departure of the brood, and was named by sociologists the "empty-nest syndrome." During the fifties, wrote Georgia Dullea, "mothers rarely admitted to feelings of joy, much less relief, in the empty nest period."[1] In the same article, sociologist Lillian Rubin further elucidated the situation: "There was a lot of guilt about the relief women felt when children left, but that couldn't be expressed in an atmosphere that didn't encourage expression."

As the decade went on, the employment rate of married women increased (as did the divorce rate), but women were not supposed to earn more than or even as much as their husbands, only enough to supplement the primary family income. Nor were they supposed to derive any personal satisfaction or growth from a job, as this would clearly be threatening to the family structure. State laws, for the most part, backed the double standard: By 1959, twenty states had equal-pay laws on the books, but only in seven of these states did the laws call for equal pay for men and women alike; in the other thirteen states, women's salaries were required to be equal—but only to those of other women.

During the 1950s it was clear that instead of staying out all night blowing their own horns, women were expected to be like June Allyson in *The Glenn Miller Story* (1954): self-sacrificing, patiently waiting mates. (Interestingly, this film, set in wartime America, conveyed more of a fifties message than many of the films made during the war years, when Hollywood brought competent, independent heroines to the screen.) In 1957, a survey taken in a college class on general psychology (103 men and 86 women) looked at the effects of sex roles engendering inferiority and passivity on women's goals, achievements, and self-image. One of its findings reflected, in microcosm, the prevailing attitudes of much of American society in general: Both performing and composing jazz were seen by these students as "masculine" pursuits, compared with ballet, reading, or listening to eighteenth-century music, which were considered "feminine."[2] When asked to rank eight musical activities in order of "femininity," the men and women alike viewed jazz as the least feminine, each group placing listening to it seventh, and performing it eighth. When it came to musical preferences, the men listed listening to jazz first and performing it third, while the women listed listening to it second and performing it eighth. Their interest in jazz was there, but, clearly, for these women active participation in the music was still far from a realistic option.

Working against the fifties tide, new female jazz talent nevertheless emerged. On keyboard, there was the gifted Detroit pianist Bess Bonnier; Massachusetts-born Barbara Carroll, classically trained but influenced early by the piano playing of Nat King Cole, was one of the most popular new pianists (and an early exponent of bop); another Detroiter, Terry Pollard, played piano and vibes and worked in a duo with Terry Gibbs from 1953 to 1957; organist Shirley Scott joined Eddie "Lockjaw" Davis's group in 1956, and, with her roaring energy and subtle delicacy on the instrument, has been at the forefront of jazz organists ever since.

Two women from abroad also appeared on the American jazz scene in the 1950s: One was German-born Jutta Hipp, who worked at the Hickory House in New York (but eventually disappeared from the jazz world); the other was the young Toshiko Akiyoshi. Born in Manchuria and raised in Japan, by the early fifties Akiyoshi was playing in coffeehouses and on Japanese television, and listening to all the jazz she could—Harry James, Gene Krupa, Teddy Wilson, and Bud Powell, the pianist who more than anyone else influenced her early style. By 1956 she was the highest-paid free-lance arranger and studio musician in the country; that year, receiving a scholarship to Berklee College of Music in Boston, she came to America, worked four nights a week at George Wein's Storyville Club in Boston, and made her debut at the 1956 Newport Jazz Festival. "In the early years in America," she told Leonard Feather in an interview, "I dealt with both racial and sexual prejudice. I played clubs and TV wearing a kimono, because people were amazed to see an Oriental woman playing jazz."[3] In 1959 she married saxophonist Charlie Mariano, with whom she worked into the sixties. (By the early seventies, with her second husband, saxophonist Lew Tabackin, Akiyoshi would go on to form one of the most outstanding big bands in jazz.)

Among vocalists, Carmen McRae began to gain recognition as a major jazz singer in the 1950s; Teddi King came out of Boston to work with George Shearing and continued as a single up until her death in 1978; Berbara Lea began to record; Long Island-born Della Griffin—with a voice uncannily like Billie Holiday's—sang with an all-female singing group, the Delltones, and later became a drummer as well; and the innovative Jeanne Lee began to work with pianist Ran Blake. A compelling newcomer, Michigan-born Lodi Carr, was singing around Detroit and New York, and in the liner notes of her "refreshingly candid debut album" (*Lady Bird*) Nat Hentoff noted that she sang "directly, musically, and with a sound and style of her own." (After her son was born in 1961, Carr devoted most of her energy to her family, but since 1979 has come back to music full-time.)

The dynamic Dakota Staton rose to prominence after *down beat* voted her the most promising new vocalist of 1955. Sarah Vaughan and Ella Fitzgerald were both adding more popular music to their repertoires (in 1955, Fitzgerald had begun her monumental series of American Songbooks), and Billie Holiday, by this time, was performing and recording some of her most chilling and affecting work.

As had been true in previous decades, the fifties were especially difficult for female instrumentalists. A number of social and musical factors militated against them. The wartime attitude that had fostered praise and support for working women who'd "pitched in" in time of crisis had been suddenly reversed, and now, more than ever, women were supposed to cook only in the kitchen, leaving the paying instrumentalist jobs free for the men. This deeply ingrained attitude was compounded by the decline of the big bands in general and the highly competitive job market. As the music moved out of the USO and dance halls into the small clubs and concert stages, women's opportunities for employment were drastically reduced; there were fewer places for them to work and, consequently, fewer of them "out there" to attract attention.

As the music departed more and more from the danceable, four-four beat (as it had begun to do in the forties), it branched out in a number of directions: the "cool" and modal music of Miles Davis; the more intellectual, experimental sounds and tempos of such West Coast musicians as Dave Brubeck; the jazz and classical synthesis of the "third-stream" Modern Jazz Quartet; and the hard bop of such players as Horace Silver, Art Blakey, and Fats Navarro, who returned to the black and gospel roots of the music. In the black world, notes Michele Wallace, during the fifties calm before the storm, jazz was the single refuge, and "it was more resistant to the dominant culture than ever."[4]

In the American mainstream, with jazz increasingly sophisticated and undanceable, the way was open for something new to propel the youth onto the dance floors. In 1954, Bill Haley had a smash hit on the theme song from the movie *Blackboard Jungle*. The song "Rock Around the Clock" for the first time blended elements of country-and-western music with elements of rhythm-and-blues (and because of the black R&B influence, Haley recalled, some radio stations refused to air the song). But the number filled the bill. By the time Elvis Presley recorded "Hound Dog" in 1956—a song that had been an R&B hit for Big Mama Thornton long before Presley ever heard it—rock-'n-roll (with its rhythm-and-blues retentions) had become the principal dance music of American youth.

Despite the unpropitious musical climate and highly repressive atmosphere of the fifties, some of the women who had worked in the big bands of the forties, as ever, went against the customs and mores of the day and were able to work in or lead their own small units. Leaders Vi Burnside, Tiny Davis, and Flo Dreyer all accomplished this; Beryl Booker had an excellent trio on 52nd Street, with Elaine Leighton on drums and Bonnie Wetzel (formerly with Ada Leonard and Tommy Dorsey) on bass; and Hetty Smith recalled the formation of another women's group in 1952: "I was contacted by Myrtle Young," she says, "alto saxist with the former Darlings of Rhythm, who had formed a sextet in Philly to play mainly the eastern-seaboard night spots. Out of the group was born the sensational Four Jewels—Willene Barton, tenor; Regina Albright, pianist; Gloria Bell [Coleman], bassist and vocalist; and myself on drums."

The bandleaders of the thirties and forties also continued to work. Ina Ray Hutton turned to television and, on her own program, led a more commercial band with such players as Jane Sager and Audrey Hall. Ada Leonard was leading an all-woman band in the early fifties, but when she came back in 1955, after a brief retirement, she did so with male personnel, explaining in *down beat* that there were so few first-rate female players around, they could name their price and get it, but it was more than she could afford. Besides which, "top-notch" female musicians did not like to work in "all-girl bands. They like to feel that they've been hired not because of their looks or sex appeal, but because they are good musicians."[5]

Longtime Sweethearts leader Anna Mae Winburn also remained active, touring the country with smaller Sweethearts units that featured such fine players as Eileen Chance on bass, Lorraine "Jazz" Walsh on piano, Jean Davis on trumpet, and Willene Barton on tenor. While Winburn continued to take racially mixed groups into the South during the mid-fifties, Eddie Durham recalls that, due to increasing racial tension, the units he was involved with had by that time begun to trade players, sending black bands south and white bands north. In 1955 Durham took a five-piece women's band into the South on a package tour with Little Richard and a six-piece male band. But that, says Durham, was the last of the women's bands.

Recording activity for female instrumentalists had also diminished compared with the 1940s. In 1954 Leonard Feather arranged an MGM date that brought some women into the studio for a session set up as a "battle of the sexes" and released as *Cats vs. Chicks*. Personnel included Corky Hale, Mary Osborne, Beryl Booker, Terry Pollard, Elaine Leighton, Bonnie Wetzel, Urbie Green, Clark Terry, Lucky Thompson, Horace Silver, Kenny Clarke, Percy Heath, and Tal Farlow. Another woman who recorded around this time was Lillian Briggs, a singer, bandleader, and former trombone player with Joy Cayler's band. After her 1955 hit on the jump blues "I Want You To Be My Baby," Briggs continued as an entertainer, more in a rock-'n-roll than jazz vein.

A number of jazz artists had gone to Europe in the late forties and early fifties, and Paris was another site of recording activity for some American jazz women: Lil Hardin Armstrong recorded there, and Beryl Booker's all-woman trio worked with Don Byas, as did Mary Lou Williams. (The Booker/Byas and Williams/Byas sessions have been recently reissued on Inner City Records.) Williams, however, greatly disillusioned with the music world at this time, walked out of a Paris club one night in the early fifties and went into a period of retreat, devoting herself instead to the Catholic Church and to her own charitable organization, the Bel Canto Foundation, dedicated to helping musicians who had fallen on hard times. (By 1957, however, she was appearing with Dizzy Gillespie at the Newport Jazz Festival, and would soon come back to the music via her compositions for the church.)

As far as the press was concerned, a Leonard Feather column in *down beat* began to focus attention regularly on the talents and achievements (and struggles) of some of the women in the field. The series, titled "Girls in Jazz," offered profiles of such players as Corky Hale, Melba Liston, Ginger Smock, Norma Carson, and Beryl Booker. And in 1953 Nat Hentoff wrote one of the more enlightened contemporary pieces on the subject of women in jazz, prompted by the negative response of a music critic to the fact that a woman had been given a first chair with one of the symphony orchestras. This reaction, said Hentoff, was an example "of what a young psychologist friend of mine likes to call scathingly, 'male chauvinism.' The psychologist (who buys her own cigarettes and pays her own checks, thank you) points out that even enlightened males may intellectually admit women's right to social equality but emotionally, there is a strong yearning for the good old medieval days when the woman's place was wherever the man decided it was."[6]

Such insights were exceedingly rare at that time, however, and the old notions and prejudices still prevailed for the most part: No woman could be glamorous "with the mouthpiece of a saxophone between her pretty red lips, or while blowing her lovely face all out of shape playing a trumpet or trombone," Mrs. Xavier Cugat—that was how she was identified—told *down beat* readers;[7] and female entertainers, even *poor* ones, would always draw an audience, said *Metronome* in an article titled "Leave It to the Girls" (December 1956, p. 18), because the men would "look first, then listen."

In the early fifties, a new black publication, *Jet* magazine, appeared, and it brought to the black community information about many black artists and musicians—both female and male—who got no mention or recognition anywhere else. Anna Mae Winburn, Vi Burnside, Tiny Davis, and Myrtle Young, for example, were the subjects of a *Jet* cover story (February 1954, p. 60) titled "Why Girl Bands Don't Click" (a headline which, unfortunately, exemplified the type of negative publicity about which Winburn had complained). The article, however, despite its use of some of the inescapable clichés of the day, made several important points about why "no female band [could] boast of beating the all-girl orchestra jinx." "Some argue," the writer said, "that chief reasons are that the girls are usually long on looks and short on talent." If this were indeed the case, Sweethearts arranger Maurice King explained, romantic interest on the part of male backers was often one major reason why: "It is difficult to get a leader who is not more interested in the girl—as girls than as artists or musicians," he said. "Since many of the all-girl bands have been organized by men or are under their direction, [the male preference for romance over musicianship] is one of the big handicaps [faced by the all-woman bands]." Tiny Davis—who, according to the article, was forming an all-white group—also pointed out that "the lack of hit records [had] hurt girl bands."

As the decade drew to a close, Barry Ulanov posed the question in a *down beat* article, "Women in Jazz: Do They Belong?" (January 9, 1958, p. 17): "Is there a place in jazz for women as instrumentalists, not simply for pianists who lead trios two-thirds of which are male," not "women regarded as oddities" who play passable horn, but a real place for women "strictly on the basis of merit," not sex? The obstacles that had kept women out of the field for so long, he said, had hurt not only the women, but also the world of jazz in general. While his point was well taken, perhaps a more apt title than the misleading "Do They Belong?" would have been the question bassist Lucille Dixon had asked in the early forties about the classical field: "Will they let me in?"

That many women had been "killed off" or discouraged by prejudice and an unreceptive culture was something no one knew better than the women themselves. (Rarely, if ever, was that side of the story written about or even acknowledged.) Although the fifties were a particularly reticent "twilight" decade for American women in general—and, compared with the forties, for many women in jazz as well—nevertheless, the voices still came through.

As Maya Angelou wrote in *I Know Why the Caged Bird Sings*: "Bible say, 'He who can hear, let him hear. He who can't, shame on 'em.'"[8]

Willene Barton

(tenor saxophone/leader)

None of 'em was as good as Willene. Willene's got that tone that touches the soul for some reason. Ben Webster had it, and Lester had it, and Coleman Hawkins had it, and Hershal Evans had it. And Louis played it on his trumpet.

—Eddie Durham

Willene Barton began her career in the early fifties, playing with the small Sweethearts unit and various other all-woman small combos. Since then she has worked as leader of her own small groups and free-lanced as a jazz, disco, and commercial-big-band player.

After thirty years of full-time commitment to the business, and after winning the respect of such formidable musicians as Johnny Hodges and Charlie Parker, it is only within the past six years, since she played briefly with a group called the Jazz Sisters, that Barton has begun to get some of the publicity and critical recognition she deserves. As a result of her exposure with that group (led by pianist Jill McManus) and her appearances at such events as the Women's Jazz Festival in Kansas City and the Universal Jazz Coalition's Salute to Women in Jazz, Barton has now been reviewed by just about every major critic in New York, she says—"and each one has been *very* generous to me." For all the years before that, she adds, "I was playing in places where they didn't come."

The places where the critics "didn't come"—local dance halls, neighborhood clubs, and hotels and resorts both here and abroad—are the places where much of the history of women in jazz occurred. Barton continued to work in such places throughout the late sixties, when, despite the recession, "there were lots of clubs and lots of extra work." By 1972, however, the state of the art and the economy forced her to take a full-time day job. "It's a nothing job," she says, "but it keeps me going, and I don't have to worry about bills and things like that."

Barton can literally bring a house to its feet as she digs deeper and deeper into a solo, whether she's swinging into a raunchy/elegant ("gruffly rhapsodic") blues or a hard, biting, up tune like "Perdido," or swirling broadly into a ballad—"Tenderly," "As Time Goes By," "What Are You Doing the Rest of Your Life?" or one of the others she says she likes to play "after twelve o'clock at night."

"Attack and get the audience's attention right away," she says, "build until you feel it peak, and then make sure you go out screamin' the same way. Hit, play, and out, and it works."

Willene Barton was born in Oscilla, Georgia. When she was ten, her family moved to Long Island, and there she started studying the clarinet, influenced by an uncle who played the instrument. When she got to junior high school, she switched to tenor saxophone.

"During those days, as far as jazz was concerned, the tenor horn was it," she says. "There was Illinois Jacquet, Budd Freeman . . . Believe it or not, one of my favorite saxophone players was Freddy Martin. I learned a lot of melodic lines from him. I guess you wouldn't call him jazz. He plays strictly big tone and strictly melody. I listened to how he played. He was more like a society type, but I happen to like that. At that time, everything in jazz or swing was tenor. Bands were made or broken because they had a good tenor player."

Most of the music in Barton's home was church music, and her earliest experience playing was in the church. "I used to play when the choir sang; I played the same hymns on the saxophone." After high school, she opted without hesitation for the world of professional music over college. At that time the music offices on New York's 48th Street were where aspiring musicians congregated. Veterans like Eddie Durham and tenor man Walter "Foots" Thomas were headquartered there, and they had helped many young women break into the business. Barton studied with Thomas and teacher Louis Arfine, working with them to develop power and her sound. At some lessons she did nothing but just blow notes. "I wanted the biggest and fullest tone I could get, and to know how to control breath and that sort of thing. All of their students sound *big*, because no matter how brilliant in technique you are, if you don't sound good, it's empty." As for the myth that women were not strong enough to play horns, all players, says Barton, build up through practice. "The boys had to go through the same thing as I do. Naturally, I think there are a lotta guys who could never have the sound that I do. They may sound louder, but [they could never achieve] the quality and tone."

In 1952, Anna Mae Winburn was getting together another small Sweethearts unit to take on the road. "I came down and took an audition through Walter Thomas and Eddie Durham and all that bunch, and I got the job," Barton says. "*Couldn't* play, didn't know anything about structure or anything. I just played, and when I got tired I stopped. Didn't matter where it was. So I could end up in the channel [the bridge] and anywhere but where it was supposed to end up. Except for the ballads. I could always play those straight through.

"At that time it was an eight- or nine-piece band. We toured the South, Southwest, in shows, and then she broke the band down to about six pieces, and she was the singer, and we toured all over the United States with that. Which meant that I played from six to seven nights a week, and I was with first-rate musicians. The only novice in the whole band was me." The other women in the group were Eileen Chance on bass, Lorraine "Jazz" Walsh on piano, Maxine Fields on trumpet, and Pauline Braddy on drums. "It was heavy action!" Barton says. "That's where I learned to play, doing that *every* night. That was the best way to do it.

"The audiences were always tremendous. If the people hadn't received me as well as they did, I'm sure I wouldn't have stayed. There were always people like Eddie [Durham] around to help, so the people who gave you a hard time, it didn't matter. There were some people within the *band* who gave you a hard time, too, just because they were so far advanced they felt it was just ridiculous to be playin' with somebody who didn't know their way around the door. What makes me feel good is that years later they wanted me to give them a job."

The unit toured the country, sometimes staying out on the road as long as six months at a stretch. They traveled by bus, station wagon, or Cadillac limousine, sometimes going 500 miles between jobs. "It was tough, but very exciting," Barton says. "This was before integration. There were no hotels. Very often you had meals of cheese and crackers or whatever you could buy in a grocery store. In the South, the white girls would put on black makeup. . . . We went to the worst states in the union—Mississippi, Louisiana, Alabama. Once in Louisiana this policeman looked in the stage door and he said, 'Well, I don't know whether you are or not, but I suggest you get outta town right now.' We did. It was hard, sometimes dangerous, in a case like that. But we had a lot of fun with all this going on—we could still be in jail today.

"We had to really want to play to put up with all that, and we did. I'd never been anywhere but Georgia and Great Neck and Flushing. To me, it was great. Every night I got a chance to play, so that was it."

When Barton left the Sweethearts, she returned to New York. "I got my own group. Then I joined other groups." (One of these was an all-woman unit that Melba Liston led briefly in 1958 and that played to capacity audiences in Bermuda.) "For a woman to work all the time," says Barton, "if you don't get a job with other groups, you get your own band." Her groups were always made up of male musicians, with the exception of one time when she and the late Elsie Smith, who played saxophone with Lionel Hampton, teamed up with a male drummer and bass player.

"In the old days," Barton explains, "with the *guys*, it was like this: It was still the old chauvinistic kind of thing. I would sort of lay back and appoint one of the guys, let him call the numbers. That way it didn't seem that I was the overbearing female. I'd make it a group kind of thing; we'd all make decisions. That's how you had to work with those guys in those days. But then you had the responsibility of getting the job, and toward the end—the groups I had later—you had people you worked with, and if somebody gave them a couple of dollars more, they'd split. They didn't care how they left you, whether it was one day or one night or one hour before performance. You'd go on the road and you'd be responsible for these people. Being a leader is not glamorous at all; it's very hard, frustrating work. [But] if you wanna work, that's what you have to do."

Much of "making it" in the music world, says Barton, has to do with politics. "I find that this business of the American Dream, of studying hard, and if you have talent—that's not it. It's good to have it, but if you don't know the right people, you're just out, no matter how talented you are." As for managers and agents, "Oh, I had some dillies," she says. "All they wanted to do was to collect the ten percent and book me all kinds of strange places. Never a promotion like somebody says, 'I have a talent here that needs to go somewhere.' I never had anybody like that. [Of all the stars she met, Dinah Washington, who ran her own agency, Queen Attractions, was the only one who showed an interest in Barton's career.] Everybody that believes in me has no money.

"Another thing—I always thought this never happened to men— they'd say, 'You've got to have an act.' The fact that I'm standing on the stage playing saxophone as well as I do is enough, as far as I can see. They don't ask singers or dancers do they play the saxophone. People tell me, 'I can give your band a job, but you gotta have an act.' What kind of act? Tell stories? Comedy? I don't dance. I certainly can't tell jokes. I sing very little. So what do they mean? The fact that I'm standing up there is an act. And you get the same thing from club owners. *People*—they like what I do."

Sometimes, says Barton, when she walks into a room with her horn, "women [will] look up at you and the look on their faces is 'Oh, my God. I hope you don't embarrass *us!*' Other women [will] say, 'What is *that?*' And the guys, 'Oh, my God, what is this?' Then when I start to play, and the women are sure [I'm not] gonna make a fool of myself and embarrass them, then smiles and 'oh's' and after the performance, 'Oh, you're just marvelous.' And they're so proud and they're so happy. When I see that look, of course, I'm gonna try to give it a little bit extra.

"The UJC [Universal Jazz Coalition] is the best thing that's happened to us, because a lot of us would be somewhere unheard of today. I think one of the nicest compliments I got recently was in Kansas City [where Barton appeared with the Big Apple Jazzwomen]. After the show, a woman came up to me and said, 'Thank you for mastering the instrument

I never could,' which meant that she had probably stopped too early or something. I'm sure a lot of them are out there. . . .

"I've knocked myself out over twenty years—I mean devoted full time, nothing else—and I don't know what else I'm supposed to do. I thought, 'I'm good enough to never touch another kind of job,' but it was one of those things.

"Because every year, you see, you get better and better, and my ambition was—it still is—to see just how good can I be, how good can you *really* get, you know, just how great. And I just decided that I was gonna *do* it!"

Jean Davis

(trumpet)

Jean Davis began her career working with small local groups around New York. She has also led her own male combos, free-lanced, and, more recently, worked with the Jazz Sisters and the Big Apple Jazzwomen. Since 1969 she has held a full-time day job that leaves time for little else, but she has never considered herself anything but a musician. "I go in the car on my lunch hour and listen to [jazz] when I feel like it, get away from all that other stuff," she says. "I come home and try to play as much as I can. Once in a while, if I'm *very* tired, I don't force myself, but I don't miss too many. I might not practice today, but I gotta make it the next. The trumpet is a horn that you can't lay off; that's a seven-day job."

Jean Davis was born in New Orleans but moved to New York as a child. Her mother, about whom she never knew too much, was reputed to have been a great singer. "I always liked music," says Davis. "I always wanted to be a singer, and I even went through a phase of being a tap dancer. I heard Ella Fitzgerald when she first came out with 'A-Tisket, A-Tasket.' I was a kid and I wanted to sing like her. You know how you go through phases. Then I went to the movies one day and I saw this picture, I think it was called *Syncopation*. I just loved the trumpet sound track. 'Oh, wow,' I said, 'I can play one of those. Just three keys, it must be a breeze to play.'" Davis's father, however, was against the idea. "He said, 'Whoever heard of a girl playing trumpet?' That's all I heard. So I said, 'Oh, well . . .' They had a guy in my junior high school playing fantastic drums, and I liked the way he played. Everybody else was playing violins, or pianos, so I said, 'Well, let me play drums while I'm trying to orient my family to a trumpet.'

"I started playing for the high-school plays, and they called me back to play for the operettas and everything. People said, 'Don't you think you should stay on the drums?' And I said, 'No, I don't think so, because with a trumpet you can play a melody and you can play *sweet*,' and that's what I wanted to do.

"Finally my father gave in. He went to Wurlitzer, and he didn't know anything about trumpets, so he said, 'Give me a trumpet—you know, for a present.' So they gave him the *worst* trumpet they could *ever* give, and with the trumpet came ten free lessons from the Wurlitzer Company." At first, Davis recalls, the Wurlitzer teacher did not take her very seriously. "He figured, well, I was a girl and after about a year I would forget about it or put it down, so why should they waste their energies. Then, after he saw I was serious, he even came up to my house and gave me lessons. After that, I started gigging or playing around, sitting in.

"I knew from the time that I can remember as a kid I was gonna be a musician. I used to [baby-sit] for the lady next door to me in the Bronx, and that's when I first heard Jazz at the Philharmonic." As soon as the woman went out, Davis would look through her records. "They used to have this particular record, 'One O'Clock Jump,' which I *loved*, and I'd turn it on and listen to that."

There were also a lot of musicians living in Davis's neighborhood— Thelonious Monk, Cat Anderson, Elmo Hope. "I'd run behind 'em. I was the only girl runnin' behind 'em, you know. 'Got a jam session?' 'Yeah.' 'Come up to my house.' My mother used to just go crazy. I used to bring the whole band up to my house. We had the piano. I used to bring the bass, bring drums, met a guy who played vibes. We'd go in the living room and it was great, because the neighbors were great. There was a guy, I'll never forget it, he was a baker, and he worked nights, so he used to sleep in the daytime, and his room was right below my room. He used to yell out the window, 'I don't care if you practice, as long as you play "Stardust" before I go to sleep.' I'd play 'Stardust' and everything was cool. He slept like a log then.

"My father kinda worried. He said, 'It's kind of hard for a woman.'" He advised Davis to stay in school and learn some more practical subjects. "Between the music, I still went to school and learned typing and all that other jive," she says, which she has had to use in other jobs outside the music field.

After her lessons with the Wurlitzer teacher, Davis took an audition with trumpet player Doc Cheatham and then began to study with him. "He took an interest," she says. "You know, it wasn't like, 'Oh, wow, here comes another girl, she's gonna get pregnant, she's gonna stop, why am I gonna waste my time.'" (Cheatham also helped her to buy a new horn immediately and had her old one turned into a lamp.) With him, she studied the "nonpressure system," a method of playing in which the power comes from the diaphragm, and she worked on breath control. "I don't like a lot of high notes," says Davis. "I like a range up to maybe high D or high E. I'm not a screamer. Some guys come around and say, 'How high can you hit?' I like to hit high enough to be comfortable for me, and I can make the full range of the scale." Her ambition now is to switch to the flugelhorn, whose melodic sound she likes. Says Doc Cheatham, who knew about Davis before she came to study with him, "If you can play beautiful, that's all that matters."

After working around New York with a number of local groups, Davis settled into a weekend location job in Westchester County with Ross Carnegie's band, which included musicians Charli Persip, Oliver Nelson, and Chris Wood. She also attended the jam sessions around the city. Count Basie's club had an open session every Monday night. "Sometimes they would call all around me, but that didn't bother me. I knew what was going on. I just waited around. Sometimes they didn't call me till maybe three-thirty in the morning and the place closes at four. I might just get in one number by the time everybody takes a solo, depends how many horns you have. All the guys used to come in before they were really makin' it. I used to sit in with all of 'em—Cedar Walton, Donald Byrd, Freddie Hubbard, Bill Hartman. I guess they looked at me like, 'This woman . . .' I didn't care, 'cause I sounded better than a whole lot of guys that were sittin' in there."

Other times, Davis's name caused problems. "'Look, miss,'" she says one leader told her when he saw her sitting out front "cooling out" before the band had started, "'we're all ready to go. Now, I see you with the horn. Where is your old man?' So I said, 'What do you mean?' He said, 'Well, we got a trumpet player hired here named Jean and where is he, man? We're late; we gotta hit right now.' So I said, 'Well, I don't know what you're talking about, but I'm Jean and I'm it for tonight.' Well, you should have seen his face. There was nothing he could do, because I was union and he had to have all these pieces. So he said, 'Okay, all right, well, what do you know how to play?' I got very indignant then. I said, 'Well, what do you know how to play? Anything you know how to play, I know how to play.' So he said, 'Okay,' and he starts playing in D flat and all kinda upside-the-wall keys you know he doesn't play in. So I told him, I said, 'When are you gonna stop playin' games and don't knock yourself out, because any key that you go to, I'm gonna play in it. This is not my first job.' After he got it together, we got along all right, but he had to go through all those changes unnecessarily."

In 1964 Davis felt the need to try something new. She accepted an offer to join Merritt Hemengeon's all-woman combo, which was going to Sweden. Hemengeon was on piano, Eileen Chance on bass, Bernadine Warren on drums, and Bert Etta "Lady Bird" Davis on alto. "It was a great group," says Davis. They stayed in Sweden for over a year, touring the country from one end to the other. When she returned to the States, Davis immediately began to work with her own group at a club in West-chester County, and did very well there until the owner renovated the place and then found that the higher prices drew too small a crowd. By the late sixties, with the economy failing and work getting harder to find, Davis took a variety of jobs, from playing muted trumpet in Shea Stadium for two years to touring with the Red Chavis band as the only woman in the group. This group was booked by a woman, and Davis recalls that "be-cause she was a woman agent, they gave her a hard time. They gave her a double hard time because a lot of people never saw a girl trumpet player before."

While a man can get up and play halfway decently without anybody saying a word, says Davis, "if a girl gets out there and plays halfway, the first thing they say, 'Ah, I knew she couldn't play.' I used to think that you [had] to be really outrageous. But you could do that and it's like [some of them] have a closed mind to you [anyway]. Not all of them, 'cause there's some guys that'll help you, but the majority of musi-cians hate [women] horn players. . . .

"Women have been playing a long time—they've always had girl groups—[only] now it's more noticeable. Most of the time, I've been working with the guys. I really don't care, as long as I'm working and playing and getting paid." Increasingly, Davis has been approached by record producers asking her to get a women's group together, but the orientation would be commercial and, to her, aesthetically unsatisfying. "I'd probably wind up playing Mickey Mouse tunes and all that stuff, and I said, 'No way. We're trying to be recognized as musicians playing good music, exerting ourselves like any male musician can do, and that's what it's all about.'"

To Davis, jazz is a feeling more than anything else. "[Of course] you have arrangements," she says, "and Count Basie [for example] has a big band and everybody reads—but when they read, they read like they're one voice, and with *feeling*! Like I try to tell people, don't try to make jazz strict. It's a blending; it's a feeling coming from the soul.

"I'm always striving to try and upgrade the music," says Davis, who tapes her practice sessions and all her jobs. "Once in a while I say, 'Yeah, that was a pretty nice set that I played,' but the majority of the time I say, 'No, I could have played a little bit better than that.'" Sometimes she asks herself, "Why did I pick this? I should have been a piano player. But I wouldn't have been happy. The horn is a challenge to me. All I wanna do now is play, make a little bit of money, and enjoy myself. Later for adventure. I know what I want to do and I know what kind of music I'm gonna play and that's it. If I make it, I make it; if I don't, I don't. I tried.

"It's not like it used to be," Davis says. "There are no places to jam anymore. The young kids coming up, they don't know what it is [to] take out their horn, go into a place, and jam. I think they need more jazz. They're brainwashed; [all they hear is] disco, disco. When I was comin' up, it was all jazz. That's all I heard around my neighborhood. You go to New Orleans and they got the funerals. One time I went to visit my aunt in New Orleans, and they had a funeral that passed by her house, and that's the first one I've seen. They don't do it too much now, I understand, but they used to do it all the time, and it was really great. They had this guy, and umbrellas. It was so enlightening. People think it's sad, but that's the way it used to be. Like I told 'em: 'Look, if I go, man, y'all better play, and leave me twenty-four bars of something, you know. Just leave it blank. Leave it blank, so if I'm down there, you know I'm in there playing.'"

Dottie Dodgion

(drums)

Dottie Dodgion started out as a singer and says she was "accidentally" led to the drums. She became serious about them in the mid-fifties, and has worked with such musicians as Zoot Sims, Benny Goodman, Marian McPartland, and Joe Venuti, as a member of Melba Liston's new group, Melba Liston and Company, and in the successful off-Broadway show of Jerry Herman's, *Jerry's Girls*. Vocalist/writer Carol Sloane has praised Dodgion's "razor-keen" time, the subtlety and taste of her accents, and her sensitivity to other musicians on the stand.[9] "I'm a supportive player," Dodgion says. "I don't need to solo. If the ensemble sound is right, it thrills me to death."

Dottie Dodgion was born in Brea, California. Her father, Chuck Giaimo, a drummer in his mid-seventies, is still working. "I didn't even think about playing drums until I was twenty-two or twenty-three," says Dodgion. "I played one time because I got stranded in Springfield, Illinois, [while] I was straight man and singer for Rosco Ates, a stuttering comedian. The Mary Kay Trio came by and I went to Springfield with them and formed a trio with Mary Kay's brother and his wife, who played piano. So we played opposite them, and that's how I got back home to San Francisco. Frank Ross [accordion player with the group] taught me enough stand-up brushes just to play 'apple pie' on a stand-up snare, and that's when I first started. Then when I got back home, drummers would be late, and I'd play brushes on a magazine or whatever. They'd say, 'Come on, Dottie, play some "time" till the drummer gets here.' Male drummers were always late! Maybe there'd be a session goin' on and the drummer would be there, but there'd be a snare or maybe a high hat or something, and—I've said this many times before—I felt needed. I never thought about playing drums; I just felt needed. So I started playing before I knew how difficult it would be. But then, after a while, I really started getting interested.

"I know that the first rhythm section that ever hit me hard—talk about cooking, really 'time' cooking, which I love—was the Buddy de Franco Quartet. He had Art Blakey [drums] and Kenny Drew [piano] and Eugene Wright [bass], and boy, that group bit me. I wanted to play drums after that. Later on, Kenny Clarke was one of the first drummers to influence me, because of the way he could swing a big band and also a small group. At that time, there weren't very many drummers who could do both. You know, they specialized in one or the other, and that always knocked me out about him. He wasn't a drummer who got in everybody's way. So many drummers play so loud and they're so busy and everything, and that impressed me about him. He knew how to lay back and listen."

In the mid-fifties, Dodgion married alto saxophonist Jerry Dodgion. (Dottie has one daughter, Deborah.) "The guys would let me sit in when they needed me, or whatever. Eugene Wright and Jerry were *very* encouraging to me when I was just beginning to play, and, of course, my father thought it was wonderful. They didn't think it was *strange*, you know. And that helped a lot, especially then, when a woman playing *piano* was odd, let alone playing drums.

"I was around so many professionals, I mean truly wonderful musicians, with Jerry that I didn't have half the trouble being accepted as a lot of women had. I was at least *accepted* by the guys, even though they didn't *hire* me for those jobs; many a time a drummer who couldn't swing half as well as I could would be hired. Those kinds of things used to hurt. In one case I would suffer, but in another case I got to play with some professionals that some ladies would have given both arms to play with. I played with the greats ever since I can remember, so to me it was easy—if you knew how."

By the late fifties, the Dodgions were in L.A. Jerry was out on the

Tiny Davis and her Hell Divers. Left to right: Helen Cole, Eileen Chance, Tiny Davis, Bert Etta Davis, Margaret Backstrum, Maureen Smith.

Ada Leonard (in spotlight) with her band. Top row, left to right: Mary Ann Gould, Joan Koupis, Helen Stompful, unknown, Bertie Lawrence, Cele Touhey, Dez Thompson. Second row, left to right: Jule Donahue, Mildred Cobb, Bernice Lobdell, Jane Sager, Bernice Little. Bottom row, left to right: Ethel Buttons, Brownie Slade, Connie Van, Midge Goodrich.

June Rotenberg, 1946.

Betty Sattley Leeds, 1945.

The Flo Dreyer Quintet in Honolulu, 1952. Left to right: Stella Mattern, Chris Reed, Fagle Liebman, Flo Dreyer, Eleanor Williams.

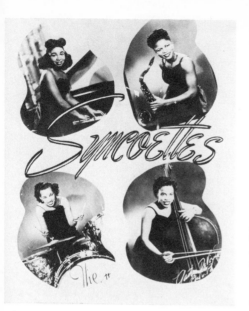

The Syncoettes: Sarah McLawler (piano), Lula Roberts (tenor sax), Hetty Smith Pasco (drums), Vi Wilson (bass).

Corky Hale in Hollywood discussing a song with Frank Sinatra.

Bridget O'Flynn at the "111 Club," 1950.

Sarah McLawler at the Universal Jazz Coalition's Salute to Women in Jazz, New York, 1979.

Sheila Jordan.

Jean Davis.

Carline Ray.

Willene Barton.

Maxine Sullivan and friends.

Lucille Dixon.

Patti Bown.

Mary Lou Williams, 1974.

Fostina Dixon.

Jane Ira Bloom.

JoAnne Brackeen.

Janice Robinson.

Melba Liston and Company. Left to right: Chessie Tanksley, Carline Ray, Melba Liston, Britt Woodman, Dottie Dodgion, Larry Smith, Erica Lindsay.

Ann Patterson's Maiden Voyage. Top row, left to right: Judy Chilnick, Valerie Sullivan, Jodi Gladstone, Louise Baranger, Anne Petereit, Stacy Rowles. Middle row, left to right: Debbie Katz, Betty O'Hara, Beth Carver, Martha Stevens, Jackie Wollinger. Front row, left to right: Carol Anderson (piano), Carol Chaikin, Barbara Watts, Ann Patterson, Lesli Dechter, Jamie MacEwing.

UJC's 1978 Salute to Women in Jazz staged on the sidewalk after lockout by club owners. Left, from drums: Barbara Merjan, Bob Cranshaw, Jimmy Rowles, Carol Sloane.

road with Benny Goodman, and Dottie was working around the city when she got a call asking her to come to Las Vegas to work with Carl Fontana and Gus Mancuso. "That was a perfect opportunity. I stayed in Vegas about a year, and I was playing *every* day, *every* night, and that's where I got my chops together."

At that time, Dottie did not know many other women drummers. Those who played with the women's groups were out on the road, getting relatively little publicity or exposure, and many of the women drummers who had been active in the forties had quit the scene by then. "There would be an occasional Las Vegas cutie coming through, but they weren't musicians," Dodgion says. "They just wore low-cut gowns and played cocktail drums and fluff music. There *were* a couple of good lady cocktail drummers in Las Vegas, but they never did play a full set, and I fought that all the time. I swore to myself that if I couldn't play the whole set, forget it. I lost a lot of jobs on account of it, but I would have gotten hung up in that trap (no pun intended), making money and then never doing what I really wanted to do.

"You have to want to play bad enough. Then there isn't any sacrifice to it. People don't understand that too well, I'm beginning to find out. You have to really be dedicated, especially to jazz, because you never make a lot of money in jazz. I mean once in a great while—Miles started making money for people in jazz, he brought the buck up—but unless you're a superstar, it still doesn't pay much. So you have to love it. You don't set your sights on overnight riches."

In 1959 Jerry Dodgion returned to Vegas and was working with the Benny Goodman band. One day while he and Dottie were jamming, she says, "Benny walked over and asked if he could sit in with us, and that was all there was to it." When she and Jerry arrived in New York sometime later for the band's opening at Basin Street East, Goodman invited her to jam again. "Got your shoes?" he asked her as she walked into the rehearsal one day. "And I said, 'Yeah, I got my shoes.' 'Well, come on up and play.' I thought we were just going to jam again, but he'd been trying out drummers all day and he hadn't found anybody he liked, so he said, 'Okay, you start tonight.' Jerry says, 'How do you like New York so far?' First day in New York, right? I had no place to go but down.

"It was quite an experience. Zoot was on that band, John Bunch, Red Norvo, Jimmy Wyble, Carl Fontana, Buddy Childers. Maria Marshall was one singer; the great Jimmy Rushing was the other. It was mean. I really enjoyed it."

Then one night Goodman forgot to introduce Dottie. The audience kept asking the name of the drummer, and when Goodman finally announced it, the applause was overwhelming. "When I came off," she remembers, "Benny's manager says to me, 'Bye.' I got my notice the next day. As Gene Krupa once told me, 'Just remember, baby, he's fired the best.'"

In the early seventies the Dodgions were still headquartered in New York, and Dottie began to get more calls and more offers to work. "That kind of took Jerry and me apart from each other. Up till then, I'd always been around. But it was time for us to go on to other things. We'd been together twenty years, and that's a nice run. It was time for us to grow and meet other people and do other things. So that took me out to L.A. for a while, and L.A. is just Death Valley to me—I don't care who knows it."

What helped Dottie through this time of transition was her music. "It was everything," she says. She landed a job in Lake Tahoe, where she lived with her daughter, and went back to her original vocation—singing and playing. "It was the only way I could get the gig. There was an organ player, Ron Rose, and he sounded like a whole big band. I was singing the old standards and playing, and I lasted there a year." She then moved to Washington, D.C., where she spent two and a half years as the music director of a jazz club, The Rogue & Jar. She brought in such artists as Lee Konitz, the Brecker Brothers, Thad Jones, Jimmy Rowles, and Carol Sloane. Then, in 1979, after joining Melba Liston and Company, she moved back to New York. "And I've been playing and learning and growing."

"Once I start playing," Dodgion says, "the music takes over. I feel like it's coming through me, not from me. Once I hear the time and I place it there, I couldn't put it any other place if I tried to. I mean, I *have* to place it there, because that's where the overall feeling is, the overall sound, the overall beat. Now, why that gut feeling is there—and that it works—I don't know. But it sure does fill me with great joy when it's right. Melba brought a lot of changes out of me, and I've gotten a bit more aggressive. I feel that I'm stronger now than I have ever been. The only way you keep growing is to keep playing. You can't just play a couple of nights a week."

As far as being a woman in the field is concerned, "I've never had a problem with a real professional," Dodgion says. "You have to keep a lot of professionalism going. The most important thing to me is that they want to play, male or female. All I want is a hundred percent. That's all I ask, because I can *give* it."

Dorothy Ashby

(harp/piano/composer)

Dorothy Ashby, an accomplished pianist, was self-taught on the harp and started out playing in Detroit in the early fifties, the beginning of what she calls the "golden years" of jazz in that city.

In the liner notes to Ashby's 1961 album *Soft Winds* (Jazzland Records), Ira Gitler wrote: "Dorothy Ashby may not be the first jazz harpist (Caspar Reardon) or the first female jazz harpist (Adele Girard), but her feeling for time and ability to construct melodic guitar-like lines mark her as the most accomplished modern jazz harpist. Apropos of her relation to the guitar, Orrin Keepnews paid her a high compliment when he said that she reminded him of Wes Montgomery."

In 1962 Ashby was given *down beat*'s Critic's and Reader's awards as best harpist. Of her album *The Fantastic Jazz Harp of Dorothy Ashby*, one reviewer said, "This isn't just novelty, though that is what you expect. The harp has a clean jazz voice with a resonance and syncopation that turn familiar jazz phrasing inside out."[10]

Despite such praise for all of her work from those who know, Ashby has not received wide recognition for what she does. Because there are so few authentic jazz harpists, "people don't know what you're doing," she says. "Nobody else knows enough to know that nobody else is doing it."

Dorothy Ashby's father, Wiley Thompson, was a jazz guitarist. "When I took to playing piano," she says, "I played the things that I heard and played along with my father, who taught me more about harmony and melodic construction than I learned in all my years of high school, college, and private study, and sacrificed more time and money than the family could afford for my musical training and instruments." (The four people, says Ashby, who "sacrificed through the years" for her talent—"the training of it, sustaining of it, challenging of it, physical and psychological well-being of it"—were her parents, brother, and husband, musician/composer John Ashby.)

"When musicians would come to rehearse with my father, I would get a chance to chord along with the adults, and they thought that was a big thing. I thought it was quite wonderful, too, because I was so young at the time. And from there, I guess my interest was always primarily jazz. My father had perhaps other aspirations for me. He didn't want me to wind up in the clubs and suffer the hard times that so many of them encountered. The excellence with which they played had nothing to do with the bucks they made.

"When I changed to the harp, I just tried to transfer the things that I had heard and the things that I wanted to do as a jazz player to the harp. Nobody had ever told me these things shouldn't be done, or were not usually done on the harp, because I didn't hear it any other way. The only thing I was interested in doing was playing jazz on the harp."

Ashby went to Detroit's Cass Tech High School, which was the alma mater of many jazz musicians. "It was a very special place because it trained so many: Gerald Wilson; Donald Byrd and I played in the marching band; Kenny Burrell was there a short time. I was playing saxophone at that time in the marching band, and I guess it wasn't the greatest saxophone, because [the band director] said she'd rather have me play bass. But it was terribly exciting in those days, and we were all growing. And there were so many talented players.

"I think if I had studied harp, perhaps I might not have been as bold a player. When I took harp, it was in the high-school classroom with usually about fourteen other girls in the class, and we had five harps and we took turns practicing. You'd get in an hour every day, if you were lucky. And when school was out, that was the end of your harp work and practice and playing and everything, so it took a little time, but I spent all my time wanting to do it my way. There were some girls who had harps of their own, but they were very few, and none of the black girls, of course, had harps. We hadn't even seen a harp before we got there."

Ashby went on to Wayne University, where she studied piano and prepared to teach (which she never did). "When I did my graduation recital, I did the Rachmaninoff Concerto. We couldn't afford an orchestra, but my teacher played the second piano part. So I was very proficient as a pianist. Harp I did on my own. Harp I liked much more."

When Ashby started to work in Detroit, it was as a pianist; in fact, she did not even own a harp then. "Detroit spawned and sent away some of its very finest representatives of jazz playing in those years," she remembers. "Most of them wound up in New York and other places, because Detroit wasn't a place where you could become very rich. You could become very well liked and very well known among your peers, but there wasn't a lot of money to be made and there weren't a lot of opportunities, especially if you were in jazz. . . . There was Paul Chambers, Doug Watkins, Milt Jackson, Kenny Burrell, Roland Hanna, Tommy Flanagan, Pepper Adams, Barry Harris, Yusef Lateef. Miles Davis spent a lot of time in Detroit, even though he wasn't a Detroiter. You could go to hear Miles often, or there would be the performances of Sonny Stitt, who was born in Flint, Michigan. You could hear saxophone battles between Frank Foster and Sonny Stitt and Billy Mitchell and just all the names that are now world famous."

Two of the other outstanding women players in Detroit then were Terry Pollard (who also plays on *Soft Winds*) and Bess Bonnier. "You couldn't sit in unless you could play," Ashby says. "The guys would not allow it. They'd let you sit in, but you wouldn't last long unless you turned out something that was worth hearing, so the standards were very high and the lady players were very few."

By 1952 Ashby had acquired her own harp, but for her the difficulties of being a female player were compounded by her choice of instrument, which was rarely thought of or accepted in jazz. "Often the harpists who got the write-ups and the media coverage were very pretty, and that seemed to be about all they were interested in. Detroiters have never been much on looks; they've always been strong on talent, 'cause there were so many talented players there. If you didn't have the talent, you wouldn't usually get to play. But, in other places, it seemed that when they thought about harpists, they thought about a beautiful, delicate girl."

Even in Detroit, Ashby says, it was hard for her to start getting jobs. "The word *harp* seemed to just scare people. Once you began to play, your work began to speak for your opportunities to play at other times, but it was very difficult. Club owners could not believe that they were gonna get anything less than chamber music. They would turn me off so quickly, you couldn't believe it. I'd say, 'Well, can't I come in and just audition?' 'No way; you can't even audition.' That went on for quite a long time, and we began to just make our own opportunities by working at some dances for young people, college dances, and people would begin to make a few little noises about the sound and the group, and then we would talk to club owners. They still wouldn't believe it, but they would say come on some night when they needed entertainment to help spark up their off night or something, but that was good only in Detroit. As soon as you'd leave Detroit, it was the same story: They had never heard you and they couldn't even imagine having a harp in a nightclub."

Ashby was initially attracted by, and quickly addicted to, the sound of the harp and to the challenge of trying to play things that were so much more difficult on harp than they were on piano. "When you want to play a chromatic scale on the piano, you just go up by half steps from the black keys to the white and vice versa. But, on the harp, well, I've never heard of anybody yet in this world who will play 'The Flight of the Bumblebee,' at least at any speed, because it's so difficult to play chromatically. I guess that's the main reason that not too many players take to jazz. They play pop things on it, but in jazz playing, which means spontaneous improvisation, you have to think *now* what you're gonna do next so that you can be prepared for it. I hate to say that harp is so complex, but it is for players. Even arrangers admit that often they don't know how to write what they'd like to write. What they would be willing to write for harp often doesn't work, because they're writing from a pianistic point of view, or maybe from another instrumental point of view, and that doesn't work on a harp, because you can only change two pedals at a time, and various other technicalities. They might write something that has several accidental changes that happen within a fraction of a beat, and you can't possibly move your feet. The instrument wouldn't even respond that fast to do it, so it has complexities that a person has to be able to work out in their head while they're spontaneously creating jazz on it. That's why most people play prearranged solos and things that they can practice and practice, so their feet know where they're going. It's like playing Wagner with a symphony. You don't sight-read Wagner; you practice it, you've grown up with it, you know what's gonna happen. There are no surprises; your feet and your mind and your eyes are all in tune to what's gonna happen well in advance—months, years in advance—and you do it the same way, never changing.

"But if I play 'I'll Remember April' twenty nights in a row, every night it's gonna be different. You might memorize an opening or an ending so that everybody can start and end together, or you might even have an ensemble section incorporated within your arrangement, but there's nothing like that free time to create your own thing. I guess that's the thing that just fascinated me about it when I heard my father play, when I heard the others play. I always had the hang-up on jazz. The challenge was so much greater.

"I don't believe the American public realizes what the jazz players are doing when they do it. It's a skill that you've developed over a number of years, to know how and when to drop the chords in in a certain amount of time and in particular rhythms that are complex, not just evenly divided but syncopated, in mysterious ways that your mind creates as you go along, and that makes it a real art form that hasn't been capitalized on or touted properly by Americans. I think the Europeans are a little bit more intellectual in their approach to it, or understand a little bit more what's going on. That's not a put-down of American taste; it's a put-down of American promotion, because American promotion promotes what's more appealing to the masses, and the masses, of course, are capable of consuming more easily the popular kind of music, the less complex kind of music."

The Dorothy Ashby Trio toured throughout the sixties, and by the end of the decade, Dorothy's husband, who was also the drummer in the group, was becoming increasingly involved with writing and presenting musicals that dealt with black life in America. He had established an all-black theater company, the Ashby Players of Detroit, and Dorothy was writing the scores and lyrics and also performing with the shows. In the early seventies the Ashbys moved to California, and after spending some years on the road, Dorothy then became firmly established in the studios and was working regularly. Two albums of her early material, *The Best of Dorothy Ashby* and *Music for Beautiful People*, have been reissued, and in recent years she has worked on albums with Earth, Wind, and Fire, Stanley Turrentine, Freddie Hubbard, Diana Ross, Helen Reddy, Natalie Cole, Barry Manilow, Dionne Warwick, Bill Withers, Stevie Wonder, and others.

"I think they have experimented more lately with harp in pop arrangements than they had before," says Ashby. "Bill Withers was one of the first to use me out here, and he approached Stevie Wonder, because there were other harpists who were not too anxious to see me come along and get in on their good thing. And I can see why they weren't—because it is much more profitable in terms of playing than nightclubs. Not quite as rewarding, but you have to do that on your own. I come home and play. I like to play when I feel like playing, and enjoy it ever so much."

Corky Hale

(harp/piano/organ/flute/piccolo/cello)

Corky Hale began her career in the Hollywood of the fifties, working in the recording studios, clubs, and on TV. She also worked briefly with several of the all-woman bands and appeared on the 1954 recording session *Cats vs. Chicks*.

Hale first discovered Dorothy Ashby playing a harp in a Detroit club in the early fifties (before she realized that anyone else was doing what she was doing on the instrument). Says Hale, "Dorothy is very wonderful. I don't want to say that Dorothy and I are the only jazz harpists, but Dorothy and I are the only ones that can go in with a group, sit down, and improvise a tune like a piano player."

Unlike Ashby, Hale has always considered herself primarily a piano player. "It's very frustrating to me," she says, "very frustrating, in that people mostly think of me as a harpist and mainly call upon me because I do something on the harp." In 1980 she appeared at the Universal Jazz Coalition's Salute to Women in Jazz, playing piano and harp. In recent years, however, Hale has chosen to do few club or concert appearances, and considers it "amusing" that after so many years in the business, she finds herself reminding people that she has not quit "or died."

Born into what she calls one of those "lovely, fortunate childhoods," Hale describes her early life in northern Illinois farm country as the most normal imaginable. No one in the family was particularly musical, but at the age of three Corky (*aka* Merylynn Hecht) started picking out songs on the piano, and her mother decided that she ought to have lessons. At seven she started attending the Chicago Conservatory, 130 miles away, being driven there once a week for her lesson.

"By the time I was eight I had seen a woman at the Chicago Conservatory playing a harp, and I threw a tantrum and said, 'I must have one of those things.' So my father bought me a small one, a very small harp—a model that's no longer made today, which is a shame. It was a great little harp, and I started harp lessons. And ten years old I started flute, and twelve years old I started cello, and the piccolo I had to play in the marching band, so I'd be in on everything." At nine she had become the youngest child to attend Interlochen Music Camp (in Michigan), where she began to get her earliest big-band experience.

Hale's earliest musical heritage was, for the most part, classical. As far as jazz was concerned, while some people around the country were listening to Charlie Parker and Dizzy Gillespie in the mid-forties, the sounds of bop had not yet reached Freeport, Illinois. "The fact that I listened to Stan Kenton and Woody Herman," says Hale, "was considered *most* far out."

At sixteen Hale left Freeport to attend a small college in Missouri. "It was across the street from the University of Missouri, so I got involved in all the university activities. I was playing the shows and arranging stuff for the bands. I always knew, of course, that I never wanted to go to school. I knew that I wanted to be in the music business from the time I was very little. So I announced to my parents that I was going to Hollywood to get in the music business. My parents screamed and carried on and said, 'Well, the only way you could do that, of course, would be to go to school.' I would have done anything to get there. I said, 'Right, right, fine, UCLA, wonderful.' And my mother drove me out and saw that I was living nicely in—what else?—a sorority house, and I never went to one class *ever*. I had been there probably two or three weeks and one of the girls said, 'Oh, my father has this local television show. It's called "Freddy Martin and His Orchestra," and gee, my dad would probably like to have you on the show.'" (These were the early days of television.)

Hale did the show, and soon offers started pouring in: "TV, tons of movie scores, everybody's record. I took *every* job that was offered to me. I was a nut!" One of her first jobs was at the Cocoanut Grove. "I was a nineteen-year-old kid and I was really making a tremendous amount of money and throwing it away as fast as I made it. I had no conception of it at all. I bought myself a white Buick convertible, and I just went crazy. All the things that I would not dream of doing today." Then came a call from George Liberace, whose brother, Walter, was starting a local TV show on which they wanted Hale to play the harp. "We started in a movie theater, which they converted to a TV studio, on Wilshire Boulevard. The first week there were ten people, the next week there were fifty, and by a month, six weeks later, there were hundreds of people lining the street. Liberace was the Beatles of his day. I had a wonderful time. I was signing autographs.

"I can't believe those days ever existed. But that was a very exciting time for me. I was still that nice, sort of well-bred little Jewish girl from northern Illinois. I guess that's what kept me from getting quite as crazy as a lot of girl friends who really freaked out." What does Hale think kept her straight? "Mainly my mother, who would fly out at the least chance and say, 'What are you doing?' I had a very strong mother and I used to scream, 'Let me live my life, leave me alone,' right? And now I'm closer—and I have been for many years—to my mother than any other woman I know. So whatever she did, I always tell her that she evidently did the right thing."

During the fifties, Corky Hale did a great deal of work with TV and studio bands—Freddy Martin, Dave Rose, Harry James, Ray Anthony, Jerry Gray—and a 1954 album with vocalist Kitty White revealed what Leonard Feather in *The Encyclopedia of Jazz* called her "exceptionally modern approach to the harp." She also worked briefly with Ada Leonard and Ina Ray Hutton. "Ada was terribly sophisticated," she says, "and boy, I was scared to death of her. And, of course, Phil Spitalny called and asked me to go on the road with his all-girl band. I didn't join Phil, and I didn't last very long with Ada or Ina."

In a Hal Holly profile titled "Corky, the All-Girl Harpist, Won't Talk on Gal Bands" (*down beat*, June 4, 1952, p. 4), Hale addressed the subject of the all-woman bands. "It's like this," she said. "If a girl is a good musician she doesn't want to work in an all-girl band because it implies she is working in it because she is a girl. A girl doesn't feel successful as a musician unless she can work with guys—just like one of them. She wants to feel she's been hired not because she's a girl but because she can play the job."

"I've always been in a man's world," says Hale. "I've always been in a man's job. Along with that, strangely enough, I always did all those womanly things. After work, at two in the morning, it was very common for maybe sixteen, seventeen guys in the band to come to my apartment and I would cook up an enormous breakfast. I was always cooking for huge mobs of people. Kind of strange, now that I think of it. I never thought of those things till just recently. I was just simply one of the guys."

By the late fifties, Hale's parents, who were in the clothing industry in Chicago, were again concerned about her stability in the wilds of Hollywood. "What stable?" she asked them. "I'm doing great."

Presenting her with her own clothing store on the Strip, across the street from Schwab's Drugstore, they told her she could run the store and do her music at the same time. The business really took off, however, and Hale found herself working less and less on the music. Then, in 1958, she met an Englishman—"the first to bring Italian knitwear to this country. And I met him, and now we have once again this small-town girl who's been dating musicians and nice Jewish doctors, lawyers, James Dean thrown in occasionally, a lot of crazy agents, managers, and so forth, and now comes this terribly cultured, world-traveled Englishman, and I thought, 'Oh, my God, this is it! This is Prince Charming!' And I married him. Disaster strikes! We spent most of the time in Europe, back and forth and back and forth, and, of course, my playing suffered. He wouldn't let me have a harp or piano in our apartment! When I look back now and I think that I let myself live like that, I *cannot* believe it! So finally I divorced him."

In 1961 Hale moved to Rome and did some performing, including a television show called "Tempo di Jazz." In '63 she returned to L.A. for another three years. "Also disastrous," she says. "I was very unhappy there. I knew I never wanted to live in L.A. anymore." In early '66 she packed up, shipped everything, including her harp, to London, and lived there until the fall of the year, when she packed up again and came back to America to work. Soon after she arrived, Hale met songwriter Mike Stoller, and it was, she says, "love at first sight." Four years later they were married.

Back in the mainstream of New York's professional music world, Hale returned to TV—the Kraft Show, where she "sang behind the stars, led them in, and did all the introductions." She turned down club jobs, which demanded five or six nights a week, and chose studio work instead. "And that's what I've been doing in the past years," she says. She has also been involved with ventures outside the music field (for example, buying and running a restaurant during the mid-seventies and, later, becoming a film producer). As a result, she says, "Most people don't know that I'm around ever because they don't see my name. I can [also] get into the kitchen and get lost for several days and be very happy, so it's really my husband who will say, 'Listen, nobody knows you play!'

"It's an effort for me now," Hale admits. "In December and January [1979–80] I did six Monday nights at the Knickerbocker in the Village, which is a real piano room. A lot of people came down. I enjoyed it a lot, got a nice review." Since then, Hale has begun to work more frequently in other New York clubs, and in 1980 she also worked in London, doing club dates and radio. She was offered a recording contract there, and intends to record again, "just so people know I'm around. Obviously, I want to do something very contemporary, in addition to maybe some old jazz tunes. But I would like to do something, of course, that's never been done on the harp before.

"People are always coming to me," says Hale, "and [telling me], 'I was in Fort Wayne, Indiana, and there's this jazz harpist who's just marvelous . . .' 'Jazz harpist'—that signifies somebody that sits alone in a hotel dining room and plays a Burt Bachrach tune as opposed to a Bach bourrée. People think everybody that plays a popular tune on a harp is a jazz harpist. Last year, when the Selby harp company had a harp convention, they wanted to call it the 'first national jazz/pop convention.' I made a big stink, and I said, 'I won't come if you're going to call it that, because you're fooling people. You're fooling harpists. It is not jazz to sit down and play popular songs.'"

The contest (sponsored by the convention) offered $1,000 to the best pop harpist, but the rules stipulated that the harpist play solo. "That is exactly why harpists never learn to play jazz," says Hale. "They can't take their instrument into a club and sit down and jam with the rest of the band. Harpists are raised on all classical music; they never listen to any jazz or have a chance to play [it]." Harpists, Hale feels, must learn to play with "time" (i.e., with drums) and with a bass. They must learn to play chords as opposed to arpeggios, and to "comp" (play accompanying chords) behind the bass. "I was raised as a piano player," she says. "I play on the harp what I play on the piano."

The reviews following Hale's London engagements were uniformly stunning. Critics noted her swing, her sensitivity, her improvisation, and her unique skill on the harp. "Unlike most harpists who dabble in popular music," wrote one, "she does not merely play jazz tunes on the harp, but treats this cumbersome but graceful instrument as if it were a piano, spurning the rippling *glissandi* and the rhapsodizing and converting it into a swinging machine." The same writer noted her "hard, gutsy approach" to the keyboard. "At the same time, there is plenty of sensitivity and she is a superb accompanist."[11] ("I just breathe with the singer," Hale explains. "I anticipate all their phrasing.") "Whether swinging sweetly at the keyboard," said another critic, "or demonstrating that the harp is a much neglected jazz instrument (though few indeed have her invention and infallible rhythmic sense), she is a performer to pay close attention to."[12]

"See," says Hale, "that's what happens when I get out of the kitchen!"

THE SIXTIES

As the apathy and conservatism of the 1950s erupted into the violence, dissension, and fragmentation of the 1960s, women—and other minorities—began to demand the right to full participation in the mainstream of American life. In 1963 President John F. Kennedy's Commission on the Status of Women issued a Report on American Women in the first government-sponsored study of the kind. That same year saw the appearance of Betty Friedan's *The Feminine Mystique*, which strongly refuted the idea that all a woman needed to be happy was marriage and motherhood (but also failed to take into account the fact that these were valid and even important roles which women should be free to choose, if they so desired). The New Feminism focused mainly on the problems of white middle-class women, and in the black community at this time, Michele Wallace notes, women were, with good reason, "admirably thorough" in shunning the movement. (Their alternative in the black world, she also points out, was a civil rights movement and black movement which not only failed to take into account their particular needs as black women, but also often denied them full participation in the broader struggle precisely because they *were* women.)[1]

On the already politicized New Left, meanwhile, both black and white women were splitting away from the men, who, as it turned out, were not prepared to give them the support and equality they wanted. In 1964, Congress passed a major civil rights bill, and Title VII of the bill outlawed employment discrimination on the basis of race, color, religion, national origin, and sex. (Ironically, the addition of the word "sex" was a conservative Virginia congressman's last-ditch effort to keep the bill from going through, since he reasoned that the provision for equal employment opportunities for women would be so unacceptable to his male colleagues, it would insure the failure of the civil rights legislation altogether.)

In the world of music, Beatlemania, folk and protest music, and soul swept the country as, more than ever before, the demarcations between music, politics, and youth culture dissolved. In jazz, too, musicians began to respond to the tragedies and violence of the times—the assassinations of John F. Kennedy, Martin Luther King, Medgar Evers, Malcolm X; the war in Vietnam; and the escalation of social and racial struggles. *Charlie Haden's Liberation Music Orchestra*, composed and arranged in part by Carla Bley, made some of the strongest and most direct statements about the political issues of the day; elsewhere in the jazz world, signs of rebellion and change were apparent in the increasingly radical departures from formal musical traditions of the past, as musicians sought to explore new textures, feelings, and technical resources. In 1959 Ornette Coleman became the chief proponent of what would become known as "free jazz," a music with no structure, no set keys, no set tempos, and no star soloists, but rather a form of collective improvisation that subordinated the individual to the group. In the liner notes to Sonny Simmons's *Manhattan Egos* (Arhoolie), Ralph Gleason cited Albert Ayler's statement that the "new" music was "more about feelings than about notes." In interpreting the powerful force behind the new and unfamiliar sounds, Gleason himself noted that the creative act had become "the only defense of life against the machine"; creativity was tantamount to religion.

Some black musicians (known as the "black nationalist musicians") began to look to Africa, Asia, South America, and India for new instruments, textures, colors; the "little instruments" were introduced; musicians created "sound sheets"; and horns began to emulate the human voice as such musicians as Sun Ra, Archie Shepp, Charlie Mingus, Cecil Taylor, Sonny Simmons, Barbara Donald, John Coltrane, and Alice Coltrane attempted to communicate increasingly on their own terms.

Musicians also began to take business matters more and more into their own hands. In 1964 Bill Dixon organized the October Revolution in jazz, during which the "free" musicians produced five nights of concerts at a New York club when no one else would give them a forum in which to present their music. In Chicago, the Association for the Advancement of Creative Musicians was founded in 1965, and around the same time, Carla Bley, who had been composing since the late fifties, helped found the Jazz Composer's Guild to service musicians writing for large groups.

During the second half of the sixties, Miles Davis would take the initiative in exploring the increased use of electronics and in synthesizing elements of rock, soul, pop, and modern jazz into a music that would become known as "fusion." Tony Williams, Wayne Shorter, Joe Zawinul, Chick Corea, John McLaughlin, and Herbie Hancock were at the forefront of those fusion artists who would create a more commercially viable—and also more controversial—branch of the music.

Two women who participated significantly in the "free" music of the decade were trumpet player Barbara Donald and pianist Alice (McLeod)

Coltrane. Detroit-born Coltrane had studied piano in America and with Bud Powell in Europe and later worked and recorded with vibes player Terry Gibbs. In the early sixties she married John Coltrane and in 1964 began working with his group. After Coltrane's death in 1967, Alice continued to explore in her own music the spiritual dimensions she had discovered in her husband's work, broadening the tonal and technical boundaries of her own compositions by adding the voices of the oud and the tamboura, and utilizing such devices as the baroque basso ostinato. During the seventies, her work showed an increasing Indian influence.

Two other leading women on the sixties scene, Dizzy Gillespie noted in his autobiography, *To BE, or not . . . to BOP*, were pianist Patti Bown and Melba Liston, both of whom worked in Quincy Jones's big band in 1960; Gloria Coleman, the powerful organist who had started her career in the fifties playing bass, was recording, working with guitarist Tiny Grimes, and leading her own group with Booker Ervin on tenor sax; Mary Lou Williams had also come back to the music, starting to compose for the Catholic Church, and in 1963 she founded her own record label, Mary Records, as a means of securing her artistic freedom; and with the blues and folk revival of the decade, such women as Alberta Hunter, Lucille Hegamin, Lil Hardin Armstrong, Lovie Austin, Sweet Emma Barrett, and Billie Pierce were brought back into the limelight (and the recording studio), and blues woman Victoria Spivey also founded her own recording company in 1967.

Nevertheless, as the music departed from the earlier traditions of swing and bop, and as the business itself went into decline—riots had closed the 1960 Newport Jazz Festival, and the fifties package-tour concept was no longer viable—the sixties proved to be a generally difficult decade for jazz, and particularly so for women in the field. Many of the instrumentalists who had worked steadily through the previous two decades were disillusioned enough with the state of the art to quit the business altogether; others were forced to take day jobs and relegate their practicing to evenings and their music jobs to weekends. Women like Norma Shepherd and Clora Bryant described the decade as "ordinary," with "not too much happening." Betty Carter, in retrospect, assessed the lull of the sixties in more explicit—and dramatic—terms: After the Beatles came along, she said, "the whole business went to pieces. For me, it got scary. On one side there was free jazz, which shook up a lot of black people. Free jazz got a lot of white audiences, but it never played to blacks. On the other side, soul music came in heavy, with free jazz on the white side, and soul on the black side. I was overwhelmed."[2] Toshiko Akiyoshi recently corroborated the general feelings about the decade expressed by these women. By the late sixties, she said, she "almost quit jazz for good. . . . All of a sudden, I felt as insignificant as the sand on the beach. I looked at the jazz scene and saw that I hadn't changed anything."[3] Akiyoshi did not quit, however, and it was her husband, Lew Tabackin, who urged her to come back, convincing her that she still had something to contribute.

If the sixties move toward artistic self-advocacy and minority rights did not, for the most part, directly affect or include women in jazz—whose growth and progress had traditionally stemmed from personal, one-on-one battles rather than from any political or ideological involvement—it did serve to draw attention to the problems women faced in general. It also established a momentum and a social climate that set the stage for the seventies, when for the first time since Ma Rainey had traveled the road with the Rabbit Foots, or Dolly Jones had played with the Harlem Harlicans, there would start to be an organized network of support available to women in the field.

Following are profiles of four women who contributed significantly to the jazz world of the sixties and continue to do so today.

Carla Bley

(composer/keyboards/saxophone/leader)

Carla Bley entered the New York jazz world in the late fifties and began composing for such players as Canadian pianist Paul Bley, George Russell, Charlie Haden (Carla was arranger and composer for parts of *Liberation Music Orchestra*), and Gary Burton (for whom she composed *A Genuine Tong Funeral*). In 1964, with musician Michael Mantler, she founded the Jazz Composer's Orchestra, and shortly after, the record label Jazz Composer's Orchestra Association (JCOA), as well as the Watt label, which produces her own and Mantler's music. Bley's albums to date include *Dinner Music, Tropic Appetites, Musique Mechanique, European Tour 1977, 13 & ¾* (with Mantler), *Social Studies*, and—to refute the notion that women cannot work in large scale—her monumental three-record "chronotransduction," *Escalator over the Hill*, "sort of a free-associative oratorio,"[4] which took her four years to produce.

Revolutionizing the business aspects of the music, in the mid-sixties Bley and Mantler also founded New Music Distribution Service, which provided artists with new options in terms of developing and recording their work without compromise and obtaining an outlet for distribution. By the late seventies Bley had started her own orchestra, which crossed the lines between jazz, rock, and "new music." "The music is by turns hilarious, sober, reflective and aggressive," wrote one reviewer, "but it is always wholly personal."[5] "She creates luminous, lyrical but also sinewy pieces," said Nat Hentoff, and ". . . I rather think that much of her work will endure longer than that of some of her more hugely shouting contemporaries."[6]

Bley is today regarded as one of the most ground-breaking and influential forces in the music world, and is also, one writer notes, "one of the very few women acknowledged as a major composer."[7]

Carla (Borg) Bley was born in California in 1938. Both of her parents were musicians, and her father, organist and choirmaster at their church, also taught piano. Bley began composing early and was greatly influenced by church hymns, as well as by classical music and "badly played scales and elementary piano pieces," which her father's students played at their lessons. Bley herself had embarked upon a formal musical education, but, she says, after exasperating her father and biting her mother on the arm, "they both gave up on me, and I developed in my own, unsupervised way." When a talent competition opened her eyes "to the deficiencies caused by my wilfullness regarding fingering and other boring technical things," she adds, "I soon stopped studying altogether."[8]

At fifteen Bley quit high school, got a job selling music, and joined up with a folk singer writing songs and singing in nightclubs. Still unfamiliar with jazz or improvisation, she took some jobs playing beautiful but, in her words, "unspontaneous" standards, and then, on an impulse, went to New York with a friend who was traveling there from California. Her first jobs were at Birdland and Basin Street—working as a hatcheck girl—and soon she started to write for pianist Paul Bley's group. (Eventually she and Bley married—"one of the few ways of locomotion for women," Bley told writer Margo Jefferson.[9]) Soon other musicians started to play and record her work—Jimmy Guiffre, Art Farmer, Charlie Haden, George Russell. Bley herself was playing in Greenwich Village coffeehouses and in Charles Moffett's group with Pharaoh Sanders.

By the mid-sixties, frustrated with the commercial aspects of the music world, Bley, as previously mentioned, helped to found the short-lived Jazz Composer's Guild. Though the effort failed at that time, the concept was sound, and by 1964, with Michael Mantler—Bley's second husband and "a composer whose music was as strange as mine"[10]—she founded the Jazz Composer's Orchestra, which, like the earlier Jazz Composer's Guild, existed to service composers writing for large ensembles. Shortly after JCO was formed, she helped to organize the Jazz Composer's Orchestra Association (JCOA), a nonprofit organization to support the orchestra and to commission and record new works.

When Bley and Mantler formed the JCOA label, Bley has said, the commercial community wanted nothing to do with them: "The recording business, like all big businesses governed by the profit motive, was fast deteriorating into a mere vehicle for providing ever cheaper and more accessible produce for consumption by the largest possible market."[11] "Will it sell?" was the prime consideration. When JCO approached major companies, their problems were more acute than those of other artists: They were innovative, unknown, and big, with at least twenty musicians plus well-known soloists, all of whom commanded high salaries. After discouraging attempts to track down recording-company notables who were forever "out to lunch," Bley and Mantler, with two albumsful of material ready, decided to put out their own album. By the fall of 1968, *The Jazz Composer's Orchestra* was ready, composed and conducted by Michael Mantler and featuring Cecil Taylor, Roswell Rudd, Don Cherry, Gato Barbieri, Pharoah Sanders, and Larry Coryell.

They next had to face the problem of distribution. The record sold well in Europe and Japan, where demand for such music allowed it to exist within the commercial structure; but, in America, they had to depend on word of mouth and mail orders, which brought small but intense reaction, and kept sales small and slow. At this time, Bley was also at work on her own extensive work, *Escalator over the Hill*. Realizing that she and Mantler were not creating "popular music in any accepted formula," they decided to create a nonprofit distribution service that would cater to "all the unpopular music labels like our own."[12] Thus, New Music Distribution Service was born, and its services were available to all those who were writing or playing "new music," with no judgments made by Bley or Mantler as to whose work they would accept.

"Instead of properly disappearing," said Bley, "we got stubborn. Step by step, never realizing how far we'd have to go, we built our own survival system. If something we wanted or needed didn't exist, we created it."[13] By the end of the seventies, NMDS's catalog contained over 200 titles, produced by over fifty record companies. (Their most successful albums—Chick Corea's *Return to Forever* and Gil Scott-Heron's *Winter in America*, for example—eventually went over to ECM.) "We were all inspired by each other's existence," Bley wrote of the Friendly Independent Record Makers, "and moved by the fact that there was so much endurance in each of us. We were the weeds, the wildflowers, the ones who had managed to survive without care."[14]

"For serious jazz and post-jazz players," Nat Hentoff wrote, this kind of "indigenous socialism may be the only way to maintain creative independence."[15]

In 1977, after working in Europe with the Jack Bruce band, Carla Bley became more interested in presenting live music. JCO had always been too big and unwieldy to take on the road, and so, says Bley, she learned to orchestrate more economically, and came up with the ideal instrumentation and material—a ten-piece band that, like Ellington's and Akiyoshi's, exists to perform its leader's music.

Onstage Bley is an antic, unpredictable, charismatic presence, and her band responds in kind, as well as by reading, playing, and improvising on her music impeccably. She draws on a wide variety of musical idioms and influences—Spanish-civil-war songs, marching-band music, Indian ragas (in western scales), the classical chamber-ensemble approach on ¾ (which one writer called "an orchestral fantasy on waltzes"[16]), the Beatles, Kurt Weill, and Ellington, among others. But, a true original, Bley brings these elements together in unique statements and whimsical confrontations; she is out to "tickle tonality," not to "overthrow it."[17]

In the mid-sixties, Bley has said, she got sick of "screaming" free music and got angry at jazz. "I'm using 'jazz' in reference to musicians who like to take long solos whether they're interesting or not—that's the jazz I object to." She came home from a Paris club one night and started work on *A Genuine Tong Funeral*. "That's when my life started. I stopped being part of the stream I was in and struck out as a protest to that stream." Ornette Coleman had freed the music so the changes followed the melody, Bley said, "but then we took the next step out and tried to free the rhythm section from following the melody, and that's where we messed up, because that was total chaos." After Coleman, she says, she stopped listening. Today, she doesn't listen to music that isn't at least twenty years old, and without exception prefers rock and classical. "I need a lot of order. I'm a very conservative person," she says.[18]

Bley discusses her approach to her music with varying degrees of whimsicality or seriousness. "The little horns get the high notes, and the big ones get the low ones," she once wrote.[19] She will also admit that her music is difficult: "It demands a state of the art reading and a naïveté and freshness that come from not knowing how to read music. . . . I'm a good composer, probably. I think that's what I've come out with, that's my one shred of true self-respect now. It's something that I've learned and I don't even have to be modest about it. I'm a good composer and I work really hard. It's not easy for me, but I'm a hard enough worker that over a period of six months I can come up with a good piece of music. That's what I'll say without modesty."[20]

Barbara Donald

(trumpet/composer/leader)

Beginning with Miles Davis, who bird-dogged Charlie Parker as a young man and played at his side during his formative years, every instrumentalist since 1950 is derivative of the Parker style. The list includes all of the important figures in jazz since 1950: Sonny Rollins, Ornette Coleman, Eric Dolphy, Sonny Simmons, Clifford Brown, Red Rodney, Barbara Donald, Bud Powell, Hampton Hawes, John Lewis, Cecil Taylor, John Coltrane, Roland Kirk, Pharoah Sanders, Albert Ayler, and Archie Shepp. In their playing is more than the foundation of Parker's jazz style. In varying degrees one also hears the religious ecstasy of Parker's music.

—Ross Russell
Bird Lives!

During the 1950s, while the last units of the International Sweethearts of Rhythm were on the road, and while Norma Carson, Terry Pollard, Beryl Booker, Corky Hale, and Mary Osborne were recording *Cats vs. Chicks*, Barbara Donald was growing up listening to her mother's big-band records and learning about such trumpet players as Harry James and Cat Anderson. When she graduated from high school in 1960 and headed for a career in music, however, she found it impossible to break into the commercial world. By the early sixties she had found her place in the avant-garde jazz community, where she was, she says, always completely accepted and respected.

Between 1966 and 1970 Donald recorded with her husband, tenor player Sonny Simmons, as well as with Burt Wilson, Ed Kelly, and Smiley Winters (but never did any albums under her own name). On such records as *Staying on the Watch, Music of the Spheres*, and *Manhattan Egos*, her work with Simmons is defined by long, precise unison lines, and her sound on solos is powerful and fluid. She can produce lightning tempo lines that suggest the intensity of light, or stretch out with classical grace on a ballad.

Donald has recently formed her own group, Unity (with Irvin Lovilette, Gary Peacock, and Carter Jefferson), and in 1978 received an NEA grant for performance. Since 1979 she and her three children have been living in the state of Washington, where Donald moved, seeking a more peaceful atmosphere in which to work on her writing. In 1981, Donald recorded her first album under her own name, featuring Unity and Carter Jefferson.

Barbara Donald was born in Minneapolis, Minnesota, in 1942. Her mother, she says, was "very musical" and had perfect pitch, as well as a collection of big-band records. "I wanted to play an instrument really bad," says Donald, who started playing the trumpet in school. "I really didn't know exactly what I was getting. I thought that they were gonna give me a flute, but instead they gave me a trumpet, and I started playing it. Then I started listening to Harry James all the time and Cat Anderson, and after that I got into Maynard Ferguson. I just went through all the big-band trumpet players, really listening to 'em, and that was up until I was about fourteen."

At fourteen Donald moved to California. "Then I started listening to another style of music besides big band. I started listening to Art Farmer and Miles Davis—early Miles a lot. And then I met Benny Harris [who played with Charlie Parker]. I was seventeen, eighteen, someplace I was sittin' in on a jam session and he started showing me a lot of stuff. Then my ears started opening more, and I started listening to Clifford Brown and Fats Navarro and even Louis Armstrong sometimes. Plus, with the real good studio teacher I had, besides the jazz, I was able to learn reading and fundamentals of music."

Donald had, in fact, already learned many of the fundamentals of music, but had really never had an opportunity to put them to use. "They wouldn't accept me," she says. "It didn't matter what I did." In high school, she recalls, the director of the stage band would not admit her because she was a woman. "I got really mad and I started my own band. The musicians weren't into that; it was just the teacher. So I started my own, only it was even better, 'cause I took the best kids from all the high schools, and then I went around and got women's clubs, dances, and weddings, jobs for the band. And the teacher came up to me and said he was mad, because I was taking all his musicians and even some of the jobs he was trying to get for the high-school band."

Donald was playing lead and first trumpet in the band, but, when graduation came, while the other players got offers to go out with Stan Kenton and Buddy Rich, she was faced with the same problem she had faced in high school: no women. "I was just as capable of anything they were capable of," she says, "but they just would not hire me. They wouldn't even *think* about hiring me. So I tried to [work in] a lot of dumb commercial bands. In fact, one of them was an all-woman's band. It wasn't really music. They wanted you to stand up there in these ridiculous shoes and a funny-looking dress with glitters all over it, and swing your horn back and forth and do a dance step, and try to play two notes or something and wear this funny-looking wig. I did it for two weeks. It was in Nevada, and I just flipped out. It was a show band, more or less. They weren't musicians."

After that misadventure, Donald went back to L.A. and started a small group of her own, which she took out on the road: "We played old-time songs for dances and stuff like that, NCO clubs, and we went down in the South, and oh, it was terrible! Back then, down in the South wasn't something I could deal with, especially when I sat at the back of the bus. We didn't make much money, but it was something to do. Then we came back."

At this point, Donald met and married her first husband, who was playing piano with Dexter Gordon. "I just couldn't deal with the commercial stuff," she says. "It wasn't that much money. I said I'd rather study more and get into playing really hard jazz. And then, of course, Benny Harris was takin' me around, showing me everything, introducing me to everybody. I got to meet people that I ordinarily wouldn't have gotten to meet, plus he introduced me to my last husband, Sonny Simmons." (Donald and Simmons, who were married in 1964, moved to New York in 1965 and stayed there through the late seventies. "It's not altogether impossible that we will play together again," Donald says.)

Her music came out of bop, she says, and went "into a totally avant-garde type of playing. I tried to play it differently. I knew my horn pretty well; I already knew the chords and had the knowledge. A lot of people during that time were just playing on feelings, not necessarily knowledge, but I used both of them. I was playing my horn in all types of intervals and all registers and creating my own melodies. I always wanted to play with energy and I still do. I guess I also had a lot of rebellion in me from not being accepted. I'm doing all the things now I really wanted to do back then, because I've developed more." (One of the things Donald is striving to achieve on trumpet is the smooth, fluid sound of the saxophone.) "The people I used to deal with, a lot of the leaders, were shocked when they found out I was accepted, and all of a sudden they got real nice." One of the musicians who "accepted" her was John Coltrane, with whom she was invited to sit in two weeks after her second son was born. "We just looked right at each other and locked up on some phrases, and some things came out of my horn I didn't know I could even play," she remembers.

Since 1979 Donald has been writing and working with her group around Tacoma, Washington. "We go inside and we go outside. We stay on fire, though; we keep everybody's attention." In general, Donald finds there are not "a whole lot of good musicians around now. A lot of the younger ones are really well schooled, but they don't have the feeling or the emotion. You have to have both; one is no good without the other. A lot of people have a lot of feeling, but they don't have the knowledge, so up here there's just a few that I can play with."

"I'm so isolated up here, it's easier to think clearer," Donald says. "And, of course, I practice all the time. If I'm not practicing, I listen. I find myself listening a lot to Cedar Walton lately—I'm going back inside again. There's not too many outside things I really enjoy now. And, of course, I listen to 'Trane. I still listen to 'Trane and Bird all the time. And I listen to JoAnne [Brackeen] a lot, too. She's really takin' care of business.

"It seems like since I picked up the trumpet I had a big tone. It's a natural tone. That's funny, 'cause a lot of people that I grew up with that went out with Stan Kenton, they have the same tone now. It may be a little more advanced, but it's still the same sound that they had when they were just learning. But I've developed mine to get bigger and bigger. It's not a physical thing that gives me a big tone; it's definitely a mental thing. I think back about Bird, and I think about Clifford Brown, and I think about *music*, how it should be strong and alive. If you listen to Freddie Hubbard, he has a big sound, and Clora Bryant has a big sound, and it's important to have that in your mind. That projects and that grabs the people, and they have to listen to it, whether you're a man, woman, child, or whatever. You can't help but listen.

"I was talking to some trumpet players that were men, and they were on a trip about mouthpieces. They're always changing their mouthpiece. It's *not* the mouthpiece, it's how you approach playing the instrument. I became aware of a lot of this stuff when I was younger, because I had a lot of good teachers. It doesn't matter what size you are or what sex you are or anything. Women should just get that out of their minds. Music is not football; it's not baseball or boxing. Not that women can't do that, too, but I'm just saying, music is meant for everybody to play. I'd sure like to see more women playing instruments. It seems like so many of them don't do it for one reason or another. It's really a hard thing, especially with the economy. But if I had it to do over, I would.

"I'm playing better now than I ever have. I could play an hour with extreme energy without stopping, because that's all I do is play. There's a lot of women that play, but they've been killed off. I was fortunate, you know: I got a little recognition before I die. I'm not quite gone yet— I'm far from that."

Vi Redd

(alto sax/soprano sax/vocals/leader)

> I think a lot of women might feel a certain commitment, but I
> think it takes more than that to hang in there with an art form
> that hasn't been supported in large, and I think that the women
> horn players who are still playing and can still play on a high
> level, I think it's hard. They have to sacrifice, and not many people
> are willing to sacrifice. For Vi Redd to be playing now took some-
> thing *extra*. Not everybody can be that dedicated.
>
> —Janice Robinson

Vi Redd was born in Los Angeles. Her father, New Orleans drummer
Alton Redd, worked with Les Hite, Kid Ory, and many other groups; her
brother was a percussionist; and her mother played saxophone, although
not professionally. Originally, Redd started out playing piano, but when
she was about ten, her great-aunt, Mrs. Alma Hightower (who had
taught Melba Liston), gave her a saxophone mouthpiece, told her to
blow on it, and informed her that from then on she was going to play
the saxophone.

Redd grew up with such schoolmates as Eric Dolphy and Martha
Young and had neighborhood sessions with the likes of Hampton Hawes.
Although she continued to sing and play while attending Los Angeles
Community College, she majored in social science. After graduating from
Los Angeles State College in 1954, Redd worked exclusively in music for
several years, but in 1957 she took a job with the county and did not
return to music full time until 1961.

In 1962 Leonard Feather wrote: "Few alto players in the last year
have a more Bird-like sound or a better blues-rooted feeling than Vi
Redd. . . . She is a singer with an impressively resonant timbre and fine
intonation and phrasing." Yet, Feather noted, despite her obvious excellence, because of her sex she was all too often thought of, not as "an
available saxophonist who plays and reads well and can hold down a
chair in any man's reed section, but rather as a novelty who can't really
be that good."[21] Nevertheless, throughout the sixties came a number of
highlights in Redd's career. During the early part of the decade she recorded the album *Bird Call*, and later did *Lady Soul*, which displays her
melismatic, bluesy vocals and, as Feather remarked in the liner notes,
her "raw, gutty quality" on alto; another date, Al Gray's album *Shades
of Gray*, contains what Redd considers her best recorded performances,
on "Dinah" and "Puttin' on Mellow." Redd also appeared at the 1966

Monterey Jazz Festival, toured Europe in 1967 (during which time she was the only American artist to work in Ronnie Scott's club in London for a ten-week stretch), and in 1968 toured Europe again, this time with Count Basie.

At the same time that Redd was pursuing her career in music, she had also been married to drummer Richie Goldberg and was involved in raising their children. In the early seventies, while her sons were growing up, she curtailed her musical activities and taught for seven years, working with retarded children. Then, around 1976, she decided to come back to the music. "I felt I had something to offer," she told Shanta Nurullah in an interview.[22] The message she tries to convey, she says, is love. "Be forgiving, understanding, just love."

In response to a question about whether she felt she had received adequate recognition for her work, Redd said, "Oh, no, not from the general public. I'm not even concerned about it anymore. I'm happy with myself. I know who I am. I know what my abilities are. I think some of the musicians know I've made a contribution of some sort . . .

"When I think of people like Diz, there were such sacrifices to keep the music. And Sarah Vaughan—Dexter Gordon once said, 'She should be paid $25,000 a night.' Maybe that would compensate for all the days she had to ride the buses. The sacrifices these musicians have made— these musicians killed on the road; the black musicians denied service, denied lodging, denied medical care . . . But they kept forging ahead, and they made a sacrifice to jazz, let's face it."

Redd also talked about what it was like being a female horn player: "I've gotten rebuked so many times in the past," she said. "Some have walked off as I came on. There's still a subtle resentment if the fella feels insecure. I often tell people, and it's true, the fact that I'm a female is an act of God and I wouldn't be anything else. I love being a female; I love being a mother. I love being a woman. But it's never really entered my mind that I played the horn. It's the other people that have the hang-ups. It doesn't really bother me."[23]

Patti Bown

(piano/composer/leader)

Patti Bown began to attract attention when she worked with Quincy Jones's big band in 1960. She has recorded with the Jones band, as well as with such artists as Aretha Franklin, Benny Carter, Jimmy Rushing, Rahsaan Roland Kirk, Duke Ellington, and George Russell, among many others. (During the late fifties and in the sixties, when family responsibilities made it difficult for Patti to go out on the road extensively, she established herself as one of the most versatile musicians in the recording field, thereby insuring that she would be able to stay in New York with her family and still earn her living in music. Women were not widely accepted in the studios at that time, she notes, which makes her success in that regard even more noteworthy.)

In 1961, her own album, *Patti Bown Plays Big Piano*, included four of her own compositions—"G'wan Train," "Nothing But the Truth," "Head Shakin'," and "Waltz de Funk." Patti has also served as musical director for Sarah Vaughan and Dinah Washington, played for Broadway shows, composed for TV and films, and taught at Bennington College. Most recently, with Kenyan poet and lyricist Japhet Okari, she cofounded Universal Arts and Folklore, a "pan-artistic" organization that, by emphasizing human encounter, hopes to foster respect, understanding, and growth among peoples of different ages, races, sex, and religion. The group, she feels, will also enable her to extend jazz beyond what she already knows, to make possible a marriage of cross-cultural musical elements.

John S. Wilson has called Bown "strictly her own woman—a forceful, ebullient, and colorful performer."[24] Whitney Balliett, after hearing her play John Coltrane's "Giant Steps," called it an "eight-minute lesson in how to make a piece of improvisation so tight and complex it would supply a dozen soloists for a week."[25] Yet, like many women, she has had to divide her energy and attention between her family and her work. There have been times, she says, when critics have written about her without being aware of the demands of her family life, which sometimes made it impossible for her to appear as often as she would have liked. "The only reason I stopped doin' what I was doin'," she explains, "was to take care of my son, because I realized that I had to stop, otherwise we would never have an opportunity to get to know each other. So you can't have everything you want when you want it. Sometimes you have it when the time is right."

Patti Bown grew up in Seattle, Washington. There were eight children in the family, and four of the girls, Patti included, demonstrated special musical ability; all four also had the gift of perfect pitch. "We were playing jazz and we were playing the classics," Bown says. "I played by ear. When the others were given lessons, I was told I was too young; I was only two years old. I didn't start studying piano till I was six. It was the best thing that ever happened to me, because I was allowed the freedom to play by myself for long periods of time. I just sat there and did my own thing at the piano whenever I got the chance, and I think that's what made me get free, and very much into my own musical personality. By the time I did get lessons, I was already very much into playing jazz. I also tried to imitate everything I heard, including car horns, fire engines, and whatever. I was supersensitive to all sounds—sometimes, in fact, this made it impossible for me to play an out-of-tune piano.

"I loved to listen to all kinds of music. One of my strongest influences for jazz, probably, was Duke Ellington. I remember hearing a record of 'Chelsea Bridge' which knocked me out. I was about two years old. It was hard to get hold of jazz records in Seattle, and that was the first recorded jazz I can remember. I was a very active two-year-old, running through the house, filled with energy. I was a terror, so by the time I found Duke Ellington my family was very happy, because that was the first time I sat still. I could sit for hours and listen to Duke Ellington, Billie Holiday, Erroll Garner, and whatever other artists we could get recordings by."

Patti's parents' house was open to people, to art, to culture. "My mother painted, and she always used to take us to museums and all kinds of concerts and tried to explore our creativity as much as possible. She and my father were always pushing us some kinda way. My father was the son of a freed slave. When he was only in the second grade, his dying father called him to his bedside and told him he was depending on him to support his mother and the rest of his family, so he had to quit school and go to work at nine years of age. My mother, the child of an Irish father and black mother, had been orphaned at twelve, but still managed to get a college education by working hard and making a lot of sacrifices. By the time they met and married, they had each paid a lot of dues, and their main priority was finding a peaceful environment in which to raise their family. So I grew up with a lot of love. I think that secure home life undoubtedly helped me to survive all the things that happened to me in the jazz world."

When Patti was old enough, she started to take piano lessons with her sisters. They studied with an old lady who, according to Patti, used to fall asleep when she was giving a lesson. "We split an hour, four sisters." In the beginning Patti never learned how to read there. Because she could play so well by ear, she would get her older sister (who could read) to play her lessons over for her, and she learned them that way. "I'd play my two little pieces fast, and get my gold star, so I could go outside and play baseball with my friends. I was a crook, I'm afraid."

Patti's musical education continued in the Catholic school she attended for twelve years. "The nun who taught me music had a long yardstick. If I made a mistake, she used to crack my knuckles and make them bleed. Eventually, she stopped using that method of discipline, and taught me from fourth grade through high school. I was determined to learn any way I could, so I went to the library and got out big, thick books about music, and I told her one day I was gonna quit music, and she wanted to know why. 'Because,' I said, 'all this is playing recitals and making your mother happy, putting on little corny dresses, and I wanna do something else besides that. I wanna know what's really happening inside the music.' So then she kept me after school, and that was the beginning of me studying with her privately. She gave me extra time and started teaching me extra things. I started studying harmony, a little counterpoint, and some composition. But I was aware that that was a limited thing, because she couldn't comprehend the jazz. I was still thinking improvisationally, so I was making up my own little songs. I didn't work in any clubs, because I was underage, but I was playing for singers, for dance classes, for masses in Catholic church, and programs in black churches. It was a sin for a Catholic to go to another church service, but I always found myself near where the music was grooving. If something was really good, I found a way to get there. I had to go hear music."

"My parents used to take us out a lot, too," Patti recalls. "If there was a really good band playing for a dance, my father would take us and park the car right underneath the window and get my sisters to go inside and open the window, make sure we heard the music before we went to sleep. They kept encouraging us to listen to and enjoy music."

Patti actually began to work professionally when she was about three, and her childhood performances took her everywhere from the governor's mansion to Sunday afternoon dances at the officers' clubs. There was also one club in town where underage people who were studying jazz hung out, and Patti always managed to get in there if there was something she really wanted to hear. She was generally the only female musician in the place, but that never bothered her at all. "I wanted to play. I didn't care. Wherever I could learn, I tried to get there."

Patti was nearing the end of high school when one of her sisters (a classically trained pianist and protégée of Orson Welles and Paul Robeson), having studied in France, returned to America to give a Town Hall concert. "She was sponsored by Sol Hurok," Patti says, "and even though she had rave reviews, because she was *black* and also because she was *female* it was the wrong time, politically, in this country. Sol Hurok told her he was very sorry, but those were two strikes against her, that he couldn't handle her, and the best he could offer her was a tour of southern Negro colleges. There was just no money, and she could not really be seen or get across. This was the plight of many gifted black artists at the time, who, because of the political climate, were not permitted to become what they certainly had the ability to be."

From childhood on, Patti had herself been winning various classical piano contests, but was still deeply involved with her own creation of jazz. Her parents, though, were eager for her to pursue a classical career. "Even though my sister was not allowed to become successful, they were still determined I was gonna make it and be an exceptional concert pianist. My mother was still fighting for all that."

By the time Patti graduated from high school, she had been offered over forty-five college and conservatory scholarships and been voted the "girl most likely to succeed." None of these schools provided what she was after, however. "They didn't even respect the things I did creatively," she says. "They were looking to make me into a concert pianist. I went to a Catholic university for about a year, and then I split and went to a nonsectarian university, and it was just as bad. So I gave up my college scholarship and went back to the Catholic university. I was also working at this time, and the schedule was too intense. I had to take some time off. Eventually, I got my degree from the conservatory, but I started realizing that there just weren't any books to play the music I was into. I had to keep developing myself, writing my own book, playing myself, and doing just like I was doing when I was two years old. I knew it was the right course. I couldn't listen to anybody else telling me how."

In the mid-fifties, Patti realized there was no way she could "possibly make a nickel playing in Seattle," and she moved to New York. "I had met and played with Dizzy Gillespie when I was a child in Seattle," she recalls, "and he got me some gigs after I first came to New York. A few people gave me some work. In those days, there were agents who booked women musicians in the so-called 'better neighborhoods' of New York. Many of them expected you to socialize with customers, and many times, you were bothered by businessmen who propositioned you. Sometimes they would turn out to be friends of the club owner or agent, and if you turned them down, you would be fired. So I lost a few jobs over that.

"I can remember one particular job I was booked on—it was all the way at the end of Flatbush Avenue in Brooklyn. I lived way up in Harlem at that time, and I remember having to go there on the subway, walking seven or eight blocks when there was ice on the ground, and then when I got paid, wondering if some street thugs were going to steal my money. I used to pay the bartender twenty dollars to drive me back home, so it meant a night's pay just to get home, to try to protect what little bit of money was there, to keep me and my son eating. So you can imagine the frustration."

In 1960 Quincy Jones, who was putting together a big band, asked Patti to be the pianist. "I grew up with Quincy in Seattle," she says, "and Quincy had the choice of any pianist he wanted, so I was happy that he chose me. He had another woman in the band—Melba Liston." Also in the band were Budd Johnson, Phil Woods, Benny Bailey, and Sahib Shihab. They went to Europe with Harold Arlen's *Free and Easy*, a blues opera, and though the show closed after only two months, the band continued to tour for another ten. "Every time there was a write-up, there was a write-up about Quincy and about me," Patti says. "Me being a female, and the fact that I was an unusual soloist or something. I didn't gear it that way, but that's just the way it went down. People would came to see the band, and right away I would be the one they'd notice because I was so flamboyant. This did not make me too popular with some of the other members of the band."

When the Jones band returned to America in 1961, Patti embarked on a long period during which she went back to the recording studios and also worked in Broadway pit orchestras. (She spent two and a half years with the hit show *Purlie Victorious*.) Most recently, she has been performing in a variety of clubs and contexts as leader of her own small groups, and has become increasingly involved with composing.

"I love to write my own compositions," says Patti. "I hope my music has grown some as I hope I've grown as a person. But I think basically I can see a lot of things in my music that reflect my earliest musical instincts. I seem to lean toward brevity and simplicity in my writing. Some things are better left unsaid. I'm really a melody writer. I think melody writers are born with a gift, and it's something that when it does happen, you know it's right. The more I do it, the more I enjoy it and the more I get great pleasure out of doing it. I love to play, and I love to hear other people play, too."

Women have been playing jazz for decades, Patti says, but many have never gotten the attention they deserve. "Maybe they got married and had a baby, or disappeared into the mainstream. Many times, their husbands demanded that they give up their careers. Many just gave up the fight because it was very hard to make it." But for Patti, the hardest choice would have been to live a life without her music.

"Other people may have their images about what the life of a jazz pianist is like," she says, "but I just try to do the best that I know how. Every time I perform, I meditate, then I go on and just try to give it everything I've got."

THE SEVENTIES

Perhaps the most important lesson to have emerged from the New Feminism of the sixties was the realization that the personal was political—the "problems" each woman considered uniquely her own were, in fact, common to other women as well. By the early seventies, as women began to share their feelings about their lives, work, and art, and to reevaluate and explore their heritage in all fields, the old myths and stereotypes that had historically surrounded them began to fall away.

In jazz, the decade was, more than anything, one of transition and diversity. As the younger generation and the public began to recognize the special value of the professionalism and experience of the older artists—and to appreciate the dues they had paid in paving the way—the jazz picture became an amalgam of women from every decade and tradition: mainstream, bop, avant-garde, even "new music" and "fusion."

At the second Women's Jazz Festival in Kansas City (1978), twelve of the original Sweethearts of Rhythm were honored, and the West Coast all-woman band Maiden Voyage performed. Vocalists Sheila Jordan and Betty Carter, who had struggled uncompromisingly through several decades, now came into their prime and received the recognition they were due. "Betty Carter's development over the past 35 years," wrote Stanley Crouch, "has been central to the evolution of jazz singing. [She is today] a sure enough jazz singer and one of the two or three best in the entire world."[1] In 1970 Mary Lou Williams initiated the jazz policy at New York's Cookery, and in 1975 blues singer Alberta Hunter scored perhaps the most celebrated jazz comeback of the decade there.

The seventies also saw the formation of two of the most important big bands: the Carla Bley band; and the Toshiko Akiyoshi/Lew Tabackin band, winner of polls both here and in Japan and a four-time Grammy winner. Akiyoshi's music is complex, original, and richly colored, drawing on Japanese culture and traditions and blending them with jazz to create a vital new music. Akiyoshi has called herself a "member of so-

ciety first and a musician second," and this sense of responsibility is reflected in her music: "Kogun" was dedicated to the Japanese soldier who
was discovered in the Philippines thirty years after the war; "Tales of a
Courtesan" deals with the falsely romanticized western image of the
courtesan ("My music," Akiyoshi said, "expresses the contrast between
the superficially luxurious life of some of these women and the tragic
denial of human rights they suffered"[2]); and "Minimata," a suite on her
album *Insights*, was her reaction to the tragedy of a small Japanese fish-
ing village contaminated by industrial pollution. Some compositions are
firmly rooted in the classic swing-band tradition, while others utilize the
Japanese "arched beat," or devices from Noh drama. "I'm trying to draw
from my heritage and enrich the jazz tradition without changing it,"
Akiyoshi told one interviewer. "I'm putting into jazz, not just taking out."[3]

Among the prominent newer names were innovative guitarist Monette
Sudler, Fostina Dixon, Jane Ira Bloom, Erica Lindsay, Janice Robinson,
Sharon Freeman (piano/French horn), Karen Borca (bassoon), Barbara
Merjan (drums), Chessie Tanksley (piano), Stacy Rowles (trumpet),
Jean Fineberg (tenor sax), Ellen Seeling (trumpet and co-leader with
Fineberg of the quintet Deuce), Mary Watkins (piano), Amina Claudine
Myers (piano, organ, vocals), flautists Andrea Brachfield and Bobbi
Humphry, vocalists Urszula Dudziak, Jay Clayton, and Janet Lawson,
keyboard player/vocalist Judy Roberts, the all-woman group Alive, and
tap dancer Jane Goldberg.

On the recording front, several small independent labels reissued
works by many historic women in jazz (see Discography). A series of
anthologies on the Stash label made available recordings by women
ranging from Dolly Jones to Mary Lou Williams, Ina Ray Hutton's Melodears to the International Sweethearts of Rhythm, the Hip Chicks to
Arizona Dranes; Rosetta Records brought out two blues-women anthologies, *Mean Mothers (Independent Women's Blues)* and *Women's Railroad
Blues (Sorry But I Can't Take You)*; and Inner City Records offered
a "Women in Jazz" series that featured such artists as Helen Humes,
Urszula Dudziak, Helen Merrill, Irene Kral, Monette Sudler, Toshiko
Akiyoshi, and Judy Roberts, to name a few.

Due to the heightening commercial orientation of the big recording
companies, during the seventies women increasingly started to produce
their own records, following Mary Lou Williams's 1963 example. Among
those who did were Marian McPartland, Jane Ira Bloom, Carla Bley
(with Michael Mantler), Toshiko Akiyoshi (with Lew Tabackin), and
Betty Carter. Said Carter, "I'm not looking for any hit records; that's
why I have my own label. The independent record label is more important now than ever, because it allows you to document your own ideas,
your *own* soul. It's about you all the way."[4]

The seventies also saw the founding of two important nonprofit organizations: the Women's Jazz Festival (founded in Kansas City by Dianne Gregg and Carol Comer); and the New York-based Universal Jazz Coalition (founded by Cobi Narita). One thing the festival has taught them, says Gregg, is "how many women are into jazz all around the world. And the one thing that is consistent in all the letters from them is they've found it very difficult for the most part to work their craft, to be accepted."

Gregg, Comer, and Narita all agree that they look forward to the day when they can "put the festivals out of business," since that will mean that women have become fully integrated into the jazz world. Until that time, they will continue to provide forums where female musicians can present their music and come together in workshops, concerts, seminars, and clinics; they also publish national directories of women in the field. The WJF hopes eventually to have a recording company to produce the work of female jazz artists, and to sponsor a jazz camp for women. ("There are many around the country," says Gregg, "but very few women ever attend them, and you rarely find female instructors.")

The UJC—one third of whose 5,000 musician members are female— encourages its membership to learn the business aspects of music, and stresses the importance of autonomy and leadership roles. Women are therefore able to become more sophisticated about the business and to take their careers into their own hands to a much greater degree than ever before. The UJC also provides its members with services they might not otherwise have access to or be able to afford, such as career guidance, printing facilities, and low-cost mailings.

At the New York Salutes to Women in Jazz (produced "with no up-front money," Narita points out), there are free day-long outdoor concerts, workshops, conferences, and six evening concerts featuring four or five groups each night. Since 1978 the UJC has featured, among others, Patti Bown, Willene Barton, JoAnne Brackeen, Melba Liston, Sarah Mc-Lawler, Jane Ira Bloom, Revella Hughes, Corky Hale, Julie Gardner, Dakota Staton, Evelyn Blakey, Sheila Jordan, Jane Jarvis, Jean Davis, Bernadine Warren, Jay Clayton, Carline Ray, Keisha St. Joan, Jill Mc-Manus, Nina Sheldon, and Sharon Freeman.

Since the inception of the Kansas City and New York women's festivals, there have been similar events produced in Rome, Detroit, Boston, Chicago, and other cities. "We'll do anything we can to help any organization that wants to put on a women's jazz festival," says Gregg, "or wants to do something to promote women in jazz. We'll work with anybody on that, because that is our whole purpose. A lot of people have the same ideas or intentions that we do. The only difference between us and those other folks is that we went ahead and did it. But I know there are a lot of people around that would like to be doing the same thing—and I wish they would."

In reviewing a concert of the Big Apple Jazzwomen, the late Jon Saunders noted with indignation that "when women perform together, the 'sexist mentality' of some males [still] insists that they are inferior musicians."[5] Some women who had been playing for twenty or thirty years said that they noticed a backlash: Men who would have played with them twenty years ago no longer wanted to play with women. Most of the women, meanwhile, remained clear about being musicians, first and foremost: The only movement *they* were really interested in was harmonic. The one thing everyone could agree on was that it was a time of transition and growth, a time, as Betty Carter had said, for women in jazz "to document [their] own soul[s]."

When the owners of the club where the second New York Salute to Women in Jazz was to be held locked the UJC out on the night of the concert because the club owners wanted their money "up front," the enterprising Cobi Narita had the musicians unpack their instruments and play the concert on the street. "Women make it work," Narita said. "They cope."

So they always have.

Following, six of the most highly respected women in the jazz world of the seventies talk about their music and their careers.

Ann Patterson

(reeds/leader)

Ann Patterson is the leader of the West Coast all-woman band Maiden Voyage. While some writers place the band in the tradition of the all-woman bands of the forties, Patterson is quick to note that there are some very crucial differences between her band and the earlier ones. In the past, she says, the purpose of women's bands was almost entirely commercial. While she recognizes that a band must be commercially viable if it is to survive, her major goals for Maiden Voyage, in addition to financial security, are: "to give women who have incredible potential some experience; to give women who are doing their thing and doing it well some exposure; and to give women musicians some work. All of those things contribute to changing attitudes toward women musicians. The most important thing to me is that it's giving women some experience, and that's gonna make them competitive with the guys. The same with the [Women's Jazz] Festival in Kansas City. There are some things that go on musically there that are not of the quality of the regular festivals. But because it's happening, eventually it will be of the quality, so that's the important thing. The experience is going to make women competitive, because the only difference between some of the women in the band and the guys that are working professional musicians, and good jazz players, is time—time and experience."

Ann Patterson grew up in a small town in Texas during the fifties. Like many of the women in Maiden Voyage, she did not start out her life, or even her career, knowing that she wanted to be a jazz musician. Patterson's early training was classical. She started piano at seven, saxophone in the school band at eleven, and two years later switched to oboe because the band director needed one. Patterson had never heard much live music at all then, and says she didn't even know what jazz was.

"But I loved to play pop things on my saxophone, and that fifties rock thing was happening and I'd try to bend those notes and play soulfully. This was the fifties, and my town was pretty segregated. I had gone to one of the black churches to play a special number on my saxophone—this was in the very beginning and I could hardly play the horn—and the music that I heard there influenced how I played that day. I think I had something inside of me that wanted to play jazz, but it just didn't even seem to be a possibility in the fifties. I didn't know that was something that *girls* could do. Girls were encouraged to do everything boys were doing in school. But it was kinda weird, you know, because once school was out, then you either went to college or you got married and had babies. During high school, there were things that girls did that they wouldn't think of doing as a profession later on.

"I'd never heard of Vi Redd or any of the women horn players, although I think at some point I heard of Ella Fitzgerald and other big singers and piano players. By the time I got out of high school, I had somehow become a classical-music snob and sort of ignored whatever feelings I had to play jazz, because it was just out of the question for me.

"My father had done this whole thing, too—'Well, if you've got to go into music, for God's sake teach; that's really the only acceptable, secure thing for a woman to do in music.'" On this advice, Patterson enrolled at North Texas University, where she continued to study the oboe (but gave up ambitions of someday playing with the New York Philharmonic), and listened to the jazz bands, wishing she were a man so she could play with them.

"I was my own worst enemy," she says. "I just couldn't picture it. I've done a lot of thinking about it. I was raised to be a lady, to be feminine and so forth, and that didn't go with playing jazz. So, besides not seeing any *other* women doing it, I also couldn't see myself doing it. And I really didn't have a lot of self-confidence, anyway." Patterson went on to get her master's degree at the University of Illinois and taught for one year at the University of Wisconsin, after which she returned to Illinois to get married. While her husband was finishing graduate school, she went for a degree in music education. Thinking she might end up a high-school band director, she also started playing in one of the school bands. In 1973 her husband was offered a job in California, and Patterson moved to L.A.

"So I got to L.A.," she says, "spent two miserable years teaching public-school music, and being all alone in California, not very happy with my marriage, and after those two years my whole life sort of turned around. I got a divorce. By that point, I knew what jazz was and that I wanted to play it. I was a much freer person, and I knew that if I wanted to play it, it was a possibility; I could be serious about it. The decision was not really to play jazz but to try to make my living as a professional musician instead of a teacher. I had never thought about the fact that when I would finally get into teaching, I would be playing so little that I would really be unhappy, because when you're at school you're playing all the time. I didn't realize that if you took playing away from me, I just couldn't deal with it."

Patterson began to attend improvisation workshops and to learn the saxophone in earnest, something she had never really done. She played as much as she could, in college bands, rehearsal bands, and, as lead alto, in Don Ellis's band for two years. At that time, Charlie Parker was her main influence; later on it was Phil Woods. "I'm a conservative jazz player," Patterson says. "I'm a bebop player." At present, most of her income comes from commercial jobs, although her two goals, she says, are to become the best jazz player she can be, as well as a top studio musician. "I'm making a living," she says. "I'm not getting rich or anything, but I'm comfortable, and the work I get each year is better. I get better each year."

At the time Patterson was embarking on a full-time career in music, there were various all-woman-band ventures on the West Coast, but her experiences with them had not been rewarding, either financially or musically. It got to the point, she says, that whenever she'd get a call for a commercial proposition, she would just hang up the phone. "They [didn't] even care if you [could] play, as long as you [were] a woman, and relatively attractive," she says. The one women's band that was playing fairly regularly already had a lead alto, former Sweetheart of Rhythm Roz Cron, as one of its co-leaders (with drummer Bonnie Janofsky), but when that alto chair became available, Patterson was called in, and this time she decided to accept the job.

"I was real taken by the seriousness of some of the women," she remarks. "Women musicians I had been in contact with before were not serious, or didn't have enough confidence. I heard some potential in a couple of people, and I had the feeling that there really could be a good all-woman big band out here." Patterson brought in some new players and arrangements, and helped to make the demo tape that got the band to the Women's Jazz Festival in Kansas City. After the festival came an offer to play the Johnny Carson Show; following that appearance, Patterson left the band and, with some former members, formed a new one.

The current Maiden Voyage is made up of women ranging from their late teens to their fifties. In selecting people, Patterson looks for what she calls "inner musicianship—something that you either have or you don't have, because the rest can be learned. I look for potential. A couple of times I've selected real good classical musicians who hadn't played in a big band at all." Her main goal now is to get the band more work. Patterson chooses music that will appeal to jazz fans as well as to the general public—"for financial reasons, but also because I want not just the music world to know that we're serious about what we're doing; I want everybody to know it." She has gotten a dance book together—"Glenn Miller and Tommy Dorsey and all that"—and is trying to book the band on dances, since that is the only way they will make any money around L.A. She has also formed two small groups from the big band, one to play Dixieland, the other jazz, for "casuals" and such.

"Because of the band's existence," Patterson says, "there's been an incredible change in the men musicians. They're more receptive to us because [now] they know that we're serious, even if we have limitations. Most of the jazz playing in the band is not as sophisticated as [that of] the better jazz players in L.A.—and the better jazz players in L.A. are the better jazz players in the world," she says. "They've been doing it all their lives. Also, there are some young, hotshot players out here who haven't been doing it that long, but they knew when they were twelve that's what they wanted to do and they started diggin' in. For a lot of the women in the band, it's taken them a while to get enough nerve and confidence—you heard how long it took me! We have some chops limitations in the brass. We don't have a screech trumpet player. Louise Burke is an incredible lead trumpet player, her range is fine, but we can't do any Maynard Ferguson charts.

"We're getting more and more jobs, because people find it incredibly interesting that here is an all-woman big band, first one that's existed since the forties, that plays well. People really respond to that. I never heard the big bands of the forties. I have a couple of records of the Sweethearts of Rhythm—sounds real good to me. Leonard Feather says that this [Maiden Voyage] is by far the best all-woman band that's ever existed, but to me it's more than that. It's not just 'pretty good for girls'; it's a good band. What matters is that we're doing it—and the band is getting better all the time."

JoAnne Brackeen

(piano/composer)

Beyond question the pianist to watch for in the 80's is JoAnne Brackeen.

—Leonard Feather

Since JoAnne Brackeen began performing and recording under her own name in the late seventies, she has quickly become recognized as one of the most original and visionary keyboard artists and a player of definitively brilliant and flawless technique. She is constantly stretching the parameters of her playing, developing her range of textures and colors. "I don't think when I'm playing at all," says Brackeen. "It's like when you fall asleep, going into a dream . . . or the collective unconscious. That's why you have to take time during the day and think, to keep that interesting at night. Keep yourself interested. You don't want to eat the same food every night. Well, some people do, but not me."

JoAnne Brackeen started playing in her native California in the late fifties. She married saxophonist Charles Brackeen in 1960, and although she continued to study (or practice) and write, performances were infrequent while she was raising their four children. In 1965 they moved to New York, where she began to play with vibraharpist Freddy McCoy. "She belongs to the same generation as Jarrett and Corea," wrote Jim Aikin, "and if she hadn't taken time out to raise a family, her name would probably be as familiar now as theirs are."[6] Another writer has said, "It's customary to speak of Brackeen as an offshoot of Chick Corea and Herbie Hancock, but, since she's currently playing a lot better than both of them, let's skip it."[7]

JoAnne Brackeen was born in Ventura, California, in 1938. She grew up hearing the tunes her father sang while bathing the children, and the pop tunes her mother listened to on the radio. "I used to notice when I was about five or six," she says, "that some of the tunes I would hope went in another direction wouldn't go. They'd be a certain place and I'd say, 'Oh, it's going there,' and it would go; and then I would want it to go somewhere else and it didn't."

Brackeen took a few lessons when she was nine, "but they gave up on me because it was the corny tunes on the radio and I didn't like it, so I never practiced. A couple of years later, my parents had these records of Frankie Carle, so I just took the records and copied the solos for about six weeks, and that's when I really learned how to play."

By the late fifties Brackeen was playing around California with such musicians as Dexter Gordon, Harold Land, and Charles Lloyd. But at this point, she says, she wasn't thinking in terms of a career. "Just playing—that's what I intended to do the rest of my life. I remember when they used to come up and ask me to do record dates, and I didn't feel like I really had anything I wanted to put on a record, I just wouldn't call them back. I didn't care. I did care what I played and how I played and who I played with. That was about it. That's the way California people think. If I had been here [in New York], I don't think I would have been allowed to. But there you just float on. It's kind of nice to have lived a few years never knowing what day it was or what time it was."

In 1965 Brackeen moved to New York, and after working with Freddy McCoy, got "down to business" with Art Blakey and the Jazz Messengers, and became "the only female Messenger of any tenure in the band's 25-year history."[8] Later she worked with saxophonist Joe Henderson, with whom she still shares an important musical relationship, and then with Stan Getz for two years before going on her own in 1977. Brackeen has made six albums as leader: *Keyed In, Prism, Snooze, Tring-a-Ling, Aft, Mythical Magic,* and *Ancient Dynasty.*

Brackeen does most of her composing at the piano and rarely performs standards. "Standards are tunes that somebody else wrote," she says, "and that was their freedom or their experience, which in many cases is a great way to start learning how to play music, but then you want to know why *you* came to the planet, and sometimes you don't want to stop where someone else left off. They might have found something that they were very comfortable with, and you like it, but you don't feel fulfilled through that. It doesn't feel like enough.

"Most people write because somebody else wrote a tune and then they want to write one, not so much because they really feel that it needs to come into being. That's okay, too, but it's not such a serious, almost like what you might describe as a religious, type of thing. I mean *very* serious and sincere. . . . People always ask me who I listen to and all of this. I've listened through the years. I've got a record collection I probably haven't added anything to in fifteen years, and it just sits there. I don't know, I hear music okay, but it's not always in the form of sound—it's kind of in the form of a feeling, a silent feeling—but it does come out in sound when I sit down to the piano. That's what's fascinating out of it, you know. It's almost like you see this seed and then all of a sudden it's a plant. There's no visual image, but I can feel the energy of it. And it feels like energy when it comes out. Then when you finish with the music, you can listen to it, and once you hear it, you can get the visual image quite clearly."

Rhythm is the basis of all her work, Brackeen has said, and she is open to all the rhythms of the universe. "I think that it [the music] comes out of a lot of different things. Like last night, when I was going to sleep— I always like to feel the flow of life coming through me before I fall asleep—for the first time I began to feel the flow of energy coming through the planet earth. It felt like the earth was . . . as temporal as someone's body. That feeling will probably come later on, in another work or another year, and I'll really want it at that point. I believe that these things come to everybody. It comes, and they don't recognize it. Not to say I'm not like that, too, but I am aware of some of it."

At the keyboard, Brackeen's fingers work with steellike precision and control, creating dense chords and rapid arpeggios that almost seem to split the piano. She "studies" at the piano during the day, so that all the tools of creativity are at her disposal when she works. "If I'm trying to play an idea and it doesn't come out exactly like I want it to, then I figure out what to do in order to cause it to come out the next time. The way you see the keyboard, that's how you improvise, so I try to figure ways that I would never see it. This is slightly abstract. Things that would be difficult for your fingers to do, that you would never do unless you thought about them, keeping your technique up with the things that you're thinking about—that's what it is; that's the whole thing. Once you hear the touch in your mind, you can't be satisfied with less."

In an interview with Nat Hentoff, Brackeen once said, "Most women do not play as well as men because their thinking and feeling, as they improvise, are not properly coordinated. But there's a matter of conditioning, of falling in with the male stereotype about women players."[9] She sees a big change ahead: "Just because people got taught there was a difference up to this time on the planet," she says, "it's not going to stay that way. I think there are going to be a lot more female musicians— on all instruments."

Since 1977 JoAnne Brackeen has been managed by Helen Keane, whom Hentoff has called "the most formidable manager in jazz. She is not only relentlessly protective of her artists against the traditional schemes of booking agents, club owners, and record companies, but she also has the audio engineering skills to take over the control room, which she has done in the past."[10]

Keane, who managed the late Bill Evans, had decided eighteen years ago that he would be her only pianist client, until Evans himself recommended that she take on Brackeen. "I get on the phone and do as much as I can," says Brackeen, "but I could never make it without her." JoAnne has done twelve European tours, and notes that, both at home and abroad, audiences respond with enthusiasm to her playing. The difference lies in the fact that in America she has to go to major cities to appear, while in Europe even the concert halls of small cities are filled for a jazz concert.

"At the moment," she says, "I think Europeans are living their lives, generally speaking, in a much more artful manner than we do here. We've got things they don't have, but I think they're into the art of living more than people in this country are. I mean, I *know* they are much more into the art of living. I find that very intriguing. It gives more of a sense of beauty and joy. It's a way of living that kind of feels more like the kind of music that I want to continue to create.

"Things occur to me all the time. They come. In fact, there's some stuff that's coming now that when it comes I don't even allow it to come, because at points it can be frightening. It's too far out for me now, so I just try to say, 'I gotta go a little slower on this stuff,' 'cause I do have to have some kind of comfort, but it is something that I do know that I want to experience. But stuff comes all the time, just like the music. You know—revelations."

Fostina Dixon

(reeds/leader/composer)

Since she started working in 1973, Fostina Dixon has worked on the road with Marvin Gaye, on the West Coast in top studio and casual jobs, in New York with Melba Liston and Company, and with a group called Folks. She was also the leader of her own group, Collage, funded in part by an NEA grant.

Dixon's musical "kids," as she calls them, include baritone, alto, and soprano saxophone, clarinet, flute, and bass clarinet. She is a player of impeccable control and skill, with a distinctly individual sense of musical time and space and highly independent ideas.

Fostina Dixon was born in Delaware. Her earliest musical inspiration came from the church, where her grandparents were solo singers. By the fifth grade she was playing clarinet, and in high school she started baritone sax. When the time came to enter college, however, people had convinced her that there was no money to be made in music, so she enrolled in Boston University's premed program. By the end of the first year, though, she realized that her primary interest was in music. She switched to Berklee College of Music in Boston, and after several years was playing clarinet, bass clarinet, baritone, and flute. Then, during a trip to Los Angeles the summer before her last year, she took a job touring with Marvin Gaye's band, and stayed with it for two and a half years.

Following the tour, Dixon settled in L.A. and immediately started to get top work there, doing recording sessions and casuals behind such artists as Sammy Davis, Jr., Teddy Pendergrass, and Nancy Wilson. She had also organized her own group, Collage, which she started not so much because she wanted to be playing her own music necessarily as because she wanted a context in which to do some consistent hard playing, which L.A. did not offer.

"Most people aren't even interested," she says. "Most of the young people, their concept of being successful is how many record dates you can get. Ninety percent of the younger musicians don't think in terms of developing personalities. To them, the biggest thing in the world is to sound like Michael Brecker. So that makes it really strange, and I'm sayin', 'Now wait a minute. Why would I want some fourth- or fifth-hand information? If I'm gonna sound like anybody, at least let me sound like the source, you know? Why sound like the Doobie Brothers? Why not just go to a Baptist church and get it right from the Baptist church?' But for some reason most people just can't see that, I guess because of the money that's involved. They don't understand that they have their personality—I mean, if you want to get hired, you got to develop your own."

In the sixties and seventies, while Dixon was growing up, she was not listening to Miles Davis's fusion or to Chick Corea or Herbie Hancock. "Oh, no no no. I was listening to James Brown, the Temptations, the Supremes, Martha and the Vandellas, the Four Tops. I just recently started listening to jazz. Since I've been here [Dixon spent 1980–81 in New York] I've heard more music than I've heard in my life, just going over to friends' houses. I've been really trying to immerse myself in it, since it's available. And I have that inspiration, too, around me, that's saying, 'Come on, don't stop, come on.'"

Dixon is constantly adding to her instrumental "family." In L.A. she started playing alto because the baritone was rarely thought of as a solo instrument; about ninety percent of the time the solo would go to the tenor or alto. "Alto is the closest to my voice, my speaking voice, so I feel a little like twin-soul type of thing with the alto," she says. "And I wanted to start going up, more *altissimo* range [three octaves above middle C]. I do treat my alto and baritone differently. I treat my baritone like it's more of a passive-aggressive instrument. I play maybe like a lion in the forest—they're very, very domineering creatures, but they're very quiet, too, and they know how to weave in and out—as opposed to a *big* elephant. I don't have the sound that I want yet on the alto, but I feel very aggressive on it. It's more projecting, it's louder, it's more of an accepted solo instrument. On the alto, I think about *fire*! Throwin' rocks at somebody or something! You know, just goin' up in front of somebody and just hollerin'!"

Dixon is also working on the soprano sax. Sidney Bechet, first master of the instrument, had a harsh, intensely vibrato sound. Dixon's tone is sweet and smooth. "I like sweet sound. It's sort of like waves. Every time I pick it up, I feel very spiritual." The tenor sax is the only one of the family Dixon has not made a commitment to. "I don't feel that sound too much yet," she says.

Dixon is also a singer, and she started to compose in 1978. "I love words. When I was a little kid, I wanted to learn all of the words in the dictionary and to know what they meant—and still have an urge to do that. I guess maybe that's the thing that draws me to singing—being able to use those *words.*" She describes her compositions as "melodic but moving on. My music would never be so complicated or so free that you couldn't sing it, because I like melody. If I don't have a good melody, to me I don't have a good tune. I'd like for anybody to be able to come and sing it, not just me because I have the musical knowledge of knowing what a seventh interval is and go down to a perfect fourth and go up to an augmented fifth. I'd like the average person to be able to sing it or feel it.

"I like Dionne Warwick's style when it comes to lyrics and tunes, and Barbra Streisand. I'm always trying to go for looseness. I think that's why, eventually, if I keep on developing my voice, maybe I can really go somewhere with it, because of the concept I have of improvising on the instrument. A lot of vocalists are limited simply because they don't have that knowledge of how to work around and weave in and out, so unless they have a great ear, or remarkable talent or something—I mean, you hear thousands and thousands of singers who all sing 'Feelings' the same way, then you hear Sarah Vaughan—but of course [she] played the piano."

Being a woman in the field, Dixon admits, can be a "bit hard. It's like they used to say, if you're black and you do something, you have to do it ten times as good. If you're a woman and you go to a jam session, you can maybe be wipin' out half the guys, but if you're still just barely makin' it, they're gonna leave there talkin' about the nonplaying woman before they're gonna leave there talkin' about the nonplaying men she wiped out. And it's like either you're gonna be *mean* or you're gonna be poor. So I mean you have to really go after being the best, because by bein' the minority still, we are put under a bit of pressure. I mean, the women's thing is cool, but on record, the quality has to come through. . . . I'm just trying to do my own thing. If it involves women, great. When I had Collage [a male group], I didn't think about women; I just wanted to hear a sound—plus, I don't like the idea of 'let's show 'em.' I'm not in a war with anybody. I pick music—either I pick it or it was chosen for me—and I'm gonna try to play it. Why do I even have to think about being as strong as a man?

"Sometimes the praise that we get bugs me, too. I mean, it works both ways. Don't let me say I play baritone—'A little girl like you?' [people ask]. First of all, size has nothing to do with strength. I mean, Bruce Lee, Mohammad Ali, Sugar Ray Robinson, none of these guys are big, fat, hefty-lookin' men. It's about developing certain muscles to do your trade. I can't stand when you get off stage and people are running up and most of them don't have anything valid to say except like, 'How can a little girl . . .' What about the music? How was the *music*? I just look at it as being ignorant, and I can't look at it beyond that point. I love attention, but I do not like that kind of attention at all.

"I figure the more secure I get with my music, the less insecure I will feel about those people who to me are ignorant. So I'm just tryin' to get secure with myself; then, at least when I feel like I'm even halfway in the race, nothing will bother me. . . . I like leadership positions, 'cause I don't like to have any limitations, like I can only play this or I can only play that. Although eventually, who can play everything well? Nobody. But at least you can be versatile enough—try to be close to being a total musician."

Erica Lindsay

(reeds/leader/composer)

Erica Lindsay was born in San Francisco in 1955 and raised in Germany. She has been living in New York since 1979, and working most notably with Melba Liston and Company. In Erica Lindsay, said Leonard Feather, "Liston has found an exciting new soloist . . . whose tenor sax and flute displayed powerful individuality."[11]

At the age of five, Erica Lindsay moved with her family to Munich, where her father was principal and her mother a teacher at the American school. Her parents, she says, liked Ray Charles and Ella Fitzgerald, but their musical orientation was essentially classical. Her mother had studied opera, and her grandmother had been a concert pianist. When she was eleven, Lindsay started studying classical piano, but, after several years, asked for a more modern teacher. She was sent to Mal Waldron, the Munich-based American composer and pianist who had worked with, among others, Billie Holiday and Charlie Mingus. Waldron was very encouraging to Lindsay, she says, and recordings also helped to set her on course. "That was my main introduction, but in a very strong way. All I had to do was hear just one or two records and that was it; I knew. I remember it was Miles Davis and Wayne Shorter—*Miles in the Sky*. In fact, I started listening to that before I even heard the older, the bebop people, and it just set me up. It definitely gave me direction, because I was always very interested in music, but I knew I didn't want to be a classical player."

At thirteen Lindsay started playing clarinet for "beginning band" at school. "When I was fifteen or sixteen," she says, "the hippest thing in the music department was the jazz band. To do that you had to play saxophone, you couldn't play clarinet, so I started playing alto. Played alto for all of high school and then started with the tenor in my last year. It was just one of those things; I picked up the tenor and that was it. Just something about the sound." Lindsay's teacher, she remembers, "encouraged women just as much as men. There was no difference at that first point. My parents were the same way. They were glad I was creatively involved in something, so they just let me go at it."

After high school, Lindsay returned to America and studied at Berklee College in Boston for one year. She then returned to Munich, where she tried the role of housewife for a couple of years while also doing music jobs. "I didn't have to support myself and that type of thing," she says, "but I had started working." By the time she was twenty-one, she was out on her own again, and began studying at the University of Maryland in Munich. "That's when my professional career really started. I was working at night and then going to school during the day, but there I studied literature, which is my other favorite thing."

Student by day, jazz musician by night, at this point Lindsay began to work in a variety of contexts. Few of the musicians with whom she played were German. Some were Polish, some Yugoslavian, but mostly the musical community of Munich was American. Lindsay worked in a big band, a sextet (where she started writing), a Brazilian jazz group, her own quartet (which played her own compositions), and the Unique Munich Saxophone Choir, which consisted of eight saxes and one drum. This group was based on more "free" compositions, she says, with everybody writing. "That started opening me up more in terms of possibilities. You wouldn't believe the sounds you can get from that."

In February 1980 Lindsay decided to come back to the United States. "People [like drummers Art Blakey and Bob Moses] started telling me I better get my ass over here. Especially for a young musician, this is the place where you learn and can be exposed to the music at its best." Her first teacher when she returned was Andy McGee, at Berklee. "He was very good for me," she says, "because he straightened me out. I was doing all kinds of things wrong, 'cause you know, when you start playing and you haven't had a teacher, fingerings, everything's wrong. He gave me a lot of freedom, because I've never been able to grow as much [via a technical approach]. I'm getting there now, but till this point, I've just been listening a lot, playing with records, and just playing more than studying. I think now I'm at a point where I should study more."

McGee was an especially good teacher, Lindsay says, because he allowed her to develop in her own way "and gave me encouragement, which I needed. He was very positive. In fact, he's the one who got me this gig with Melba. Melba phoned him up and said, 'I need a saxophone player,' and I had just phoned him and told him I had arrived in New York, so it worked out well."

Lindsay auditioned for Liston and bassist Carline Ray, who was with the group at the time, and was hired to fill the tenor, alto, and flute chair. "I played better after I got in the band," she says. "She [Liston] did it more on taking Andy's word. For me, it was very beautiful, because I hadn't even started making connections here or even meeting people. I'm not an extroverted type, anyway, so it was just perfect. And since then other things have been happening." Lindsay has worked other jobs around New York, toured Europe and the Far East with Liston's group, and has been singled out by critics and other musicians as a player to pay attention to.

When she is not busy playing or working, Lindsay works on her writing. As a composer, she considers herself a "harmony freak." "Sound," she says. "I hear one sound and then that'll make me think of another to follow it. It's just like writing. Sometimes it can be a melody, but it's mainly colors and trying to make sounds out of colors. Combinations of notes will make a certain mood that has a color to it, and you can try to go deeper into that or move that mood into another mood. Once you get to a point where you have an idea of what your individual concept is, the rest of your life you just spend working on that and trying to shape and develop it."

Jane Ira Bloom

(tenor sax/alto sax/soprano sax/leader/composer)

Jane Ira Bloom is one of the most highly respected musicians to have started working during the seventies. She has led her own groups, appeared at New York, Rome, and Kansas City Women's Jazz Festivals, and been featured in the Broadway musical *The 1940's Radio Hour*. Bloom's first record, *We Are*, released in 1979 on her own label, Outline, won critical praise. "In her first album as leader," wrote Nat Hentoff, "she should finally begin to get the national jazz attention she so unmistakably merits."[12] Said another critic, "I am firmly convinced that hers is a voice destined to be at the cutting edge of tomorrow's music."[13]

Since the release of *We Are*, Bloom has continued to work with her own or other groups (most recently in a duo with bassist Ratzo Harris and in a group with vibist David Friedman), and has also brought out her second Outline album, *Second Wind*.

Born and raised in a suburb of Boston, Jane Ira Bloom began her musical training on the alto sax, then started studying soprano with Joe Viola in Boston. "[The soprano sax] became very important to me," says Bloom. "Joe's a woodwind doubler as well. He happened to have a special feeling for the soprano, which I kind of like to think he helped communicate to me." Eventually, Bloom also took up tenor sax.

"I didn't grow up in the city," Bloom says. "I would go into Boston any time I could, but I didn't go to clubs a lot, although I wanted to. I couldn't get to them. So I learned, I think in retrospect, a lot of what I hear inside my internal musical head from records. If anything influenced me in my listening taste, my mother had a very, very complete collection of Ella Fitzgerald albums, and I can remember learning the American songbook, really, American lyrics and the show-music tradition, by listening to [those records]. And then as I started getting more interested in instrumentalists, my teachers would throw Charlie Parker my way, and Sonny Rollins, and gradually build up. So it's a slow process, but I think those Ella Fitzgerald records were there before I knew about *nothin'*."

Bloom received a B.A. and an M.A. from Yale, where she also worked for three years with bassist Kent McLagan, developing the music that would become the material of her first album, *We Are*. "Over the years, we had developed our own compositions, and I felt, if I don't get it down, it's gonna be lost. So, it was time to make a record." The sessions were recorded in 1978; Bloom then embarked on the long learning process of producing and distributing one's own record.

"It's a real learn-by-doing process with a little help from your friends," she explains. "Basically, the first step to me was that I had something of artistic importance to put down on record. Fortunately, I knew some very expert recording people and had decided about the situation I wanted to do. Once you have the music per se on the tape and in the can, then you start learning about record-manufacturing companies where you get the electronic impulses turned into a disc, and all the processes that are involved in your mastering, reproduction, and packaging." Much of this is a long, slow process of waiting, "because independent record producers are treated very scarcely by the manufacturers, who would much rather, I'm sure, do big labels quickly and more efficiently."

When the records are made, "and you have, say, a thousand sitting on your doorstep, then you have to go out and talk to the distributors. This is all one on one. Once the distributors have it, which is on a consignment basis, you're never gonna see a cent until they have sold it, and that's maybe months and months later. Then, hopefully, your record will get in the hands of those few people that you want to reach, that could not hear your music if you just performed. That's why you record."

Bloom was helped with the distribution end of the project by New Music Distribution Service in New York. As a result of their expert handling of the record, getting it out across the country, Bloom did receive a great deal of recognition through the critics' polls. "Really, what does it mean?" she asks. "I don't know. Someone has heard your record and has liked it, so there'll be future opportunities for you. That's how it works. That's the success story. I haven't made any money. I just put out a lot. How much? I never tallied. About three, four thousand dollars. There are guys who have done it cutting the budget even more, but that's the homemade version."

On the album, Bloom strove to explore ways in which compositions could be structured so that they might sound more spontaneous. At a saxophone workshop she ran at one of the UJC salutes, she emphasized the importance of formalizing one's ideas in compositions (as well as in practice exercises), no matter what level of proficiency one is at. Many of her own pieces, she says, are loose skeletons that suggest a framework—for example, whole tones within a certain pitch, or birdlike figures drawn on the staff, indicating birdlike sounds on the high register of the horn—but that leave the player room for improvisation.

"One of our strongest concerns," she wrote in the liner notes to *We Are*, "was that the music, whether improvised or composed, should always have an impelling sense of motion and flow." She and McLagan used a variety of musical sources for their ideas—from Billy Strayhorn and Miles Davis to an original, chantlike composition, to another based on the blues. Nat Hentoff praised Bloom's mastery of the "often resistant soprano": "Her sound is strong, clear and actually sings. Moreover, she is an unusually resourceful, cohesive melodist—creating what sound like 'spontaneous compositions.' . . . The sound is as clean and vivid as Jane Ira Bloom's playing. Like her, it's honest."[14]

From the duo, Bloom went on to explore larger ensembles, and during the second New York Salute to Women in Jazz, did a composition for thirteen pieces. "Not that my music is getting bigger and bigger," she says, "but it's just an area that I want to work on in addition to my quartet things. Orchestral writing, just another thing to keep me busy. I guess doing improvised music as an individual writer and player in the city, there's no set schedule or plan, really, except what you would internally decide yourself. So it's a process of trying to get the money together, trying to put out a substantial concert of your music and ideas, I guess every two or three months, which people seem to do, and maybe you get a club engagement where you can work some of your own material into what has to be a little more commercially viable. Maybe an occasional gig comes your way. That's basically the kind of plodding-along existence that I've been having, at least a year. Not knowing too many people.

"With all the rigorous criteria of this crazy lifestyle, you have to move from here to there. If you decide to work with a big band, you're gonna do one-night stands on a band bus, with all men. It's rough. It's just a simple fact if you're gonna live in New York and you're a woman alone, you gotta think, how the hell are you gonna get around at night? What are you gonna do to take care of yourself? But everybody seems to find their own way around it. . . . Your growth depends on yourself. If you're the kind of person that likes to keep doing different things, then it'll happen kind of naturally. But again, part of the personality thing that helps you deal with that kind of lifestyle has to do with a very driven kind of commitment. I think I was always one of those people who's never cared about what anybody else thought, including my parents. I always did what I wanted to."

Today, says Bloom, "certain opportunities are available to women that just never crossed anybody's mind ten years ago: possible gigs, grant support, even the fact that a woman saxophonist could be coming up and playing with some of the better male players. The fact that you can work and be accepted at whatever level you're at is a new concept."

Still, says Bloom, "what you have to go through time and time again, especially with musicians a generation or so older, is an initiation rite. Once these guys hear you play, just close their eyes and listen, somehow you get to be friends a little bit faster. But I think that's plain human nature. So you have to go through that a lot of times, and it takes a lot of perseverance, and it happens with women, too, where other women are not used to women who can play, either. One thing I've found that I think is kind of common among a lot of women who are out and working in the music world right now is that you, by nature, have to have a set of defenses that are like a brick wall, and I put them up every time I talk to a club owner. I put 'em up any time I encounter some small bit of hostility. Maybe it's male/femaleness, maybe it's musicians, but you have to have a defense that comes up to protect you as a *person* because of all the hard things that are involved in dealing in the business of the music world, which isn't pretty at all.

"I remember one of my first experiences when I came to New York. George Coleman, a very important, well-established tenor player in the city, was a teacher of mine, and he spent some time one night taking me around to a lot of the clubs in the city. I think we covered about five or six clubs downtown in the Village just to check out the scene. But, even more important than that, he was very concerned that a nice person had to know how to be hard—you know, to deal with all the music business world—and that was his way of showing me how to toughen up a little bit when you get in that environment. 'Cause, you know, I don't look like a linebacker for the Dallas Cowboys, like that man does, and I don't have a deep, resonant voice, like Dexter Gordon. So there's gotta be something else there; you have to have, I think, a certain resilience and a kind of internal strength to communicate your strength. You don't really think about that, but, in retrospect, I think that's what happens. Nobody likes to be an ugly person or anything like that [but] there are times when it just has to come out. It would be so nice if it didn't have to be—but I guess that's life."

Her first priority, though, says Bloom, is and always has been her music—"being the best musician I can possibly be. That's the way I've always gone about it, and I hope the way I'll always continue."

Janice Robinson

(trombone/leader/composer)

In 1966, when Janice Robinson was still in high school in Clairton, Pennsylvania (a suburb of Pittsburgh), she entered the Ted Mack Amateur Hour at the local county fair, and shortly afterward she wound up on the first Bill Cosby television special. At twenty-one she graduated from the Eastman School of Music, moved to New York City, and at once became part of the New York music world, taking auditions, substituting for other musicians, and sitting in. One of her first appearances was with Marian McPartland at Youth and Jazz Day at the Newport Festival. She then went on to work in Broadway shows, as well as with the Thad Jones/Mel Lewis Orchestra, Slide Hampton and his World of Trombones, the Jazzmobile Big Band, Clark Terry's Big Bad Band, with Marian McPartland, the Janice Robinson–Sharon Freeman Quintet (which evolved after the two women played a UJC concert together), the Collective Black Artists' Ensemble, and Frank Foster's Loud Minority and Living Color—the Twelve Shades of Black. She has also worked with the National Orchestral Association, the Symphony of the New World, the Dance Theater of Harlem, and the American Symphony, in addition to composing for and leading another group of her own. In 1978 and '81 Robinson won an NEA grant for composition.

"If you heard me play a year or two ago," she says, "I think I'm a different player now. I know I'm a 'professional' musician, but people sometimes forget that there's a lot of growth involved in that. Sometimes I've been concentrating on all the things I want to do in the technical aspects of music, in developing my playing, more than the business, making records and stuff. Eventually I would like to do that. I just haven't explored that avenue. But I'll probably be forced to, because you can't get a whole lot of work unless you have a record, or at least a professional tape."

Meanwhile, says Robinson, who is disenchanted with much of the "business side" of music, she is "racking her brain" to come up with other paths musicians can explore in the eighties and still keep their art and their integrity intact.

Janice Robinson was born in Pennsylvania in 1951. (Her family, whose history she has traced back to 1869, migrated north from South Carolina.) There was little jazz around the house, she recalls, and more television than stereo, but her mother, who sang in church, started teaching her piano when she was seven, and eventually sent her to a neighborhood teacher. Later on in school, Robinson took a musical-proficiency test. "If you had some talent," she says, "they'd offer you an instrument. I wanted the trumpet or the drums, but my parents said the drums were out, so naturally it fell to the trumpet. There was a girl around the corner who had played the trumpet in the high-school band, so we were able to get a used trumpet very easily."

Robinson spent several years on the horn before the band directors decided she could not play high enough and switched her to trombone, something she says she "didn't appreciate at all. I didn't like the [trombone parts] that were written [for] the school band. [They] were fairly simple, and because I wanted to be a trumpet player, I didn't want to accept anything [else]." Robinson was also already studying trumpet privately with a neighborhood teacher. "Same guy taught all the instruments," she says, and when she finally decided to "go along with the program," she continued to study with him and just switched from the trumpet to the trombone.

At first, she found the trombone "pretty easy. I set out to prove, since I wanted to be a trumpet player, that the trombone was easy and it was beneath me somehow. So I didn't initially confront a lot of problems on the [instrument]. I don't remember any specific problems until after I'd been playing about three years and was able to play some of the solo literature, regular band music, 'Blue Bells of Scotland,' a lot of Italian kind of music. Then I started running into some solos and some music that I thought was interesting and technically challenging, and that's when I really started to work on the instrument. I got a teacher who was specifically for trombone, and I started checking out little contests and things that certainly encouraged me to become more proficient."

In junior high school, Robinson played in the marching band. "They were doing this thing [the Ted Mack Amateur Hour] at the county fair," she says, "and they had auditions. I went to school and I said, 'I'd like to play for this, but I don't really have any hip music or anything.'

One of the teachers, Joe Campus, was an arranger for Enzo Stuarti, and he wrote this little arrangement and I played 'A Taste of Honey.'" Shortly after this, she appeared on Bill Cosby's television special out in California. "I got to see a lot of the music world *very* quickly," she says. "It taught me a lot. By that time, I had decided that I was gonna do something in music." Around her hometown, she began doing little guest spots, playing in marching bands and stage-band camp, and was also interested in playing in orchestras. At one band festival, fellow musicians and Eastman alumni told her about the Eastman School of Music, and Robinson decided to go there, "basically because they had a variety. They were just starting a jazz program. Naturally, they had an orchestra."

At the Eastman School, Robinson branched out. "I just liked all kinds of music . . . and I wasn't gonna cut anything off. I sang in the Gregorian-chant choir, played in the jazz ensemble, had a chance to do some writing for the jazz ensemble there, and was also preparing for an orchestral career." She also began to meet some of the musicians and writers who would be important later in her career: Oliver Nelson, Thad Jones, Mel Lewis, Clark Terry, Alec Wilder, Marian McPartland, and Mary Lou Williams (who, she remembers, lost no time advising her to leave school at once).

On graduation day, 1973, Robinson went to New York. One of her first appearances was with Marian McPartland at the Youth and Jazz Day at the Newport Festival. "I was also balancing this with other music. I went to California and played at the Santa Barbara Music Academy, then I came back and Marian McPartland and I did 'What's My Line?' [Melba Liston and tuba player Barbara Dreiwitz are other female musicians who have appeared on "What's My Line?"] I used to pay my rent playing in orchestras, the National Orchestral Association." In Los Angeles she worked with Oliver Nelson, and in New York with Thad Jones and Mel Lewis, first sitting in, then subbing, then working for a year. She also worked, toured, and recorded with Clark Terry's band.

"It's important," says Robinson, "ensemble work; also to get next to the writing, to listen to those players." By 1974 she had become a member of the Thad Jones/Mel Lewis Orchestra and at that point decided to concentrate on jazz. "Being around musicians who did that for life and were really committed to that," she says, "I could see a lot of other things that were happening in music that I couldn't see from being in school. They were able to help me establish some kind of direction. At that time I was still auditioning [for orchestral work]. I think the last audition I took was for the Metropolitan Opera. I was in Boston with Thad and Mel and I was supposed to go for a Boston Symphony audition, and I called them and didn't go. So I guess I started improvising seriously in the last five years.

"When I went into the band, I took [Quentin] Butter Jackson's place. Butter used to play the plunger, and so I played plunger because that was what was called for. That was a little different, but I enjoyed it. I enjoyed the band. Plunger has a little entertainment thing involved. But you know, the other guys in the band, they could really play. They had a lot of facility on the instrument and everybody sounded different, and I found out you really had to have something to play consistently well. That was a challenge. You had to start thinking about some stuff not to be stale.

"They would talk sometimes about different approaches to chords. And you can hear it right there in the band. Every guy in the band has a different approach to the changes, a different sound. One of the guys, Billy Harper, used to say, 'Why don't you try this? This is something that trombone players usually do. Try that, see how it sounds. And practice that until it's perfect. And these are the chords that it relates to and this is how it's important.' And then the more I got into the music, I could see how it was important and how it did relate. It was a good place for me to be. I learned a lot, even though I wasn't able to produce it all at that time. I found it's one thing to listen to the music or to play and have a general appreciation, and another to really be closely involved with the directions that one goes within the music.

"When I came to town, I also had an opportunity to sub for some guys who were real busy [playing Broadway shows]. Contractors get to know you; it operates mostly by word of mouth. When Butter died, I started to do *Guys and Dolls*. It's really rough. I think there were maybe more things happening then, but I also had it in mind that I was gonna do all of these things. It helped, you train and prepare yourself to read anything on the spot and to pick up things quickly.

"I used to get tired, though," says Robinson, even after eight-night runs in out-of-town theaters. "You just knew the music. There weren't gonna be very many changes. During the Broadway show, you carried the show around with you all day; that was the only music you could hear, the music you'd been playing every night. You can imagine, if you're trying to improvise or trying to create, this conflicts, or it did for me at that time. As I say, now I can handle it a little bit more. But I just didn't see myself as that kind of musician. I didn't have that particular temperament. There has to be a little bit of freedom.

"But it is very hard for a jazz musician to be able to pay rent. Some people go from club to club, they make a little bit of money at every club, and they make enough to keep themselves together. A few that have really good records establish a kind of touring thing. I think the road work is really hard for *anybody*. Tears on your personal life and everything." As for the organized "jam sessions" sponsored by loft or club owners, Robinson says, they "take a learning experience and turn it into a business" in order to minimize musicians' salaries.

"And this whole fusion thing—I don't know if they've realized it, but it's opened up a whole different kind of thinking among younger musicians. I know for myself, if I were to decide to play a different kind of music, I wouldn't have to worry about anything. That music has a place; they've made a place for it. I know everybody has financial responsibilities, but when you're an artist and you're supposed to be presenting a certain thing in life, if a businessman from a certain record company says 'Do this' and you do it, that doesn't say a whole lot. For a guy to do that, he sacrifices an art form to pay his rent. I have nothing against that. I think people have to do any number of things. But so many people did it, and they really thought they were gonna make a lot of money, that they opened up a whole set of musicians who don't even know where *they* came from. A person has to be careful when they're very popular and very highly respected. I guess my ideas about what an artist is and a musician's supposed to be are old-fashioned. I've been really racking my brain this year to figure out some other way, some other avenues that I could pursue—art shows, museums, dance concerts, concert halls."

When Robinson was still in high school, a Pittsburgh trombone player, Harold Betters, was her idol. "He was real barrelhouse. He impressed me as having real strong iron chops, kind of rough in a way. I sort of started listening to J. J. Johnson and later Slide [Hampton], but I think, of anybody, Harold Betters was more the one that I tried to play like at that time. The other people I enjoyed, and I think they have their influence on you in some respect, but it's important to learn a lot from them and then develop your own particular style.

"After I got through with Harold Betters, I wanted to sound like J.J. [He] has a very kind of mellow sound, very solid. I used to try to play really long, long tones, try to fill up the room with your sound. You have something in your head that you really like, a certain kind of sound that you always hear. I like a rich sound, whatever that means. I associate the sound with warmth. To me, the trombone is the vehicle for what I want to express. But when I'm playing, I'm just thinking about the music, you know. We're gonna move *here*, and there's a different color that can be put in here, and sometimes building the solo performance, and different times you're listening to different people playing in the band, and creating off of that.

"I've found out how difficult it is to have a woman in a small-group situation. Somehow I feel there are people that I would enjoy playing with and that I've had a chance to play with in New York, but when you're talking about being a permanent member and going on the road, there are other problems that come in. There were problems with Thad and Mel. I'm sure a lot of other women have a *lot* of stories. I think sometimes with a singer it's different, because they're star status. There are problems in a big band, and I'm not sure, maybe those problems are larger in a small group. Recently some guys have been telling me, 'Yeah, well, I know you can do this gig, but the leader is kind of shaky about women in the group.' And I've never really paid attention to this up to now, because I've always been able to work doing something. But now I'm looking at it and I'm seeing that there are certain problems that would come up in that situation, and so I'll probably be put in the position where I have to create more work for myself, create an environment.

"You also have to have your personal principles really together, because they will be challenged on *all* levels no end." With the Thad Jones/Mel Lewis band, says Robinson, she "hung out with the guys who didn't smoke and drink and who were interested in touring the places. There wasn't any problem among those." On her first tour with Clark Terry's band, she says, she was "really naïve. I used to ask a lot of questions, and the older guys, they'd sort of look out for you. It was a brother kind of relationship for me.

"I'm sure people have jealousies. Sometimes the woman gets a lot more applause maybe when she hasn't played the level—that's happened in a lot of situations. I've realized that so-and-so is *really* playing and people don't appreciate it, and if a woman can play twelve bars, that's *fantastic*. So I figure, well, if I can really play, that should be more the better. But I can see jealousies in men, and I think basically the guys have to come to terms on this. I think in jazz, especially, men can come to a degree of honesty, because they have to be honest with themselves when they're playing. I think if they accept you, if they feel that you're being honest with yourself and you're doing the job that you're supposed to do, they can understand that."

As far as all-woman groups are concerned, Robinson says they have been "a good commercial idea always. I personally think that the music is the most important thing, if the people get along well and if they play well. It's difficult to have an all-woman band that does that. You have a smaller group of people to pick from, first of all. If you were to go across the country, you could put together an ideal band of women, that's certainly possible. I had thought of that myself. But, at the same time, in improvising music, there's a certain thing that everybody brings. There are women musicians who want to play in a surrounding of all women, and to me, I'm thinking that life is not like that, and there are certain things that men bring to the music that I enjoy."

"I think maybe the weight of a musician's lifestyle has kind of contributed to not seeing as many women playing. But all of a sudden I'm looking and putting everything in line—all aspects of one's life," Robinson says. "Max Roach says, 'Oh, you have to be married to that trombone.' I love playing the trombone and I like being involved in the music, but there are other things in life. People sort of hint you shouldn't count on it [family life] if you're gonna be involved in the music, because it's another thing that's gonna take a lot out of you and it's gonna take you away from your dedication to the music. I'm not seeing things in that way. At the same time, I realize that it demands a lot—both are gonna demand a lot—but there's a certain kind of life that I have to live, or that I wish to live, and I'm willing to do things to live it.

"A friend of mine, a string player that's doing shows, we were just thinking about it, and we said, 'Name one black female musician—instrumentalist—who has a family, that's living as a typical American family.' At that point, we came up with two names. It's difficult, but I think it's certainly possible. Anyway, music is still the thing; that remains the focus, but everything that happens in life is reflected in the music, in what I play or what I write. To me, it's not separate.

"When I get ready to write something, I have a form in mind. For an ensemble, I hear certain colors, the colors that I want to bring out. I usually start with a tune that has structure." Robinson's compositions include "Crying to Be" (a piece that she composed under an NEA grant in 1978), "Soul Music," "Gorre," and "The Sound of Light." Recently she has begun to write lyrics. "I always had some ideas that more could be done with lyrics to help people relate. I have often squelched a lot of my creative ideas because I felt they always say, well, if you wanna play, play, and that's what you should do *only*. But I found out in order for me to create and to be really active, it seems that I have to do more than one thing. So I'm going to do some more songs with lyrics, and I will present them to some singers and to some writers and maybe try to get them recorded or at least performed."

Robinson's practicing now consists basically of "studying" herself, she says. "I try to take some of Bird's solos off the records. I like Bird and 'Trane. There are so many people who have contributed to the music, but there are certain people who have really gone a particular direction—John Coltrane, Dizzy Gillespie, Charlie Parker. They have really set up something that there's just a lot to learn from. There are certain tunes that are always good tunes for musicians to play on, because of the form, or because they presented some interesting harmonic structure or had a good melody. Practicing comes from all those angles, and when it's time to play, you're supposed to create on the stuff you've been practicing. The whole thing of improvisation is, you have to play *on* the spot.

"The more I learn about playing, the more directions I feel that I can go in. The more I learn, the freer I feel. Sometimes it's difficult to play exactly what you hear, and I think that's the main idea that I'm trying to do in my practicing. It's like giving myself dictation. If I'm playing through a tune with a record, just trying to hear the harmonic movement of the tune, I'm gonna stumble over some passages. I try to stop and go over that and clear it up. You find out that there are certain sounds that you hear all the time, and that's also an area you can grow from. You know—I seem to like that sound, and I play that a lot. How can I develop it? When you're taking stuff off a record, that's like having something dictated to you. It improves your hearing, so that eventually you won't stumble, you'll be able to play exactly what you are hearing in your inner ear. I think the really great musicians have been able to do that. That's why the jazz thing to me is so exciting. Sometimes guys can play tunes they only heard once, and they can play on it like they *own* the tune. That's something that I'm really working on.

"And I've been working on increasing my range; when I practice, I try to play to the high F. . . . I practice playing two-fives [II-V's]—certain harmonic movements, cadences that happen often, especially in the bebop era. The more ways that you know how to get over them and through them, the better. That's another thing you practice, is trying to be as flexible as possible on the instrument, so that when you have an idea you can execute it. Improvising is difficult. It's like life, you know. You try to prepare yourself to meet all the different circumstances in life."

EPILOGUE

When Mary Lou Williams began to perform extensively during the late seventies, she began to present a pianistic "history of jazz," which moved from the spirituals to *her* style of ragtime, to blues, to the Kansas City style, which she illustrated with her own seminal piece "Night Life," recorded in 1930. As she played each phase of the music, it was as if she were giving away—and yet replenishing—precious pieces of her soul.

"What is wonderful about this music," says choreographer Alvin Ailey, whose company dances to *Mary Lou's Mass*, "is that it is a sum total of black music, a retrospective."[1] Said Williams on her solo piano recording *The History of Jazz* (Folkways Records), "It was my pleasure to bring you through the history of jazz. You may not realize this, but you're lucky. On the other hand, to bring this history to you, I had to go through muck and mud."

In 1977, Mary Lou Williams recorded an album called *My Mama Pinned a Rose on Me*, and the title song was the only one she ever sang. Tom Piazza called the album a "record full of exquisite moments, fragile and strong at the same time . . . one of her most enduring statements."[2]

Said another writer: "Williams is one of the three great jazz pianists still with us who grew up with the music as it came of age. It's about time that we recognize that of the three [Teddy Wilson and Earl Hines are the other two he cites] she has been the most creative and aesthetically rigorous in recent years, never resting on her laurels or trading on nostalgia" (LCL-M).

Like Coleman Hawkins, Williams was one of the very few musicians to have been active, creative, inspired, and inspirational pan-generationally. She had come the route of the music itself, from the lessons of love and loss of the early days (as she once said, "Never be that close to anyone, they told me; otherwise, if somebody dies, what happens is that you can't play"[3]); from the days of good-time swing through her own "scenic route" of bop; from jazz in the era of what she considered the "evilness" of rock to the avant-garde, which she, of all the pianists who had started in the Swing Era, dared to meet and challenge on her own terms. In the sixties she found new faith in the Catholic Church, which soon became the setting for her offerings of jazz masses.

Williams had come full circle, from knowing the spirituals at the root of jazz, to learning and reaffirming in all her work the healing power of the blues. When she wanted to put more feeling into her playing, she once said, she would return to the blues for a number or two and then go on. "Listen," she would implore inattentive customers in a nightclub. "Listen—this will heal you."

Mary Lou Williams not only worked to preserve and pass on the truth of the music and its roots in the black world (in the last decade of her life, she taught full time at Duke University in Durham, South Carolina); she had also, throughout her lifetime, created that truth.

Mary Lou Williams died of cancer on May 29, 1981. Her entire estate went to the Mary Lou Williams Foundation, which she founded in 1980 to enable gifted young children, ages six to twelve, to study one on one with professional jazz musicians. The truth of the music, Williams knew, lay in the blues and the early spiritual roots; her hope for the future lay in passing on that knowledge to the very young.

Notes

PREHISTORY (1619-1900)

1. Cited in Eileen Southern, *The Music of Black Americans: A History* (New York: W. W. Norton & Company, Inc., 1971), p. 17.
2. Cited in Robert Tallant, *Voodoo in New Orleans* (New York: Collier Books, 1946), p. 74.
3. Susan Cavin, "Missing Women: On the Voodoo Trail to Jazz," *Jazz Journal*, Vol. 3, No. 1, Fall 1975, p. 15.
4. Sidney Bechet, *Treat It Gentle* (New York: Da Capo Press, Inc., 1975), p. 8.
5. Cited in Cavin, "Missing Women," p. 15.
6. Cited in Tallant, *Voodoo in New Orleans*, p. 56.
7. Adrienne Rich, "Disloyal to Civilization," *On Lies, Secrets, and Silence: Selected Prose 1966–1978* (New York: W. W. Norton & Company, Inc., 1979), p. 287.
8. Tallant, *Voodoo in New Orleans*, pp. 34–35.
9. Cited in Southern, *Music of Black Americans*, p. 209.
10. Alice Walker, "In Search of Our Mothers' Gardens," *Working It Out*, eds. Sara Ruddick and Pamela Daniels (New York: Pantheon Books, Inc., 1977), p. 94.

THE TWENTIES

1. E. Simms Campbell, "Blues Are the Negroes' Lament," *Esquire*, December 1939, p. 100.
2. Paul Oliver, *Conversation with the Blues* (New York: Horizon Press, 1965), p. 121.
3. Albert Murray, *The Hero and the Blues*, the Paul Anthony Brick Lectures, ninth series (Columbia: University of Missouri Press, 1973), pp. 36–37.
4. Charles Edward Smith, "Ma Rainey," *Notable American Women, 1607–1950*, ed. Edward T. James, Vol. 3 (Cambridge: Harvard University Press, 1971), p. 110.
5. Sterling Brown, "Ma Rainey," *Southern Road* (New York: Harcourt, Brace and Company, 1932).
6. Sandra Robin Leib, *The Message of Ma Rainey's Blues: A Biographical*

and Critical Study of America's First Woman Blues Singer (Ann Arbor, Mich.: University Microfilms International, 1979), pp. 28–29.

7. Charles Edward Smith, "Ma Rainey and the Minstrels," *The Record Changer*, Vol. 14, No. 6, 1955, pp. 5–6.

8. Dan Morgenstern, liner notes, *Ma Rainey*, Milestone Records.

9. Barbara and Arnold Caplin, liner notes, *Gertrude "Ma" Rainey, Queen of the Blues, 1923–1924*, Vol. 3, Biograph Records.

10. Morgenstern, *Ma Rainey*.

11. Ibid.

12. Smith, "Ma Rainey and the Minstrels," p. 6.

13. Nat Shapiro and Nat Hentoff, eds., *Hear Me Talkin' to Ya* (New York: Dover Publications, Inc., 1966), p. 243.

14. Chris Albertson, *Bessie* (New York: Stein & Day Publishers, 1974), p. 130.

15. Willie the Lion Smith, with George Hoefer, *Music on My Mind* (New York: Da Capo Press, Inc., 1975), p. 29.

16. Albert Murray, *Stomping the Blues* (New York: McGraw-Hill Book Company, 1976), p. 17.

17. Richard Hadlock, *Jazz Masters of the Twenties* (New York: Collier Books, 1965), p. 223.

18. Ibid., p. 219.

19. Ibid., p. 227.

20. Donald Bogle, *Brown Sugar: Eighty Years of America's Black Female Superstars* (New York: Harmony Books, 1980), p. 28.

21. Albertson, *Bessie*, p. 145.

22. Ibid., p. 197.

23. Sidney Bechet, *Treat It Gentle* (New York: Da Capo Press, Inc., 1975), pp. 138–9.

24. Smith, with Hoefer, *Music on My Mind*, p. 102.

25. Ibid., p. 104.

26. Ibid.

27. Leonard Kunstadt and Bob Colton, "Mamie Smith, First Lady of the Blues," *Record Research*, Vol. 31, November 1960, p. 7.

28. Ethel Waters, with Charles Samuels, *His Eye Is on the Sparrow* (New York: Jove Publications, Inc., 1978).

29. Ibid., p. 21.

30. Ibid., p. 201.

31. Ibid., p. 219.

32. Ibid., p. 238.

33. Ibid., p. 242.

34. Ibid., p. 247.

35. Langston Hughes, *Famous Negro Music Makers* (New York: Dodd, Mead & Company, 1955), p. 112.

36. Albertson, *Bessie*, p. 191.

37. Leonard Kunstadt, "Rosa Henderson Yesterday and Today," *Record Research*, Vol. 75, April 1966, p. 3.

38. Jim O'Neal, *Rolling Stone*, November 19, 1976, cited in Sheldon Harris, *Blues Who's Who* (New Rochelle, N.Y.: Arlington House, 1979), p. 482.

39. Amy O'Neal, *Living Blues*, September 1976, p. 5, cited in Harris, *Blues Who's Who*, p. 482.

40. Oliver, *Conversation with the Blues*, p. 112.

41. Ibid., p. 113.

42. Ibid., p. 114.

43. Leonard Kunstadt, "Victoria Spivey," from Ann Arbor Blues and Jazz Festival program notes, courtesy Spivey Records.

44. Victoria Spivey, "Blues Is My Business," *Record Research*, Vol. 53, July 1963, p. 12.

45. Alain Locke and Sterling Brown, "Folk Values in a New Medium," *Folk-Say: A Regional Miscellany, 1930*, ed. B. A. Botkin (Norman: University of Oklahoma Press, 1930), p. 344.

46. Cited in Leonard Kunstadt, liner notes, *The Blues Is Life: Victoria Spivey*, Folkways Records.

47. All Alberta Hunter quotes in this section are from the transcript of the Chris Albertson interview with Alberta Hunter, taken for the National Endowment for the Arts' Jazz Oral History Project at the Institute of Jazz Studies at Rutgers University.

48. Chris Albertson, liner notes, *Classic Alberta Hunter*, Stash Records, Inc.

49. Norman Stevens, liner notes, *Clara Smith*, Vol. 1, VJM Records.

50. Carl Van Vechten, *Vanity Fair*, 1926, cited in Harris, *Blues Who's Who*, p. 467.

51. Cited in Eileen Southern, *The Music of Black Americans: A History* (New York: W. W. Norton and Company, Inc., 1971), p. 51.

52. W.E.B. DuBois, "The Damnation of Women," *Darkwater: Voices from Within the Veil* (1921; reprint ed., Millwood, N.Y.: Kraus-Thomson Organization, Ltd., 1975), p. 163.

53. Theo Zwicky, comp., "Lloyd Hunter's Serenaders and the Territory Bands," *Storyville*, Vol. 35, June–July 1971, p. 163.

54. Mary Lou Williams, liner notes, *Jazzwomen: A Feminist Retrospective*, Stash Records, Inc.

55. Edward Kennedy Ellington, *Music Is My Mistress* (Garden City, N.Y.: Doubleday & Company, Inc., 1973), p. 21.

56. Frank Driggs, liner notes, *Women in Jazz: Pianists*, Stash Records, Inc.

57. This and all other unidentified Mary Lou Williams quotes in this section are from the transcript of the John S. Wilson interview with Mary Lou Williams, taken for the National Endowment for the Arts' Jazz Oral History Project at the Institute of Jazz Studies at Rutgers University.

58. Shapiro and Hentoff, *Hear Me Talkin' to Ya*, p. 30.

59. Al Rose, *Storyville, New Orleans: Being an Authentic, Illustrated Account of the Notorious Red Light District* (Alabama: University of Alabama Press, 1974), p. 105.

60. Smith, with Hoefer, *Music on My Mind*, p. 94.

61. Item courtesy *Kansas City Call*, January 5, 1923, cited in *Goin' to Kansas City*, eds. Howard Litwak and Nathan Pearson (Kansas City: Mid-America Arts Alliance, 1980), p. 10.

62. Southern, *The Music of Black Americans*, p. 341.

63. Pops Foster, *Pops Foster, the Autobiography of a New Orleans Jazzman*, as told to Tom Stoddard (Berkeley: University of California Press, 1971), p. 106.

64. Ibid., p. 103.

65. Ibid., p. 122.

66. John S. Wilson, cited in Lil Hardin Armstrong obituary, *The New York Times*, August 28, 1971.

67. Herman Kogan, "The Blues Moan Low, But Lil Armstrong Sings 'Em with a Grin," *Chicago Sun-Times*, undated clipping, Institute of Jazz Studies at Rutgers University.

68. Unless otherwise indicated, this quote and those that follow are from the 1961 Riverside album *Satchmo and Me*.

69. Shapiro and Hentoff, *Hear Me Talkin' to Ya*, pp. 92–93.

70. Ibid., p. 93.

71. Ibid., p. 95.

72. Ibid.

73. Ibid., p. 102.

74. Ibid.

75. Ibid., p. 101.

76. Paul Whiteman and Mary Margaret McBride, "Jazz," *The Saturday Evening Post*, February 27, 1926, p. 5.

77. Mary Cass Canfield, "The Great American Art Form," *Grotesques and Other Reflections* (New York and London: Harper & Brothers, 1927), pp. 38–47.

78. Carol Hymowitz and Michaele Weissman, *A History of Women in America* (New York: Bantam Books, Inc., 1978), p. 287.

79. Edith Lynwood Wynn, "Women Musicians and the War," *The Musical Observer*, Vol. XVIII, October 10, 1919, p. 47.

80. This and the three quotes that follow are from press releases of the day, courtesy Audrey Hall.

81. Miles Jordan, "Women Jazz in the Afternoon," *Pacific Sun*, August 19–25, 1977.

82. Philip Elwood, "Tale of Two Pianos in North Beach," unidentified press clipping, courtesy Norma Teagarden.

83. Pat Beeman, "The Stars Shone in Old Sacramento," *And All That Jazz*, June 1977, p. 2.

84. Dick Young, "Two for Teagarden," unidentified press clipping, courtesy Norma Teagarden.

85. Mildred Hamilton, "The Teagarden Legend Plays On," *San Francisco Examiner & Chronicle*, September 7, 1975.

86. Ibid.

THE THIRTIES

1. Ted Toll, October 15, 1939, p. 18.

2. Albert Murray, *Stomping the Blues* (New York: McGraw-Hill Book Company, 1976), p. 170.

3. Mary Lou Williams, liner notes, *Jazz Women: A Feminist Retrospective*, Stash Records, Inc.

4. Stanley Dance, *The World of Earl Hines* (New York: Charles Scribner's Sons, 1977), p. 63.

5. Brian Rust, liner notes, *Valaida: High Hat, Trumpet and Rhythm*, EMI Records.

6. Jeff Aldam, "The Lady with the Unfeminine Vibrato," *Melody Maker*, July 7, 1956, p. 6.

7. Harrison Smith, "Valaida's Gone," *Record Research*, Vol. 9, May–June 1956, p. 12.

8. Sharon A. Pease, "Swing Piano Styles: Betty Roudybush with Ina Ray Hutton Shows Her Skill on 'Someday Sweetheart,'" *down beat*, May 1939, p. 22.

9. "Ina Ray Hutton: 'Blonde Bombshell' Has Hottest Gal Swing Band," *The Orchestra World*, unsigned, undated clipping, LCL-M.

10. George T. Simon, *The Big Bands* (New York: The Macmillan Co., 1967), pp. 260–61.

11. Henry Jerome, "Bands Dug by the Beat," *down beat*, April 1, 1943, p. 12.

12. Peter S. O'Brien, S.J., liner notes, *Mary Lou Williams: The Asch Recordings, 1944–1947*, Folkways Records.

13. Dance, *The World of Earl Hines*, p. 181.

14. Unpublished correspondence between Irene Kitchings and Callie Arter, courtesy Callie Arter.

15. John Lucas, "Cats Hepped by Connee's Chirping," *down beat*, October 15, 1944, p. 4.

16. Leonard Feather, review of *Mildred Bailey: Her Greatest Performances, down beat*, October 11, 1962, p. 28.

17. Richard Gehman, "Red Means Go," *Esquire*, November 1954, p. 138.

18. Studs Terkel, "Two Artists with Much in Common," *Chicago Sun-Times*, April 16, 1950, Section 2.

19. John S. Wilson, review of *Duke Ellington Presents Ivie Anderson*, *High Fidelity*, Vol. 23, No. 11, November 1973, p. 92.

20. Edward Kennedy Ellington, *Music Is My Mistress* (Garden City, N.Y.: Doubleday & Company, Inc., 1973), p. 124.

21. David Tipmore, "Ella Fitzgerald Is 'Just Middle Class,'" *The Village Voice*, December 9, 1974, p. 21.

22. Lester Young radio interview taken by Chris Albertson, August 26, 1958.

23. Dan Morgenstern, liner notes, *Swing, Brother, Swing*, CBS Records (Encore).

24. Michael Levin, review of *Sullivan, Shakespeare, Hyman, down beat*, March 16, 1972, p. 30.

25. Ibid.

THE FORTIES

1. "Strictly Ad Lib," *down beat*, March 1, 1943, p. 13.

2. "Gal in Studio Ork," *down beat*, May 15, 1944, p. 9.

3. *down beat*, February 1, 1941, p. 2.

4. Marvin Freedman, *down beat*, February 1, 1941, p. 9.

5. Cited in Leonard Feather, *Inside Jazz*, originally published as *Inside Bebop* (New York: Da Capo Press, Inc., 1977), p. 16.

6. Whitney Balliett, *Such Sweet Thunder* (New York: The Bobbs-Merrill Company, Inc., 1966), p. 151.

7. Michael Levin, *down beat*, April 23, 1947, p. 2.

8. Typescript for "We the People" radio broadcast, February 3, 1948, courtesy Bridget O'Flynn.

9. Henry Jerome, "Bands Dug by the Beat," *down beat*, April 1, 1943, p. 12.

10. Evalyn Elbaum, "Billie Rogers Discusses Horns," *down beat*, March 15, 1943, p. 12.

11. Frank Driggs, "Women in Jazz: A Survey," © Stash Records, Inc., p. 21, booklet accompanying *Forty Years of Women in Jazz*, Stash STB 001.

12. Carol Hymowitz and Michaele Weissman, *A History of Women in America* (New York: Bantam Books, Inc., 1978), p. 314.

13. "Want a Job?", *Metronome*, January 1946, p. 21.

14. Mort Goldsen, "Jazz Harvest," *Metronome*, January 1946, p. 32.

15. Cited in Art Napoleon, liner notes, *Women in Jazz: All-Women Groups*, Stash Records, Inc.

16. "All-Girl Mixed Ork Knocks Out Harlem," *down beat*, October 15, 1941, p. 3.

17. Barry Ulanov, *A History of Jazz in America* (New York: The Viking Press, 1955), p. 233.

18. Dizzy Gillespie with Al Fraser, *To BE, or not . . . to BOP* (Garden City, N.Y.: Doubleday & Company, Inc., 1979), p. 415.

19. Leonard Feather, "Mary Osborne: A TV Natural," *down beat*, May 18, 1951, p. 4.

20. Cited in Wilma Dobie, "Dorothy Donegan: Lady Dynamite!" *Jazz Forum*, Vol. 56, June 1978, p. 26.

21. John S. Wilson, "Jazz: Dorothy Donegan and Combo," *The New York Times*, March 16, 1980.

22. Feather, *Inside Jazz*, p. 26.

23. "Dinah Washington," *Ebony*, Vol. 5, No. 8, June 1950, p. 59.

24. Barbara Van Rooyen and Pawel Brodowski, "Betty's Groove: An In-depth Interview with Betty Carter," *Jazz Forum*, Vol. 57, January 1979, p. 30.

25. Abdul Josh Alexander, "Sheila Jordan's Wide Range Allows Her to Take Chances," *Bay State Banner*, February 2, 1978.

26. Ray Murphy, "Sheila Jordan's Singular Style," *Boston Evening Globe*, December 9, 1975.

27. Mark Rowland, *The Real Paper*, April 8, 1978.

28. Cited in Nat Hentoff, liner notes, *Portrait of Sheila*, Blue Note Records.

29. Hentoff, liner notes, *Portrait of Sheila*.

THE FIFTIES

1. Georgia Dullea, "The 'Empty Nest': Chance for a Fuller Life," *The New York Times*, November 24, 1980.

2. Paul R. Farnsworth, "The Effects of Role-Taking on Artistic Achievement," *Journal of Aesthetics and Art Criticism*, Vol. XVIII, No. 3, March 1960, p. 4.

3. Leonard Feather, "Toshiko Akiyoshi: The Leader of the Band," *Ms*, November 1978, p. 34.

4. Michele Wallace, *Black Macho and the Myth of the Superwoman* (New York: Warner Books, Inc., 1978), p. 64.

5. Hal Holly, "Why Ada Selected Men to Replace Girls in Band," *down beat*, February 23, 1955, p. 5.

6. Nat Hentoff, "Cherchez-Les Femmes," *down beat*, December 3, 1952, p. 5.

7. Hal Holly, "Mrs. Cugat Can't See Gals as Tooters: Kills Glamor," *down beat*, May 4, 1951, p. 13.

8. Maya Angelou, *I Know Why the Caged Bird Sings* (New York: Random House, 1969), p. 127.

9. Carol Sloane, "A Drum Is a Woman: The Swinging Dottie Dodgion," *down beat*, March 20, 1969, p. 17.

10. Robert Ostermann, "Records in Review," *The National Observer*, undated clipping, courtesy Dorothy Ashby.

11. Peter Hepple, *Stage and Television Today*, May 1, 1980, p. 4.

12. Anthony Shields, "Night Life," *What's On in London*, May 2, 1980, p. 78.

THE SIXTIES

1. Michele Wallace, *Black Macho and the Myth of the Superwoman* (New York: Warner Books, Inc., 1978), p. 5.

2. John S. Wilson, "Betty Carter Sings Jazz on Broadway," *The New York Times*, November 24, 1978.

3. Annalyn Swan, "Jazz with Oriental Spice," *Newsweek*, July 14, 1980, p. 52.

4. Jon Pareles, "Carla Bley's Playground," *The Village Voice*, May 22, 1978.

5. Robert Palmer, "Carla Bley and Her Band at the Public," *The New York Times*, January 29, 1980.

6. Nat Hentoff, "Indigenous Music," *The Nation*, August 6, 1977, p. 126.

7. Margo Jefferson, "Crossing the Borders," *Newsweek*, September 2, 1974, p. 61.

8. Carla Bley, *The Music of Carla Bley* (Indiana: Alrac Music, Studio P/R, Inc., 1981), Introduction.

9. Jefferson, "Crossing the Borders," p. 61.

10. Bley, *The Music of Carla Bley*, Intro.

11. Carla Bley, "The New Music Strikes a Responsive Chord," *Unicorn Times*, May 1976.

12. Ibid.

13. Bley, *The Music of Carla Bley*, Intro.

14. Bley, "The New Music Strikes a Responsive Chord."

15. Hentoff, "Indigenous Music," p. 126.

16. Pareles, "Carla Bley's Playground."

17. Ibid.

18. Howard Mandel, "Carla Bley, Independent Ringleader," *down beat*, June 1, 1978, p. 18.

19. Unpublished liner notes.

20. Mandel, "Carla Bley, Independent Ringleader," p. 19.

21. Leonard Feather, "Focus On: Vi Redd," *down beat*, September 13, 1962, p. 23.

22. Shanta Nurullah, "Vi Redd: Interview," *Cadence*, Vol. 3, No. 9, January 1978, p. 3.

23. Ibid.

24. John S. Wilson, "Jazz Piano: Patti Bown at Weston's," *The New York Times*, July 16, 1979.

25. Whitney Balliett, "Jazz: Newport News," *The New Yorker*, July 16, 1979, p. 79.

THE SEVENTIES

1. Stanley Crouch, "Betty Carter: A Sure Enough Jazz Singer," *The Village Voice*, December 31, 1981.

2. Leonard Feather, "Toshiko Akiyoshi: The Leader of the Band," *Ms*, November 1978, p. 34.

3. Peter Rothbart, "Toshiko Akiyoshi: Arranging on a Steady Ascent," *down beat*, August 1980, p. 14.

4. Crouch, "Betty Carter: A Sure Enough Jazz Singer."

5. Jon Saunders, "Universal Jazz Coalition Liberates Women 'Axes,'" *N.Y. Amsterdam News*, April 28, 1979.

6. Jim Aiken, "Records," *Contemporary Keyboard*, May 1980, p. 62.

7. Rafi Zabor, "Jazz Short Takes," *Musician*, No. 28, November 1980, p. 82.

8. Bob Blumenthal, "The Arrival of JoAnne Brackeen," *Rolling Stone*, March 6, 1980, p. 35.

9. Nat Hentoff, "The Natural Swing of JoAnne Brackeen," *Books & Arts*, September 28, 1979.

10. Ibid.

11. Leonard Feather, "A Festival of Jazz in Nice Style," *Los Angeles Times*, August 3, 1980.

12. Nat Hentoff, "A Jazz Woman and a Jazz Immortal," *Modern Recording*, November 1979, p. 112.

13. Chuck Berg, review of the album *We Are*, in *Radio Free Jazz*, September 1979, p. 20.

14. Hentoff, "A Jazz Woman and a Jazz Immortal," p. 112.

EPILOGUE

1. Anna Kisselgoff, "Ailey Dancers Return to Give *Mary Lou's Mass*," *The New York Times*, December 7, 1971.

2. Tom Piazza, "Mary Lou Williams Keeps the Faith," *The Village Voice*, November 19, 1979.

3. Melinda Mousouris, "Mary Lou Williams: Musician as Healer," *The Village Voice*, July 23, 1979.

Selected Discography

Some records listed below were out of print and no longer available at the time this book went to press. They were nevertheless included, either because they were mentioned in the text or because they represent what in some cases may be the only recorded work by women discussed in the book. Interested scholars and listeners should refer to the Schwann catalogs 1 and 2, jazz-record specialty outlets, or archival collections for the most up-to-date information on availability of albums or reissues.*

TOSHIKO AKIYOSHI

Akiyoshi-Tabackin Big Band, *Insights*. RCA AFL1 2678.
Akiyoshi-Tabackin Big Band, *Kogun*. RCA AFL1 3019.
Akiyoshi-Tabackin Big Band, *Long Yellow Road*. RCA AFL1 1350.
Akiyoshi-Tabackin Big Band, *Road Time*. RCA CPL2 2242.
Akiyoshi-Tabackin Big Band, *Tales of a Courtesan*. RCA AFL1 0723.
Toshiko Akiyoshi Trio, *Dedications*. Inner City IC 6046.
Toshiko Akiyoshi Trio, *Finesse*. Concord Jazz CJ-69.
see *Women in Jazz: Pianists*.

ALIVE

(Barbara Borden, drums; Carolyn Brandy, congas/percussion; Rhiannon, vocals; Janet Small, keyboards; Susanne Vincenza, bass; Barbara Edwards, manager)

Alive! Urana STWWE 84.
Call It Jazz. Redwood RR 8484.

IVIE ANDERSON

Duke Ellington Presents Ivie Anderson. Columbia KG 32064.

* Records and cross references under the main entries of this discography are alphabetized according to the first major word. Thus a reference to an album titled *Dinah Washington*, for example, or a cross reference to the same artist would be alphabetized under the letter "D."

LIL HARDIN ARMSTRONG

on *Jazz, Vol. 5 (Chicago No. 1)*. Folkways 2805.
see *Jazz Women: A Feminist Retrospective.*
on *King Oliver and His Creole Jazz Band*. VJM VLP-49.
Lil Armstrong and Her Swing Band, 1936–'40. Gardenia 4005.
on *The Louis Armstrong Story, Vol. 1*. Columbia CL 851. Louis Armstrong's
      Hot Five.
————, *Vol. 2*. Columbia CL 852. Louis Armstrong's Hot Seven.
see *Mean Mothers: Independent Women's Blues.*
Satchmo and Me. Riverside RLP 12-120. Oral history by Lil Hardin Armstrong.
see *Women in Jazz: Pianists.*
on *Young Louis: "The Side Man."* MCA 1301. Lil's Hot Shots and Louis
      Armstrong's Hot Five.

DOROTHY ASHBY

Afro-Harping. Cadet 809.
The Best of Dorothy Ashby. Prestige PRS 7638.
Dorothy Ashby Plays for the Beautiful People. Prestige PRS 7639.
Dorothy's Harp. Cadet 825.
The Fantastic Jazz Harp of Dorothy Ashby. Atlantic ATC 1447.
The Rubiyat of Dorothy Ashby. Cadet 841.
Soft Winds: The Swinging Harp of Dorothy Ashby. Jazzland JLP 961. Also
      features Terry Pollard.

LOVIE AUSTIN

on *Alberta Hunter with Lovie Austin's Blues Serenaders*. Riverside RLP 418.
Lovie Austin 1924–26. Fountain FJ-105. With her Blues Serenaders.
see *Women in Jazz: Pianists.*

MILDRED BAILEY

All of Me. Monmouth-Evergreen MES 6814.
Mildred Bailey. Archive of Folk & Jazz 269.
Mildred Bailey: Her Greatest Performances, 1929–1946. Columbia Special
      Products P3L22.
Mildred Bailey, with Paul Baron's Orchestra, 1944. Hindsight HSR-133.
Radio Show 1944–45. Sunbeam 209.
see *Red, White & Blues: Women Sing of America.*

SWEET EMMA BARRETT

see *New Orleans: The Living Legends.*
Sweet Emma Barrett and Her New Orleans Music. GHB 141.
Sweet Emma Barrett at Disneyland. GHB 142.

GLADYS BENTLEY

on *Bertha "Chippie" Hill and Gladys Bentley*. Raretone RTR 24010.
see *Mean Mothers: Independent Women's Blues.*

BILLIE, ELLA, LENA, SARAH.

Columbia PC 36811.

CARLA BLEY

The Carla Bley Band European Tour 1977. Watt 8.
on *Charlie Haden's Liberation Music Orchestra.* Impulse AS 9183. Bley as
    composer and arranger.
Dinner Music. Watt 6.
Escalator over the Hill. JCOA 3LP-EOTH.
on Gary Burton, *A Genuine Tong Funeral.* RCA (French) PL 42766.
Social Studies. ECM-11.
on *13 & ¾.* Watt 3.
Tropical Appetites. Watt 1.

JANE IRA BLOOM

on David Friedman, *Of the Wind's Eye.* Enja 3089.
on Jay Clayton, *All Out.* Anima 1 J35.
Second Wind. Outline OTL-138.
We Are. Outline OTL-137.

BERYL BOOKER

see *Cats vs. Chicks.*
on *Don Byas.* Inner City IC 7081. Beryl Booker Trio (Elaine Leighton and
    Bonnie Wetzel).
see *Jazz Women: A Feminist Retrospective.*
on *Modern Jazz Piano.* RCA Victor LPT-31. 10" lp.
see *Women in Jazz: All-Women Groups.*
see *Women in Jazz: Pianists.*
see *Women in Jazz: Swingtime to Modern.*

BOSWELL SISTERS

The Boswell Sisters, 1932–1934. Biograph BLP-C3.
Nothing Was Sweeter Than the Boswell Sisters. Ace of Hearts AH 116.
On the Air. Totem 1025.

CONNEE BOSWELL

Bing and Connee. Decca DL 5390. 10" lp.
Bing and Connee. Spokane 18.
Connie [sic] Boswell: The Early Solos. 1931–35. Take Two TT 209.
Sand in My Shoes. MCA MCFM 2739.
Singing the Blues with Connee Boswell. Decca DL 5445. 10" lp.

PATTI BOWN

Patti Bown Plays Big Piano. Columbia CL 1379.

JOANNE BRACKEEN

Aft. Timeless/Muse TI 302.
Ancient Dynasty. Columbia JC 36593.
on Art Blakey, *Jazz Messengers 70.* Catalyst CAT 7902.
Keyed In. Tappan Zee JC 36075.
Mythical Magic. Pausa 7045.
New True Illusion. Timeless/Muse TI 103.

Prism. Choice CRS 1040.
Snooze. Choice CRS 1009.
on Stan Getz, *Getz Gold.* Inner City IC 1040-2.
Tring-a-Ling. Choice CRS 1016.
Trinkets and Things. Timeless/Muse TI 123.

CLEO BROWN

on *Kings & Queens of Ivory, Vol. 1.* MCA Jazz Heritage Series (S) 1329.
see *Women in Jazz: Pianists.*

CLORA BRYANT

Gal with the Horn. Mode LP 106.

VI BURNSIDE

see International Sweethearts of Rhythm.

ANN BURTON

By Myself Alone. Inner City IC 6026.
New York State of Mind. Inner City IC 1094.

JACKIE CAIN

on Charlie Ventura, *Euphoria.* Savoy SJL 2243.
on *Charlie Ventura and His Band in Concert.* GNP 1E.
Jackie and Roy: Concerts by the Sea. Studio 7 ST7-402. With Roy Kral.
Jackie and Roy, Star Sounds. Concord Jazz CJ-115. With Roy Kral.

BLANCHE CALLOWAY

Blanche Calloway and Her Joy Boys (1931). RCA (French) Black and White
Series, Vol. 185, PM 42393. Also features Mary Lou Williams.

UNA MAE CARLISLE

see *Jazz Women: A Feminist Retrospective.*
see *Women in Jazz: Pianists.*
see *Women in Jazz: Swingtime to Modern.*

LODI CARR

Lady Bird. Laurie LLT-1007.

BARBARA CARROLL

At the Piano. Discovery DS-847.
Barbara Carroll. Blue Note BN-LA-645(G).
From the Beginning. United Artists UAR (S) LT-778.
see *Women in Jazz: Pianists.*

NORMA CARSON

see *Cats vs. Chicks.*
see *Jazz Women: A Feminist Retrospective.*
see *Women in Jazz: All-Women Groups.*

BETTY CARTER

Betty Carter. Bet-Car MK 1001.
————. Bet-Car MK 1002.
Betty Carter with the Audience. 2-Bet-Car 1003.
Finally. Roulette ROU (S) 5000.
Inside Betty Carter. United Artists UAR 5639.
Now It's My Turn. Roulette ROU (S) 5005.
on Ray Charles, *Ray Charles and Betty Carter*. ABC Paramount ABC (S) 385.
Round Midnight. Roulette ROU (S) 5001.
Social Call. Columbia (S) JC 36425.
What a Little Moonlight Can Do. ABC Impulse (ASH) 9321 (2).

CATS VS. CHICKS.

MGM E-255. Features Terry Pollard, Elaine Leighton, Bonnie Wetzel, Beryl
    Booker, Norma Carson, Mary Osborne, Corky Hale. 10" lp.

ROSEMARY CLOONEY

Blue Rose. Rosemary Clooney and Duke Ellington and His Orchestra. Columbia
    Special Products P 13085.
Everything's Coming Up Rosie. Concord Jazz CJ 47.
Here's to My Lady. Concord Jazz CJ 81.
Rosemary Clooney and Harry James, *Hollywood's Best*. Columbia Special
    Products P 13083.

GLORIA COLEMAN

Gloria Coleman LTD. Sings and Swings Organ. Mainstream MRL 322.
Soul Sisters. Gloria Coleman Quartet. Impulse A 47.

ALICE COLTRANE

Cosmic Music. Impulse AS 9148.
Journey in Satchidananda. Impulse AS 9203.
Lord of Lords. Impulse AS 9224.
Transfiguration. Warner Brothers 3218.
Universal Consciousness. Impulse AS 9210.

IDA COX

Blues Ain't Nothin' Else But . . . Milestone MLP 2015.
Ida Cox, Vol. 1. Fountain FB-301.
————, *Vol. 2*. Fountain FB-304.
see *Mean Mothers: Independent Women's Blues*.
The Moanin' Groanin' Blues: Ida Cox. Riverside RLP 147. Accompanied by
    Lovie Austin and her Blues Serenaders.
on *Spirituals to Swing. The Legendary Carnegie Hall Concerts of 1938-9*.
    Vanguard VRS 8523/4.
on *Stars of the Apollo Theater*. Columbia KG 30788.
Wild Women Don't Have the Blues. Foremothers, Vol. 1. Rosetta RR 1304.

DARDANELLE

Colors of My Life. Stash ST 217.
see *Jazz Women: A Feminist Retrospective*.
on *New York, New York*. Stash ST 204.
Songs for New Lovers. Stash ST 202.

ERNESTINE "TINY" DAVIS

see International Sweethearts of Rhythm.

FOSTINA DIXON

on *Our Music Is Your Music: The Leslie Drayton Orchestra*. Esoteric ER 1001.

DOTTIE DODGION

see *Now Is the Time*.

BARBARA DONALD

Barbara Donald and Unity, Featuring Carter Jefferson. Live at the Gnu Delhi. Cadence CJR 1011. Also includes Cookie Marienco.
on Ed Townsend, *Townsend, Townsend, Townsend*. Casablanca CCLP 2007 DJ.
on Huey (Sonny) Simmons, *Burning Spirits*. Contemporary 7625/6.
on Smiley Winters, *Smiley ETC*. Arhoolie 8004/5.
on Smiley Winters, *That Nigger Music*. Touché TRL TPS 101.
on Sonny Simmons, *Manhattan Egos*. Arhoolie S-8003.
on Sonny Simmons, *Music of the Spheres*. ESP S-1043.
on Sonny Simmons, *Rumasuma*. Contemporary 7623.
on Sonny Simmons, *Staying on the Watch*. ESP S-1030.

DOROTHY DONEGAN

At the Best of Harlem. Four Leaf Clover 5006.
The Explosive. Progressive PRO 7056.
see *Jazz Women: A Feminist Retrospective*.
The Many Faces of Dorothy Donegan. Mahogany 558.101.

ARIZONA DRANES

She Shall Wear a Golden Crown. (Sanctified Pianist 1926–28). Herwin 210.
see *Women in Jazz: Pianists*.

URSZULA DUDZIAK

Future Talk. Inner City IC 1066.
Michal Urbaniak and Urszula Dudziak, *Heritage*. Pausa 7047.

ELLA FITZGERALD

on *The Best of Chick Webb*. MCA (S) 2-4107.
The Best of Ella Fitzgerald, Vol. 1. MCA (2)-4047.
————, *Vol. 2*. MCA (2)-4016.
see *Billie, Ella, Lena, Sarah*.

on *Chick Webb 4. Ella Swings the Band 1936–1939.* MCA 1327.
The Cole Porter Songbook. Verve VE2 2511.
The Duke Ellington Songbook. Verve VE 2-2535.
Ella & Duke at the Cote d'Azur. Verve V 6 4072.
Ella Fitzgerald Abaca Jobim. Pablo 263021.
Ella Fitzgerald at Carnegie Hall. Columbia PG 32557.
Ella Fitzgerald and Her Orchestra Live from the Roseland Ballroom, 1940. Sunbeam 205.
Ella & Louis. Verve 2V6S 8811.
Ella Sings, Chick Swings: Ella Fitzgerald and Chick Webb. Olympic 7119.
Ella Sings Gershwin. MCA 215 E. With Ellis Larkins.
The Gershwin Songbook. Verve VE 2-2525.
Lady Time. Pablo (S) 2310825.
Live in Berlin. Verve V6 4041.
Porgy & Bess. Verve VE 2-2507. With Louis Armstrong.
The Rodgers and Hart Songbook. Verve VE 2-2519.
Whisper Not. Verve UMV 2668.

FORTY YEARS OF WOMEN IN JAZZ.

Stash STB 001. (Five-record box set including Stash *Jazz Women* and *Women in Jazz* albums 109, 111, 112, 113, plus Frank Driggs's 24-page booklet, "Women in Jazz: A Survey.")

ADELE GIRARD

see *Jazz Women: A Feminist Retrospective.*
on *Joe Marsala and His Orchestra.* Aircheck 14.

ROSE GOTTESMAN

see Mary Lou Williams, "Harmony Grits."
see *Women in Jazz: All-Women Groups.*

DELLA GRIFFIN

Della Griffin Sings. Dobre 1009.

CORKY HALE

see *Cats vs. Chicks.*
Corky Hale Plays George Gershwin & Vernon Duke. GNP Crescendo 9035.
Kitty White–Corky Hale. Pacifica 2002.

LUCILLE HEGAMIN

Lucille Hegamin: Blue Flame. VJM VLP-50.
see *Songs We Taught Your Mother.*
see Victoria Spivey, *Basket of Blues.*

ROSA HENDERSON

see *Mean Mothers: Independent Women's Blues, Vol. 1.*
on *Rare & Hot! 1923–1926 Female Vocals with Accompaniment.* Historical HLP-14.

JUTTA HIPP

At the Hickory House, Vol. 1. Blue Note BLP 1515.
————, *Vol. 2.* Blue Note BLP 1516.
Jutta Hipp with Zoot Sims. Blue Note 1530.
see *Women in Jazz: Pianists.*

BILLIE HOLIDAY

All or Nothing at All. Verve VE 2-2529.
see *Billie, Ella, Lena, Sarah.*
Billie Holiday. Archive of Folk & Jazz 265.
————, *Vol. 2.* Archive of Folk & Jazz 310.
Billie Holiday/Ella Fitzgerald. MCA 4099.
Billie Holiday at Jazz at the Philharmonic. Verve UMV 2520.
Billie's Blues. Columbia (S) C-32080.
The Billie Holiday Story, Vol. 1. Columbia PG 32121.
————, *Vol. 2.* Columbia PG 32124.
————, *Vol. 3.* Columbia PG 32127.
The Billie Holiday Story. MCA (2) 4006E.
Body and Soul. Verve UMV 2597.
on *Count Basie: At the Savoy Ballroom.* Everest EVR (S) 318.
Fine and Mellow. Columbia Special Products Commodore Series XFL 14428.
The First Verve Sessions. Verve VE 2-2503.
Gallant Lady. Monmouth-Evergreen MES 7046.
God Bless the Child. Columbia CG 30782.
Greatest Hits. Columbia CL 2666.
Greatest Hits. MCA 275.
Guess Who?—Billie Holiday. Two Flats Disc TFD 5-006.
The History of the Real Billie Holiday. Verve 2-V6S-8816.
I'll Be Seeing You. Columbia Special Products Commodore Series XFL 15351.
     With Eddie Heywood.
on *Jazz at the Philharmonic: The Historic Recordings.* Verve VE 2-2504.
Lady Love. United Artists UA 5635. Accompanied by Beryl Booker and Elaine
     Leighton.
see *Mean Mothers: Independent Women's Blues.*
Lady Sings the Blues. Verve UMV 2047.
The Original Recordings. Columbia C-32060.
on *The Sound of Jazz—TV Soundtrack.* Columbia Special Products P 104.
Stormy Blues. Verve VE 2-2515.
Strange Fruit. Atlantic ATC (S) 1614.
Swing, Brother, Swing. Columbia Special Products P 14388.

LENA HORNE

see *Billie, Ella, Lena, Sarah.*
A Date with Lena Horne. 1944. Sunbeam 212. With Fletcher Henderson.
For Someone in Love. Stanyan 10138.
Lena & Gabor. Gryphon G 908. With Gabor Szabo.
Lena Horne: The Lady and Her Music. Qwest 2 QW 3597.
on *Stormy Weather.* Sandy Hook 2037. Sound track from the 1943 film.

HELEN HUMES

on *Black California, Vol. 1.* Savoy SJL 2215.
————, *Vol. 2.* Savoy SJL 2242.
Helen. Muse MR 5233.
Helen Humes. Audiophile AP 107.
Helen Humes & the Muse All-Stars. Muse MR 5217.
The Incomparable Helen Humes. Jazzology 55.
Let the Good Times Roll. Classic Jazz CJ 120.
see *Red, White & Blues: Women Sing of America.*
Sneakin' Around. Classic Jazz CJ 110.
Songs I Like to Sing! Contemporary (S) 7582.
" 'Tain't Nobody's Business If I Do." Contemporary (S) 7571.

BOBBI HUMPHRY

The Best of Bobbi Humphry. Epic EPC (S) JE 36368.
The Good Life. Epic EPC (S) JE 35607.

ALBERTA HUNTER

Alberta Hunter with Lovie Austin's Blues Serenaders. Riverside RLP 418.
Amtrak Blues. Columbia (S) JC 36430.
on *Chicago: The Living Legends.* Riverside RLP (9) 389/90. With Lil's Hot
    Shots.
Classic Alberta Hunter. The Thirties. Stash ST 115.
The Legendary Alberta Hunter: The London Sessions, 1934. DRG SL 5195.
Remember My Name. Columbia JS 35553. Sound track from the motion
    picture, for which Alberta Hunter wrote the songs.
see *Songs We Taught Your Mother.*
see *Women of the Blues.*

INA RAY HUTTON AND HER MELODEARS

see *Jazz Women: A Feminist Retrospective.*

MARJORIE HYAMS

on *The George Shearing Quintet: Lullabye of Birdland.* Verve (E) 2683/029.
see Mary Lou Williams, on *Cafe Society* and "Harmony Grits."
see *Women in Jazz: All-Women Groups.*
see *Women in Jazz: Swingtime to Modern.*
on *Woody Herman: The Greatest Hits.* Columbia CS 9291.

INTERNATIONAL SWEETHEARTS OF RHYTHM

"Hey—Mr. Postman." Magic 715-42. (Vocal by Mildred McIver Presented by
    the International Sweethearts of Rhythm.) 78 rpm.
see *Jazz Women: A Feminist Retrospective.*
"Temptation." Magic 715-13. (Vocal by Carline Ray Presented by the Inter-
    national Sweethearts of Rhythm.) 78 rpm.
see *Women in Jazz: All-Women Groups.*
see *Women in Jazz: Swingtime to Modern.*

JAZZ WOMEN: A FEMINIST RETROSPECTIVE.

Stash ST 109. Includes Dolly Jones, Lil Hardin Armstrong, Memphis Minnie, International Sweethearts of Rhythm, Ina Ray Hutton and Her Melodears, Dardanelle, Norma Teagarden, Billie Rogers, Sarah McLawler, Mary Lou Williams, Beryl Booker, Norma Carson, Dorothy Donegan, Valaida Snow, Una Mae Carlisle, Marian McPartland, Melba Liston, Adele Girard, Jewel Paige, and Kathy Stobart; see also *Forty Years of Women in Jazz.*

DOLLY JONES

see *Jazz Women: A Feminist Retrospective.*

ETTA JONES

Don't Go to Strangers. Prestige PRS (S) 7186.
Etta Jones' Greatest Hits. Prestige PRS (S) 7443.
If You Could See Me Now. Muse MR 5175.
Ms. Jones to You. Muse MR 5099.
My Mother's Eyes. Muse MR 5145.

SHEILA JORDAN

Confirmation. East Wind EW 8024.
on *George Russell: Outer Thoughts.* Milestone M 47027.
Home: Music by Steve Swallow to Poems by Robert Creeley. ECM 7-7760.
Portrait of Sheila. Blue Note 9002.
Sheila. Steeple Chase SCS 1081. With Arild Anderson.
The Steve Kuhn/Sheila Jordan Band, *Playground.* ECM-1-1159.

NORA LEE KING

(aka *Lenore King, Lenore Kinsey, Susan King, Susan Lenore King*)

on "Larry and Lenore," *Travelin' Guitars.* Request RLP 10037.
on Lawrence Lucie, *Cool and Warm Guitar.* Toy T-1001.
on Lawrence Lucie, *Mixed Emotions.* Toy T-1006.
on Lawrence Lucie, *Sophisticated Lady/After Sundown.* Toy T-1003.
on Lawrence Lucie, *This Is It.* Toy T-1003.
see Mary Lou Williams, *The Asch Recordings, 1944–'47.*
Nora and Delle, "Army Camp Blues." Decca DL 7852. 78 rpm.
Nora and Delle, "Get Away from My Window." Decca DL 7852. 78 rpm.
Nora and Delle, "You Ain't Been Doin' Right." Decca DL 7858. 78 rpm.
"Why Don't You Do Right?" Decca DL 7866. 78 rpm.
see *Women's Railroad Blues.*

TEDDI KING

Lovers and Losers. Audiophile AP 117.
Marian Remembers Teddi. Halcyon HAL 118. With Marian McPartland.
Someone to Light Up Your Life. Audiophile AP 150.
Teddi King Sings Ira Gershwin . . . this Is new. Inner City IC 1044.

JANET LAWSON

Janet Lawson Quintet. Inner City IC 1116.

BARBARA LEA

The Devil Is Afraid of Music. Audiophile AP 119.
Remembering Lee Wiley. Audiophile AP 125.

JEANNE LEE

on Gunter Hampel, Anthony Braxton, Jeanne Lee, *Familie.* (Concert in Paris, April 1, 1972.) Birth 008.
on Gunter Hampel, *The 8th of July 1969.* Birth 001.
on Gunter Hampel, *Spirits.* Birth 007.
on Gunter Hampel, *Waltz for Three Universes in a Corridor.* Birth 010.
on Gunter Hampel & His Galaxie Dream Band, *All the Things You Could Be If Charlie Mingus Was Your Daddy.* Birth 031.
on Gunter Hampel & His Galaxie Dream Band, *A Place to Be with Us.* Birth 032.
on Gunter Hampel and the Galaxie Dream Band, *Angel.* Birth 009.
on Gunter Hampel and the Galaxie Dream Band, *Life on This Planet 1981.* Birth 0033.
Gunter Hampel & Jeanne Lee, *Oasis.* Horo HDP 33-34.
Gunter Hampel-Jeanne Lee Duo, *Freedom of the Universe.* Birth 010.
The Newest Sound Around/Jeanne Lee and Ran Blake. RCA (French) PM 42863.

PEGGY LEE

on *Benny Goodman: All-Time Greatest Hits.* Columbia (S) PG 31547.
The Best of Peggy Lee. 2-MCA 4049E.

KATHERINE HANDY LEWIS

W. C. Handy Blues. Sung by His Daughter, Katherine Handy Lewis. Folkways FG 3540. Accompanied by James P. Johnson.

ABBEY LINCOLN

see Aminata Moseka

MELBA LISTON

on *Bebop Revisited, Vol. 1.* Xanadu 120.
see Dinah Washington, *The Jazz Sides.*
see *Jazz Women: A Feminist Retrospective.*
on Johnny Griffin, *White Gardenia. Johnny Griffin with Strings & Brass. A Tribute to Billie Holiday.* Riverside RLP (9) 387. Liston as arranger.
on Randy Weston, *Little Niles.* Blue Note BN-LA 5988 (112). Liston as arranger.

SARAH McLAWLER

see *Jazz Women: A Feminist Retrospective.*

MARIAN McPARTLAND

At the Festival. Concord Jazz CJ 118.
At the Hickory House. Savoy SJL 2248.
Elegant Piano. Halcyon HAL 106. With Teddy Wilson.
see *Jazz Women: A Feminist Retrospective.*
Live at the Carlyle. Halcyon HAL 117.
Marian and Jimmy McPartland and the All-Star Jazz Assassins. Improv 7122.
see *Now Is the Time.*
Portrait of Marian McPartland. Concord Jazz CJ 101.
see Teddi King, *Marian Remembers Teddi.*

CARMEN McRAE

After Glow. Decca DL 8583. McRae also on piano.
Blue Note Meets the L.A. Philharmonic. Blue Note BLN LKAO-870.
Carmen/Billie. Carmen McRae Sings "Lover Man" and Other Billie Holiday Classics. Columbia PC 37002.
Carmen McRae. Chiaroscuro CHI 2023.
Finest of Carmen McRae. Bethlehem BCP 6004.
At the Great American Music Hall. Blue Note LWB-709.
The Great American Songbook. Atlantic SD2-904 0996.
The Greatest of Carmen McRae. MCA 2-4111.
Here to Stay. Coral COR (S) 20018.
Take Five. Carmen McRae–Dave Brubeck Recorded Live at Basin Street East. Columbia Special Products P 9116.
Two for the Road. Carmen McRae/George Shearing. Concord Jazz CJ (S) 128.

MEAN MOTHERS: INDEPENDENT WOMEN'S BLUES, VOL. 1.

Rosetta RR 1300. Includes Bessie Brown, Martha Copeland, Maggie Jones, Susie Edwards, Bernice Edwards, Gladys Bentley, Mary Dixon, Bertha Idaho, Rosa Henderson, Harlem Hannah, Lil Hardin Armstrong, Blue Lou Barker, Rosetta Howard, Ida Cox, Lil Green, and Billie Holiday.

MEMPHIS MINNIE

Memphis Minnie. Blues Classics 1.
Early Recordings, Vol. 2. Blues Classics 13.
on *I'm Wild About My Lovin'.* Historical Jazz HJ 32. With Joe McCoy.
see *Jazz Women: A Feminist Retrospective.*

HELEN MERRILL

Autumn Love. Catalyst CAT 7912.
Chasin' the Bird. Inner City IC 1080.
Helen Merrill and Teddy Wilson: Sings, Swings. Catalyst CAT 7908.
The Nearness of You. EmArcy EXPR 1018.
Something Special. Inner City IC 1060.

LIZZIE MILES

Hot Songs My Mother Taught Me. Cook 1183.
Moans & Blues by Lizzie Miles. Cook. 1182.
Torchy Lullabies My Mother Sang Me. Cook 1184.

AMINATA MOSEKA (ABBEY LINCOLN)

Abbey Is Blue. Riverside (Japanese) SMJ 6088.
Golden Lady. Inner City IC 1117.
on Max Roach, *We Insist! Freedom Now Suite.* Columbia JC-36390.
People in Me. Inner City IC 6040.
Straight Ahead. Barnaby (the Candid Series) KZ 31037.
That's Him. Riverside (Japanese) SMJ 6155.
What It Is. Columbia JC 36581.

AMINA CLAUDINE MYERS

Poems for Piano. Sweet Earth SER-1005.
Salutes Bessie Smith. Leo LR 103.
Song for Mother E. Leo LR 100.

NEW ORLEANS: THE LIVING LEGENDS.

Riverside RLP 356/7. Sweet Emma Barrett and her Dixieland Boys; Billie and
    De De Pierce.

NOW IS THE TIME.

Halcyon HAL 115. Features Marian McPartland, Lynn Mylano, Vi Redd,
    Dottie Dodgion, and Mary Osborne.

ANITA O'DAY

Angel Eyes. Emily 13081.
Anita O'Day Sings the Winners. Verve UMV 2536.
The Big Band Sessions. Verve VE 2-2534.
Gene Krupa with Anita O'Day. Columbia JCL 753.
Live at the City. Emily 102479.
Live at Mingo's. Emily 11579.
Live in Tokyo. Emily 9578.
At Mister Kelly's. Verve UMV 2550.
My Ship. Emily 11279.

BRIDGET O'FLYNN

see Mary Lou Williams, on *Cafe Society*, "Humoresque," and "Waltz Boogie."
see *Women in Jazz: All-Women Groups.*

MARY OSBORNE

see *Cats vs. Chicks.*
on *The Complete Coleman Hawkins, Vol. 2, "Low Flame" (1941-'47).* RCA
    (French) Black and White Series, Vol. 181, PM 42046.
see Mary Lou Williams, on *Cafe Society* and "Harmony Grits."
"Mary's Guitar Boogie." Mary Osborne Trio. Signature 15077. 78 rpm.
Now and Then. Stash ST 215.
see *Now Is the Time.*
see *Women in Jazz: All-Women Groups.*
"You're Gonna Get My Letter in the Morning." Mary Osborne Trio. Decca DL
    74308. 78 rpm.

BILLIE PIERCE (WITH DE DE PIERCE)

Billie & De De Pierce: New Orleans Music. Arhoolie 2016.
Billie & De De Pierce: Vocal Blues & Cornet in the Classic Tradition. Riverside RLP 370.
on *Jazz at Preservation Hall.* Atlantic ATC (S) 1409.
At Luthjen's. Biograph CEN 15.
see *New Orleans: The Living Legends.*

TERRY POLLARD

on *Bethlehem's Finest, Vol. 2.* Bethlehem BET (S) FCP 4002.
see *Cats vs. Chicks.*
see Dorothy Ashby, *Soft Winds: The Swinging Harp of Dorothy Ashby.*
on Terry Gibbs, *Mallets-A-Plenty.* MRC MG 36075. Pollard on piano.
see *Women in Jazz: All-Women Groups.*
see *Women in Jazz: Swingtime to Modern.*

GERTRUDE "MA" RAINEY

"Blame It on the Blues." Milestone MLP 2008.
Blues the World Forgot: Ma Rainey and Her Georgia Jazz Band, 1924–'28. Biograph BLP 12001.
Down in the Basement. Milestone MLP 2107.
Gertrude "Ma" Rainey: Queen of the Blues, Vol. 3, 1923–'24. Biograph BLP 12032.
The Immortal Ma Rainey: First of the Great Blues Singers. Milestone MLP 2001.
Ma Rainey. Milestone M-47021.
Oh My Babe Blues: Ma Rainey and Her Georgia Jazz Band, Vol. 2, 1924–'28. Biograph BLP 12011.

RARE AND HOT! 1923–1926, FEMALE VOCALS WITH ACCOMPANIMENT.

Historical HLP-14. Includes Rosa Henderson, Viola McCoy, and others.

RED, WHITE & BLUES: WOMEN SING OF AMERICA.

Rosetta RR 1302. Includes Bessie Smith, Helen Humes, Mildred Bailey, and others.

VI REDD

on Al Gray, *Shades of Gray.* Tangerine TRC (S) 1504.
Bird Call. United Artists UA 15016.
Lady Soul. Atco 33-157.
see *Now Is the Time.*
see *Women in Jazz: Swingtime to Modern.*

JUDY ROBERTS

The Judy Roberts Band. Inner City IC 1078.
Judy Roberts: The Other World. Inner City IC 1099.

JANICE ROBINSON

on The Clark Terry Big Band, *Live at the Wichita Jazz Festival.* Vanguard VSD 79355.
on Frank Foster's Living Color, *For All Intents and Purposes.* Leo 007.
on Frank Foster's Loud Minority, *Manhattan Fever.* Nippon Columbia YX 7521.
on Frank Foster's Loud Minority, *Shiny Stockings.* Nippon Columbia YX 7545.
on Thad Jones/Mel Lewis Orchestra, *New Life.* Horizon (ANM) SP701.
on Thad Jones/Mel Lewis Orchestra, *The Suite for Pops.* Horizon (ANM) SP707.

BILLIE ROGERS

see *Jazz Women: A Feminist Retrospective.*
One Night Stand with Billie Rogers. "Womens' Lib in 1944." Joyce LP-1018.

JUNE ROTENBERG

see Mary Lou Williams, "Harmony Grits," "Humoresque," and "Waltz Boogie."
see *Women in Jazz: All-Women Groups.*

JEANETTE SALVANT

on *Celestin's Original Tuxedo Jazz Orchestra. Recorded in New Orleans 1926–1928.* VJM VLP-33.

SHIRLEY SCOTT

The Best of Shirley Scott. Prestige PRS (S) 7773.
Blue Flames. Prestige PRS (S) 7338. With Stanley Turrentine.
Blue Seven. Prestige PRS (S) 7376.
Eddie's Function. Bethlehem BCP 6035.
Great Scott! Shirley Scott Trio. Impulse Mono A-67.
One for Me. Strata-East 7430.
Queen of the Organ. Impulse Mono A-81.
Satin Doll. Prestige PRS (S) 7283.
Soul Is Willing. Prestige PRS (S) 7845.
Soul Shouting. Prestige PRS (S) 7312. With Stanley Turrentine.
Soul Sister. Prestige PRS (S) 7392.
Sweet Soul. Prestige PRS (S) 7360.

CAROL SLOANE

Carol Sings (1978). Progressive 7047.
Carol Sloane and Ben Webster, *Carol & Ben.* Honeydew HD 6608.
Cottontail. Choice CRS 1025.

BESSIE SMITH

Any Woman's Blues. Columbia CG 30126.
on *Bessie Smith, Louis Armstrong, Cab Calloway (Legendary Jazz Stars in Their First Films).* Biograph BLP-M-3. Sound track from *St. Louis Blues.*

The Empress. Columbia CG 30818.
Empty Bed Blues. Columbia CG 30450.
Nobody's Blues But Mine. Columbia CG 31093.
see *Red, White & Blues: Women Sing of America.*
see *Women's Railroad Blues: Sorry But I Can't Take You.*
The World's Greatest Blues Singer. Columbia CG (S) 33.

CARRIE SMITH

Carrie Smith. West 54 8002.
Do Your Duty. Classic Jazz CJ 139.

CLARA SMITH

Clara Smith, Vol. 1, 1923. VJM VLP-15.

MAMIE SMITH

on *Jazz Odyssey, Vol. 3: The Sound of Harlem.* Columbia Jazz Archive Series
    C3L-33.
see *Women of the Blues.*

VALAIDA SNOW

on *Americans in Europe, Vol. 2.* Swingfan 1012.
Hot Snow: Valaida Snow, Queen of the Trumpet, Sings & Swings. Fore-
    mothers, Vol. 2. Rosetta RR 1305.
see *Jazz Women: A Feminist Retrospective.*
Swing Is the Thing. World (EMI) SH 354.
Valaida: High Hat, Trumpet and Rhythm. World (EMI) SH 309.

SONGS WE TAUGHT YOUR MOTHER.

Prestige/Bluesville 1052. Features Alberta Hunter, Lucille Hegamin, Victoria
    Spivey.

VICTORIA SPIVEY

Basket of Blues. Spivey LP 1001. Also features Lucille Hegamin and Hannah
    Sylvester.
The Blues Is Life. Folkways FS 3541.
The Queen and Her Knights (The Tops in Blues Royalty). Spivey LP 1006.
see *Songs We Taught Your Mother.*
Three Kings and the Queen. (Individualism, Artistry, and Longevity). Spivey
    LP 1004.
Three Kings and the Queen, Vol. 3. Spivey LP 1014.
Victoria and Her Blues. Spivey LP 1002.
Victoria Spivey's Recorded Legacy of the Blues, 1927–'37. Spivey LP 2001.
Woman Blues! Bluesville 1054. With Lonnie Johnson.
see *Women of the Blues.*

JEAN STARR

see *Women in Jazz: All-Women Groups.*
see *Women in Jazz: Swingtime to Modern* (Hip Chicks).

DAKOTA STATON

The George Shearing Quintet with Dakota Staton. In the Night. Capitol ST
1003.
The Late, Late Show. Capitol (T) 876.

MARY STRAINE

"Ain't Got Nothin' Blues." Black Swan 14155. 78 rpm.
"Chirpin' the Blues." Black Swan 14150. 78 rpm.
"Downhearted Blues." Black Swan 14150. 78 rpm.
"I Wish I Could Shimmy (Like My Sister Kate)." Black Swan 14123. 78 rpm.
"The Last Go Round Blues." Black Swan 14123. 78 rpm.

MONETTE SUDLER

Time for a Change. Inner City IC 2062.

MAXINE SULLIVAN

on *Cafe Society.* Onyx 210.
Earl Hines & Maxine Sullivan. Live at the Overseas Press Club. Chiaroscuro
CHI 107.
Maxine Sullivan/Art Hodes Orchestra, *We Just Couldn't Say Goodbye.* Audio-
phile AP 128.
Maxine Sullivan/Bob Wilbur. Close as Pages in a Book. Monmouth-Evergreen
MES 6919.
Maxine Sullivan/Jack Teagarden. Archive of Folk & Jazz 307.
Sullivan, Shakespeare, Hyman. Monmouth-Evergreen MES 7038.
on *Swing Street.* Columbia JSN 6042.

NORMA TEAGARDEN

on *Big T and the Condon Gang.* Pumpkin 106.
on *Big T and Mighty Max: Jack Teagarden and Max Kaminsky.* Columbia
Special Products Commodore Series FL 14940.
on *Big T's Jazz.* Decca DL 8304.
see *Jazz Women: A Feminist Retrospective.*

VAUDEVILLE BLUES.

VJM VLP-30. Includes Mary Stafford, Susie Smith (Monette Moore), Laura
Smith, Josie Miles, Julia Moody, Frankie and her Jazz Devils, Mandy
Lee, and Helen Gross.

SARAH VAUGHAN

After Hours. Columbia Special Products 660.
on *Basie, Getz, & Vaughan Live at Birdland.* Roulette Echoes of an Era RE
126.
see *Billie, Ella, Lena, Sarah.*
Copacabana—Exclusivamente Brazil. Pablo 2312 125.
on *The Count Basie Vocal Years.* Roulette Echoes of an Era RE 107.
"The Divine Sarah." *Sarah Vaughan/The Early Years.* Musicraft MSV 504.
With Tadd Dameron and Bud Powell.

Duke Ellington Songbook, Vol. 1. Pablo 2312 111.
———, *Vol. 2.* Pablo 2312 116.
Golden Hits. Mercury MER 60645.
How Long Has This Been Going On? Pablo 2310 821.
I Love Brazil. Pablo 2312 101.
In Hi-Fi. Columbia Encore Star Series P 13084.
Linger Awhile. Columbia Special Products P 14364.
Recorded Live. EmArcy EMS 2-412.
Sarah Vaughan. Roulette Echoes of an Era RE 103.
Sarah Vaughan. EmArcy EXPR 1009.
Sarah Vaughan, Vol. 1. Archive of Folk & Jazz 250.
———, *Vol. 2.* Archive of Folk & Jazz 271.
———, *Vol. 3.* Archive of Folk & Jazz 325.
Sarah Vaughan & Dizzy Gillespie. Ozone 17.
"*Send in the Clowns.*" Sarah Vaughan and the Count Basie Orchestra. Pablo
    2312 130.

HELEN WARD

on *The Complete Benny Goodman, Vol. 1.* RCA Bluebird AXM2-5505.
The Helen Ward Songbook, Vol. 1. Lyricon 101.

DINAH WASHINGTON

The Best of Dinah Washington. Roulette ROU (S) 42014.
Dinah Jams. EmArcy EXPR 1013 (mono).
Dinah Sings Bessie Smith. Trip TLP 5556.
Dinah '62. Roulette ROU (R) 25170.
Dinah Washington. Archive of Folk & Jazz 297.
Dinah Washington/Immortal. Roulette RE 125.
Discovered. Mercury MER 6119.
The Dinah Washington Years. Roulette Echoes of an Era RE 104.
The Jazz Sides. EmArcy EMS-2-401. Also features some Melba Liston arrange-
    ments.
The Queen of the Blues. Roulette RE 117.
Two of Us. Mercury MER (S) 60232. With Brook Benton.
Unforgettable. Mercury MER (S) 60232.
What a Difference a Day Makes. Mercury MER (S) 8006.

ETHEL WATERS

Ethel Waters' Greatest Years. Columbia KG 31571.
Ethel Waters 1938–'39. RCA (French) 741067.
Jazzin' Babies' Blues. Ethel Waters, 1921–'27, Vol. 2. Biograph BLP 12026.
Miss Ethel Waters. Monmouth-Evergreen MES 6812.
Oh Daddy. Ethel Waters, 1921–'24. Biograph BLP 12022. Accompanied by
    Lovie Austin's Serenaders.
On Stage & Screen. Columbia Special Products P 2792.

LEE WILEY

Back Home Again. Monmouth-Evergreen MES 7048.
Jess Stacy/Lee Wiley, and Friends. Columbia Special Products Commodore
    Series XFL 15358.
Lee Wiley. Early Recordings 1931–'37. Philomel 1000.

Lee Wiley Sings the Music of George Gershwin and Cole Porter. Monmouth-Evergreen MES 7034.
Lee Wiley Sings Rodgers and Hart and Harold Arlen. Monmouth-Evergreen MES 6807.
Night in Manhattan. Columbia Special Products P 656.
On the Air. Totem 1021.
————, *Vol. 2*. Totem 1033.

MARY LOU WILLIAMS

on *Andy Kirk and His Clouds of Joy: Instrumentally Speaking, 1936–1942*. MCA Jazz Heritage Series 1308.
Best of Mary Lou Williams. Pablo (S) 2310 856.
Black Christ of the Andes. Mary 101.
on *The Black Swing Tradition*. Savoy SJL 2246.
see Blanche Calloway, *Blanche Calloway and Her Joy Boys (1931)*.
on *Cafe Society*. Onyx 210. With Mary Osborne, Marjorie Hyams, Bridget O'Flynn, and Bea Taylor (Billy Taylor).
on *Don Byas*. Inner City IC 7018.
First Lady of the Piano. Inner City IC 7006.
Footnotes to Jazz, Vol. 2. Rehearsal. Folkways FJ 2292. 10″ lp.
Free Spirits. Inner City IC 2043.
From the Heart. Chiaroscuro CHI 103.
"Harmony Grits." Mary Lou Williams Girl Stars (Mary Osborne, Marjorie Hyams, June Rotenberg, and Rose Gottesman). RCA Victor VIC 20-2174. 78 rpm.
History of Jazz: Ragtime to Avant Garde (Solo Piano and Narration). Folkways FLK 2860.
"Humoresque." Mary Lou Williams Trio (June Rotenberg and Bridget O'Flynn). RCA Victor VIC 20-2025. 78 rpm.
on *Jazz Pioneers*. Prestige PR 7647.
see *Jazz Women: A Feminist Retrospective*.
on *Kings & Queens of Ivory, Vol. 1*. MCA Jazz Heritage Series (S) 1329.
Live at the Cookery. Chiaroscuro CHI 146. With Brian Torff.
In London. GNP Crescendo 9029.
Mary Lou's Mass. Mary 102.
Mary Lou Williams. Folkways 2843.
Mary Lou Williams. Stanyan 24.
Mary Lou Williams. The Asch Recordings, 1944–'47. Folkways FA 2966.
Mary Lou Williams Quartet. Crescendo CRS (S) 9030.
The Mary Lou Williams Quintet. GNP Crescendo 9030. Featuring Don Byas.
on *Modern Jazz Piano*. RCA Victor LPT-31. 10″ lp.
My Mama Pinned a Rose on Me. Pablo 2310 819.
Praise the Lord in Many Voices, Vol. 2. Avant Garde AVD (S) 103.
Solo Recital/Montreux Jazz Festival 1978. Pablo L 2308 218.
"Waltz Boogie." Mary Lou Williams Trio (June Rotenberg and Bridget O'Flynn). RCA Victor VIC 20-2025.
see *Women in Jazz: Pianists*.
Zodiac Suite. Folkways 32844.
Zoning. Mary 103.

EDITH WILSON

He May Be Your Man but He Comes to See Me Sometimes. Delmark DEL 637.

WOMEN IN JAZZ: VOL. 1. ALL-WOMEN GROUPS.

Stash ST 111. Includes Jean Starr, Marjorie Hyams, Marian Gange, Rose Gottesman, Beryl Booker, Norma Carson, Mary Osborne, Bridget O'Flynn, Terry Pollard, Bonnie Wetzel, June Rotenberg, International Sweethearts of Rhythm, Ginger Smock, Edna Williams, Vivian Garry, and others; see also *Forty Years of Women in Jazz*.

WOMEN IN JAZZ: VOL. 2. PIANISTS.

Stash ST 112. Includes Arizona Dranes, Lovie Austin, Lil Hardin Armstrong, Mary Lou Williams, Rose Murphy, Una Mae Carlisle, Cleo Brown, Beryl Booker, Nellie Lutcher, Hazel Scott, Jutta Hipp, Toshiko Akiyoshi, Barbara Carroll, and others; see also *Forty Years of Women in Jazz*.

WOMEN IN JAZZ: VOL. 3. SWINGTIME TO MODERN.

Stash ST 113. Includes Mills Cavalcade Orchestra, Mike Riley and his Round and Round Boys (with L'Ana Webster), Una Mae Carlisle, International Sweethearts of Rhythm, Hip Chicks, Marjorie Hyams, Vi Redd, Terry Pollard, Beryl Booker, and others; see also *Forty Years of Women in Jazz*.

WOMEN OF THE BLUES.

RCA Victor Vintage Series LPV 534. Includes Mamie Smith, Victoria Spivey, Sweet Peas (Addie Spivey), Lizzie Miles, Alberta Hunter, Susie Smith (Monette Moore), Sippie Wallace, and Margaret Johnson.

WOMEN'S RAILROAD BLUES: SORRY BUT I CAN'T TAKE YOU.

Rosetta RR 1301. Includes Trixie Smith, Clara Smith, Bessie Smith, Bertha Chippie Hill, Ada Brown, Sippie Wallace, Martha Copeland, Bessie Jackson, Lucille Bogan, Blue Lou Barker, Sister Rosetta Tharpe, and Nora Lee King (Lenore King).

Selected Bibliography

Albertson, Chris. *Bessie*. New York: Stein & Day Publishers, 1972.

Balliett, Whitney. *American Singers*. New York: Oxford University Press, 1979.

Bechet, Sidney. *Treat It Gentle*. New York: Da Capo Press, Inc., 1975.

Bogle, Donald. *Brown Sugar: Eighty Years of America's Black Female Superstars*. New York: Harmony Books, 1980.

Chilton, John. *Billie's Blues: The Billie Holiday Story, 1933–1959*. New York: Stein & Day Publishers, 1975.

Driggs, Frank. "Women in Jazz: A Survey." © Stash Records Inc., 1977.

Ellington, Edward Kennedy (Duke). *Music Is My Mistress*. Garden City, N.Y.: Doubleday & Company, Inc., 1973.

Feather, Leonard. *Inside Jazz*. New York: Da Capo Press, Inc., 1977.

Forrest, Helen, and Libby, Bill. *I Had the Craziest Dream*. New York: Coward, McCann & Geoghegan, 1982.

Gleason, Ralph J. *Celebrating the Duke and Louis, Bessie, Billie, Bird, Carmen, Miles, Dizzy and Other Heroes*. New York: Delta Books, 1976.

Handy, D. Antoinette. *Black Women in American Bands and Orchestras*. Metuchen, N.J., and London: The Scarecrow Press, 1981.

Handy, W. C. *Father of the Blues*. New York: Collier Books, 1970.

Harris, Sheldon. *Blues Who's Who*. New Rochelle, N.Y.: Arlington House, 1979.

Holiday, Billie, and Dufty, William. *Lady Sings the Blues*. New York: Doubleday & Company, Inc., 1956.

Horne, Lena, and Schikel, Richard. *Lena*. Garden City, N.Y.: Doubleday & Company, 1965.

Hymowitz, Carol, and Weissman, Michaele. *A History of Women in America*. New York: Bantam Books, Inc., 1978.

Jones, LeRoi. *Blues People*. New York: William Morrow and Company, 1963.

Leib, Sandra R. *Mother of the Blues: A Study of Ma Rainey*. Massachusetts: University of Massachusetts Press, 1981.

Murray, Albert. *The Hero and the Blues*. Missouri: University of Missouri Press, 1973.

———. *Stomping the Blues*. New York: McGraw-Hill Book Company, 1976.

O'Day, Anita, and Eells, George. *High Times, Hard Times*. New York: G. P. Putnam's Sons, 1981.

Oliver, Paul. *Conversation with the Blues*. New York: Horizon Press, 1965.

Rich, Adrienne. "Disloyal to Civilization: Feminism, Racism, and Gynephobia," in *On Lies, Secrets, and Silence*. New York: W. W. Norton & Company, 1979.

Shapiro, Nat, and Hentoff, Nat, eds. *Hear Me Talkin' to Ya*. New York: Dover Publications, Inc., 1966.

Smith, Willie the Lion, with Hoefer, George. *Music on My Mind*. New York: Da Capo Press, Inc., 1975.

Southern, Eileen. *The Music of Black Americans*. New York: W. W. Norton & Company, Inc., 1971.

Stewart-Baxter, Derrick. *Ma Rainey and the Classic Blues Singers*. New York: Stein & Day Publishers, 1970.

Tallant, Robert. *Voodoo in New Orleans*. New York: Collier Books, 1974.

Walker, Alice. "In Search of Our Mothers' Gardens," in Ruddick, Sara, and Daniels, Pamela, eds., *Working It Out*. New York: Pantheon Books, 1977.

Wallace, Michele. *Black Macho and the Myth of the Superwoman*. New York: Warner Books, 1980.

Waters, Ethel, with Samuels, Charles. *His Eye Is on the Sparrow*. New York: Jove Publications, Inc., 1978.

MUSIC BOOKS

Bessie Smith, Empress of the Blues. Commentary by Chris Albertson and Gunther Schuller. New York: Schirmer Books, A Division of Macmillan Publishing Co., Inc., 1975.

The Best of Billie Holiday. New York: Edward B. Marks Music Corporation, 1962. Also includes songs by Irene Kitchings and Irene Higginbotham.

Billie Holiday, Anthology: Lady Sings the Blues. California: Creative Concepts Publishing Corp., 1976. Also includes songs by Ann Ronell and Irene Higginbotham.

The Music of Carla Bley. Indiana: Alrac Music, Studio P/R, Inc., 1981.

Index

Adams, Billy, 35
Adams, Dolly, 43
Adams, Pepper, 240
Adler, Henry, 171
Aikin, Jim, 273
Akiyoshi, Toshiko, 222–223, 250–251, 266–267
Albertson, Chris, 30–31, 38
Albright, Regina, 224
Aldam, Jeff, 94
Ali, Bardu, 180
Allen, Red, 35
Allen, Viola, 46
Altman, Robert, 37
Ammons, Gene, 197
Anderson, Cat, 162, 232
Anderson, Frank, 190
Anderson, Ivie, 75, 113–114
Andrews, Ward (Dope), 21
Angelou, Maya, 227
Anthony, Ray, 245
Archey, Jimmy, 39
Arfine, Louis, 228
Arlen, Harold, 264
Armenra, Dolly Jones, 46, 47, 64–66, 149, 267
Armstrong, Lil Hardin, 37, 58–63, 86, 225, 250
Armstrong, Louis, 9, 10, 15, 19, 24, 35, 37, 43, 47, 58, 60, 63, 64–65, 85, 92, 94, 108, 119, 216
Arter, Ann, 111
Arter, Callie, 110, 111
Ashby, Dorothy, 239–243
Ashby, John, 239
Ates, Roscoe, 236
Attles, Joseph, 26, 28, 94
Austin, Lovie, 15, 18, 29, 38, 39, 43–44, 127, 250
Ayler, Albert, 249

Backstrum, Margaret, 86, 87, 150, 198
Bailey, Benny, 264
Bailey, Buster, 63
Bailey, Jessie, 96
Bailey, Mildred, 20, 113, 122, 125
Bailey, Rector, 199–200
Baker, Josephine, 26, 38, 85
Balliett, Whitney, 24, 128, 261
Banning, George, 172
Banning, Sally, 171, 172

Barbieri, Gato, 253
Barefield, Eddie, 34, 65
Barker, Danny, 18
Barnet, Charlie, 90, 103, 104, 107
Barrett, Sweet Emma, 250
Barrie, Gracie, 127
Barris, Harry, 113
Barton, Willene, 224, 227–231, 268
Basie, Count, 92, 97, 114, 124, 133, 203, 216, 233, 260
Bayron, Gracie, 132
Bayron, Judy, 132
Bechet, Sidney, 5, 9, 18, 20, 22, 38, 47, 94, 278
Beiderbecke, Bix, 73
Bell, Brenda, 34
Bell, Gloria. See Coleman
Benford, Bill, 64
Benford, Tommy, 64, 93
Bennett, Eloise, 110
Benny, Jack, 26
Bently, Gladys, 9
Bernhardt, Clyde, 9, 13, 14, 26, 39, 40, 46, 93
Berry, Ananais, 94
Berry, Bill, 155
Berry, Chu, 45, 63, 99
Berry, Connie, 192
Bethune, Mary McLeod, 150
Betters, Harold, 289
Blaine, Alberto Valdez, 186
Blake, Ran, 223
Blakey, Art, 223, 236, 274, 280
Blakey, Evelyn, 268
Blesh, Rudi, 15
Bley, Carla Borg, 249, 251–254, 266, 267
Bley, Paul, 251, 252
Bloom, Jane Ira, 267, 268, 281–285
Boas, Gunter, 23–24
Bogan, Lucille, 9
Bolar, Juanita, 108
Bonnier, Bess, 222, 241
Booker, Beryl, 130, 164, 167, 169, 186, 192, 199, 224, 225
Borca, Karen, 267
Boswell Sisters, 23, 112–113
Bown, Patti, 250, 260–265, 268
Brachfield, Andrea, 267
Brackeen, Charles, 273
Brackeen, JoAnne, 258, 268, 273–276
Braddy, Pauline. See Williams

Bradford, Perry, 21, 22
Brady, Mae, 46
Braud, Wellman, 63
Brecker Brothers, 238
Briggs, Lillian, 225
Bronson, Art, 67
Brown, Cleo, 43, 108
Brown, Clifford, 166, 258
Brown, Lawrence, 183
Brown, Les, 162
Brown, Ray, 191
Brown, Sterling, 15, 35
Brubeck, Dave, 223
Bruce, Jack, 253
Bryant, Clora, 152–156, 250, 258
Bryant, Mel, 155
Bryant, Willie, 137
Bucher, George, 136
Buel, D. W., 5
Bunch, John, 237
Burg, Doris, 172
Burke, Louise, 272
Burnside, Vi, 133, 134, 139, 147, 163,
    165, 199, 224, 226
Burrell, Kenny, 240
Burrs, Glen, 123
Burton, Gary, 251
Butler, Toby, 134, 163
Byas, Don, 100, 128, 192, 225
Byrd, Donald, 233, 240
Byrd, Ina Belle, 136

Cain, Jackie, 213
Calloway, Alice, 46, 47
Calloway, Blanche, 93
Calvin, Robert, 34
Campbell, E. Simms, 7
Campus, Joe, 287
Canfield, Mary Cass, 68
Capone, Al, 110
Carlisle, Una Mae, 108
Carnegie, Ross, 233
Carr, Lodi, 223
Carroll, Barbara, 222
Carson, Norma, 158, 164–167, 225
Carter, Benny, 96, 110, 111, 119, 260
Carter, Betty, 6, 213, 250, 266, 267, 269
Carter, Consuella, 132, 135
Carter, Rae, 139
Castro, Concepcion, 87
Catlett, Sid, 64, 136
Cauette, Frenchy, 186
Cavin, Susan, 5
Cayler, Joy, 130, 162, 225
Chambers, Paul, 240
Chance, Eileen, 136, 224, 229, 234
Chappell, Gus, 178
Charles, Ray, 63
Chavis, Red, 234
Cheatham, Doc, 30, 40, 64–65, 95,
    232–233
Cherry, Don, 253
Chester, Bob, 186
Childers, Buddy, 237
Chilton, John, 115
Christian, Charlie, 128, 147, 185
Clair, Natalie, 175
Clark, George, 61, 63

Clarke, Kenny, 128, 225, 236
Claxton, Rozelle, 108
Clayton, Jay, 267, 268
Clifford, Gene, 158–159
Clooney, Rosemary, 213
Coates, Pauline, 51
Cole, Nat (King), 222
Cole, Natalie, 243
Coleman, Bill, 128
Coleman, George, 284
Coleman, Gloria Bell, 199, 224, 250
Coleman, Ornette, 249, 254
Colton, Bob, 22
Coltrane, Alice McLeod, 249–250
Coltrane, John, 181, 249, 257, 258, 261
Comer, Carol, 183, 268
Condon, Eddie, 71, 72
Cook, Olivia, 43
Corea, Chick, 249, 253
Cortez, Alma, 132, 150
Coryell, Larry, 253
Cosby, Bill, 285, 287
Coston, Helen Saine, 143–145
Cox, Adler, 29
Cox, Ida, 8, 10, 11, 28–32
Crawford, Joan, 127
Crawford, Vivian, 139
Crayton, Pee Wee, 154
Creath, Charlie, 51, 52, 53, 55
Creeley, Robert, 214, 219
Cron, Roz, 134, 135, 271
Crosby, Bing, 113
Crosby, Bob, 122, 125
Crouch, Stanley, 266
Crowley, Arthur, 197
Crump, Jesse, 30

Dade, Al, 142
Dameron, Tadd, 128, 212
Damita Jo, 155
Damrosch, Walter, 188
Dance, Helen Oakley, 65, 86, 110, 112,
    115, 122–126
Dance, Stanley, 65, 94, 125
Dandridge, Vivian, 155
Daniels, Billy, 153
Davis, Bert Etta (Lady Bird), 92, 153,
    234
Davis, Bette, 127
Davis, Desdemona, 49, 50
Davis, Eddie (Lockjaw), 222
Davis, Ernestine (Tiny), 86, 90–93, 104,
    133, 134, 139, 153, 199, 224, 226
Davis, Jean, 199, 224, 231–235, 268
Davis, Miles, 223, 240, 249
Davis, Sammy Jr., 155, 277
Davis, Wild Bill, 199
Dédé, Sanité, 4, 5
de Franco, Buddy, 236
De Paris, Wilbur, 202
Desdoumes, Mamie, 43
Dickens, Charles, 14
Dickerson, Garvinia, 43
Dixon, Bill, 249
Dixon, Fostina, 135, 179, 267, 276–279
Dixon, Lucille, 175–178, 226
Dodgion, Dottie, 179, 187, 235–238
Dodgion, Jerry, 236, 237

Doggett, Bill, 199
Dolphy, Eric, 259
Donald, Barbara, 249, 255–258
Donegan, Dorothy, 193–195, 197
Door, Anita, 146
Dorsey, Jimmy, 77, 90
Dorsey, Tommy, 96, 213
Dorsey Brothers, 85, 108
Douglas, Memphis Minnie, 9
Dranes, Arizona, 44, 267
Dreiwitz, Barbara, 287
Drew, Kenny, 236
Dreyer, Flo, 92, 156, 159, 161–164, 224
Driggs, Frank, 44, 86, 130
DuBois, W. E. B., 7, 42
Dudziak, Urszula, 267
Dullea, Georgia, 221
Dunbar, Paul Laurence, 50
Dunham, Katherine, 103, 107
Dunn, Johnny, 22, 64
Dupont, Ann, 87
Durham, Eddie, 86, 87, 92, 96, 97, 100,
    108, 129, 133, 139, 224–225, 228, 229;
    All-Star Girl Orchestra, 149–151
Duvivier, George, 129, 209

Eckstine, Billy, 120, 197, 212
Edison, Harry (Sweets), 171
Edwards, Bernice, 34
Edwards, Earle, 95
Edwards, Gus, 96
Edwards Sisters, 139
Egan, Babe, 70, 80, 87, 99
Eldridge, Roy, 31, 65, 90, 104, 208, 209
Ellington, Duke, 44, 48, 85, 97, 99, 113,
    114, 122, 124, 125, 126, 203, 216, 260
Ellington, Mercer, 188, 191
Elliott, Ernest (Sticky), 21
Ellis, Don, 271
Ervin, Booker, 250
Europe, James Reese, 188, 203
Europe, Mary, 203
Evans, Bill, 275

Farlow, Tal, 225
Farmer, Art, 252
Feather, Leonard, 165, 173, 192, 212,
    222, 225, 245, 259, 272, 279
Fields, Maxine, 229
Filmore, Lazy Daddy, 34
Fineberg, Jean, 267
Finney, Mrs. Theodore, 42
Fitzgerald, Ella, 6, 114, 124, 223
Fitzpatrick, Leo, 118
Flanagan, Tommy, 240
Fleisher, Leon, 169
Fletcher, Dusty, 180
Fontana, Carl, 237
Forrest, Helen, 112
Foster, Frank, 241, 285
Foster, Pops, 54, 55
Foxx, Redd, 139
Franklin, Aretha, 260
Freeman, Sharon, 179, 267, 268, 285
Friedlander, John, 76
Friedman, David, 282
Fuller, Walter, 110

Gale, Moe, 198
Gange, Marian, 97, 130, 173
Gardner, Julie, 268
Garner, Erroll, 100
Garrison, Amy, 139
Garry, Vivian, 129
Garson, Greer, 127
Gaye, Marvin, 276, 277
Gaynor, Gloria, 201
Gee, Jack, 19
Gee, Lottie, 93
Getz, Stan, 274
Giaimo, Chuck, 235
Gibbs, Terry, 222, 250
Gibson, Marjorie, 86
Gilbert, Peggy, 80, 82–84, 89, 107
Gillespie, Dizzy, 128, 154, 179, 180, 181,
    182, 212, 216, 225, 250, 264
Girard, Adele, 192
Gitler, Ira, 239
Glaser, Joe, 92, 162, 200, 201
Gleason, Ralph, 249
Glenn, Tyree, 178
Goff, Nettie, 46
Gold, Sanford, 186
Goldberg, Jane, 267
Goldberg, Richie, 260
Goldman, Emma, 69
Gonsoulin, Bertha, 44
Gonzales, Antonia, 46
Goodman, Benny, 27, 84, 85, 105, 108,
    122, 124, 125, 213, 235, 237
Gordon, Dexter, 181, 257, 260, 274
Gottesman, Rose, 102, 131, 173–175
Graham, Billy, 28
Grant, Henry, 203
Gray, Al, 259
Gray, Jerry, 245
Gray, Marlene, 102
Green, Charlie (Big), 15, 19, 64
Green, Joe, 9
Green, Juanita, 20
Green, Ruth, 51
Green, Urbie, 225
Greer, Sonny, 34, 114
Gregg, Dianne, 179, 183, 268
Grice, Bobbie, 70, 78, 79
Griffin, Della, 223
Griffin, Johnny, 179, 182
Grimes, Tiny, 204, 250
Grupp, Maurice, 124
Guiffre, Jimmy, 252
Guinan, Texas, 108

Hackett, Bobby, 103, 107, 121
Haden, Charlie, 251, 252
Hadlock, Richard, 18–19
Hale, Corky, 164, 225, 243–244, 268
Haley, Bill, 224
Hall, Al, 128
Hall, Audrey. See Petroff
Hall, Ed, 124
Hall, Juanita, 17
Hammerstein, Oscar, 38
Hammond, John, 19, 31
Hampton, Lionel, 83, 171, 209, 212
Hampton, Slide, 285
Hancock, Herbie, 249

Handy, D. Antoinette, 42, 46
Handy, W. C., 7, 13, 46
Hanna, Roland, 240
Hardin, Lil. See Armstrong
Harper, Billy, 288
Harris, Barry, 240
Harris, Benny, 256, 257
Harris, Estella, 46
Harris, Ratzo, 282
Harris, Wynonie, 213
Hart, Clyde, 124, 212
Hart, Mrs. Henry, 42
Hartman, Bill, 233
Hawes, Hampton, 259
Hawkins, Coleman, 19, 22, 31, 33, 184, 186, 216
Hawkins, Erskine, 188, 190, 203
Heath, Percy, 226
Heckman, Don, 218
Hegamin, Lucille, 10, 24, 34, 250
Hemengeon, Merritt, 234
Henderson, Fletcher, 9, 22, 26, 29, 33, 60, 85, 99, 122, 197
Henderson, Horace, 197
Henderson, Joe, 274
Henderson, Rosa, 10, 32–33
Henderson, Skitch, 188, 191
Henderson, Slim, 32
Hentoff, Nat, 218, 223, 225, 252, 253, 275, 281, 283
Herman, Jerry, 235
Herman, Woody, 130, 131
Herzog, Arthur Jr., 109, 111
Hesser, Fie, 96
Hightower, Alma, 179–180, 259
Hightower, Lottie, 43
Hill, Alex, 96
Hill, Bertha (Chippie), 10
Hill, Ethel, 46
Hines, Earl (Fatha), 94, 123, 146, 151, 177, 197, 212
Hipp, Jutta, 222
Hite, Les, 84, 259
Hite, Mattie, 10
Hodges, Johnny, 125, 227
Holder, T., 50
Holiday, Billie, 6, 24, 110, 111, 126, 139, 189, 216, 223
Holly, Hal, 245
Holly, Major, 191
Holmes, Algretta, 27
Hope, Elmo, 232
Hopkins, Claude, 123
Hopkins, Linda, 17
Horne, Lena, 112
Howard, Jack, 44
Hubbard, Freddie, 233, 243, 258
Hughes, Langston, 28
Hughes, Revella, 268
Humes, Helen, 114–115, 209, 267
Humphry, Bobbi, 267
Hunter, Alberta, 8, 10, 11, 18, 36–39, 250, 266
Hunter, Lloyd, 35, 146
Hurok, Sol, 263
Hutchinson, Dolly Jones, 61, 65, 86, 110
Hutton, Ina Ray, 73, 80, 82, 95–98, 133, 224, 245, 267

Hyams, Marjorie, 129, 131, 167, 173
Hyman, Dick, 121
Hymowitz, Carol, 131

International Sweethearts of Rhythm, 132–148

Jackson, Bull Moose, 213
Jackson, Cliff, 120
Jackson, Mahalia, 18
Jackson, Milt, 240
Jackson, Preston, 59, 60
Jackson, Quentin (Butter), 287
Jackson, Tony, 37, 46
James, Etta, 139
James, George, 43, 46, 47
James, Harry, 155, 222, 245
Janofsky, Bonnie, 271
Jarvis, Brian, 211
Jarvis, Jane, 208–212, 268
Jaxon, Frankie (Half-Pint), 209
Jefferson, Blind Lemon, 34
Jefferson, Carter, 255
Jefferson, Margo, 252
Jerome, Jerry, 186
Jett, Sammy Lee, 149
Johnson, Bobby, 67
Johnson, Budd, 110, 212, 264
Johnson, Buddy, 213
Johnson, Ella, 213
Johnson, J. J., 289
Johnson, J. Rosamond, 50
Johnson, James P., 19, 22, 33, 44
Johnson, Jesse, 34, 54
Johnson, Lonnie, 34, 35
Johnson, Manzie, 63
Johnson, (Countess) Margaret (Queenie), 91, 108
Johnson, Mildred L., 50
Jolson, Al, 37
Jones, Dolly. See Armenra; Hutchinson
Jones, Dyer, 47, 64–66, 93
Jones, Etta, 213
Jones, Flo, 149
Jones, Helen. See Woods
Jones (Papa) Jo, 92, 136, 174, 208
Jones, Jonah, 61, 62, 63
Jones, Laurence Clifton, 132, 135, 141
Jones, Lillian, 198
Jones, Quincy, 179, 182, 250, 260, 264
Jones, Rae Lee, 132, 143, 147
Jones, Thad, 238, 285, 287, 289, 290
Joplin, Janis, 20
Jordan, Duke, 217
Jordan, Sheila, 213–220, 266, 268
Jordan, Taft, 133, 178
Josephson, Barney, 31, 36, 108
Julius, Lela, 86, 87, 149

Kapell, Billy, 169
Kay, Mary, 236
Keane, Helen, 275
Keaton, Buster, 67
Keaton, Myra, 67
Kelly, Ed, 255
Kelly, George, 178
Kelly, Peck, 72
Kenton, Stan, 83
Keppard, Freddie, 61

Kern, Jerome, 38
Kewit, Marge, 163
Kimball, Jeanette Salvant, 43
King, Jackie, 189
King, Maurice, 133, 139, 189, 226
King, Nora Lee, 128
King, Teddi, 223
Kirby, John, 23, 118, 119
Kirk, Andy, 45, 49, 50, 85, 96, 99, 108
Kirk, Mary Colston, 49
Kirk, Rahsaan Roland, 260
Kitchings, Elden, 111
Kitchings, Irene, 65, 109–112, 126
Knectges, John, 82
Knopf, Paul, 219
Konitz, Lee, 209, 217, 238
Kral, Irene, 267
Kral, Roy, 213
Krupa, Gene, 124, 136, 174, 213, 222, 238
Kubly, Herbert, 172
Kuhn, Steve, 214, 217, 219
Kunstadt, Leonard, 22, 24, 33, 34–35, 36
Kyle, Billy, 124
Kyle, Marcella, 51, 52

Lacy, Mayme, 86
Ladnier, Tommy, 9, 15, 29
Lamar, Nappy, 56
Land, Harold, 274
Lang, Eddie, 79–80
Lang, Irving, 174
Larkins, Ellis, 119, 188
Lateef, Yusef, 240
Latrobe, Benjamin, 5
Laveau, Marie, 4, 5
Laws, Enola, 188
Lawson, Janet, 267
Lea, Barbara, 223
Leadbelly, 35, 113
Lee, Jeanne, 223
Lee, Jean Ray, 86, 150
Lee, Julia E., 43, 91, 108
Lee, Peggy, 213
Leeds, Betty Sattley, 90, 96, 97, 99–101, 127
Leeds, Charlie, 100, 127
Leeman, Cliff, 174
Leighton, Elaine, 164, 192, 224, 225
Leonard, Ada, 73, 76, 84, 103, 105, 130, 156, 158, 164, 165, 224, 245
Leslie, Lew, 96
Lewis, John, 181
Lewis, Mel, 285, 287, 289, 290
Liberace, 245
Liebman, Fagle, 156–161
Lindsay, Erica, 179, 267, 279–281
Liston, Melba, 179–184, 188, 191, 213, 225, 229, 235, 238, 250, 259, 264, 268, 276, 279, 281, 287
Lloyd, Charles, 274
Locke, Alain, 35
Lovilette, Irvin, 255
Lucas, Marie, 46
Lucas, Roxanna, 134, 177, 198
Lucas, Sam, 46
Lucas, Tony, 46

Lunceford, Jimmie, 85, 107, 108, 133, 174, 203
Lutcher, Nellie, 192
Luter, Claude, 56
Lynn, Gloria, 199

Mabley, Moms, 139, 200
Major, Addington, 21
Manilow, Barry, 243
Mancuso, Gus, 237
Mantler, Michael, 251, 252, 253, 267
Maples, Ida, 43
Mares, Paul, 124
Mariano, Charlie, 222
Markham, Pigmeat, 180
Marsala, Joe, 192
Marsh, Warne, 217
Marshall, Maria, 237
Martin, Freddy, 244, 245
Martin, Sara, 10
Mason, John, 32, 33
Masten, Will, 93
Matlock, Matty, 73
McConnell, Shorty, 177
McCoy, Freddy, 273, 274
McDaniel, Hattie, 46, 50
McDonnell, Winifred, 185
McGee, Andy, 280–281
McGee, Evelyn. See Stone
McGee, Nova Lee, 132, 133, 149
McGinty, Artiebelle, 15
McKay, Deloyd, 204
McLagan, Kent, 282, 283
McLaughlin, John, 249
McLawler, Sarah, 195–201, 268
McLintock, Guthrie, 27
McManus, Jill, 227, 268
McPartland, Jimmy, 192
McPartland, Marian, 184, 187, 192, 235, 267, 285, 287
McRae, Carmen, 223
Memphis, Slim, 34
Merjan, Barbara, 267
Merrill, Helen, 213, 267
Mezzrow, Mezz, 56
Micheaux, Oscar, 65
Mieux, Leora, 61, 86
Milano, Lynn, 187
Miles, Lizzie, 9
Miley, Bubber, 22
Miller, Glenn, 85, 133
Miller, Henry, 172
Miller, Irvin C., 17
Millinder, Lucky, 174
Mills, Florence, 46, 85
Mills, Irving, 95, 96, 124
Mingus, Charlie, 170, 217, 249
Mitchell, Billy, 241
Mitchell, Blue, 155
Mitchell, Leroy, 216
Moffett, Charles, 252
Monk, Thelonious, 128, 232
Montgomery, Frank, 33
Moore, Orvella, 86
Moore, Shirley, 163
Moreland, Mantan, 33
Morgan, Lee, 154

Morgan, Richard, 19, 20
Morgenstern, Dan, 16, 115
Morrison, George, 46, 49, 50
Morse, Ella Mae, 213
Morton, Jelly Roll, 29, 43, 45, 53, 59
Mosby, Curtis, 22
Moses, Bob, 219, 280
Mosier, Gladys, 117, 118
Moten, Bennie, 85, 133
Mullins, Mazie, 44
Mundy, Jimmy, 86
Murray, Albert, 18, 90
Murphy, Rose, 192
Myers, Amina Claudine, 267

Narita, Cobi, 201, 268, 269
Navarro, Fats, 165, 178, 223
Nazarro, Nat, 189
Nelson, Oliver, 233, 287
Newman, Bob, 164
Newton, Frankie, 124, 128
Nicholas Brothers, 139
Nichols, Herbie, 217
Norvo, Red, 113, 122, 125, 237
Nurullah, Shanta, 260

O'Brien, Peter S., 108
O'Connell, Helen, 213
O'Day, Anita, 213
O'Flynn, Bridget, 129, 130, 168, 171–
    173, 192
Okari, Japhet, 261
Oliver, King, 35, 44, 59, 60
Oliver, Sy, 188
Ory, Kid, 259
Osborne, Mary, 164, 184–187, 225
Otis, Johnny, 207, 208
Otto, Richard, 196, 200

Page, Lips, 105, 124
Page, Walter, 85
Palmer, Robert, 214, 218
Park, Mungo, 4
Parker, Charlie, 128, 197, 212, 213, 214,
    216, 227, 271
Parker, Dorothy, 68
Parker, Leroy, 21
Parks, Jean, 151
Pasquale, Don, 61
Pastor, Tony, 213
Patterson, Ann, 269–272
Payne, Sonny, 178
Peacock, Gary, 255
Peavey, Doris, 67, 70, 71–73
Peavey, Hollis, 71, 72
Peek, W. I., 139
Pendergrass, Teddy, 277
Perkins, Red, 146
Perry, Kathryn, 110, 112
Persip, Charli, 233
Peters Sisters, 139
Petroff, Audrey Hall, 78–82, 88, 90, 95–
    96, 224
Pettiford, Marjorie, 139
Pettiford, Oscar, 139, 212
Phelan, Ruby, 92
Piazza, Tom, 293
Pierce, Billie, 43, 250

Polcer, Ed, 209
Pollack, Ben, 73, 84
Pollard, Terry, 164, 222, 225, 241
Pope, Jean, 197
Powell, Bud, 128, 222, 250
Powell, Specs, 176
Powers, Ollie, 60
Pridgett, Thomas, 12, 16
Prima, Louis, 84, 100
Pullum, Joe, 34

Quinichette, Paul, 67, 110

Ra, Sun, 249
Rainey, Gertrude Pridgett (Ma), 8, 10,
    11, 12–16
Rainey, Will (Pa), 13
Randall, Doc, 53
Ray, Carline, 136, 179, 187–192, 268, 281
Redd, Alton, 259
Redd, Vi, 180, 187, 206, 259–260
Reddy, Helen, 243
Redman, Don, 86
Reed, Dale, 171
Reese, Lloyd, 171
Reilly, Jack, 217, 219
Rice, Eli, 86
Rice, Johnny Mae, 132
Rice, Sylvester, 86
Rich, Adrienne, 5
Richards, Johnny, 103, 105–106
Riley, Mike, 87
Rinehardt, Django, 185–186
Rinker, Al, 113
Rio, Rita, 88, 103, 104
Roach, Max, 290
Roberts, Judy, 267
Roberts, Lula, 198, 199
Robeson, Paul, 263
Robinson, Bill, 46
Robinson, Ikey, 64, 66, 94, 109
Robinson, Janice, 267, 285–292
Rogers, Billie, 130
Rose, Al, 46
Rose, Dave, 245
Rose, Ron, 238
Rosner, Betty, 163
Ross, Diana, 243
Ross, Frank, 236
Rotenberg, June, 129, 130, 167–170, 172,
    175, 186, 192
Roudybush, Betty, 96
Rowles, Jimmy, 109, 238
Rowles, Stacy, 267
Rubin, Lillian, 221
Rudd, Roswell, 253
Rushing, Jimmy, 24, 114, 237, 260
Russell, George, 217–218, 251, 252, 260
Russell, Luis, 35, 190, 191
Russo, Danny, 34
Rust, Brian, 94
Ryan, Jimmy, 202

Sager, Jane, 70, 89–90, 96, 103–107, 224
St. Joan, Keisha, 268
Saloppé, Marie, 4
Sanders, Pharaoh, 252, 253

Sattley, Betty. *See* Leeds
Saunders, Gertrude, 19
Saunders, Jon, 269
Saxon, Lyle, 4
Scaffidi, Ralph, 184, 186
Schiffman, Frank, 18, 151
Scott, Alma Long, 61, 86
Scott, Hazel, 31, 61, 108, 192, 197, 204
Scott, Raymond, 124
Scott, Ronnie, 260
Scott, Shirley, 222
Scott-Heron, Gil, 253
Seeling, Ellen, 267
Selkin, Pat, 163
Sellers, Brother John, 8
Senter, Boyd, 83
Shand, Terry, 186
Sharp, Belle, 162
Shavers, Charlie, 184, 186
Shaw, Artie, 85, 124, 133
Shearing, George, 131, 223
Sheldon, Nina, 268
Shepherd, Norma, 202–205, 250
Shepp, Archie, 249
Shihab, Sahib, 264
Shirley, Fran, 158
Shorter, Wayne, 249
Silver, Horace, 223, 225
Simmons, Alberta, 44
Simmons, Sonny, 249, 255, 257
Simms, Alfred, 193
Simon, George, 98
Sims, Zoot, 235
Singleton, Marge Creath, 51–57
Singleton, Zutty, 18, 35, 51, 53, 55–56, 57, 90
Sissle, Noble, 38
Slaughter, Vesterine, 196
Slavin, Estelle, 96, 100, 101–103, 130, 173–174
Sloane, Carol, 235, 238
Smith, Andrew, 17
Smith, Bessie, 6, 8, 10, 11, 16–21, 38, 39
Smith, Carrie, 17
Smith, Charles Edward, 16
Smith, Clara, 10, 11, 39–40
Smith, Clarence, 17
Smith, Edna, 136, 188, 190
Smith, Elsie, 229
Smith, Harrison, 94–95
Smith, Hetty, 197, 198, 224
Smith, Jabbo, 124
Smith, Joe, 22, 26
Smith, Laura, 10
Smith, Mamie, 9, 10, 11, 21–24
Smith, Pinetop, 43
Smith, Stuff, 61, 84, 100
Smith, Tab, 124
Smith, Trixie, 10
Smith, Viola, 17
Smith, William (Sweet Singing Smitty), 21
Smith, William and Laura, 17
Smith, Willie, 90
Smith, Willie (the Lion), 18, 21–22, 46, 73
Smock, Ginger, 130, 225

Snow, Alvaida, 93
Snow, Lavaida, 93
Snow, Valaida, 64, 85, 93–95
Spaulding, Fern, 82
Spight, Skeeter, 216
Spiller, Isabelle Taliaferro, 46
Spitalny, Phil, 87, 245
Spivey, Addie (Sweet Pea), 34
Spivey, Elton, 34
Spivey, Victoria, 8, 10, 11, 23, 24, 29, 33–36, 250
Stabile, Dick, 127, 186
Stacy, Jess, 210
Stafford, Mary, 10
Starr, Jean, 107, 130–131, 149, 150, 173
Starr, Kay, 213
Staton, Dakota, 223, 268
Sterling, Jack, 186
Stevens, Ashton, 26–27
Stewart, Rex, 105, 202
Stewart, Sammy, 64
Stewart, Slam, 192, 204
Sticht, Betty, 96
Stitt, Sonny, 240, 241
Stoller, Mike, 246
Stone, Evelyn McGee, 135, 136, 138–141
Stone, Jesse, 22, 23, 92, 133, 134, 136, 138, 139, 141, 177
Stone, Joe, 154
Straine, Mary, 8
Sudler, Monette, 267
Suleiman, Idress, 129
Sullivan, Maxine, 23, 24, 116–121, 209
Sutton, Della M., 46
Swallow, Steve, 217, 219
Swartz, Harvie, 219
Sylvester, Hannah, 34

Tabackin, Lew, 223, 251, 266, 267
Tadler, Mary, 102
Tampa Red, 15
Tanksley, Chessie, 179, 267
Tate, Buddy, 34, 178
Tate, Grady, 209
Tatum, Art, 104, 169, 189, 190, 195, 204, 207
Tatum, May, 191
Taylor, Billy, 129
Taylor, Cecil, 249, 253
Teagarden, Charlie, 74, 75, 77
Teagarden, Clois (Cub), 74, 75
Teagarden, Jack, 73, 74, 75, 76
Teagarden, Norma, 67, 70, 73–78, 210
Terkel, Studs, 113
Terry, Clark, 165, 179, 209, 225, 285, 287, 290
Thigpen, Ben, 136
Thomas, Edna, 43
Thomas, Joe, 63
Thomas, Walter (Foots), 228
Thompson, Ellarize, 132, 150
Thompson, Lucky, 165, 225
Thompson, Wiley, 239
Thornton, Big Mama, 224
Thornhill, Claude, 117–118
Todd, Camilla, 43
Todd, Sterling, 193

Tolen, L. C., 34
Traill, Sinclair, 108
Tristano, Lennie, 217
Tucker, Sophie, 21, 26, 37
Turner, Big Joe, 24, 92
Turner, Jessie, 149
Turnham, Edythe, 8, 47–49, 108
Turnham, Floyd Jr., 47, 48
Turrentine, Stanley, 243

Ulanov, Barry, 172, 226

Valentine, Gerald, 212
Vance, Dick, 61–62, 128
Van Vechten, Carl, 19, 40
Vaughan, Sarah, 6, 128, 189, 197, 212,
    216, 223, 260, 261
Ventura, Charlie, 213
Venuti, Joe, 27, 79–80, 186, 235
Vidor, King, 35
Viola, Joe, 282

Waldron, Mal, 279–280
Walker, Alice, 6
Walker, T-Bone, 126, 154, 213
Wallace, Michele, 223
Wallace, Sippie, 8, 10, 11, 34
Waller, Thomas (Fats), 44, 96, 104, 108
Walsh, Lorraine (Jazz), 224, 229
Walton, Cedar, 233, 257
Ward, Helen, 112
Warren, Bernadine, 234, 268
Warwick, Dionne, 199, 243
Washington, Dinah, 6, 17, 212–213, 230,
    261
Waters, Ethel, 10, 24–28, 38, 46, 94
Watkins, Doug, 240
Watkins, Mary, 267
Webb, Chick, 85, 114, 122, 124, 125
Webster, Ben, 67, 168, 204, 216
Webster, L'Ana, 87, 130, 173
Wein, George, 222
Weiss, Sid, 167
Weissman, Michaele, 131
Welles, Orson, 263
Wells, Gertie, 44
Wesley, Charles, 40
Weston, Randy, 179, 182
Wetzel, Bonnie, 164, 192, 224, 225
Whipper, Leigh, 24
White, George, 96
White, Josh, 35
White, Kitty, 245
White, Princess, 10
White, Slappy, 139
White, Thelma, 99
Whiteman, Paul, 68, 113
Whiteman, Wilberforce J., 49
Whiting, Margaret, 213
Whiting, Napoleon, 67
Wilbur, Bob, 209

Wilder, Alec, 287
Wiley, Lee, 112
Williams, Bert, 8, 46, 142
Williams, Billy, 155
Williams, Cootie, 162
Williams, Edith, 108
Williams, Edna, 130, 132, 139, 149
Williams, John, 45
Williams, Josie, 46
Williams, Mary Lou, 44–45, 68, 86, 91,
    108, 128–129, 130, 131, 167, 168, 169,
    171, 172, 173, 186, 188, 191, 192, 210,
    225, 250, 266, 267, 287, 293–294
Williams, Ned, 124
Williams, Pauline Braddy, 104, 132,
    134–137, 141, 190, 229
Williams, Tony, 249
Wills, Alyse, 96
Wilson, Burt, 255
Wilson, Dick, 99, 108
Wilson, Edith, 10
Wilson, Gerald, 179, 180, 181, 240
Wilson, Harriet, 84
Wilson, John S., 28, 58, 114, 120, 193,
    261
Wilson, Nancy, 277
Wilson, Teddy, 109, 110, 111, 124, 222
Wilson, Vi, 198, 199
Winburn, Anna Mae, 91, 136, 143, 145–
    148, 224, 226, 228
Winters, Smiley, 255
Withers, Bill, 243
Witherspoon, Jimmy, 154
Wonder, Stevie, 243
Wong, Willie Mae, 132
Wood, Chris, 233
Wood, Mary, 185
Woodman, Britt, 179
Woods, Helen Jones, 132, 134, 141–143
Woods, Phil, 179, 264, 271
Work, John, 197
Wright, Eugene, 236
Wyble, Jimmy, 237
Wynn, Al, 12, 64
Wynn, Edith Lynwood, 69

Yenney, George S., 71
Young, Alice, 180
Young, Irma, 47, 66–67, 206
Young, Lee, 66, 67, 171
Young, Lester, 66, 67, 115, 168, 206, 207–
    208, 216
Young, Martha, 206–208, 259
Young, Myrtle, 163, 224, 226
Young, Willis B., 206

Zanuck, Darryl F., 27
Zawinul, Joe, 249
Zimmer, Vicki, 131, 173
Zimmerman, Fred, 176
Zirl, Cecilia, 102, 131, 173